ZOO

A HISTORY OF ZOOLOGICAL GARDENS IN THE WEST

ZOO

ERIC BARATAY AND ELISABETH HARDOUIN-FUGIER

REAKTION BOOKS

Published by Reaktion Books Ltd
79 Farringdon Road, London EC1M 3JU, UK

www.reaktionbooks.co.uk

First published in English 2002

First published in French as *Zoos: Histoire des jardins zoologiques en
occident (XVIe–XXe siècle)* © Editions La Découverte & Syros, 1998

Translated by Oliver Welsh

English-language translation © Reaktion Books 2002

This work has been published with the support of the Centre
National du Livre, French Ministry of Culture.

The publication of this book is supported by the
Cultural Service of the French Embassy in London.

Printed in Hong Kong.

British Library Cataloguing in Publication Data

Baratay, Eric
    Zoo : a history of zoological gardens in the West
    1.Zoos – history
    I. Title II.Hardouin-Fugier, Elisabeth
    590.7'3

ISBN 1 86189 111 3

CONTENTS

⊙ INTRODUCTION: THE CALL OF THE WILD

Zoological gardens draw crowds all over the world. In 1995, six hundred million people walked the paths of some eleven hundred establishments listed world-wide. In many countries, a day at the zoo ranks among the most popular of leisure pursuits, both because zoos attract such a varied public, often people of modest means, and because they do so in greater numbers than most cultural or sporting activities. In Germany, for example, zoological gardens receive more visitors than museums, theatres or sports stadiums. In Canada, in 1989, their attendance figures were double those of museums, and triple those of libraries. In France, 24 per cent of the population visits the zoo at least once a year, a smaller proportion than for cinemas, historical monuments or museums, but greater than for sporting events, theatres or concerts of light or classical music.[1]

Wild animals clearly fascinate people. They reveal unknown worlds and diverse life forms; they pose the eternal questions of identity, challenging or reinforcing life's certainties. The exhibition of wildlife in the midst of civilized societies has been a constant of human history because it has helped people to place themselves in relation to the rest of the world. Human beings need the wild and endlessly seek it out.[2] But people are also attracted by animals in captivity, because they symbolize the intentions and actions of human societies towards wildlife and, in a more general sense, towards nature: exploitation, through hunting, consumption and dissection; control, through acclimatization, reproduction and domestication or reintroduction; curiosity, with the aim of collection; domination or examination, through the accumulation of cages and fences or artificially reconstructed habitats. All of these actions and attitudes have evolved, intertwined and displaced one another as societies' viewpoints have shifted.

Indian elephants bathing, Hannover Zoo.

Because it is a place of forced meeting between animal and human, between nature and culture, where one stares at the other and where the second appropriates the first, the zoological garden brings the various aspects of societies' relationship with the wild into focus – their thoughts about

A caged monkey in a Paris menagerie, 1980s, by J. C. Nouet.

it, conduct towards it and utilization of it. Consequently, zoos help in the identification and compilation of these aspects, and in the study of their complexity, interaction and development. But this observational space – the zoo – is also the constantly renewed and transformed product of the views and attitudes which it helps to shape. The staging of the zoo says just as much as the practices within it about the relationship of human beings with nature.

This book is not intended to record the technical history of individual aspects of such places – their architecture, their integration into processes of urban development, the sociology of their founders and personnel, their scientific or artistic relevance – although these significant themes will contribute to our analysis. It is our hope to shed light on humanity's view of wild animals in the context of the zoological garden, approached as a perfect laboratory, while considering the concepts, customs and intellectual interactions relevant to the history of zoos, in an effort to understand why human beings keep wild species near them in enclosed spaces, and why these spaces are so attractive to the curious.

The answers to these questions vary according to period, and a sound understanding of the current fascination with zoos or of their transformation in the contemporary period can only be achieved with reference to the history of these acts and places. The history of the zoo is a long one, dating from antiquity, perhaps even from the Neolithic period, when people kept animals, mostly ungulates, for hunting and food.[3] The expression 'zoological garden', taken in the generic sense of an enclosed space containing a collection of wild animals, in fact covers a broad range of realities across space and time, from hunting reserves to today's wildlife parks, via seraglios of fighting animals and the menageries of private collectors. We have chosen not to retell this entire story, but rather to seek to understand the genesis and evolution of zoological gardens as they exist today. In order to do this, we go back to the sixteenth and seventeenth centuries, when new curiosities began to inform age-old practices, when great discoveries in Asia and the Americas heightened interest in the exotic species that were arriving in Europe in ever greater numbers, and when those species became symbols of the wild. At the same moment, the West, having

Rotterdam Zoo, 1999, by Candida Höfer.

Berlin Zoo, 1991, by Candida Höfer.

Lar gibbon, London Zoo, 1992, by Britta Jaschinski.

already eliminated part of its own wildlife, was waging war on those animals that it considered to be the worst nuisances, such as bears and wolves. Along with these two species, it was exotic creatures that became the focus of human curiosity, questions, fears, fantasies and dreams of domination. The idea of establishing a single place for their exhibition, as opposed to numerous locations scattered among seigniorial abodes, developed during this period. Thus the first theatres of the wild were created in the grounds of grand princely residences; these establishments, which turned the act of keeping animals into a spectacle, foreshadowed the zoos of today.

Having looked carefully at the use of captive wild animals during the early modern period, and the intentions informing the spaces in which they were kept, we hope to reveal the perceptions and ambitions that gradually trans-formed them, that imposed them over and above other means of detention (reserves, travelling menageries and so on), which either fell into decline or were adapted to the new model, and that finally, after a long process of democ-ratization, established them as popular venues for walking and recreation. Our perspective is a European one because these modern forms of zoological garden were invented in Europe and spread from there beginning in the nineteenth century.

Every aspect of humanity's relationship with nature can be perceived through the bars of the zoological garden: repulsion and fascination; the impulse to appropriate, master and understand; the progressive recognition of the complexity and specificity of the diverse forms of life; and so on. The story of this microcosm is thus linked to vast parallel histories of colonization, ethnocentrism and the discovery of the Other; violence in human relationships and the moderating effect of the civilizing process on morals and behaviour; the creation of places of collective memory such as museums; the complication of social practices; the development of leisure activities. To tour the cages of a zoo is to understand the society that erected them.

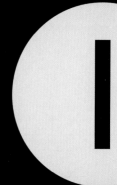

THE PASSION FOR COLLECTING (1500s to 1700s)

I ANCIENT TROPHIES

An interest in wild animals – in particular, a desire to own them and be near them – was widespread among the European aristocracy of the sixteenth, seventeenth and eighteenth centuries, because animals were considered to be prestigious, luxury items indispensable to the nobility and a symbol of its distinct nature. From the late fourteenth century on, many royal, princely and even seigniorial courts exhibited wild beasts, either indigenous or exotic ones, in what were called *serragli* in Italy; this term was subsequently exported to the rest of Europe, becoming *serrallo* in Spain, *serralho* in Portugal, and *serrail*, followed by *sérail*, in France (there, the terms *hostel* or *maison de lions*[1] were also used). In fact, this custom dated back to antiquity and beyond, to the earliest civilizations.

ANIMALS IN ANTIQUITY

The practice of hunting – and the desire to relocate quarry from one region to another or to control its procreation – has no doubt led humankind to keep wild animals in pens since Neolithic times. The earliest significant accounts of this practice come from Egypt and China. In Egypt, as far back as the fifth and fourth millennia BC, sacred beasts were kept in or near temples, and captured herbivores (gazelles, antelopes and others) grazed in enclosures. In the second millennium, when cheetahs and lions were used for hunting and warfare, a fascination with exotic beasts developed. In the Thirteenth Dynasty, at Thebes, Queen Hatasou created the first

Alexander the Great in an elephant-skin headdress.

known zoological gardens. In the fourteenth century BC, the emperors of China collected animals from various regions and gathered them together in their palaces. In the ninth century BC, Emperor Wen-Wang established a park of 375 hectares – called the Garden of Intelligence since it was thought of as a divine creation – for hunting and fishing. (Much later, in the thirteenth century AD, the Great Khan visited by Marco Polo kept big cats in his residence and herbivores in his grounds.[2]) In India, princes tamed and housed elephants, lions, tigers and panthers for war and hunting from very early on. In the first millennium BC, the kings of Assyria possessed animals which they used for display, sacrifices to the gods or hunting in their parks. The kings of Persia did the same, while in Babylon, whether independent or enslaved, a royal *paradeisos* (wooded garden) was maintained and populated with various animals. (Another example of this type of garden was found in the capital of the Aztec Empire when it was discovered by Europeans in 1519.[3])

The ancient Greeks, on the other hand, did not create grand seraglios, although more or less domesticated birds, other fowl and monkeys inhabited the grander residences, as well as temples and their surroundings, signals of pomp and luxury. The taste for big cats and elephants did not develop until the time of Alexander the Great and his successors, under the influence of Persian displays and in line with the interplay of diplomatic relations and the symbolism of power. The wealthiest citizens of ancient Rome liked to possess exotic birds, once again as a sign of the highest luxury. Near their villas, they kept aviaries, fish-ponds and animal pens, the latter filled initially with hares and then, in the last days of the Republic, with stags, deer and wild boar kept for pleasure, hunting and food. Under the Empire, a taste for 'ferocious' animals developed alongside that for circus games; such beasts were housed in or near residences.[4]

It was in the third and second centuries BC that the consuls of Rome gradually developed the habit of parading and then massacring elephants and big cats captured during their campaigns in order to avenge the losses inflicted by military pachyderms, to signify the destruction or appropriation of their adversaries' riches and land – in short, to celebrate the power of Rome.[5] This practice, which seduced a population already accustomed to gladiatorial combat, took on considerable importance under the Empire; emperors and citizens receiving triumphal honours and plundered riches presented animals (exotic ones, for the most part) in public exhibitions, sumptuous processions, hunts and fights, to which were added bouts with gladiators and the slaughter of condemned men by big cats.

For these purposes, there existed more or less temporary seraglios of 'ferocious' animals – which served as holding pens before the games or as markets that sold to private individuals – as well as enclosures for herbivores. The emperors of Rome also used domesticated and trained big cats for hunting and ceremonies, harnessing them to chariots in order to emphasize their own strength, glorious divinity and ascendancy over what were considered to be the cruellest of nature's beasts. All of these customs were fed by diplomatic gifts, by spoils of war and, above all, by the systematic hunting of wild animals, which led both to huge convoys of beasts converging on Rome and to the depopulation of sizeable parts of North Africa and the East. In the Empire's last days, the increasing scarcity of these species was such that living animals had to be kept and exhibited over and over again, and the number of combats reduced in favour of feats of prowess.[6]

Such games were discontinued in Rome around the sixth century AD, but continued in certain western provinces. In Gaul, Clovis organized animal combats in the sixth century, and the eighth-century emperor Charlemagne revived Roman custom by receiving a few animals as gifts from Eastern princes, keeping an elephant and some rare birds (peacocks, pheasants, ducks). However, all of this became less common (though this question has

Elephant and other animals, 1398.

not been resolved) during the early Middle Ages. The traditions of seraglios and games were kept alive for the most part in the Byzantine Empire, at least until the twelfth and thirteenth centuries. It was through contact with Byzantium and the Muslim world, which was in the process of becoming the West's supplier of wild animals, that the Crusaders to the Holy Land acquired a taste for hunting with leopards and an interest in the upkeep of exotic species. Indeed, the first seraglio of any importance seems to have appeared in the thirteenth century in the court of Frederick II, King of the Two Sicilies. Frederick possessed camels, dromedaries, elephants, big cats, monkeys, bears, gazelles and a giraffe, which he used for hunts or parades. The custom spread gradually to the princely courts – first to those of the Italian peninsula, then to the rest of Europe – thanks to favourable economic conditions, and as knights sought to define their positions further by engaging in exclusive pastimes. In this way, grandees took to keeping curious beasts – mostly birds and monkeys – in their homes, while fishponds, aviaries and small seraglios were established in the fourteenth and fifteenth centuries next to the warrens that had been there since antiquity. Also inherited were the great hunting parks of several hundred hectares that were common in the Middle Ages, for example in Burgundy, Brittany and England, where deer, wild boar and even bears imported from other regions were kept for hunting to improve the local game.[7]

BIG CATS AT THE CASTLE

Western seraglios of the sixteenth and seventeenth centuries followed late medieval practice while undergoing a clear change in both their scale (with increasingly abundant and well-rounded collections of livestock) and the breadth of their geographical distribution (with their first appearances in a number of regions). Until the seventeenth century, the two most common groups of wild animals to be found at castles were the 'ferocious' kind (bears, lynxes, wolves, lions and, more rarely, tigers, snow leopards, cheetahs and leopards) and the various species of game animal (stag, deer). The less costly indigenous beasts were still the most numerous, but exotic animals were much sought after since they reinforced the impression of their owners' power, particularly when ferocious and shown in pairs.

In Renaissance Italy, where the phenomenon was already well developed, seraglios could be found in Naples, in Parma, at the court of the Duke of Ferrara (who maintained a very rare and very precious tiger in the late fifteenth century), at the Duke of Calabria's villa at Poggio Reale and elsewhere. The most successful and best-known example is that of the Medici in Florence, who possessed a seraglio from the fifteenth century. Lorenzo the Magnificent (1469–92) brought this establishment to its peak, accommodating hunting leopards, lions, elephants, bears, bulls and wild boar. The Medicis' successors, the grand dukes of Tuscany, maintained this tradition from the second half of the sixteenth century. In Renaissance Rome, the popes received quantities of animals in tribute from various princes. It was with Leo X (1513–21), Lorenzo's son, that this practice reached its apogee in the small courtyards of the Vatican. Roman cardinals did the same in the grounds of their villas.[8]

In the first half of the sixteenth century, the Age of Discovery and of the first colonial empires, the other area where this predilection was widespread was Portugal, one of the great maritime powers. Royal seraglios were established in the capital, Sintra and Ribeira and housed a great many wild cats, as well as rhinoceroses, elephants and other

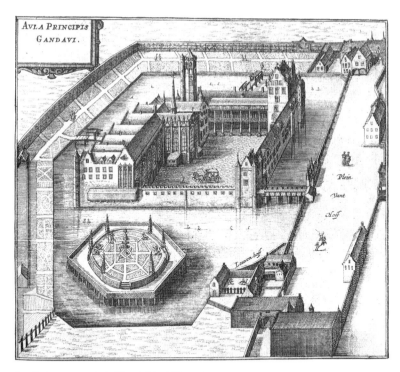

A private menagerie in Ghent, late 16th century.

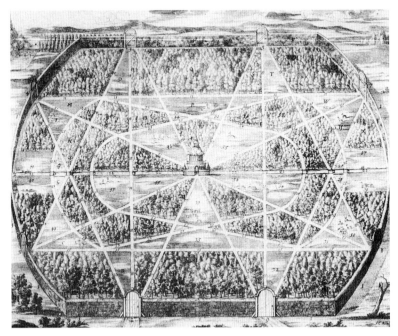

A hunting park, late 17th century.

animals. The great lords, such as the dukes of Bragança, Coimbra and Aveiro, imitated their monarch. At one point abandoned under Spanish rule, the tradition was then restored, but in a reduced form on account of the political and economic decline of the country, which had lost a good part of its empire. In Spain, the custom does not seem to have taken hold to the same extent, doubtless due to the less ostentatious and more austere character of the court there. It is known, however, that Charles V and several great aristocrats, such as the Duke of Infantando, kept animals in their palaces. A century later, Philip IV (1621–65) maintained bears, tigers and lions at the Casa del Campo. In England, the practice was less developed than in other Western European countries, but it was traditional for sovereigns to keep big cats – lions in particular – in the pits of the Tower of London. The governor-generals of the Spanish Netherlands did the same at Ghent during the sixteenth and seventeenth centuries.[9]

In the Germanic lands, many lords kept an example of the species that appeared on their coats of arms (lions, bears, wolves). Large seraglios appeared there in the second half of the sixteenth century, imitating the customs of the Italian and Portuguese powers. The imperial electors of Saxony, for example, possessed lions, bears, lynxes and other species at

Dresden from 1554, and then at Neustadt Castle from the eighteenth century. The landgraves of Hesse did the same at Kassel from the mid-sixteenth century, and it was also from this time that the emperors of the Holy Roman Empire established seraglios on Austrian soil. The future Maximilian II (1564–76) had the first one built at Ebersdorf in 1552 to house an elephant and some hunting leopards brought back from Spain, where he had spent his childhood. He repeated this gesture at Neugebäu Castle, where the seraglio, which did not reach its full extent until the late seventeenth century, remained in service until 1781, while that at Ebersdorf disappeared in the 1600s.[10]

The Italian wars had given the sixteenth-century French monarchs a taste for luxury and pomp. Sites there varied according to the movements of the court, being distributed in a way that favoured the châteaux of Paris and the Loire. Major lords also maintained big cats, lions in the great majority of cases.[11] These beasts would usually be housed near residences, in enclosures, pits or outbuildings transformed for the purpose, but certain more or less domesticated cats found their way into the princely apartments themselves in the sixteenth and seventeenth centuries. Francis I sometimes had a lion or snow leopard lie at the foot of his bed. In 1682, at Versailles, Moroccan ambassadors, having come to sign a six-year peace treaty with France, presented one of their gifts in the Queen's bedroom: a 'personal tigress' as gentle as a dog which let itself be stroked by the ladies of the court.[12]

In England, the exhibition of birds spread among the aristocracy of the fourteenth, fifteenth and sixteenth centuries. King Charles I, for example, was a great bird-lover. Men opted for parrots, often left free to fly around their apartments. Ladies preferred smaller, caged birds. Cages were often beautiful wooden constructions, designed by prominent architects, decorated with glass, jewels and precious stones, and shaped like castles or cathedrals (sixteenth–seventeenth centuries) or lanterns (eighteenth century).[13]

MEANS OF POSSESSION

While indigenous beasts were hunted with traps and nets, exotic species could be obtained from a variety of sources. First, there were the gifts made by Asiatic powers to mark alliances, submissions or peace treaties, such as that of the Ottoman Empire to its ally Francis I in 1534, or indeed that of the sovereign of Cambodia to his Portuguese counterpart in 1515. But donations, or even exchanges, between European monarchs were also very important. In 1514, the King of Portugal offered an elephant and a snow leopard to Pope

Turkish animal hunters with a captive giraffe, 16th century.

Leo X in recognition of the division of new territories performed by the Holy See in 1493. In 1591, Henry IV of France gave the Queen of England a pachyderm which he had had for some time, and which she coveted. One can gain some idea of the importance of this custom from the example of Francis I, who received a convoy of beasts and birds on behalf of the 'roy' of Tunis in 1532; lions and tigers brought by the Turkish embassy in 1534; a sheep from the Indes, proffered by a Norman lord in 1538; and two seals sent by Mary of Hungary, Regent of the Netherlands, in 1539. The diplomatic value of these presents expressed the rare and precious nature of the animals, which were often accompanied by choice items like the vases, diamonds from the Indies and tapestries which arrived in Rome in 1514.[14]

Another means of procurement was trade, the role and scope of which grew in parallel with European expansion. In the fifteenth and even the early sixteenth centuries, it was the towns of Genoa, Pisa, Livorno and Venice, masters of Mediterranean trade with the East, that ensured the importation essential to the development of animal seraglios at the Italian courts. But the great discoveries of the time also gave a powerful impetus to this process. Travel diaries show that Europeans were always anxious to take home a few specimens, most notably birds and monkeys. The Italian towns were thereafter subjected to increasing competition from Portugal, which imported, via the new shipping routes in the southern Atlantic, great quantities of animals of which many, such as the rhinoceros, were virtually unknown. This commerce began with Alvise Ca'da Mosto's travels along the African coasts in 1454. The formative wars of the colonial empires also created some useful opportunities. In Melaka in 1511, the Portuguese captured seven elephants, including the one that would ultimately be offered to Pope Leo X in 1514.[15]

While Mediterranean ports like Marseilles retained some trade, it was those on the Atlantic and the northern seas that became predominant from the sixteenth century. The principal venues for importation and sale were therefore Lisbon in the first half of the 1500s, Antwerp after 1560, and Amsterdam, London and Lorient in the following centuries, thanks to the development of various East India trading companies. Thus the Dutch East India Company became the main supplier for north-western Europe. The Company had sheds built on the quays of Amsterdam's port which served as holding pens before sale. The Company's importance is apparent, for example, in the work of the Dutch scholar Peter Camper, who was able to cite the origins of the exotic animals he described.[16]

Although the transport of animals represented only a minor enterprise for these companies when compared to the sum total of their traffic, it assumed great diplomatic importance since it helped maintain relations with sovereigns and grandees. Thus, in eighteenth-century France, the heads of trading syndicates took the initiative by sending animals straight to Versailles, even if it meant selling them on to showmen if they were refused. Conversely, the court regularly placed orders to replenish the livestock of the menagerie at Versailles or to satisfy the enthusiasms of courtiers. In 1750, for example, the general supervisor requested, on the latter's behalf, a delivery of eight hundred small birds, a hundred or so budgerigars and 25 parakeets.[17]

In addition to using the commercial channels that rose to prominence in the eighteenth century, monarchs were not afraid to mount their own expeditions. Francis I sent explorers, the most famous of whom was André Thévet, to the East under orders to bring him back rare manuscripts and local wildlife. In 1532, he dispatched Pierre Pitou to Fez. This gentleman of the King's household purchased and sent back lions, wolfhounds, camels, ostriches, birds and other species. In 1683, the great Colbert advised vessels sailing in the Levant to bring back the largest possible number of partridges from the Barbary Coast, as Louis XIV was particularly found of them. He dispatched a 'tartan to Tunis, expressly' to find some. Consuls were mobilized to smooth the way for the King's agents, if not to find beasts themselves and organize their return. Governors of colonies and even corsairs got involved, including a certain Jean Doublet who brought back llamas in 1711.[18]

In the eighteenth century, some of these expeditions were led by scientists charged with a more rational kind of collecting. In 1732, the Elector of Saxony sent a doctor from his court to northern Africa to seize Roman antiquities and exotic animals. The doctor landed at Algiers, crossed the Atlas Mountains and arrived in Tunis with lions, jackals, ostriches and chameleons. In 1754, Marie-Thérèse of Austria instructed the botanist Nicolas Jacquin to scour tropical America for plants, birds and mammals, and bring them back to the menagerie at her palace at Schönbrunn. Another botanist conducted a similar expedition in 1783, but this time to North America.[19] In 1764, a vessel of the East India Company was chartered to bring back exotic beasts, among them two tigers, destined for the Duke of Cumberland, son of King George II.[20]

On each of these occasions, transporting the animals caused innumerable problems. In 1675, Le Mosnier had to leave some creatures behind in Alexandria because his ship was too small. He had some difficulty accommodating the others, which had to spend 50 days on deck, unprotected, in heavy weather. Once in Marseilles, he had to wait for a period of quarantine to end before he could land. Voyages tended to be long (from six to fifteen months from the Indies to Lorient, for example), given that itineraries were dependent on the vagaries of cargo and the requests of passengers. Food too had to be planned for: three to four hundred sheep and a great quantity of fodder were taken on board a ship of the Compagnie des Indes in 1770 to feed two tigers between Chandernagor and Lorient.

The other difficulty, on arrival in Europe, involved the land transport necessary to convey the beasts to their destinations. Not only did cages have to be constructed, wagons fitted out, food planned and gathered, and men found who knew something about animals and how to feed and look after them, but the length of each stage and rest period of the journey had to be determined. An eighteenth-century letter from a French minister to an official in Marseilles illustrates the improvised nature of such transportation. On the arrival of a caracal from Alexandria, the minister asked the official to recruit someone experienced in the transportation of beasts and to issue him with instructions after asking the ship's captain about the animal's habits; it was apparently carnivorous, but was it big, or dangerous? How much food would it consume? Would a cage have to be made for it?[21]

These questions help to explain the high mortality among animals during shipping and the difficulty of acclimatization on arrival. The numerous shipwrecks which killed beasts and people alike must also be taken into account: in 1517, a boat conveying a rhinoceros from Portugal to Rome sank off Genoa; in 1771, it was an orang-utan from Borneo, en route to Peter Camper, which disappeared in the Indian Ocean. The French Consul at Cairo drew up a sombre account in 1714–15: the fourteen ostriches which he had sent to Malta had died for want of care, the 80 blue grouse he had obtained had been engulfed by the Nile, and most of the creatures he had purchased in Alexandria had expired en route. At the end of the century, A. Vosmaer reported that twelve of the fourteen goats from Guinea that had been dispatched to Holland in 1762 had died en route, and another on arrival.[22]

All of this activity represented a considerable outlay of cash. The rhinoceros brought by the Compagnie des Indes in 1770 cost Louis XV 5,388 *livres*, of which 1,650 were for the journey by sea, 1,200 for the stay in Lorient and preparations for transit, and 2,530 for delivery to Versailles. This amount was equivalent to four-and-a-half years' upkeep for a landed ship's captain, or double the sum (2,400 *livres*) paid to master artists for each of the paintings in the series of 'Exotic Hunts' destined for the King's apartments. Purchases of numbers of animals, or of species of imposing size, were therefore confined to the highest aristocracy, while more humble amateurs often limited themselves to birds and small monkeys. A 1750 order for a thousand birds, for example, came to a modest 840 *livres*.[23]

SYMBOLS OF POWER

Until the seventeenth century, the favoured 'ferocious' group of animals was primarily used in parades. On the Italian peninsula, noblemen would appear with their cheetahs perched on the rumps of their horses. In Ghent, the Governor of the Spanish Netherlands maintained 'cruel and fierce beasts from strange lands' for 'parades of grandeur and magnificence'.[24]

These living trophies, which inspired the public's imagination, were sometimes included in processions to recall the pomp of classical times, a practice that remained current until the seventeenth century. As early as the end of the 1400s, Lorenzo the Magnificent held parades of lions and elephants. These animals were favoured because their strength and supposed domination over other species made them symbols of power and kingship; in the following century, sovereigns were in any case often the only people to possess them. The association between lions, elephants and worldly power is conveyed in such literary works as the *Hieroglyphica* of Horapollon (1505) and Valeriano (1556), and in such paintings as Mantegna's *Triumph of Caesar* (1506) and Hendrick Pot's *Triumph of William I* (1620), in which three pachyderms process before the Prince. An elephant played a similar role in Maximilian's coronation as King of Hungary in 1552. In 1514, the ambassador of Manuel I of Portugal made a triumphal entry to Rome with a domesticated elephant called Hanno. It became customary to parade him during festivals with his body gilded from head to foot, which practice caused his death by suffocation in 1516.[25] Pomp was ever-present and extremely significant. When Francis I kept, not a small dog in the bourgeois manner, but 'some lion, panther or other such proud beast which had become as dear as the pet in some peasant's house' by his bed, he was asserting his symbolic kinship with the wild, sharing in its power, passion and courage. He was putting more distance between himself and the plebeians lined up in fearful, placid docility, while at the same time proclaiming his victory over the brutal forces of nature.[26]

Such animals were also assembled for spectacular eruptions of violence, in the fights between species that the aristocracy liked to stage and that the Humanists likened to the practices of ancient Rome. The most extravagant of these were incorporated into major festivities: for the arrival of Charles V and Prince Philip at Ghent in 1549, for the birth of a child to the Elector of Saxony in Dresden in 1613, in honour of the son of the King of Denmark and the Persian ambassador in 1663 and 1682 at Vincennes, and so on.[27] Others took place regularly at the behest of courtiers,

for example at Windsor Castle under Elizabeth I or James I of England, where more or less permanent installations were required. The Grand Duke of Tuscany possessed a wooden arena in Florence, 'surrounded by a row of very well-decorated boxes from whence the fighting can comfortably be seen'; a similar installation could be found in Berlin at the start of the eighteenth century. Some mêlées even took place indoors: in 1611, while still a child, Louis XIII was present at a bear and dog fight in the oval room of the Château de Saint-Germain.[28]

The most common battles pitted wild beasts (bears, boar, lions, tigers, leopards, elephants) against domestic animals (bulls, mastiffs, horses, cows and donkeys). It was a matter of measuring the power of the former against the well-known strengths of the latter, of seeing whether nature or humanity would carry the day. There were also combats between wild beasts (lion against bear, elephant against

tiger or rhinoceros) which either mixed or segregated indigenous animals – favoured for this purpose – and exotic ones. These events fostered the foundation of a rudimentary zoology based on comparison and ranking. For example, the arrival of an elephant and a rhinoceros at Lisbon in 1517 provoked a debate at court about their mutual antipathy, as claimed by classical authors, which the King decided to test with a confrontation between them.[29]

This custom also corresponded well with the nobility's code of ethics, in that it proclaimed the profuse generosity of the host, who was sacrificing some of his most precious possessions for the pleasure of his guests. The intention was to entertain. These fights would be played out in an abundance of brutality and blood, and the most Dantesque of encounters (elephant versus rhinoceros) or the most unfair (lion versus cow) were allowed to take place, the better to create carnage. These encounters satisfied the voyeuristic desires of what was still a warlike society in the sixteenth and seventeenth centuries. In the 1700s, while these contests survived, they seemed rather to constitute a means of release for an aristocracy that was engaged in a process of civilizing itself. Thus, in Dresden in 1719, the attraction of violence mingled with delight in refinement:

An animal fight in a private lion house, 16th century.

[The] King, the Prince and the Princess were in a great hall, where there were several tables piled with preserves and refreshments ... The ladies of the town and a great number of outsiders were lined up on three tiers of balconies which fully surrounded the space. We found three bulls there, and another called *Auru Ochb* [aurochs] of prodigious grandeur and size ... Some time later, a fine, unharmed horse was made to enter, and it went straight to the large bull to attack it; but with one blow from the bull's horns it was put out of action for the rest of the day. There then appeared a lioness, a tiger and a lion, but none of these did much damage. The former two ran hither and thither, appearing to be frightened, and the lion calmly lay down during these goings-on. One would have said that he was no more than a spectator and referee of the fight. After this, no fewer than six bears were released, who in fighting over a small basin of water in the middle of the space did each other the most terrible harm. Yet they did not fail to fight a few more times against one of the ordinary bulls, which was furious and knocked them down one after another. There then appeared one of the biggest and ugliest monkeys I have ever seen, which tried several times, but in vain, to climb to the balcony. It attacked one of the bears and knocked it down, chased the tiger all around the space and fought with success one of the seven or eight boars which had been made to enter for the conclusion of the festivities. The King killed them all with musket shots, excepting one that the lion strangled in passing, and another that was mortally wounded and then dragged into the basin of water by one of the bears. So ended the festivities, from whence one went to the Italian *Comedia*.[30]

For people of the time, these encounters were considered failures when the animals refused to fight and did not assume the roles that had been assigned to them, in ignorance of their ethology. In Portugal in 1517, for example, an elephant fled at the sight of a rhinoceros. This incident caused disappointment, and jibes were aimed at these unfortunate creatures, whose combat had allegorical significance for the aspiring nobility. It was important for them to highlight the value of bravery and strength, and reinforce the supremacy of the heroic. The struggles between wild beasts that served as emblems in England and the Germanic lands mirrored the duels between valiant knights, and those who pitted the wild against the domestic must surely have been symbolically reiterating the aristocracy's privileged position. The frequent conflicts between big cats kept in castles and cattle purchased from butchers certainly carried this underlying message, and victories by domestic animals caused astonishment. Such was the case with the cow that, at Vincennes in 1682, defeated a lioness, two tigers, a lion and a wolf, 'even though one of them had flayed her haunches, which had made her lame and half-witted'.[31] This victory was interpreted as that of culture over nature.

If menageries proclaimed the human victory over the wild through the imprisonment of animals, then animal combat confirmed this domination by reducing the latter to performing for the pleasure of the former. Although unusual, apparently limited to the unrefined sixteenth century and often involuntary, the sudden appearance of a nobleman or even the Prince himself in the mêlée realized this symbolism in a brutal way and allowed mastery to be reclaimed. In 1515, at Amboise, Francis I felled with his sword a boar that had escaped from the arena and was provoking terror among the spectators.[32]

Wild animals were similarly used in hunting parks, where men sought to claim other kinds of trophies from game largely composed of indigenous species (stags, roe-deer, boar roaming in herds), but including a few acclimatized species such as fallow deer. This did not include the warrens that were a frequent element of provincial manors. Smaller in scale than parks, and enclosed by walls or ditches to guard against predators, poachers and herds of cattle, warrens made animal management and hunting easier, but by the sixteenth century they were often no more than simple reserves for rabbits, which were neither truly wild nor clearly domesticated.[33]

More significant were the large parks that Western aristocrats created almost everywhere, siting them near their castles or favouring them with residences. The Duke of Ferrara did this, as did the Duke of Calabria at Poggio Reale, or indeed Cardinal Riario at Bagnaia, near Viterbo, where he demarcated a *barco* of 25 hectares in 1514, walling it in and populating it with game. Game parks were common in England. Windsor Park contained, over an area of 720 hectares, a great quantity of deer; in 1764, the Duke of Cumberland entertained himself by setting his tigers on this prey.[34] In France, sovereigns scattered castles around good hunting areas and often equipped them with reserves: the Château de Chambord, on which work began in 1519, was at the centre of a park of 5,500 hectares. The same was true in Spain, where monarchs used the grounds of the Casa del Campo in the seventeenth century, and in the Germanic lands, where, for example, the Prince-Bishop of Würzburg had a summer residence built at Veitshöchheim to which he added a large game reserve in 1686. These creations continued into the eighteenth century, an example being the King of Sardinia's property at Stupinigi, constructed in 1759.[35]

The establishment of such parks did not put an end to hunting in the open forest, but it did allow game to be controlled and released in other areas, and meat to be obtained 'as readily as from a kitchen or larder', as Charles Estienne wrote in 1564.[36] They must also have allowed for the close observation of animals' habits or the progress of hunts. Theorists of residential and garden design were insistent on this point. In Italy, from the fifteenth century, it was felt that the ideal park should be centred on a hill topped with a pavilion and planted with sufficiently well-spaced copses for easy viewing. In France, such parks were composed of plantations of trees and meadows roughly square in form, called *parquets*, and were probably criss-crossed by paths radiating like stars, a scheme applied to the royal forests, for example at Compiègne from the time of Francis I. In the Germanic lands, parks were surrounded by crenellated walls and observation towers, although seventeenth-century designers synthesized Italian and French influences by advocating pavilions and avenues set out in the shape of a star.

At Anet, Philibert de l'Orme created perspectives with a system of terraces and recesses which allowed one to follow the pack without leaving the château. At Stella Castle near Prague, constructed by Archduke Ferdinand of Tyrol, the hunting pavilion was situated inside the reserve, and its star shape multiplied the available sight-lines. At Clemenswerth, built between 1737 and 1747, an octagonal pavilion occupied the centre of the park. Thanks to the landscaping, Francis II and his court could admire fights between stags, in the image of chivalrous tournaments, at Saint-Germain, and Louis XV was able to see the morning ceremonies of the rut at Fontainebleau.[37]

Mostly, however, these parks facilitated hunting, which occurred frequently thanks to efficient management of the abundant game, and which could be included in such festivities as the torch-lit pursuit at Chantilly one evening in 1718. They made it possible for the scale of the slaughter to escalate (up to a thousand boars a day at Dresden in 1670), communicating an increased taste for ostentation and hosts' boundless generosity. Finally, they allowed the confrontation with the wild to be staged anew, and dominance to be asserted in the midst of landscaped, domesticated nature.[38]

A change in aristocratic practices emerged in the seventeenth century. Hunting with the aid of exotic wild cats, notably cheetahs, declined during this period despite the efforts of Emperor Leopold I to revive it at Neugebäu, and despite a few echoes in the eighteenth century, such as the hunt featuring tigers that was arranged at Windsor in 1764. The hunting of big cats themselves suffered the same fate and, by the 1700s, the nobility could barely maintain its interest in animal combat. It disappeared in France from the beginning of the century, and stagnated in Italy and England, although George II (1727–60) did organize a few fights, and it only really survived in Eastern Europe and Russia. In 1775, Abbot Coyer visited Florence and observed the change:

> You won't need to be told about a show that enjoyed fame under the Medici! A fight between beasts, in imitation of ancient Rome. Today, it is hardly worth more than that bit of mischief on offer in Paris [the bullfight], since the animals are not free to fight each other without interference; to prevent them from tearing each other apart, men hidden in a machine on wheels use devices to frighten and separate the combatants, which are few in number: two lions, two tigers and a wolf. The only thing left worth seeing is the amphitheatre. I asked to know the reason for this decline; I was told that it was too expensive as it was.[39]

Over and above the possible financial considerations, there was a change in mentalities as a result of the civilizing process that has been described by the historian Norbert Elias. Over time, this engendered – at first in European courtly society and then, through social mimicry, among the bourgeoisie – the cultivation of morals, the control of self and of passions and impulses, a retreat from physical and verbal brutality, and a taste for more refined entertainments. Henceforth seen as barbaric, bloody events involving animals lost their appeal. A parallel can be drawn with the decline of the tournament, and then of the duel. The transformation accelerated to such an extent that fights were appropriated and quasi-institutionalized by the people, with bullfights in Spain, fights between bulls in France and mastiffs in England and so on. The aristocracy withdrew from such activities, although this was not true of the great slaughters of the hunt (using either traditional means or firearms), because these were the privilege of the nobility, and because ceremony seems to have sublimated violence. The inveterate hunter, however, was somewhat decried, and the subject henceforth excluded from polite conversation.[40]

2 THE ARISTOCRACY'S NEW-FOUND CURIOSITY

The most significant development of modern times for the history of zoos lies in the growing influx of exotic animals caused by the expansion of trade and the great discoveries of the fifteenth and sixteenth centuries. In fact, it was in the 1500s that the term *exotique* first appeared in French literature, used to describe objects from distant lands. Rabelais seems to have been the first to employ it when, in 1552, he described the markets at the port of the island of Medamothi, which exhibited 'various paintings, various tapestries, various animals, fish, birds and other exotic and well-travelled merchandise' brought by merchants from Asia and Africa.[1] First adopted in the late sixteenth century, the English word *exotic* was initially used to designate a more or less barbarous foreigner; from 1645, its use extended to plants or animals from other continents and, in 1650, to distant lands themselves.

The European aristocracy's interest in rare and curious animals began to develop in earnest in the 1500s, alongside an increasing curiosity about the marvels of nature, from flora to fauna, from stuffed specimens to living, breathing creatures. For among the characteristics of the so-called Renaissance Man were his wonderment at the works of nature, his taste for extravagance and his productivity. This state of mind was a consequence of exploration, which revealed new worlds and brought as many curios to Europe as it did new commodities. To this was added the effect of the printing press, which made it possible to disseminate classical literature in copious quantities from the end of the 1400s. Many classical authors, such as Pliny in his *Natural History*, delighted in evoking astounding stories and fantastic beings; some, like Ovid in his *Metamorphoses*, glorified nature's creative power, mostly manifest in monsters and curiosities. Thus as the Scientific Revolution unfolded slowly, the concept spread of nature as a living organism, nature endowed with a soul, as were its various elements (earth, rocks, plants), and possessing a certain autonomy in relation to God, who permitted it to invent, to play, to decorate the world with its admirable and singular creations.

The desire to collect these rare and curious, and therefore costly and precious, *naturalia* spread almost

An imaginary 'man-eating dromedary', early 18th century.

everywhere in parallel with this concept. Initially, this penchant of the aristocracy allowed its members to assert their dignity and superior character; it was encouraged by groups that hoped to provide or study such items (travellers, merchants, scholars and artists). In terms of status, the accumulation of objects that were devoid of any concrete use was close to the collection of works of art; it expressed a taste for the gratuitous and a disdain for vulgar utility, distancing the nobility yet further from the rest of society, which was constrained as always by necessity and material considerations. Collecting was an instrument of prestige, and the loftier one's position, the more impressive the number and quality of the assembled elements had to be. If some, like Rudolf II, Holy Roman Emperor from 1576 to 1612, took to collecting with a passion, many others practised it out of obligation and in emulation of their peers.[2]

CABINETS OF CURIOSITIES

Due to considerations of time and the difficulty of transport, collectors' choices prioritized imperishable objects of minimal size, and the collecting spirit expressed itself first and foremost through cabinets containing curiosities that were relatively easy to obtain. A number of princes began to assemble such collections in the sixteenth century: Francis I; William IV, Duke of Bavaria; Cosimo I, Grand Duke of Tuscany; Ferdinand of Tyrol, Archduke of Austria. There was a noticeable rise in the number of exhibition rooms, also called cabinets, in the second half of the sixteenth century that was accompanied by their spread not just among the aristocracy but also among scholars (Leonardo da Vinci), doctors and the affluent bourgeoisie – a phenomenon that became more pronounced in the seventeenth and, especially, the eighteenth centuries. Cabinets were common

in eighteenth-century England. Sir Hans Sloane, doctor, doyen of British naturalists and (in 1727) Newton's successor as president of the Royal Society, mustered a fabulous collection that was celebrated throughout Europe; Linnaeus travelled in order to study it in 1736.[3]

These cabinets of curiosities were rarely specialized and would be just as likely to display *artificialia* created by human agency (works of art and ethnological items) as *naturalia* (minerals, stones, fossils, plants, fruit, specimens of wood and animals). They were envisaged as microcosms, as condensations of the perceivable, understandable world. They contained disparate collections of all the rare and curious things that would best express the diversity and power of human, divine and natural invention. There was therefore no rational classification or sorting in the sense that we might understand it, because the division between natural and supernatural did not exist, God and nature being all-powerful, and because creative forces made themselves seen and understood to best advantage in accumulations of extraordinary objects that symbolized the extent of their potential.[4]

In the sixteenth century, the part played by *naturalia* varied from region to region. In Venice, cabinets contained scarcely any *naturalia* before the end of the century. The rest of the Italian peninsula as well as the south of France seemed to prefer antiquities, in contrast to northern Europe. This geographical divergence began to blur in the 1600s, but *artificialia*, especially medals and antiquities, continued to take pride of place until the years 1730–50. From this point on, with natural history becoming fashionable among the nobility and the cultured élite (as indicated by the success of the French naturalist Buffon and the fame enjoyed by the Swedish botanist Linnaeus), collections of shells, minerals, plants and animals took on growing importance. Adopted by courtiers, they were mostly the work of scholars versed in

An Italian cabinet of curiosities, *c.* 1600.

medicine or pharmacology. They became a popular diversion for members of high society just as the exhibits themselves became more specialized, a process that began in Italy at the end of the 1500s and that led to the formation of the natural-history cabinet.[5] Every wealthy milieu was involved: royal families, the court, the legal profession, provincial lords. It was the same in Venice as it was in Sweden, where Linnaeus' renown prompted King Adolphus Frederick, the Count of Ticino and other aristocrats to collect *naturalia*.[6]

Among these *naturalia*, two kinds of specimens held a particular fascination for collectors from the sixteenth through the eighteenth centuries: deformed animals (together, in the eighteenth century, with embryos), because they spoke of the power of nature; and exotic, curious or rare creatures, because these characteristics illustrated both the variety inherent in nature and the value of the collection, and justified the effort expended by its owner. Indigenous animals were not highly valued.

In the French cabinets of the seventeenth and eighteenth centuries, the most common species were those that fired the imagination while being easy to collect thanks to their small size or ease of preservation. Visitors would find fish (sawfish, sunfish and remora, which were thought to be able to bring ships to a standstill, for example); skeletons or bones of dolphins, whales or porpoises that were too large to be preserved in their entirety; the shells of tortoises or armadillos; dried crocodile or chameleon skins that would not decay; great numbers of crustaceans, insects, butterflies and birds, notably ostriches, parrots and toucans. Quadrupeds were few in number, represented by small stuffed examples or by a few teeth, horns and bones from more sizeable mammals such as elephants, rhinoceroses and gazelles.[7]

In princely exhibits such as those of the kings of France or the grand dukes of Tuscany, mammals, preserved by a variety of methods (in jars or in the form of bones, skeletons or stuffed skins), were much more numerous and indicated the owners' social standing. But this was not always the case. The collection personally assembled by the King of Sweden at Ulriksdal Castle showed a preference for species that were easier to display: 'animals preserved in alcohol, innumerable stuffed birds, an incredible number of insects on pins and shellfish, arranged in little boxes', as Linnaeus wrote, having been called upon to classify the collection according to the classification system he had just invented.

Travellers and, later, scholars were often entrusted with the supervision of these cabinets, for example those of the Italian princes or the French monarchs from the 1500s on. Under the influence of the Scientific Revolution, they imposed a new reading of nature, investigating regular (and less interesting) rather than extraordinary phenomena, the laws rather than the wonders of nature.[8] However, the fascination of exotic animals did not wane, even if they continued to intrigue and be coveted because they were little known rather than because they were considered to be miraculous.

A TASTE FOR RARE ANIMALS

It was in this context that the attraction of living animals and a new impulse to collect them began to develop. In Prague, under Rudolf II, rare beasts could be seen in three places: at the menagerie, in the cabinets and in the albums of drawings of live or dead animals made to preserve their memory. In Dresden, in the seventeenth century, one could visit the castle of the Elector of Saxony and see mineralogical collections, paintings, medals, automata, an apothecary and his mummies, an exhibition of animal skeletons and, outdoors, living African species.[9]

In the 1500s, curious animals had still been very rare, as sought after as sugar, the finest spices or the most beautiful precious stones or furs. On the Italian peninsula, noblemen would promenade with parrots or monkeys on their shoulders. Popes and cardinals before the Counter-Reformation, Portuguese sovereigns, Emperor Charles V, Margaret of Austria and Catherine de' Medici were all fond of the company of such animals. The practice spread through social mimicry among the old aristocracy and the wealthy bourgeoisie, in keeping with their increased wealth and the relative fall in prices thanks to the increasing number of imports. Eighteenth-century memoirs and journals often recall these animals and the tribulations some of them endured. In 1768, for example, the Queen of Sweden resolved to give her monkey to Linnaeus because it had become insufferable at court, where it would rip the buckles off courtiers' shoes.[10]

But true collections were the sole preserve of princes and the aristocracy for reasons of cost; the inadequacy of accommodation gave rise to high rates of mortality and necessitated the incessant renewal of stock. Ordinary collectors, among whom were many lesser nobles, often had to content themselves with stuffed specimens or a few pieces that were cheap and easy to preserve. The power and riches of princes were therefore emphasized even further. Cabinets, on the other hand, became progressively more and more popular, although their inherently private nature (the animals were often arranged in cupboards) did not declare the possessors' prestige emphatically enough. This remained the case even as the reputations of such collections spread throughout Europe and they opened their doors to visitors.

This symbolic importance of living collections explains why they were rarely supervised by scholars. Grandees devoted a lot of attention to their animals, sometimes placing orders with merchants themselves and sending agents to locate rare beasts. Thus, in 1682, Abbot Bernard Lenet ran from one Parisian *animalier*'s boutique to the next for the Comte du Grand Condé:

> The bird-seller having notified me that he had an extraordinary bird freshly arrived from the Indies, I went to see it, and I found it as rare in its figure as in its plumage. It is a little larger than a big lark; it is all fire-coloured, with a crest on its head, and a large reddish bill too, well made and steady on its feet, very cheerful, very lively and eating well. It has, says the bird-seller, a warbling song like a nightingale's, but I did not hear it, although I did hear an occasional whistle which was very pretty and gracious; and if one were assured that it would live a long time, it should not be passed up; it is true that it seems healthy and eats well, of a certain seed that is called *alpiste*, which it likes very much. If Y.M.S.H. [Your Most Serene Highness] would like it, I will make the trip, pay for it and send it to you.[11]

The Condé menagerie at Vineuil, 17th century.

Birds occupied a predominant place which remained unchallenged until the eighteenth century. In the 1500s and 1600s, they were sometimes the only animals to be present alongside big cats. Thus, in Florence, the great aviary at Pratolino formed a counterpart for the old lion house in the town. Henry IV had an aviary installed at Fontainebleau along with facilities for staging big cat fights. With the decline of the latter, some menageries of the late sixteenth and seventeenth centuries contained only birds, since they were less costly to buy, and their upkeep and conservation were simpler. This course of action was taken mostly, but not exclusively, by provincial lords. The Earl of Portland possessed, near The Hague, an aviary and ponds teeming with birds. The Vineuil menagerie founded by the princes of Condé held, in the years 1677–1709, almost nothing but birds of every kind.[12]

Parrots and macaws imported from South America by the Portuguese were among the most prized specimens in the 1500s. It was mostly for their sake that the future Emperor Maximilian II had a building, intended solely for exotic animals, built at Ebersdorf in 1552. Many such birds were also to be found at the Vatican or at the residences of Roman cardinals. The small exotic birds of Asia and South America (birds of paradise, hummingbirds, canaries), brought to Europe by the Portuguese and the Dutch, could be found in most contemporary aviaries. But there were also larger birds, and these seem to have formed the majority of discoveries and imports in the sixteenth and seventeeth centuries, with the exception of big cats: exploration and trade favoured, besides the Levant, the lands of South America, the Indies and the ocean islands, all of which were rich in bird life. Without making an actual inventory, one can list ostriches, various breeds of crane and heron, curassows, pelicans and cormorants. Rarer and more sought after were gannets, dodos and penguins, discovered in 1598 and 1599, and condors, as well as cassowaries, the first example of which reached Amsterdam in 1547 and caused a sensation. It was purchased by the Archbishop of Cologne, who presented it to the Emperor.[13] Although the number of different species seems to have increased in the 1600s and 1700s, birds ceased to have the same degree of novelty and curiosity. It must be stressed how difficult it is to assess their distribution. Despite the arrival, effectively, of more and more exotic animals, they remained few in number and often appeared intermittently, meaning that one European generation would see some while the next would discover others.

Birds were housed, according to their size, in aviaries, in enclosures equipped with pools, on ponds or even in apartments. In fifteenth- and sixteenth-century England, the aristocracy had luxurious birdcages made, in wood and glass, often decorated with precious stones, and in varied architectural designs (castles, abbeys, cathedrals and palaces) and styles (Doric, Ionic and Gothic). In the seventeenth and eighteenth centuries, there was a proliferation of treatises on the subject of birds, informing owners how to avoid an 'often prompt' death and the loss of a sizeable investment. Feeding methods were proposed, as well as models for cages and aviaries: for some, wooden enclosures, open on all sides to allow the creature to become familiar with its environment, and high enough to allow it to fly, to thrive and to avoid the onset of fatal melancholy; for others, open-air cages made from iron mesh.[14]

It was primarily the diversity of birds that attracted monarchs and grandees: this justified collection as an enterprise because it allowed inventories of these marvels of nature to be compiled, and because it also made collectors' reputations. In 1665, a visitor to Versailles discovered 'more than 40 species that I had never seen before, nor even heard spoken of'.[15] The splendour of their songs, shapes and plumage was also seductive. Birds appeared to be nature's own works of art, and the fascination they aroused illustrates the growing refinement of Western courts. Visiting the menagerie at Versailles with Racine, Boileau and Molière, the French fabulist La Fontaine wrote:

It is a place filled with many kinds of fowl and quadruped, most of them very rare and from far-flung lands. They admired how one single species of bird multiplied into many different kinds, and praised the artifice and diverse imagination of nature at play in animals, as in flowers. What pleased them most were the Numidian dragonflies and some fishing birds [pelicans] which have uncommonly long bills with skin hanging beneath that serves them as a pocket. Their plumage is white, but a brighter white than a swan's; although close up it seems flesh-coloured, and verges on a pink colour towards the root. There is nothing more beautiful.[16]

Pelicans at Versailles in the time of Louis XIV.

Attention also fell on more or less wild, or even domesticated, exotic fowl imported (from the sixteenth century) mainly from Asia (such as Chinese peacocks and pheasants) but also from Africa (such as guinea fowl) or from America (such as turkeys). They were grouped with their indigenous congeners and installed in farmyards, in specially constructed pheasantries with sheds and pools, as well as in game parks. These species seem to have been by far the most numerous and were present at a great many noble residences. In the Holy Roman Empire, the breeding of pheasants was one of the privileges of the nobility. Most French lords, noble or bourgeois, possessed no other kind of exotic animal. However, they could also be found in the most prestigious seventeenth- and eighteenth-century princely menageries at Versailles, Schönbrunn, Potsdam and elsewhere.

Pheasants were mostly intended for consumption. Their recent introduction, their relative rarity, their sometimes delicate breeding, and hence their expense, kept them exclusively on aristocratic tables in the 1500s and 1600s. The élite's disaffection at that time with large ceremonial birds such as swans, cranes and herons, whose flesh was considered too tough for refined palates, made room for other birds thought to be more delicate in flavour. The turkey, the consumption of which was popularized somewhat in the seventeenth and eighteenth centuries with its occasional appearance on the tables of the wealthy bourgeoisie, took its place alongside the pheasant, which remained costly and precious throughout the period. This domestic use highlights the instability of the lesser menageries. At the mercy of royal and noble successions, developing fortunes, the whims of their proprietors and the arrival of new animals, they often veered from being handsome ceremonial collections of various species to being pure pheasantries or simple farmyards with poultry, cattle, sheep and pigs. Such was the case at Weimar for example. After the death of Duke Ernest-Augustus in 1751, his successor scaled down the menagerie, thought to be too expensive, by selling the rare species and keeping just the pheasantry, which itself only contained fowl destined for the table.[17]

Some of these birds were also hunted in game parks, which were frequently replenished by the release of bred animals. The menagerie at Kew Palace in England possessed, in the eighteenth century, pheasants from China and Tartary.[18] At Versailles in 1684–5, nearly six thousand pheasants were released into the park. Finally, pheasants were used for decoration in pleasure gardens, especially in the eighteenth century. Pheasantries thus became substitutes for overly costly ceremonial menageries. For example, at the castles of Augustus near Brühl in 1747–54, of Clemensruh at Poppelsdorf in 1758, and of Karlsruhe in 1764, they were transformed into or established as promenades with pleasure rooms at their centres where visitors would dine, amuse themselves and admire the birds, notably pheasants and peacocks, these seldom being eaten after the seventeenth century.[19]

With the exception of big cats, exotic quadrupeds were still exceptional in the 1500s. Indian elephants enjoyed an ambiguous status somewhere between fighting animal and grand curio. When Henry III deserted Poland in 1574 to take the throne of France, he passed through Vienna, where the Emperor had him admire his 'most singular' possession: his pachyderm.[20] It seems that only a handful of giraffes or rhinoceroses arrived in the course of the sixteenth century, and virtually no crocodiles, as these were mostly collected stuffed. More common were the various species of monkey (poorly differentiated by contemporaries), stags, deer, gazelles or antelopes and, above all, those domestic crea-

tures that were less dangerous, easier to transport and satisfied just as fully the requirements of curiosity and collection: camels, dromedaries, horses, sheep and goats. Most came from the Levant and Asia, and a few from the coasts of southern and western Africa or from America, where quadrupeds of decent size were rare.

These animals still formed the core of most menageries in the seventeenth and eighteenth centuries, and their numbers increased (elephants, for example, became less rare in the 1700s), but at the same time the range of species grew. Europe saw the arrival, through the channels detailed in Chapter 1, of a few orang-utans, one of the first appearing in Holland around 1640; of crocodiles at Versailles in 1687; of African hartebeest and zebras from the Cape in Portugal; of seals at Versailles; of llamas at Potsdam; and of kangaroos in England. While Asia remained prominent and America remained marginal, Africa began to furnish specimens despite being fairly unexplored – a foretaste of the massive consignments of the nineteenth and twentieth centuries. These new sources did not replace the old ones, however. The menagerie founded in Madrid in 1774 received animals from the Philippines, South America and the Indies, but also from Constantinople.[21]

In fact, countries of origin varied according to the European state in question, the structure of its trade and its patterns of colonization. While the Italian courts supplied themselves from the Levant, sixteenth-century Portugal, followed by the United Provinces of the Netherlands, received mostly Asiatic species via the Cape of Good Hope or the Gulf of Guinea. In France, as in the Germanic lands, sources were more diverse, and there was a progressive broadening of horizons, from the Levant and North Africa to more remote regions. The inventory of animals received at Versailles between 1664 and the French Revolution clearly

Exotic birds at Versailles in the time of Louis XIV.

demonstrates the influence of India, North Africa and the Levant, and the modest part played by the Americas (llamas and a few Canadian animals: foxes, lynxes and beavers).[22]

The diversification in livestock was again emphasized in the eighteenth century thanks to a fashion for landscape gardens, with hamlets adorned with sheepfolds and cowsheds, which stimulated an interest in European domestic animals. Such an interest had existed previously, for example among the princesses of the court of Louis XIV, who kept livestock destined for the dinner table in their menageries. But it was for decorative effect that Mme de Pompadour, a favourite of Louis XV, introduced cows from Holland to the menagerie at the Trianon at Versailles, and Queen Marie-Antoinette had cattle and sheep brought from Switzerland in 1785.[23] These foreign breeds, being little known and therefore curious local species, allowed people to collect animals and play at being farmers without

descending into vulgarity, all the while maintaining a distance from the world of the peasants and preserving the aristocracy's distinction. In England, following the troubles of the seventeenth century, a number of different animals were introduced to the handful of aristocratic menageries, above all to the grounds of stately homes (those of the dukes of Portland and Richmond, for example); these included zebras, Ganges stags, collared pheasants and goldfish.[24]

The list of curious animals grew even longer in the eighteenth century thanks to a change in the status of big cats, henceforth included among rare and singular creatures. The scientific expedition dispatched by the Elector of Saxony in 1732 returned with lions. In 1750, the Duke de Luynes mentioned three lions and two tigers alongside a condor, a pelican, a seal and a dromedary as being among the most significant animals at Versailles.[25] This was no doubt an effect of the decline in animal fighting and the increasing scarcity of big cats in North Africa and the Levant, which made them more precious. From this point on, the Western perception of big cats changed to focus more on their appearance than their ability in combat.

BROADER INTERESTS

The desire to own exotic animals was consistent with an increasing desire to collect all living things, everything from plants to human beings. The owners of cabinets accumulated exotic objects obtained from other peoples through gift, barter or conquest: tools of war (bows, arrows, axes), trade (baskets, gloves) and transport (canoes). The logical extension of this collecting instinct was a desire to see the human beings who had created the objects. Christopher Columbus, for example, presented Native Americans to the Spanish court, as did Cortez in 1528. In the fifteenth century, René d'Anjou had 'kept' Turks, Blacks and 'barbarians'. In Rome at the beginning of the 1500s, Cardinal Hippolyte de' Medici also maintained a troupe of 'barbarians', comprised of Turks, Moors, Blacks, Indians and others that spoke more than twenty different languages – a veritable image of the world after Babel. A century later, the Danish King Christian IV (1577–1648) exhibited captured Greenlanders at his palace. Deformed people were considered manifestations of nature's creative fancy at this time. Petrus Gonzalus, born around 1540 in the Canary Islands and covered in hair from birth, was brought young to the French court, raised there and then presented at a number of European palaces in the 1580s.[26]

While the 'collecting' of human specimens remained exceptional, this was not the case with plants. The great discoveries stimulated the importation of dried plants to supply the herbariums that began to spring up in the Italian universities in the mid-sixteenth century. One of the oldest, dating from 1563, was that of the botanist Andrea Cesalpino. A century later, plants could be found in most cabinets of curiosities, in effect constituting medicine chests containing every kind of vegetal product: plants, flowers, fruit, roots, bark and wood. The introduction of seeds, bulbs, tubers and living plants also began, albeit with considerable loss due to the difficulty of acclimatization and conditions in transit. Plants arrived from the East in Italy, from Canada in Paris, from Virginia in London, and from Cape Town and Asia in Amsterdam, which served as Europe's revolving door from the second half of the sixteenth to the beginning of the eighteenth centuries.

The channels through which plants were introduced were similar to those used for animals. They included travelling scholars, who initially journeyed alone – like Pierre Belon, who explored the Middle East in the middle of the sixteenth century, and the German, Rauwolff, who did the same beginning in 1573 – and then gathered in expeditions, which became quite common in the eighteenth century. There were also diplomats like Ogier de Busbecq, posted in Constantinople in the second half of the sixteenth century, who introduced several exotic plants to the West, notably the tulip. And finally, there were merchants, particularly active in the United Provinces of the Netherlands in the sixteenth and seventeenth centuries, who imported ethnographical curiosities, stuffed animals, fruits, seeds, bits of wood and plants. These merchants developed an intensive production of acclimatized plants in the Low Countries, to be sold locally – Holland was famously overcome by tulipomania in the seventeenth century – or sent on into Europe.

The enthusiasts of this period sought out the greatest possible number of exotic species, or of different varieties of the same species. The meagre estimate of the number of existing plants (five to six thousand in 1600) inspired the belief that it might be possible to form a collection that would be a microcosm, a more or less perfect reflection of the entirety of nature. The vertiginous rise in the number of new discoveries shattered that illusion, while the taste for the rare and bizarre gradually gave way to aesthetic sentiment and pleasurable sensation, both olfactory and visual (predominant in the 1600s). The layout of flowerbeds in this period was based on the alternation of colours, while a hundred years later there was a preference for grouping 'families' together and for producing what might be considered to be a more natural effect.

These collections blossomed thanks to the creation of botanical gardens. The foundation of chairs of botany in the Italian universities of the mid-sixteenth century brought with it the design of gardens (the first being in Padua and Pisa in 1545) that were often associated with cabinets of curiosities and conceived as microcosms intended to promote knowledge. This initiative was picked up by the rest of Europe, from Leiden (1587) to Berlin (1679) via Montpellier (1593), Oxford (1622), Paris (1635) and elsewhere. This first wave was followed by another, beginning in the late 1500s, of private gardens centred more around ornamentation, the fashion for which spread among the bourgeoisie. While numerous in the Netherlands, England, France and Italy, they were rarer in the Germanic lands until the late seventeenth century due to the ravages of the Hundred Years' War.

Monarchs and princes supported the intitatives of scholars to create botanical gardens. Such was the case with the Grand Duke of Tuscany, Cosimo I de' Medici (the first of that dynasty to possess a cabinet of curiosities), at Pisa. Some had their own gardens, which they entrusted to botanists or doctors specializing in the study of medicinal plants. A number of aristocrats also had ornamental gardens near their residences. But, as with cabinets, their social diffusion, aided by the fact that plants were less expensive and easier to acclimatize and maintain than animals, prevented them from being established as signs of noble distinction on a par with seraglios.[27] Botanical gardens and ornamental parks nonetheless inspired the creation of menageries of animal curiosities.

THE CREATION OF MENAGERIES

A distinction was seldom made in the sixteenth century between animals intended for ceremony, combat, pleasure and curiosity. This explains the ambiguity in status of the elephant, for example, and the gathering together of all types of beasts in the same places. Emperor Maximilian II placed his pachyderm and parrots in outhouses at Ebersdorf Castle alongside bears, lions, tigers and wolves. There were similar arrangements at sovereigns' castles in the Netherlands, Italy, Portugal and France. The menagerie at the Tower of London presented the same mix of animals in the eighteenth century as it had in the sixteenth: lions, leopards and tigers alongside bears, eagles, ostriches, monkeys and so on.[28]

This situation perpetuated itself in Europe in the seventeenth century since a great many princes and lords were happy just to adapt the surroundings of their residences to accommodate ever greater numbers of curious creatures. This was true of the Elector of Saxony at Dresden and the landgraves of Hesse at Cassel, who possessed a lion house, a cowshed containing cockatoos, parrots and a bear, a courtyard with a cassowary and two porcupines, and an enclosure for two aurochs. Many seraglios for fighting animals were transformed in this way into more eclectic

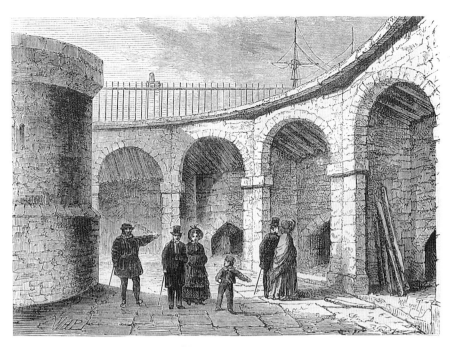

The Tower menagerie, London, early 19th century.

places that mixed all kinds of creatures, as in Parma, Florence and Madrid and at the Tower of London.[29]

The fondness for curiosities and the example of botany led some collectors to establish sites for unusual animals. These were still rare in the sixteenth century, and only seen in certain Italian villas or in the grounds of Portuguese princes at the peak of trade with the Indies. The practice developed later as many princes found that they no longer had anything but curious creatures in their collections. In Brussels, Archduke Albert possessed only an aviary of birds and some dromedaries. In the mid-sixteenth century, at Honsholredijk Castle near The Hague, Frederick Henry of Nassau kept exclusively rare animals, an orang-utan among them.[30]

This process of evolution was accelerated by Louis XIV, who made the distinctions between animals official by separating the places where they were kept. Around 1661, he had a seraglio of 'ferocious' beasts built at Vincennes for the organization of fights. Surrounding a rectangular courtyard, a two-storey building with balconies allowed spectators to view the scene. The animals were housed on the ground floor in cells bordering the courtyard, with small yards on the outside where they could take a bit of exercise. In 1662–4, Louis established a menagerie at Versailles, reserving it for exotic, rare and curious creatures. This particular enterprise marked a decisive step in the creation of menageries of curiosities and was imitated to some extent throughout Europe. The practice of distinguishing between sites was picked up in the Germanic lands in the 1700s, at Dresden, Potsdam and elsewhere. In Austria, the previously versatile Neugebäu Castle was reserved for ferocious creatures, while peaceful animals were installed at Belvedere and then at Schönbrunn.

Animal fights were halted at Vincennes around 1700, the site fell into disuse, and the animals were installed at Versailles with the others. This decision would prove to be a landmark. The Neugebäu seraglio was done away with in 1781 and its animals transferred to Schönbrunn.[31] This initiative also gave impetus to the abandoning of the old seraglios of big cats, which began in the seventeenth century: at Ghent in 1649, in Italy and Dresden during the eighteenth century, in London in 1831. In the early 1800s, the Tower of London's menagerie was in a state of neglect. Buildings were dilapidated, animals were few, and deaths

Pavillon de la Menagerie à Kew.

A pavilion in George III's menagerie at Kew Gardens.

'The Kingfisher', seen at Osterley Park menagerie, 1782.

were common. The pens were renovated and the collection restocked. In 1831, the menagerie lost the seraglio-like aspect it had had since the 1500s; fighting animals were replaced with birds, reptiles, herbivores and monkeys.[32]

Consequently, only menageries of curiosities were created after the late seventeenth century. Princes and important lords built them in France (Chantilly from 1663), England (Kew, Osterley), the United Provinces (Het Loo from 1748), Portugal (Belém in 1726, Quelez around 1780), Spain (Madrid in 1774) and Austria (Belvedere in 1716, Schönbrunn in 1752), as well as in the Germanic lands following the ravages of the Thirty Years' War and the ensuing reconstruction. Frederick William, Elector of Prussia, equipped Potsdam with a menagerie around 1680. The Palatine Elector, the Prince Regent of Westphalia and many others followed suit.[33] One should not draw false conclusions from this list, however. Due to their cost, menageries and even ponds of aquatic birds were quite rare. It was in the second half of the seventeenth century that these new sites took the French name *ménagerie*. Derived from the term *ménages*, which had been used from the thirteenth century to refer to housekeeping, *ménagerie* indicated the

The Menagerie of William III at Het Loo, by Melchior de Hondecoeter.

administration of a farm in the 1500s. From the 1580s, it designated the place that contained all the constituent parts of a farm, including the animals, while in the seventeenth century it was used to indicate the 'place constructed near a country house for the feeding of cattle and poultry'.[34] By extension, it was used in January 1664 in the *Comptes des bâtiments du roi* to designate the site of the animal collection at Versailles. In 1680, Pierre Richelet wrote in his *Dictionnaire français* that 'it is a place at the Château de Versailles where one finds, in the maintenance of all kinds and species of animal, everything necessary to make country life diverting and agreeable.' The great dictionaries gave the term its modern sense; that of the Académie Française (1684) refers to a site where princes 'keep rare and foreign animals'. The

term and its sense were adopted in German-speaking countries,[35] England, the Low Countries and the United Provinces in the eighteenth century, although the Italian peninsula, either occupied or in decline during the 1600s and 1700s, mostly retained the word *serraglio*.

3 BAROQUE SCENOGRAPHY

In the sixteenth and often in the seventeenth centuries, wild beasts, whether they were intended for combat, for use in ceremonies or as collector's items, were housed in gardens, courtyards, annexes and apartments, depending on the space available. At Amboise, King Francis I dispersed his animals throughout rooms, courtyards equipped with wire-fenced pens, and the grounds. The situation was the same at Kassel, at Ebersdorf in the time of Maximilian II, and at Prague, where Emperor Rudolf II placed animals in a park at Bubenec, near his castle, as well as in the castle's courtyard, moat and gardens.[1] Between the sixteenth and eighteenth centuries, animals at the Tower of London were distributed randomly around the available spaces, in pits, vaulted rooms, even corridors.[2] However, a more orderly approach to the deployment of wild animals at princely courts gradually developed under the influence of Baroque scenography, beginning in the sixteenth century in Italy.

ITALIAN VILLAS

Italy's aristocracy were able to escape the austere, inward-looking urban palaces of the fifteenth century by having sumptuous residences built on the outskirts of cities, such as the Villa d'Este at Tivoli, Pratolino near Florence, and the Madam, Lante, Medici and Montaldo villas at Rome. Influenced by Humanism, nobles of the time abandoned old designs and rejected the trope of the enclosed garden, which had been intended as a refuge from the violent, disordered and disturbing urban world, fostering intimacy, reflection and private conversation. Henceforth, gardens would be planned to allow their owners to let the world in, contemplate it and take control of it. The new villas, perforated by windows and loggias and flooded with light and air, looked outwards rather than inwards onto courtyards, allowing gardens, the surrounding sprawling countryside and the horizon to be viewed and enjoyed. In his work of 1485, *De re aedificatoria*, the Italian architect Leon Battista Alberti was the first to consider the garden as an integral part of the design of a villa and a continuation of the proprietor's living space. Gardens also came to be places where culture and nature could meet. By accommodating statues and antique reliefs, they paid homage to the ancient world by recreating the atmosphere of Greco-Roman gymnasiums, academies and sacred woods. They helped to realize the dream, driven by the myth of the Golden Age, of a return to perfection, to universal fulfilment through the study and celebration of the splendour and variety of God's creation. But they also revealed the elements and methods that had gone into their creation, thus highlighting their owners' imagination, taste and authority. Because all of their parts bore his signature, and because they were marvellous spectacles in their own rights, gardens were a means for their proprietors to assert their glory and nobility and, by extension, those of humanity at large, around which nature fell into ordered ranks.

In order to achieve this, each aspect of a garden had to be exceptional and provide food for the eyes and minds of visitors who came there to enter into a dialogue with the world. Three elements were crucial in this process. Perspectival effects accorded importance to sight-lines, organizing a garden according to axes and viewpoints, and giving the various elements a symbolic structure. The ordered succession of areas, from the regular flowerbeds surrounding the

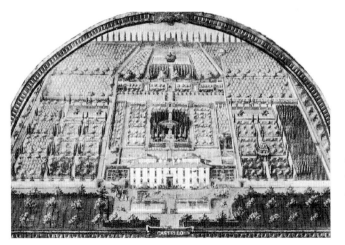

Grounds of the Villa Medici, Pratolino, late 16th century.

villa to the forests on the horizon reached via the *bosco* – a designed and developed wooded area – confirmed the subordination of nature to culture as the visitor approached the house, where great artworks would be on display. An abundance of fountains, streams and waterfalls, as well as the many works of artifice, such as water features, hydraulic machines and grottoes, loggias, mazes or covered alleyways constructed of trimmed greenery, celebrated nature's domestication; vegetation bent itself to the will of the designer, and channelled water submitted to his wishes.

One explanation for the development of this kind of theatrical fantasy lies in the conception of courtly magnificence as a means of government, a widespread practice among Italian courts which was notably expressed in urban festivals or triumphal processions. It also fell into line with contemporary curiosity about the wonders of the world. Works of art were 'liberated' from villas and installed in many corners of their gardens, invoking the goddesses of water or woods and praising nature's mysteries. Cabinets of curiosities, whose desiccated treasures were on display indoors, were extended outside in collections of exotic plants and trees (cedars, orange trees, bay trees, jasmine), preserved in winter in greenhouses or orangeries, which became fairly common in the late 1500s.[3]

Animals had a part to play in this *mise en scène*. At Pratolino, a villa conceived by Francis I de' Medici and known throughout Europe, the residence housed galleries of art and plant and mineral exhibits, while half of the garden/park was devoted to the glories of the past and the other half to the marvels of the present. This latter part exhibited mechanical theatres, grottoes filled with coral or depicting metal and silver mines, hydraulic organs and water features, mechanisms that imitated birdsong, aviaries with real exotic birds, fishponds and coppices populated with hares, goats and partridges.[4] Thus the animals housed at villas were no different to those found elsewhere: rare or indigenous fish in fishponds fed by fountains, birds large (peacocks, pheasants, turkeys, guinea fowl) and small in aviaries. Others were present in the coppices and the surroundings area. At the Villa Barbarigo near Padua, a rabbit warren was installed in 1693 as a symbol of peaceful refuge and restoration of the countryside to its original state.

The role played by animals in such schemes was expanded at the end of 1500s by the creation of parks adjacent to villas and their formal gardens. The Bishop of Viterbo had the Villa Lante built in 1573–8 in a *barco* (hunting park) at Bagnaia. Pope Sixtus X purchased 65 hectares between 1585 and 1588 to grace the Villa Montaldo and establish an enormous reserve there. The Roman villas of the early seventeenth century (Borghese, Ludovisi, Doria Pamphili) have similar profiles.[5] Most of these parks accommodated animals, and some presented visitors with approaches that intentionally dramatized their scenographic aspects. At the Villa Lante, visitors had to enter by the park, situated on a hill. They were welcomed by a fountain depicting Pegasus, the winged horse of classical antiquity, and busts of the Muses, suggesting that they were about to climb Mount Parnassus. This symbolism was supported by the presence of ilex trees, which, according to

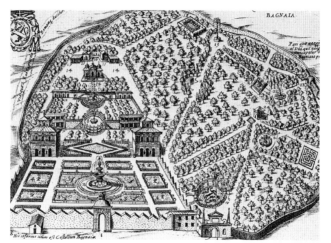

Grounds of the Villa Lante, Bagnaia, late 16th century.

Ovid, produced honey during the Golden Age. Visitors then passed a fountain dedicated to Jupiter and another to Bacchus, in memory of that same blessed time when wine flowed in streams, if Vergil is to be believed. A few animals, mostly deer, roamed freely in this blissful domain. Once atop the hill, visitors would enter the gardens at the back of the villa, marked by a fountain representing the Flood that announced the end of the Golden Age. They would then descend the terraces, sampling the views and crossing copses of trees arranged in lines, where huge suspended nets formed natural cages for birds who joined their songs to the sound of a channelled stream cascading from fountains. On the final terrace, two similar buildings served as aviaries, quite real this time, where birds could be admired. The approach to the villa ended among gardens whose symmetrical beds of low plants announced the definitive victory of culture over nature.[6]

The presence of animals was even more significant at the Villa Borghese, a veritable triumph of the Baroque style at Rome, representing a major step in the theatricalization of menageries. In the early 1600s, a nephew of Pope Paul V, Cardinal Scipione Borghese (1576–1633), a great Humanist, patron of letters (as well as a poet himself), art lover and collector with a permanent court of scholars and artists around him, decided to build a villa to attest to his own munificence and high culture by becoming the site of great artistic, botanical and zoological collections. This lengthy undertaking spanned the years 1608 to 1628. The building, begun from plans by Flaminio Ponzio, was finished by G. Vasanzia, who concerned himself especially with the decoration of the façade, studded with sculptures and bas-reliefs, and the placement of many antique statues recovered from Rome. The rooms of its two storeys were intended for exhibition as much as for reception, and famous paintings and sculptures, contemporary and Antique, were assembled there, including Bernini's *Apollo and Daphne*, the *Gladiator* attributed to Agasias of Ephesus, and many others.[7]

Outdoors, art mingled with exotic flora and fauna in a sumptuously composed setting intended to recall the mythological garden of the Hesperides, the daughters of the Titan Atlas. The formal garden, situated in front of the palace, was made up of squares of evergreen trees separated by a grid of paths. It was decorated with fountains and statues at each intersection. The 'perspective garden', reserved for the Cardinal and his closest friends and relatives, was situated at the rear of the residence and presented the visitor with copses of trees planted in rows, cleared of undergrowth and adorned with numerous statues and bas-reliefs in an effort to recreate an antique orchard. In the mid-seventeenth century, gazelles roamed this garden, released from a bordering *serraglio*. On each side of the villa, and therefore adjacent to the art collections, were the two 'secret' gardens dedicated to the marvels of nature: one, called the garden 'of melancholy', was devoted to flavours, and exotic citrus fruit was cultivated there; the other had colours as its theme and displayed the rarest flowers, as well as an aviary of remarkable birds built between 1617 and 1619. Composed of two symmetrical buildings, both topped with gables of wire mesh which let in rainwater to collect in basins for the birds to drink, the aviary allowed its inhabitants to be viewed from several sides. The interior was decorated with frescoes depicting the countryside, flowers and birds, following the Baroque habit of mixing artifice and reality, in this case to give an illusion of liberty that could not be granted to such costly beasts. At mid-century, a courtyard at the building's rear housed exotic gallinaceans, or domestic fowl.

Next to these gardens, a park of 40 hectares was created on old agrarian countryside of uneven topography. Plantations of trees, some (such as plane trees) imported from the East, were intended to recreate untamed nature and recall the sacred sites of antiquity where philosophers would gather to debate. Many animals were left at liberty in the park to reinforce this effect: hares, Syrian goats, stags and deer pacing the coppices; swans and other aquatic creatures on a lake; pheasants, peacocks and ducks around a poultry house. These animals could be observed from the villa's windows, and some of them were hunted. At mid-century, tortoises and lions were installed, and the *serraglio* also contained tigers, bears, wolves and boars.

As at the Villa Lante, a route through the grounds of the Villa Borghese lent a coherent dynamic to their scenography. Entering through the main gate, visitors crossed the formal garden, the palace's halls and the secret gardens, passed through the perspective garden, explored the park and then left through a second gate after crossing a newly cultivated area of vines and rare flowers. Thus there was first a gradation – from humanized nature (the formal gardens) to areas of culture in both senses of the word, artistic (the palace) and vegetal (the fruits and flowers) – and then a degradation, from those same places back to humanized nature (the perspective garden) and then to the 'wild' (the park), with a final gradation (fields of crops) announcing a return to the agrarian countryside. All of these shadings were embodied in a series of collections, living and inert, exterior and interior, and in a confusion or communion of the natural and artificial.[8]

DIFFUSION OF THE MODEL

While this model was well established in Rome, this was not the case across the whole of Italy. Venice, haughtily independent and governed by a patrician class of great traders,

Menagerie at the Villa Crivelli Sormani-Verri, *c.* 1740.

gave it only a lukewarm reception, for Venetian villas were integrated into the agricultural economy and served mostly to oversee the exploitation of the land, which left only meagre space for gardens. Residences designed by the great architect Andrea Palladio, for example, had vegetable plots, orchards and sometimes flower gardens, the whole augmented by farmyards, fishponds and dovecotes for domestic use.[9] This situation changed in the early seventeenth century, however. The garden became a sign of nobility and wealth, increased in magnitude and was adorned with exotic plants and trees. Venice came under the influence of France and Austria, which were expounding a Roman ideal that had been revisited, revised and given a foreign (and therefore acceptable) flavour, and a taste for the theatrical developed there. Common areas were hidden; water features, fountains, grottoes, mazes, statues and other elements multiplied. Aviaries graced by exotic birds also began to spread, but to a lesser extent, while adjacent parks remained rare.[10]

The Roman style quickly became the Italian model adopted throughout Europe and was enormously influential in France. The constituent elements of the garden (grottoes, fountains) were already well known, but the introduction of the Italian style of *mise en scène* systematized and dynamized them through the play of perspective and symbolism. Thus the design of Pratolino was reprised at Saint-Germain-en-Laye by Henry IV, who mixed nature and artifice by installing both aviaries and machines that imitated the birds' song.[11] Conversely, England, undergoing political upheaval during the seventeenth century and deprived of a centralized government, failed to adopt the Roman model, remaining faithful to the style of residences flanked by enclosed courtyards.

Treatises on gardens from the seventeenth and

eighteenth centuries theorized about scenography while often ignoring the symbolic and cosmographical aspects of sixteenth-century schemes (which corresponded less comfortably with contemporary sensibilities) and retaining only the visual effects. Thus in his *Jardin de plaisir* (1651), André Mollet describes the ideal garden as an ensemble of flowerbeds, lawns, coppices and carefully placed pathways:

> And, in order to perfect the work, let statues be placed on pedestals and grottoes be constructed in suitable places, then let paths be elevated and terraced according to convenience, not forgetting aviaries, fountains, water displays, canals and other such ornaments, each being duly put in its proper place, and all forming the perfect pleasure garden.[12]

Although vulgarized in this way, this model remained the preserve of princes and nobles. For reasons of cost, aviaries and even pheasantries were among the rarest of garden elements. But at the same time, those châteaux that did have precious animals on display often had only these types of installation and consequently held true to the principles of Italian scenography.[13]

The Italian ideal received just as warm a welcome in Spain and in the Germanic lands. At the royal castle of Buen Retiro in Madrid, the park alternated paths, lakes, hermitages, grottoes, salons and small outhouses, each containing a few animals. In his treatises dating from the first half of the seventeenth century, Joseph Furtenbach adopted not only garden scenography with all its characteristic elements – including the fishpond, the wire-mesh aviary and bird nets in coppices – but also that of the park with its plantations and buildings for the shelter and feeding of 'wild' animals in semi-liberty. On the other hand, the two spaces were separated by no more than a moat, which opened out the view and somewhat blurred distinctions between culture and nature. Princes began realizing similar plans in the late sixteenth century, for example the Archbishop of Salzburg in 1615. Rudolf II (at Hellbrun near Prague) and Ferdinand II (at Vienna) imitated the Villa Pratolino.[14] But the Thirty Years' War and the ensuing reconstruction stalled this movement until 1680–90, when another model began to emerge.

VERSAILLES, THE FIRST THEATRE OF THE WILD

In 1660, Louis XIV decided to adapt the hunting lodge at Versailles, built by his father, for more frequent visits by an ever-larger court which at that time was moving constantly around the Île-de-France. The work, which began in 1661, principally concerned the gardens, which were considered an indispensable entertainment, the château having no theatre. Under the direction of the architect Louis Le Vau, the hunting lodge took on the aspect of a *palazzo* with a busy façade and Italian-style gardens. Le Vau developed a theatrical scenography through the play of axial perspectives, the creation of terraces, and visual associations with surrounding spaces. He peopled the gardens with statues and filled them with fountains and water features (a passion of the King's) according to plans similar to those for the papal villa of Caprarola in Umbria. He built a grotto to Thetis, embellished with a rockery, coral, mirrors and a hydraulic organ. He also erected a menagerie,[15] most of which was constructed in 1664, when the first animals were introduced, although the interior fittings were not finished until 1668–70.[16] Situated in the south-west of the park, it was Louis XIV's first major project at Versailles and one of several pleasure houses that were gradually assembled around the château. The menagerie was accorded major importance in the 1668 revisions caused by the digging of the great canal, since it formed the southern end of the canal's cross-arm, becoming a counterpart to the Trianon and thus contributing to the ensemble's overall symmetry.[17] Above all, it represented the first modern menagerie in the West, not only because it contained only rare and unusual animals, destined solely for viewing by visitors, but also because it put an end to the earlier practice of dispersing creatures around princely residences, gathering them together in one place to exhibit them to advantage instead.

The menagerie was entered through a forecourt which heralded the little pleasure château. An interior staircase led to the first floor, where there were two apartments, to the left and right, and a central gallery leading to an octagonal pavilion in front of the main body of the building. Seven of the eight sides of its sole room, called the 'salon de la ménagerie', had windows that opened onto a balcony that looked out onto an octagonal courtyard surrounding the pavilion on seven sides, around which, in turn, seven animal enclosures were arranged. A staircase descended from this salon to the ground floor, decorated in the style of an Italian grotto, and gave access to the central courtyard, which boasted, according to Mlle de Scudéry in the earliest known account, 'a circle of six fountains issuing from six marble pillars. It is strewn with little pipes hidden underground, and whenever one wishes it can become, so to speak, a forest of criss-crossing fountains'. The animal yards – equipped with huts, ponds and fountains, and planted with turf – were separated from each other by walls and enclosed by iron railings to allow visitors to see into them; these railings were joined by architectural features illustrating scenes from Ovid's *Metamorphoses*.[18]

Behind these yards – the majority of which were devoted to the rarest of creatures, mostly exotic birds, but in which

Menagerie at Versailles in the reign of Louis XIV.

other species (ducks, camels, an elephant) lived from time to time – there could sometimes be found enclosures for horses, stags, deer, gazelles and so on. In the early eighteenth century, Louis XIV had the menagerie expanded: a second series of pens was created, partly surrounding the original seven, but not respecting their layout. These held deer and domestic fowl, as well as lions, tigers, panthers and leopards brought from the Vincennes *seraglio*, which was then abandoned.[19]

It is impossible to be certain of the influences behind Le Vau's extremely original design because no documents by him have survived. It is nonetheless possible to place it in a larger artistic and intellectual context. The central pavilion indicates a desire to observe animals from a particular vantage point, to be the audience to the spectacle of nature, that was already apparent at certain earlier castles and at the Villa Borghese. The same architectural device had been implemented in hunting parks. The radial layout of the pens, which reinforced the dominance of particular sight-lines, recalls the star-shaped schema applied to paths in some princely forests or hunting reserves. Realized in the forest of Compiègne in Francis I's time, theorized by Louis Savot in a treatise of 1624, this schema was reprised by Le Nôtre in the grounds at Versailles. It may have owed its architectural application to Vitruvius, who proposed a radial, concentric urban template in place of the Romans' usual orthogonal one, an idea that was revived in the treatises of the Italian Renaissance. Thus Alberti in 1485, Francesco di Giorgio Martini in 1500 and Fra Giacondo all proposed circular or octagonal towns, each with a major edifice at the centre and a system of concentric and radial streets. This model, occasionally realized, for example in the fortress city of Palmanova in 1593, was popularized in France by Jacques Androuet du Cerceau.[20]

Le Vau may indeed have synthesized these influences, but the animals' assembly in one place, a concept prefigured at those Italian villas where a particular route was suggested for visits, seems also to have been a product of the development of theatrical performance. The importance of festivities and entertainment in court life in the sixteenth and seventeeth centuries must be mentioned here. This was more than just diversion and frivolity. Such events were used to please the nobility, to control them, to glorify and exalt the King; they also were responses to the growing preoccupation of King and courtiers alike with being on perpetual display. Louis XIV elevated this fixation to the status of a form of government, enshrining it in the permanent ceremonial prescribed by etiquette, a choreography in which everyone had their place.[21]

Louis XIV adored the theatre. The absence of permanent theatres in the royal châteaux, and the taste for grand spectacles in the Italian style that united architects, sculptors, painters, musicians and actors of the time, required that scenery be installed in the vast spaces of the gardens. This was not a new development. In Italy, the creators of gardens, subsequently drawn to France, as we have seen, had organized ballets, and the first garden theatres had appeared at the Villa Mondragone and Villa Borghese. This initiative was adopted at Philip IV's Buen Retiro in 1637 and, above all, at Vaux-le-Vicomte during the glory days of the powerful government official Nicolas Fouquet, and Louis XIV was keen to surpass his predecessors at Versailles.[22]

Louis' entertainments made the most of the gardens, the menagerie and its animals. 'The Pleasures of the Enchanted Island' began on the evening of 7 May 1664 with a procession led by the King, followed by a ballet of the Seasons, who made their entrances as heralds of a light supper, Spring on a prancing Spanish horse surrounded by gardeners bearing preserves; Summer riding an elephant and commanding a troupe of harvesters; Autumn astride a dromedary and followed by grape-pickers; Winter perched on a bear's back and accompanied by old men and bowls of

ice. There followed, until 14 May, a succession of races and open-air comedies staged on temporary sets. On 11 May, the King led the court to the menagerie to admire its architecture and animals. The festivities of 1674 to celebrate the conquest of the Franche-Comté saw a sequence of promenades by coach and gondola, fireworks and illuminations, shows staged in specially adapted corners of the grounds, and banquets, often in those same places. On the third day, the King took all the ladies to the menagerie for tea.[23]

These entertainments were always organized around set routes, thus recalling medieval processions or mystery plays, and Renaissance triumphal entries. Interludes of merry-making and spectacle were concentrated at particular sites in the grounds where art and nature mingled, thus creating 'artificial theatre in a theatricalized reality'. For the two visual arts of theatre and garden design were, after all, seeking to fashion their respective worlds through identical means: perspective, with its singular axis and point of view, giving the illusion of reality and infinity; and the symbolic language of objects, integrating real space and lofty ideas. Installed in the gardens, theatre played with the panoramas of paths and waterways, the backdrops of greenery, the water features, the horizons. Conversely, the garden scene was a widespread convention in Italian and then French plays of the seventeenth century.

The menagerie formed one of these theatricalized places and, like the others, offered a dreamed-of spectacle, that of the marvels of nature, and a rarely seen reality. This is why it seems to have been structured according to the literary and architectural conventions of contemporary theatre: unity of place and of time, influenced by the rediscovery and pastiche of literary classics and translated into an assembly of beasts at a single point; the use of perspective and radial layout for this end, permitting the creation of 'real' décor and putting a stop to the narrative flux of time; the introduction of more or less symbolic elements to suggest environment and lend atmosphere (the ostrich enclosure used gravel to suggest the desert, and that of the aquatic birds had a vast pond); changing scenery (evoked by walking round the balcony); and staged accommodation for spectators (the pavilion's salon).[24]

After 1682 and the King's final move to Versailles, indoor festivities supplanted those that took place outdoors, for the gardens were considered too beautiful to risk damage by temporous installations or crowds of people. Although the menagerie now found itself isolated, it remained a destination for promenades – particularly after the digging of the great canal, which made it possible to get there by boat – and the site of informal meals and parties for members of the aristocracy, especially during the time the Duchess of Burgundy, wife of one of the Sun King's grandsons, spent there.[25]

Distinguished guests also visited the menagerie. In July 1664, the Cardinal-legate 'admired the great diversity of animals to be seen there, as well as the layout of the place'. King James II of England in 1689 and Emperor Joseph II in 1777 did the same. Between 1689 and 1705, Louis XIV composed several versions of a text entitled *Manière de montrer les jardins* which had to be followed to the letter by the park servants during official visits. The standard itinerary was restricted to the lesser park, as far as the Pool of Apollo, which gave a view over the château and great canal. The tour of the great park took in the menagerie and the Trianon, which were reached by boat. The King insisted on particular stopping points and certain views so that visitors could fully appreciate the patterns and perspectives. Once at the door of the menagerie, visitors were obliged to turn round to admire the cross-arm of the canal and the Trianon;

then they would 'go to the central salon. One will enter all the yards where the animals are. Afterwards, one will embark for the Trianon'.[26]

The menagerie's purpose was therefore to celebrate the King in all his glory. By its exceptional nature it illustrated, as did the rest of Versailles, his majesty and power, his ascendancy over the nobility and his subjects, his prestige and his supremacy over foreign powers. But it also exalted his power over the universe. By mixing culture and nature, the menagerie's architecture not only met the Baroque requirements of artifice and representation; it allowed culture to enclose nature, to gather it around the monarch, who from the central salon could take everything in at a single glance, and who so dominated all he surveyed that all of creation paid him homage, offering itself to him. This idea lived on in the eighteenth century. 'It is as if', wrote Dézallier d'Argenville in 1755, 'Africa has paid a tribute of its progeny, and the other parts of the world have paid the King homage with their rarest and most singular animals and birds.' The decoration of the gallery and octagonal salon at Versailles reinforced this symbolic appropriation. Around 60 pictures attributed to the animal painter Bernaerts Nicasius represented the menagerie's animals 'as if to prepare one for what one [was] about to see', wrote Mlle de Scudéry, 'or to remind one of it afterwards'. Drawn 'so naturally and with such life that nothing else compares', according to another visitor, these pictures confirmed the capturing and control of the actual beasts in their artificial surroundings. This development seems to have had its origin in the decoration of hunting lodges and was widely copied in eighteenth-century menageries.[27]

In fact, the menagerie formed part of a general desire to master nature on the part of the Sun King that was expressed symbolically in every element of the gardens. The networks of pathways, dense at first to define borders and copses, then broadening as they radiated out towards infinity, proclaimed control of the King's territories. The efforts to level out land through terracing, to transform marshland into ornamental lakes and ponds into pools, forced the site to conform to his designs. Water was diverted from its natural course, forced into pipes and transformed into liquid crystal in the form of fountains. Vegetation was severely disciplined: trees gave way to copses restricted to a height of 13 metres and converted, through incessant trimming, into curtains and palisades lining the paths. Other practices demonstrated an ambition to alter places and master situations: the importation and acclimatization of plants and trees (ilexes, fir trees, orange trees); the use of techniques (greenhouses, orangeries, wood-burning heating systems) to advance or prolong the harvest of fruit and vegetables, or even allow them to be produced out of season.[28] Louis XIV was asserting himself as a new demiurge, almost as a god.

THE FRENCH INFLUENCE

The prestige of the Sun King and his court inspired the spread of the Versailles model throughout Europe. Its influence was without doubt strongest in the Germanic lands, where formal gardens in the style of Le Nôtre first appeared in the 1690s. The radial design was quickly adopted as the style of princes. In his *Traité complet des palais pour les grands seigneurs* (1718), Leonard Christoph Sturm used the design in his proposal for a star-shaped park with a pleasure palace gracing its centre, a semi-circular courtyard with animal enclosures fanning out from it, and, behind this, a small circular yard surrounded by more pens. In 1802, Johann Krünitz defined the 'French menagerie' as the menagerie of princely courts.

The first example to be realized in the Germanic lands, and the most beautiful in the eyes of its contemporaries, was that of Prince Eugene of Savoy, famous for leading Austrian armies to victory against the Turks. First, he had Lower Belvedere Castle built between 1714 and 1716, along with a French-style garden equipped with a huge wire-mesh aviary that housed nearly a thousand birds. Then, between 1721 and 1723, he had the gardens extended, built the Upper Belvedere and created a large menagerie on the eastern flank of this rectangular building. The menagerie's layout systematized the design of Versailles and gave it more coherence. Around a semi-circular courtyard with a pool placed against the side of the palace, seven enclosures, arranged according to length, were arranged in the shape of a fan. Each one ended with a building at the back and was separated from its neighbours by walls, and from the courtyard by a railing adorned with paired features again illustrating Ovid's *Metamorphoses*: representations of Greek gods transforming themselves into animals or symbolizing the powers of nature. The view that unfolded from the castle satisfied more than just curiosity; the desire to collect, the thirst for power, and human domination of the animal world were all expressed, the garden being conceived as a microcosm, an image of the ordered universe, itself an indication of the ongoing interest in sixteenth-century cosmography in this region.

Schönbrunn Castle near Vienna was another large-scale undertaking. On the orders of Emperor Francis I, it was enlarged from 1744, while the gardens were redone in a Rococo style that left more room for imagination and the autonomy of various elements than did the French model: flowerbeds, copses, woods, a maze, grottoes, ruins, pyramids, fountains, waterfalls, pools, an aviary and a menagerie were all included. The menagerie was created in

Eugene of Savoy's menagerie at Schloss Belvedere, *c*. 1730.

Menagerie, Schloss Schönbrunn.

1751–2 by the French architect Jadot de Ville-Issey on the border between the gardens and the park. A circular yard situated at the intersection of three pathways, one leading to the castle and another to the neighbouring botanical garden, was ringed by thirteen enclosures of equal size. As at Belvedere, they were demarcated by buildings at the rear, walls at the side and a railing at the front. At the centre of this yard stood a single-storey octagonal pavilion, raised to provide a better view and containing a single room whose French windows let in light and permitting viewing of the enclosures. The interior was decorated with paintings depicting the menagerie's rare animals and, as at Belvedere, Greek gods celebrating the fruits of the earth or the metamorphoses of nature.

The radial design was reprised in 1702 at the menagerie of the Orangebourg residence of Frederick William, the Great Elector of Prussia, who had just crowned himself King; in 1715–18 at the menagerie of Karlsruhe Castle, built by the Margrave of Baden-Durlach; and again around 1730 at the Duke of Weimar's pleasure palace. Its frequent appearance in architectural projects confirms a success that was not restricted to the Germanic territories. In 1774, Charles III established a small menagerie at Buen Retiro in Madrid, where a building housing wild beasts took the form of an octagonal arena. The design's influence can also be detected at the Stadtholder of Holland's Het Loo; obliged to share power with the merchant oligarchy, he was keen to distinguish himself from them.[29] The scheme was therefore adopted by princes with an absolutist tendency, or absolutist desires, and by aristocrats celebrating military victories, doubtless because it symbolized mastery of the world. Interestingly, it was barely even echoed in England, which in the seventeeth century was in the grip of political turmoil, and which subsequently saw a slow decline in royal

power in favour of an aristocracy that was profoundly resistant to French influences and that developed another kind of garden, as will be explained later.

From the mid-eighteenth century on, the radial scheme encountered competition, as did the French-style garden. Jacques-François Blondel, one of the few architects to conceive of menageries as integrated parts of larger projects, proposed a U-shaped design with a salon on the short side, shelters on each wing and a garden in the middle, a perspective that was adopted at that time (1763), with a few alterations (no salon and a pool in place of the garden), at Schwetzingen Castle, the residence of Prince Carl Theodore of Neubau. At the Château de Lunéville, home of the exiled King of Poland, the menagerie was comprised of small buildings in a rectangular enclosure, while at Chantilly it was composed of a succession of terraced courtyards bordered by pavilions. At Lord Halifax's Horton, it took the form of a rectangular building which served as a reception room and was flanked on each side by an animal yard, itself enclosed by a wall sporting square towers. Again, the model was different at Castle Ashby.[30] In all of these cases, the pavilion or salon served as a venue for meals and concerts.

Whatever their design, integration with the garden and unity of place were invariably of paramount importance in these building programmes. The menageries of this period all relied on a system of Baroque scenography based on theatrical arrangement, the confusion of reality and artifice, and an integration with aristocratic customs of celebration and entertainment.

4 POPULAR PLEASURES

In the sixteenth century, access to aristocratic menageries was mostly restricted to friends of the owners or honoured guests, as it was in the cases of cabinets of curiosities. In Prague, Emperor Rudolf II cultivated his taste for privacy and seldom displayed his collections, animate or inanimate. There was, however, a growing need to appear in society and especially to proclaim the splendour, power and high culture of the master of the house, alongside a desire to satisfy the nascent, and essentially bourgeois, phenomenon of public opinion as it was being expressed in newspapers and books. This led in the seventeenth, and particularly in the eighteenth, centuries to the public opening of gardens, menageries and cabinets, which became visitor attractions described in guidebooks.[1] This development mostly affected large urban residences and princely estates on the outskirts of cities. Pleasure houses like the Trianon, tucked away in the countryside or in parks, remained the preserve of intimates of their owners. Lord Halifax's residence at Horton, in Northamptonshire, built in the 1750s, was a typical English pleasure house far from the public gaze. It consisted of a central building with a large reception room and one enclosed courtyard on each side where tigers, bears, storks, racoons and other animals were kept.[2]

Public opening was already occurring at Italian villas during this period. The French philosopher Montaigne, like many others, visited the Pratolino at Florence. At the Villa Lante and Villa Borghese, the gardens and parks were closed when the cardinals and their retinues were in residence, but the public could tour them at any other time. Later, during the early years of Versailles, the public could enter the menagerie only if armed with tickets and if Louis XIV was absent. It was thus that Boileau, Molière, Racine and La Fontaine discovered it in 1669. The King later decided to open the park, but vast throngs of visitors, especially after his final move there in 1682, led him to restrict access to the court in 1685 and again in 1699.[3] This measure was rescinded on both occasions because the monarchy had to heed its public, and because the presence of the Trianon made it possible to reconcile this obligation with the sovereigns' need for privacy. From then on, the park and the menagerie could be visited without hindrance throughout the eighteenth century. It had been so at the Tower of London for many years, for the British monarchy barely took an interest in the Tower, situated as it was away from their residences. The same was true at Schönbrunn from the 1760s and at the Prince of Orange's palace of Het Loo at the same time.[4]

PUBLIC SPACES

Places other than princely menageries did exist where the public could satisfy their curiosity about animals. In regions where power was divided, those towns with solid patrician governments that either enjoyed long-term political independence (as on the Italian peninsula or in the Germanic lands) or benefited from powerful cantonal or provincial autonomy (as in the Swiss Confederation or the United Provinces of the Netherlands) possessed small menageries. Venice had lions and eagles; Frankfurt kept stags in a pit in the 1500s. Amsterdam and Kampen kept lions in towers, and many of the cities in the United Provinces had parks with swans. Swiss towns such as

Bear enclosure, Bern, 1940s.

members of the public had the chance to see wild animals just as they had done in ancient Mesopotamia, Greece and Rome. For the most part, showmen were content to travel from town to town to present indigenous animals: usually bears trained to dance, do turns or fight other beasts, sometimes wolves or boar that had been hunted, but also marmots (such as those led by Piedmontese children in the eighteenth century). Exotic animals, especially monkeys and lions, grew in number between the sixteenth and eighteenth centuries, the most extraordinary of them crossing one or more borders. The first tiger seen for a very long time in Europe toured the Italian peninsula, stopping in

Zurich, Bern and Lucerne maintained bear pits. Those at Bern were made permanent after 1513, after local mercenaries brought back a bear they had seized from vanquished French troops in Italy as a trophy. As with the aristocrats whose customs such towns were consciously imitating, these animals, often big cats, communicated the independence, power and wealth of the localities in question.[5]

Other towns received animals as gifts or on bond from princes. This was the case with the stuffed specimens exhibited in public buildings – especially crocodiles, which were seen until the eighteenth century as proof of the existence of the biblical Leviathan and were suspended from the vaults of churches to assert victory over the Devil. In the 1500s, it sometimes happened that sovereigns entrusted their live animals to cities before undertaking their various peregrinations.[6]

But it was mostly thanks to itinerant showmen that

Savoyard with a Marmot, c. 1716, by Antoine Watteau.

The Display of the Elephant, 1774, by Pietro Longhi.

Turin in 1478.[7] An elephant visited Austria around 1550; others were in Ghent in 1642, in England in 1765, in Madrid in 1770 and in Turin in 1774 (it is not always possible to tell whether these were different beasts or one travelling from one country to another). The elephant Hansken crossed part of Europe, arousing great curiosity and becoming quite a celebrity. He appeared in Paris and Rouen in 1627, in Ghent in 1628, in Rome in 1630, in Toulon in 1631 and in the Netherlands in 1633.[8] One of the rare rhinoceroses of the early modern period, imported from Asia in 1747 by a Dutch ship's captain and called Clara, travelled the length and breadth of Europe on a horse-drawn chariot, accompanied by said officer, who made a fortune because he charged people to view her. Clara and the Captain appeared in the Netherlands in 1747, in the Germanic lands in 1748, in France (Reims, Paris, Lyon, the Midi) in 1749, and in Rome,

The Rhinoceros, 1751, by Pietro Longhi.

Naples and Venice in 1750–51.[9]

These showmen would assemble for the fairs which were held throughout Europe. Much documentation (exhibition permits, advertising bills, complaints) survives and provides an insight into their activities. At Reims, for example, three-quarters of them were French, mostly from the Paris Basin, and the others were Italian or German. They set up shop among the actors and acrobats in wooden huts and enclosures, where they exhibited their beasts for money. Although many only had one on show, the diversity of animals gradually increased, especially in the second half of the eighteenth century: rhinoceroses, elephants, camels, ostriches, seals, dolphins, crocodiles, iguanas, tigers, panthers, bears, various trained or untrained monkeys and perhaps some great auks. The same patterns were in evidence at the great Saint-Germain fair in Paris, which attracted merchants and showmen from all over Europe between February and April each year.[10] True travelling menageries, consisting of several species and moving from town to town and country to country, appeared during this period.

In the eighteenth century, fixed menageries were also created in the largest towns, initially in Amsterdam, the hub of animal importation into Europe. Blaauw Jan, an establishment named after a blue-dye factory which had previously occupied the building, was a menagerie-*cum*-inn which presented animals in wire cages. The public paid an entry fee, could drink beer or wine, and could stay as long as they wished. The manager brought animals from all over the world to the town *kermis* and then sold them on into Europe, for example to Schönbrunn's new menagerie in 1752. In London, Exeter 'Change opened in 1773 above the boutiques of the Strand and showed animals in minuscule cages whose walls were decorated with tropical foliage. In Paris, fairground stall-holders rented boutiques on the banks of the Seine or the Boulevard du Temple to accommodate monkeys, lions, birds and other species for exhibition or sale.[11]

THE LURE OF THE EXTRAORDINARY

Exhibitions invariably met with considerable success. In Dublin, in 1682, a huge crowd gathered to see the corpse of an elephant they had been denied the chance to admire when alive by inflated admission prices. A dromedary and a 'performing' elephant drew crowds in Paris in 1763 and 1771. The aristocracy, who were not averse to mixing with commoners at fairs in the evenings, came to see the more spectacular beasts that they could not afford or that were rarely seen in princely menageries. Even monarchs proved susceptible: the rhinoceros Clara was presented to Louis XV, who declined to buy her, the Captain having asked for 100,000 écus! William V of Orange and Emperor Joseph II visited Blaauw Jan in 1776 and 1781.[12]

In the eighteenth century, the more extraordinary animals even inspired fashions. Clara provoked sales of rhinoceros prints, engravings and pamphlets, and caused 'à la rhino' ribbons, harnesses, bonnets, wigs and even hairstyles to be invented. Showmen and salesmen also promoted social mimicry, as the bourgeoisie imitated the aristocracy in the 1600s and 1700s by buying monkeys and birds, a widespread practice in the Netherlands and the great European capitals.[13] Public interest settled on the biggest, most curious or most 'ferocious' species, and perceived them through the prism of the extraordinary. The testimony of Mrs Cradock, an Englishwoman who encountered a sea-lion in 1784 at the Saint-Laurent fair in Paris, is typical:

> We went first of all to see an excessively curious animal. It had been captured alive in the strait of Magellan ... This animal has the head of a leopard, large brilliant eyes, teeth resembling those of a lion, and a long moustache; a little below the head it is equipped with short flippers ending in webbed feet like a goose's, at the extremities of which there are five strong claws. The body, of about five feet in length, thickens in the middle to about the size of a big dog, and ends in a fishtail with a fin on each side. These fins resemble a dog's hind feet, but shorter, and end in the same way as the front flippers. Its skin is without scales, like an eel's, and a dark grey colour that is not so much flecked as intermingled with black. It seems voracious, swallowing the raw fish it is given gluttonously. It is fairly tame, letting its keeper embrace it, and lifting its head and puffing noisily at his command. I have never seen such an extraordinary creature.[14]

Attention was focused principally on exploring anatomy through comparison with better-known animals, an approach that had been used by Herodotus and Pliny. These points of reference made it possible to describe the animal, to decipher it, to find its place in the great variety of life. This explains the habit of projecting the fauna of the land onto that of the ocean, conjuring up, for example, the sea calf or sea elephant. But this form of interpretation also responded to a notion, put forth by eighteenth-century scholars but still current even today, that nature, and God, could act directly to create bizarre or hybrid animals, monsters and people according to their whims and fancies.

Observers were also concerned with animals' diets, which helped to give an impression of their way of life, and with the quantity of food they consumed, which was taken to be a measure of their monstrosity. In 1741–51, many writers noted with terrified delight the 50 pounds of hay, fifteen loaves of bread and fifteen buckets of water devoured and drained each day by Clara the rhinoceros.[15] Diet was also thought of as an indication of a beast's character, be it ferocious or docile. Interest in the possibility of commanding obedience from an animal was aimed at the symbolic confirmation of the right, natural or divine, of domination, and the possibility of realizing this over other species or distant lands. For species that were better known (whether at first hand or from images), such as primates or elephants, the question of their intelligence, already posed by classical authors, was examined through their ability to mimic humans, who were thus used as a yardstick because they were perceived to be the only creatures to possess rational souls. At Versailles around 1770, the public was enraptured by an Indian elephant that uncorked and drank bottles of wine or eau de vie, and chewed tobacco.

This sensationalist approach was shared and encouraged by the showmen, who would emphasize animals' remarkable dimensions, bizarre or composite forms, and fantastical appearances in order to attract customers. They often refrained from naming their animals to avoid making them seem commonplace to a predominantly uneducated or ill-informed public; in this period, information travelled slowly, verification was almost impossible, and the real was hard to distinguish from the false. In Paris, in 1774, the famous Gangan was displayed, a creature with the head of a Russian, an elephant's eyes, a rhinoceros's ears, a snake's neck and a beaver's tail. It was, in fact, a camel!

The showmen also hindered the emergence of a more rational, less distorted view of the animal world by invoking ancient or biblical myths that even scholars found it hard to dismiss. At the Saint-Germain fair in 1750, a showman claimed that his pelican opened its stomach to feed its young in an allusion to a verse of the Bible (Psalms 102:6) which had long since caused the bird to be seen a symbol for Christ. At Reims in 1754, another showman attributed to an iguana all the distinguishing characteristics of the basilisk, as recorded by Pliny. It scorched the stones on which it lay, killed all plants with its poison, and froze the blood and breath of any cattle it looked at. Scholars were only quoted when, due to their ignorance, they supported the showmen's extraordinary claims.

Showmen also made much of their beasts' human feats.[16] They were inclined to do so given that the public's attraction to exotic animals formed part of a broader appetite for the curious. Fairs offered multiple shows of trained animals performing tricks. These were mostly dogs and horses, but also stags, birds that pulled chariots or counted, hares that played drums and even, in Paris in 1804, fleas that pulled a coach, and two flies that fought a duel with pieces of straw! Such attractions became more elaborate during the eighteenth century. At Reims, a man presented an 'Academy' of dogs and monkeys costumed as soldiers and labourers that attacked a town, played cards, danced and ate at table. Monkeys enjoyed pride of place. At Paris, in 1714, one monkey – dressed as Harlequin, a musketeer or a young lady – saluted the company, sat on a chair and performed infantry exercises and acrobatics. At the same time, men exhibited their prowess as acrobats, puppeteers, tightrope walkers, conjurors and strongmen. The 1700s saw a fashion for wax figures, automata, Chinese shadow plays, optical effects and hydraulic machines in Europe. All of these trends occurred as the result of an interest in transcending the normal order of things: objects functioned on their own, animals imitated men, and men became superhuman.

This appetite for the extraordinary was also met by those marvels of nature, exotic animals and monsters. All fairs offered deformed animals, for example an enormous ox, conjoined twin heifers, a monkey with five feet, a three-legged horse. Unusual people were also well received: dwarves, giants, children covered in hair, strong women such a certain young lady named Cruel who lifted 400 pounds with her hair at the Saint-Germain fair in 1668.

Albino black men were displayed and, in 1747, a child that stayed for 31 years in the belly of its mother, who lived to the age of 62.[17]

Alongside the spectacles sponsored by the nobility, showmen organized fights between bears, lions and boar, or of bulls against mastiffs. These violent battles fulfilled the same fantasies regarding the extraordinary, and allowed spectators to believe that they were discovering the animals' true nature. They were institutionalized in the eighteenth century by the creation of special sites for them in large towns. The Hertz Theatre, for example, was founded in Vienna in 1755. London's Vauxhall, which opened in the same period, was a sort of permanent circus where animal combat was staged, as well as shows by lion tamers, jugglers, puppeteers and wrestlers.[18] In Paris, the 'Bull Fight' was established at the Sèvres gate at the beginning of the century, moving to the Chemin de Pantin around 1780. It took place in an amphitheatre on Sunday afternoons and religious holidays (the only public holidays) and pitted mastiffs against various wild beasts or bulls. These fights ended with the *peccata*, a contest between dogs and a donkey.[19] New sites of this type formed part of the eighteenth-century diversification of fairground attractions. They mostly attracted commoners, while the nobility scorned them due to social repulsion and a distaste for combat.

A SCHOOL OF ARTISTS

The rise of publishing multiplied the opportunities for the representation of rare and curious animals in book illustrations, the decoration of palaces, and paintings of historical, mythological or hunting scenes. The rarity of exotic animals, and the dependence on questionable texts from antiquity or accounts written by travellers, who had long confused seeing and believing, did not make the assembling of accurate information particularly straightforward. It was also necessary to leave behind the iconography of the Middle Ages according to which elephants, for example, had assumed the appearance of pigs or dogs and lost their flat ears, keeping only their tusks and trunks in variously imagined forms.[20] There were, consequently, still wild inaccuracies in sixteenth-century representations of elephants, as well as in the appearance of rhinoceroses' carapaces and horns and the look of lions' bodies; these remained quite fantastical until the 1600s.

It was during this period that artists, mostly in Italy but to an extent in the Germanic lands, began to study live animals. They took advantage of passing shows and sometimes kept their own menageries (Il Sodoma in Siena or Leonardo da Vinci in Milan), but above all visited the collections of their protectors and patrons. Raphael drew Hanno the elephant, given to Pope Leo X in 1514. Albrecht Dürer made an engraving of a sleeping lion, observed at the princely menagerie of Ghent in 1520. In 1566, the Flemish artist Stradanus drew a snake in the menagerie of Cosimo I de' Medici, who had commissioned sketches of wild animal hunts from him. This desire to see animals in the flesh was encouraged in the second half of the sixteenth century by growing criticism of and scepticism about earlier literary and iconographic traditions[21] and developed mostly in the maritime cities of Flanders in the decades that followed. The many animal painters and their public in the Calvinist, bourgeois United Provinces preferred realist art centred on local fauna, and specialists in the exotic were rare. In 1637, however, Rembrandt created one of the most accurate portrayals yet of an Indian elephant. The Catholic courts of the Netherlands, on the other hand, appreciated the power-

Drawings of a lion, c. 1520, by Albrecht Dürer.

ful art of Rubens, who took the representation of exotic animals to its pinnacle. Rubens painted hunts of tigers, lions, boar, crocodiles and hippopotami in 1615. In 1618, he drew a lion from life, a composition which he used three years later to paint a dramatic hunt symbolizing the struggle between good and evil.

The representation of exotic animals was refined and enriched by the spread of the technique of copper engraving, which permitted great precision. Christiane Luz has shown how realism developed in the representation of animals from the Renaissance into the eighteenth century,[22] but development was slow, because specimens remained rare until the 1800s, and many artists continued to base their work on earlier prints. This caused the perpetuation of errors. The *Exotic Hunts* in Louis XV's lesser apartments at Versailles show how the presence of actual animals in a menagerie did not necessarily lead to the correcting of pictorial inaccuracies. These history paintings of hunts featuring a lion, an elephant, a leopard, a crocodile, an ostrich, a tiger and so on were commissioned between 1735 and 1739 from such renowned painters as Charles Perrocel, François Boucher and Carl Van Loo. None of these masters

actually visited the menagerie to see the animals there, instead using prints reproducing works by Stradanus, Antonio Tempesta and Rubens and thus perpetuating their mistakes. Some were inspired by the work of artists who observed actual animals, but this was nothing new, Rubens having already used Jan Brughel, Paul de Vos and Franz Snyders as collaborators.[23]

This hunt format was favoured by princes, who ordered such compositions in multiples to decorate various buildings. At Versailles, Nicasius painted the menagerie's animals in its octagonal salon, and Pieter Boël of Antwerp drew some that were represented in Gobelins tapestries there. Similarly, Johann Georg d'Hamilton painted some beasts for the halls of Belvedere, Gregorio Guglielmi depicted birds in the pavilion-salon at Schönbrunn, and canvases of the menagerie's animals adorned the natural-history cabinet at Het Loo. This custom spread during the eighteenth century. In France, for example, the vogue for natural history led the aristocracy to hang representations of exotic animals in their châteaux and Parisian *hôtels*.[24]

Beginning in the 1500s, princes also commissioned anthologies of sketches, watercolours or gouaches as inventories of the marvels of nature. Some were representations of their personal collections, often of the animals of their menageries. When they were published, these anthologies celebrated the princes' glory. Maximilian II and Rudolf II had drawings made of the beasts at Ebersdorf and Prague. At Versailles, Louis XIV asked Nicasius, Pieter Boël or François Desportes to paint each animal as it arrived, while Nicolas Robert, in 1676, and Nicolas Bertin, in 1710,

Drawing of an elephant, c. 1637, by Rembrandt.

Crocodile and Hippopotamus Hunt, c. 1615–16, by Peter Paul Rubens.

published anthologies of the menagerie's inhabitants. Salomon Kleiner published a work on the animals of Belvedere in 1732, as did Franz Fuxeder for Schönbrunn's birds in 1774. Even if some of these works, such as those at Schönbrunn, were copies of earlier drawings or pictures of stuffed animals, these paintings and anthologies were usually accurate and full of life, and inspired other artists. Boël's sketches, for example, helped Le Brun to paint animals without ever visiting the menagerie at Versailles. To a great extent, such works also inspired the spread of realism in tapestry design, gold and silverwork, porcelain (Sèvres or Saxony) and, above all, the sciences.[25]

THE SCHOLARS' DREAM

The opening of Europe to other parts of the world during the sixteenth century demonstrated as we have seen that the authors of antiquity (especially Aristotle and Pliny the Elder) and their medieval commentators had been mistaken on a number of points and ignorant of a great number of species. So it was that, encountering a hippopotamus in Constantinople, Pierre Belon, who toured the East at mid-century, realized that Herodotus and Aristotle had fabricated their accounts.[26] At the same time, there was growing mistrust of the reports and inventories of explorers, conquistadors, seamen and missionaries, as the importance of careful observation began to become apparent. Many naturalists condemned the inaccuracies, the appropriations from literature disguised as observations, the fabrications and contradictions that were widespread. This critical stance was reinforced by the Scientific Revolution. In the eighteenth century, direct observation became a guarantee of credibility in scholarship. Buffon, for example, believed in a nature that was complex, multifaceted and composed of

imperceptible nuances, and that required ceaseless observation: 'Nothing is well defined unless exactly described: and to describe exactly, one must have seen, examined, and re-examined.' The naturalist Pierre Belon classified exotic mammals according to those he had personally seen and dissected, personally seen but not dissected, and neither seen nor dissected.[27]

However, the rarity of specimens and the difficulty of travel forced scholars to make use of existing materials until the eighteenth century. To describe a rhinoceros and confirm the existence of its various different types, the Dutchman Pierre Camper, in addition to observing a live specimen at Versailles, used skins and stuffed examples, and examined treatises, drawings, bronze statues, Roman coins and reproductions of mosaics from Palestine. When required to describe an elephant, a species he had never seen, Louis Daubenton had to make do with a statue erected in Naples in 1745 and an account of a dissection of 1681. The ornithologist C. Temminck used the same processes at the end of the century. Thus drawings and etchings acted as stand-ins for rare and expensive species that scholars and collectors alike were unable to acquire. The British doctor William Hunter, for example, commissioned *Pygmy Antelope* (1763), *Nilgai (Indian Antelope)* (1763) and *Moose* (1773) from the famed artist George Stubbs for his work in comparative anatomy. Such images preserved the forms of rare species, disseminated knowledge and promoted analysis. But they suffered from two handicaps, especially in the sixteenth and seventeenth centuries. The expense of publication kept the popularization of the princely anthologies in check; as an economy, booksellers would reissue old engravings or publish mediocre ones which duplicated errors.[28]

The hides, bones and stuffed specimens that formed the basis of scholarly study could be found in the cabinets that

Cheetah with Two Indian Attendants and a Stag, 1764–5, by George Stubbs.

aristocrats were happy to put at researchers' disposal, although these were not always good enough for their purposes. In the late eighteenth century, the French naturalist Jean-Baptiste Lamarck asserted that most of them, poorly organized and purely decorative, were useless. Consequently, scholars made attempts to acquire their own specimens. Animals, either captured or raised in captivity, began to be slaughtered before being sent to Europe. In this way, a doctor in Santo Domingo had his two-year-old jaguar sent to Buffon 'quite whole and well preserved in a carefully prepared fluid'. In the sixteenth and seventeenth centuries, animal remains were preserved by salting, reduction to the skeleton or hide, or rudimentary taxidermy by stuffing with straw. Progress was made beginning in the 1600s through the use of arsenic soap to disinfect skin, feathers and fur, and of spirits to preserve entire animals. Treatises on the preparation and transport of animals (and also plants) multiplied in the second half of the seventeenth century,

describing techniques for skinning, treating, wrapping, preparation and the sealing of cases and jars.[29]

Once in Europe, these examples were measured, described and drawn. But problems were regularly encountered. Fur and other soft parts frequently decomposed, were eaten by insects or rats, or were shrivelled by preservatives. Hides stretched, distorting measurements and shapes. In this way, a belief in monsters was kept alive in the sixteenth century: Belon, for example, describes a winged serpent which must have been a deformed iguana. Such distorted skins were difficult to mount on moulds, and imagination had to be used to compensate for a lack of information, thus resulting, for example, in a rather too human pose for an orang-utan, or a twisted neck for a giraffe. In the 1700s, this led to demands that consignments be accompanied by pictures or text. Scholars such as Buffon or Camper, who wished to get past simple descriptive anatomy, judged that an indispensable variable was missing:[30] it seemed more and more essential to see live animals.

Major establishments for the viewing of animals began to seem indispensable, as was suggested by Francis Bacon, who with René Descartes was one of the early theorists of experimental science. In *New Atlantis* (1627), Bacon presented a utopian scientific city. Enclosures and ponds held various species for vivisection, dissection, crossbreeding and the modification of appearance. This idea spread in the eighteenth century. The Dutchman Vosmaer asserted that a scholar could not succeed without working in a park well supplied with animals, supported by a natural-history collection to fill in the gaps.[31]

Scholarly use of princely menageries became a bit more systematic. In 1667, the doctor Claude Perrault led the members of the new French Academy of Sciences in an ambitious programme of study based largely on the beasts of Vincennes and Versailles, the first results of which were published between 1669 and 1676. Louis XIV, affirming himself as protector of the arts and sciences, intended thus to emulate Alexander the Great, who had allowed Aristotle to study in his own menagerie.[32] Louis' lead was followed by other princes who wished to present themselves as enlightened, at Madrid and at Schönbrunn, where construction of the menagerie was extended by the establishment of an adjacent botanical garden, and at Het Loo, which supplanted a declining Versailles in the 1700s and which benefited from the colonial empire and active maritime relations of the United Provinces of the Netherlands.

During the Enlightenment, scholars assumed control of the menageries, in order to reshape them as true scientific establishments. The mathematician Pierre-Louis Maupertuis, for example, wished to apply the same grafting procedures to animals that botanists had already effected on plants and hoped to conduct experiments on hybridization.

At Het Loo, in 1771, Vosmaer, who was already managing the collections, found himself entrusted with the administration of the menagerie. At Madrid, Charles III created the scientific centre evoked by Bacon and, in 1700, by the German philosopher and mathematician Gottfried von Leibniz, when he established a botanical garden, an observatory and a natural-history collection in close proximity to the menagerie. No such changes were made either at Schönbrunn or at Versailles, however, although Louis XV gave Buffon and his assistant Louis Daubenton every opportunity for study.[33]

OBSERVATION AND DISSECTION

The zoology of this period was descriptive in its aims and considered outward appearances to be the sole valid criteria for classification. Grand compilations and summaries of natural history began to appear, notably those by Conrad Gesner, Ulisse Aldrovandi and Johnston, as did more specialized works. Thus Charles de Lécluse depicted the animals, plants and fruits brought back to Europe by the Dutch in his *Exoticum libri decem* (1605), and the Dutch doctor Nicolas Tulp gave the first description of an anthropoid ape (chimpanzee, bonobo, orang-utan?) in his *Observationes medicae* (1685). From the second half of the seventeenth century, the spread of experimental science led naturalists to undertake precise monographic studies of particular species. Claude Perrault, for example, restricted himself to the measurement and description of limbs, colours, skin, eye movement, feet, mouths and so forth. This approach satisfied his mechanistic conception of living beings, which derived from the Cartesian philosophy fashionable in Europe at the time. At Het Loo, Vosmaer studied animals' sleeping and eating habits, character and intelli-

Illustration of an 'orang-utang', 1685, by Nicolas Tulp.

gence, powers of adaptation and relationships with humans. Camper did the same. Concerning an orang-utan seen at Het Loo, he examined the working of its mouth, 'which one would never have been able to discover in a dead animal', as well as of the lips and nose, its way of running, bending its arms, retracting its fingers and squatting, all of which showed that it was made to live in trees. In other specimens, he observed the effects of ageing or the process of dying.[34]

The desire for information was aided by the spread of dissection, an investigative method that provided information on internal anatomy. The first dissections of wild animals, especially exotic ones that had died in Europe or been preserved, date from the first half of the seventeenth century, but the technique truly developed in the second half of the century under the influence of Cartesianism, which compared living beings with machines that needed to be dismantled to be understood. The Englishman Edward Tyson wrote celebrated monographs, most notably on chimpanzees (1699). François Redi, an Italian, studied parasites in lions, bears and seals from menageries. The Dutchman Blaes worked in the menageries of Amsterdam. In France, Perrault's group produced a major body of work by organizing a programme of study and working as a team. At the Academy, in the King's garden or on site, they dissected many animals from royal menageries, notably the Versailles elephant which died in 1681:

The Academy was summoned to dissect it; M. du Verney performed the dissection, M. Perrault the description of its principal parts, and M. de La Hire made the drawings: anatomical dissection has perhaps never been so dazzling, be it in the scale of the animal, in the exactitude that was brought to the examination of its different parts or, finally, in the quality and number of the assistants: the subject had been laid on a kind of theatre stage, quite high: the King was content to be present at the examination of some of the parts; and when he entered, he asked eagerly where the anatomist was, for he absolutely could not see him; M. du Verney immediately rose from the flanks of the animal, where he was, so to speak, engulfed.[35]

The obvious advantages of dissecting animals that had died recently and not decomposed very much bolstered interest in specimens from menageries and showmen. Daubenton dissected anything he could get his hands on in the area around Paris. Camper plundered Amsterdam and Het Loo. Dissection permitted scholars a tacit share in menageries' increasingly coveted livestock: live beasts were reserved for the glorification of princes, while dead ones were left to those who wished to study them. Dissection also laid the foundations for comparative anatomy in the nineteenth century and, above all, for the study of wild species.

The study of living or recently dead specimens also advanced the development of scientific drawing, which favoured exactitude and a critical approach to specimens. Even if artists continued to be somewhat subjective, there were fewer and fewer errors in the representation of animals. The etchings of fish published by Rondelet are accurate in every detail. Perrault's team applied the same standards of precision and control to drawings as to accompanying text: the former were executed as dissections were taking place and were then verified by the participants before being engraved. Drawings of dead animals detailed the greatest possible number of anatomical characteristics without seeking to render realistic poses. Drawings of live specimens, on the other hand, portrayed animals in natural attitudes or hinted at their place in appropriate environments: a chameleon perched on a tree, a beaver standing in water and so on.[36]

Having touched the tusks of Hansken the elephant, Peiresc noted that they corresponded to tusks discovered on the Tunisian coast, which must therefore have belonged to a pachyderm. Perrault demonstrated that chameleons did not become furious when placed in fig trees, as had been claimed by Pliny. But such iconoclasm was difficult to defend when it came to rare or unknown animals, and most naturalists continued to use classical texts as starting points for their research or as sources. Camper, when he finally saw a real rhinoceros in 1777, thought it worth checking Pliny's assertions regarding the creature's antipathy towards elephants and its way of urinating. Among members of the public, in particular among the well-read, knowledge derived directly from classical traditions. This was true for elephants, information about which had been compiled by Gesner in the 1500s and then translated by Priézac in his *Histoire des éléphants* (1650). The two pamphlets that were published with great success on the occasions of Hansken the elephant's and Clara the rhinoceros's visits to France, in 1627 and 1749 respectively, copied Aristotle, Pliny and Strabo; the author of the 1749 version limited his encounter with the living animal to a few measurements and a touch of the tongue![37]

Looking at a beast in a cage was certainly not sufficient to truly see or get to know it, and the decline of credulity was just as much the fruit of the new rationality as of the development of menageries. At the same time, certain aspects of the latter contributed to a reduction in their use and attraction. From the end of the seventeenth century on, scholars' increasing mistrust of received ideas caused them to focus on individual specimens rather than on species. The rarity of lions and elephants, for example, obliged them to avoid making any general statements until they could see other live specimens, which happened rarely. Buffon, meanwhile, was not satisfied with the use of anatomy, morphology or even physiology to describe and define an animal, unlike the majority of his colleagues, who had a passion for systematic analysis. He preferred to study 'the natural' – that is, the behaviour of animals in nature, alone or in groups (he insisted that animal societies existed and, late in his life, wrote about animals' intelligence); his work can thus be identified as an early precursor of ethology. This idea was articulated by others, such as Georges Leroy, who believed that the complete study of a carnivore might show, for example, not just how it seized its prey but how the experience rendered it more confident, how scarcity of food emboldened it, and how its actions could reveal memory and thought processes.[38]

To further his research, Buffon kept animals in semi-liberty at Montbard, for he was convinced that being cooped up in menageries somehow disabled them: they were often scrawny and passive. This fact was recognized by Camper in relation to the size of elephants, and also at Schönbrunn, where animal studies were in fact curtailed as a result.[39] In fact, we know little of the conditions under which animals were detained at this time. At Versailles, visitors marvelled at the yards, especially the lawns and the exceptional running water that was distributed to fountains and ponds. In the late 1700s, the elephant was given a walk and a bath every morning, while the rhinoceros had an enclosure of almost 400 square metres. Naturalists were not so enthusiastic about these arrangements; Perrault remarked that a beaver remained in confinement for several years without being able to swim, and Buffon described a tiger vegetating in a narrow pen.[40] The cold, and insufficient or unsuitable food, seemed to exacerbate mortality. At Prague under Rudolf II, there was not enough money to feed the big cats. At Madrid, the lack of space and exercise curtailed the animals' survival. At Het Loo, the menagerie's insalubrity decimated its livestock. The death toll was similar among caged birds kept by private individuals.[41]

Consequently, although such specimens had great value for Daubenton, entrusted as he was with the study of anatomy and morphology, Buffon accorded them only a few pages in his works before returning to earlier treatises or travellers' accounts to describe life in the wild, even if it meant remaining a hostage to their inaccuracies. Even Linnaeus made little use of his menagerie and worked mostly from cabinet specimens or travel records. At Madrid, only 1.5 per cent of the studies made between 1774 and 1783 by the scientists involved in the pursuit of natural history took place in the seraglio.[42] Doubtful as they were regarding the suitability of princely menageries, a number of scholars began to wonder what a truly scientific establishment might offer.

Previous page: *An Afternoon in the Jardin d'Acclimatation*, 1882, by Jean-Richard Goubie.

◐ 5 THE ELITE AND THE INVENTION OF THE ZOO

Opposition to princely menageries surfaced in France during the Enlightenment. Thus the *Encyclopédie* proclaimed that 'at a time when people have no bread, the menageries must be destroyed; it would be shameful to feed beasts at great expense when men die of hunger all around.' This position must be linked to the same publication's condemnation of aristocratic hunts (they were accused of destroying the work of peasants), its redirection of scholarly study, its advocacy of the responsible exercise of power and of progress in agriculture, and its condemnation of worldly curiosity. True natural-history collections were excepted as the only such pursuit to further scholarly work.[1] This increasingly widespread sentiment led to the disappearance of princely menageries during the Revolution and to the creation, under the aegis of the naturalists at the Jardin des Plantes (formerly the Jardin du Roi) in Paris, of a new type of establishment intended to serve the entire nation rather than a select few.

This model was followed throughout the whole of Europe during the nineteenth century. In England, opposition to princely menageries surfaced in the early 1700s, born out of an opposition to French-style formal gardens; the latter were considered to be the expression of a despised absolutist power which had been fought and defeated in the previous century. The oppression of nature characteristic of such gardens was thought to mirror the oppression of human beings. Various theorists and practitioners, including Charles Bridgeman and William Kent, criticized formal gardens for being cut off from the surrounding environment, for being artificially composed, for subjecting nature to a regularity and symmetry that constrained its profusion, and for creating a uniform and boring space in which human beings shared the same fate. These ideas – current among members of the rural aristocracy, who favoured moderate, controlled and decentralized political power – were expressed in a new type of garden, which we shall examine later.[2]

THE REVOLUTIONARY JARDIN DES PLANTES

In France, the origin of a parallel transformation lay in the lack of attention accorded to the Versailles menagerie by the King and his court in the 1700s. After the death of Louis XIV, the Regent sold some animals and gave others

Panther's quarters, Versailles, 1739.

away, no doubt with the aim of erasing a potent symbol of absolutism and evoking the division of power. Returning to Versailles in 1722, Louis XV also paid little attention to the menagerie, seemingly never visiting it. His successor was no more involved than he, and the menagerie does not feature at all on a map of Versailles made in 1781 that indicates the places and paths to be maintained for the royal family's promenades.[3]

It was not that Louis XV was indifferent towards rare animals. He had them brought to him at the château when they arrived at the menagerie or passed through the capital. What he disliked was the theatricality and symbolism of public displays. Monarchs of his time were less fond of the onerous ceremony and meticulous etiquette favoured by the Sun King; they continued to maintain such practices in public while privately taking refuge in the intimate spaces of lesser apartments or retreats. Under Louis XVI, the court only really functioned on Sundays or festive occasions; otherwise, the aristocracy stayed in Paris or in the grounds of the château. At this point, the Trianon menagerie, installed by Louis XV and then Marie-Antoinette as a place for the inner circle to relax, and populated by domestic species (Dutch cows, rare hens, various pigeons) to create an idealized rural setting, became the focus of visits by the sovereigns. A similar change in attitude can be detected towards the symbolism of the park at Versailles at this time. If its general appearance changed little, its geometric rigour was abandoned; coppices grew into mature forests. It was another type of garden entirely that Marie-Antoinette created at the hamlet of the Trianon.[4]

These developments explain the contemporary lack of investment in the menagerie at Versailles, the reduced budget and the endlessly postponed plans for renovation. The buildings deteriorated, and the yards turned into quag-mires when the water system flooded. Nevertheless, members of the aristocracy who had no access to the princes' private gardens, and still less the sovereign's, continued to visit. Queen Marie walked there on several occasions, while Louis XV visited the Trianon with Mme de Pompadour. A series of renovations finally taken in hand around 1750, 1774, 1782 and 1791 suggest a balance between disinterest and the need to keep the menagerie in a reasonable state. In any case, the animals remained numerous, and new arrivals were accommodated. Those of a two-horned rhinoceros in 1770 and an elephant around 1775 revived public interest in a place that was undoubtedly less remarkable than it had been in the previous century, its public having become more knowledgeable in the interim.[5]

After the royal family's departure for Paris in the wake of the Revolution, the menagerie was reformed in 1791 for reasons of economy, and a great number of its birds disappeared. Shortly after 10 August 1792, the local Jacobins arrived to abolish this symbol of tyranny, handing monkeys, stags and birds over to skinners. The plan was to install a stud farm, a symbolic project intended to substitute the menagerie's useless beasts with a breeding ground that would benefit agriculture, transport and the army. The steward of the Versailles region decided to offer the last of the animals to Bernardin de Saint-Pierre, steward of the Jardin du Roi, in order that, stuffed and exhibited in the natural-history rooms, they might become an 'object of public education'.[6] Bernardin de Saint-Pierre modified this proposition when he addressed a memo to the French National Convention 'on the necessity of joining a menagerie to the national Jardin des Plantes in Paris'. The idea, which had been proposed in 1790, received the backing of the scientific community; it succeeded because the ground, as we have seen, had already been prepared.

Bernardin de Saint-Pierre noted that the Jardin du Roi only represented the first two kingdoms of nature, that it lacked live animals altogether, that comparative anatomy was an insufficient discipline and that it was essential to observe the behaviour of live creatures. Others spoke out in favour of the acclimatizing, domestication and improvement of exotic species. Further arguments were put forward regarding the usefulness of a national menagerie to artists and as an educational tool, although they remained secondary. Scholars, not sharing the aristocratic taste for surface appearance and extravagance, despised the Versailles menagerie as costly and unnecessary, an emblem of a pompous despotism that glorified itself while crushing its subjects. They responded with a proposal for an establishment stripped of all luxury, devoted entirely to research, which would bring scientific and economic advantages to the nation. Its displacement to Paris was intended to symbolize this change in status. Changing the nature of the stock of animals itself would differentiate the new establishment from the monarchy and its hunter's instincts. This could be achieved by a reduction in the ferocious species that exemplified devastating cruelty, supported the belief that nature sanctioned the rule of force, and illustrated and legitimized tyranny. Docile animals were to be favoured instead, placed under the banner of public utility and functioning in essence as an allegory for the hardworking citizenry.[7]

In fact, the trial and execution of Louis XVI, internal conflicts and the worries of war caused any decision to be postponed. The first relevant step was taken by the administrators of the Paris police, who in 1793 ordered that all animals exhibited on public highways should be transported to the Jardin des Plantes, and that their owners should be compensated. Perhaps they sought to enforce the law passed in 1790 that entrusted the municipality with 'the responsibility to obviate or remedy the unfortunate events that could be occasioned by madmen left at liberty or by the ravings of harmful and ferocious animals'; perhaps they were aware of the scholars' interests described above. In the event, the latter were divided on the issue, because there were neither the premises, the keepers nor the money to accommodate these animals, and because the beasts were better suited to spectacular exhibition than to careful study. But the decision to keep them prevailed, and during 1794 they were housed in sheds, with fairground stall-holders recruited as keepers. The precariousness of this situation persuaded the Committee of Public Safety to equip temporary shelters with grilles and cages from Versailles, and to allocate funds for the animals' maintenance, which amounted to an official recognition of the menagerie.[8]

This decision can be explained in the context of the general reform of scholarly establishments. In 1792 and 1793, all universities, academies and faculties of medicine were eliminated because they were thought to symbolize intellectual tyranny. But the Jardin des Plantes, open to the public and already dedicated to the popularization of science and to experimentation, was preserved. In June 1793, it was turned into the national natural-history Muséum. The Muséum's foundation formed part of a trend for the creation of great establishments, including the Musée du Louvre, all of which were marked by an identical process of destruction, appropriation, reconstruction and justification.[9]

To begin with, a lack of funds forced the Muséum to retain its temporary installations in the stables, an old greenhouse and the surrounding copses. The overcrowding in these tight spaces, conditions worse than those of a fairground menagerie, and a lack of food due to national shortages, caused high mortality and wild fluctuation in the numbers of animals. Most of those which arrived in 1794 disappeared the following year, thus making it necessary to rebuild the collection almost from scratch.[10]

Requisition from princely menageries therefore joined the usual methods of acquisition (travel, purchase, gift, scientific expedition).[11] This process began with the arrival in 1794 of the survivors of Versailles (a lion, a guagga and a bulbul hartebeest –the latter two now extinct), as well as about 30 animals from the Duke d'Orléans' estate at Raincy. In 1798, birds and mammals, a famous elephant pair among them, arrived from the menagerie of Het Loo, seized by French forces from the Stadtholder of Holland, who fled to England. That same year, military victories permitted the seizure of bears from Bern and a range of animals from Italian menageries. These appropriations were in keeping with a policy of systematic capture that soon looked like pillage to the rest of Europe. It was thus that, in 1794, the Convention sent commissioners, among them two professors of the Muséum, to the armies on the Rhine to gather works of art, books and scientific objects. The invasions of the Austrian Netherlands and the United Provinces in 1795 put not just the animals but also plants, seeds, agricultural tools and specimens from the natural-history chambers of the Brussels Academy and the Stadtholder of Holland within the grasp of the French. The same policy was put into practice in Italy, and great numbers of works of art, curios and exotic animals made their entrance into Paris on 27 July 1798 in a triumphal procession.[12]

THE PICTURESQUE GARDEN

After the difficult times of the Revolution, several construction projects were completed over a period of about 40 years, spurred on by Geoffroy Saint-Hilaire, who ran the menagerie of the Jardin des Plantes from 1802 to 1841, and Frédéric Cuvier, named warden of the menagerie in 1803. These included the monkey and bird house in 1801–5, the bear pits in 1805, the rotunda for large herbivores (elephant, giraffe) in 1802–12, the building for ferocious animals in 1818–21, the aviary for birds of prey in 1825, a pheasantry in 1827, a new monkey house in 1835–7 and, in the old building, a vivarium in 1838. A garden was laid out around the earliest buildings, destined to accommodate the more peaceful animals from the 1810s on. The grounds were

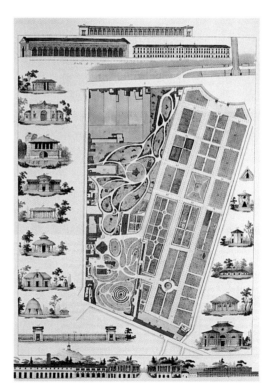

Plan of the Jardin des Plantes, Paris, 1819.

torn apart in order to create uneven terrain. Trees were planted alone or in copses, in the middle of lawns and among flowerbeds. Enclosures containing ponds were marked out, and rustic cottages were built in wood and stone with thatched roofs. A system of winding paths made it possible to move around the site in all directions. A break with the Baroque tradition was achieved through the abandoning of radial design and a new integration with the garden. The menagerie was thus no longer a separate entity surrounded by a garden, but was distributed instead over the whole area. This approach multiplied viewpoints, spaced them out along the length of a promenade, and gave the sensation, for the docile animals at least, of natural surroundings.[13]

This 'Swiss Valley' (an allusion to what was, at the time, thought of as one of the most exotic of European countries) was directly inspired by the landscaped gardens that had appeared in England in the first half of the eighteenth century and whose conception rested on a new vision of nature. Nature was no longer thought of as the creation of an engineer God, following the simplest possible course, as had been believed in the 1600s. Instead it was conceived as the product of an abundant and fluctuating energy which was best expressed in the diversity of organic life – hence the need for variety, wildness and disorder. This idea was reinforced in the second half of the century by a current of opinion, typified by the philosophy of Jean-Jacques Rousseau, which held nature to be a haven of peace protected from the corrupting city. A beautiful garden was therefore no longer one that kept nature in check, but one that restored its many facets to it.

The Swiss Garden (of the Jardin des Plantes, Paris), 1816, by John Forbes.

The irregular garden was based on a method of fragmentation and collage. It was the product of a combination of forms, designed not by the human mind but by nature itself, that had been judged by human viewers to be the most characteristic or beautiful and then gathered together in a given place in a quest for variety, asymmetry and sinuosity: small hills and valleys, lakes and streams, woods, glades, thickets and meadows, shadows and light. The whole was set within a planned perspective, linked visually

The 'Swiss Valley', Jardin des Plantes, Paris, after Jean-Baptiste Huet.

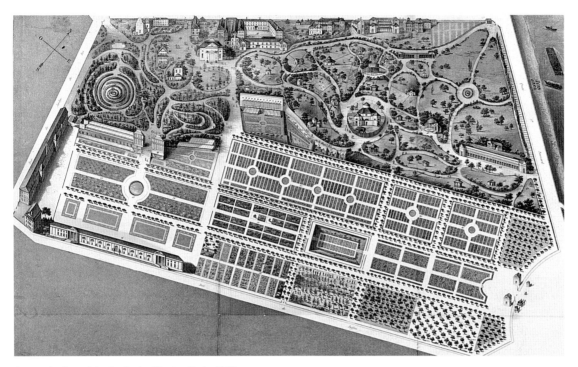

Isometric view of the Jardin des Plantes, Paris, 1842.

to the outside world – walls often being replaced with ditches – and assembled in such a manner that the traces of human intervention were invisible. The influence of seventeenth- and eighteenth-century painting on the creation of such gardens is well known, especially its presentation of landscape, models of perspective, and the play of light and shadow. 'It is as a poet and a painter that one must compose landscapes, if one is to engage the eye and the mind at the same time,' wrote R. Girardin, one of the theorists of the picturesque garden, in 1777.[14]

This style spread throughout Europe in the second half of the eighteenth century. The Landgrave of Hesse set the example in 1758 in the grounds of Bellevue Castle at Kassel, and the fashion became widespread in the Germanic lands and the Italian peninsula, for example at the Roman villas, whose parks were remodelled as a result.[15] The first examples in France, at Ermenonville and Raincy, date from the 1760s. But the movement did not gain real impetus until changes were made at the Château de Bellevue by the daughters of Louis XV in 1781 and at the Trianon hamlet by Marie-Antoinette from 1783. The aristocracy followed their

example, developing a French version of the picturesque garden consisting of an English-style landscape augmented with a hamlet or farm, retreats, mazes, pavilions, bridges and islands, rockeries, grottoes and ruins, all showing a persistent taste for a rugged artificiality.[16]

Those gardens, usually the larger ones, that had animals on display evinced a preference for domesticated, indigenous species (ducks, pheasants, bovines) left in semi-liberty around a farm, dairy, aviary and island to lend a sense of life to the tableau. This arrangement was advocated by such theorists as Girardin in France (1777), Horace Walpole in England (1785) and C.C.L. Hirschfield in the Germanic lands (1779–85), who felt that it expressed the rediscovered freedom of the open landscape and made the latter seem more natural. Rustic buildings, varied and adapted to their settings, were recommended as housing for the animals.[17]

The adoption of this style by the Muséum's menagerie was without doubt eased by the political interpretation it invited. The picturesque garden, linked by its creators and supporters to an implicit challenge to absolutist power was considered a symbol of liberty. The author of the *Guide des*

Pen, Jardin des Plantes, Paris, c. 1821–3.

jardins de Franconville-la-Garenne (1784) for example, asserted that one day, 'it will be little understood why man, born free, with a horror of slavery, should once have taken pleasure in enclosing himself in the middle of his estate just as one confines a criminal to a prison'.[18] The Jardin des Plantes was the first example of the union of a picturesque garden with a large menagerie of exotic animals. This was true even though the monkeys and more dangerous creatures remained confined to buildings that were not integrated with the landscape, because they were thought to represent another, more scientific view of nature, one that we shall explore later.

EUROPEAN FASHIONS

The example of the Jardin des Plantes was followed throughout Europe thanks in part to the contemporary prestige of France, many of whose initiatives were more or less directly imposed, even in hostile countries and even after its own defeat. The spread of these influences strengthened and accelerated, and menageries came into being throughout Europe. This development was encouraged by guidebooks produced first in Paris and then in London, and to the lithographs and, later, photographs that illustrated or accompanied them. The appearance of the railway from mid-century facilitated visits to establishments at the forefront of progress, thereby encouraging the rapid propagation of innovations. In 1858, for example, a delegation of Parisians travelled to London, Brussels, Antwerp and Amsterdam to examine the installations there, before establishing a menagerie in the Bois du Boulogne. From 1863 to 1900, the supervisor of London's zoological gardens went each year to study its Continental counterparts. For the model was changing yet again. Once the Jardin des Plantes began to seem old-fashioned, the menageries of London and Antwerp came to be regarded as exemplary for the quantity of their animals and the quality of their equipment. These monumental institutions were joined by Berlin after 1870.[19]

Despite these advances, two characteristics of the Jardin

Painting of black swans at Malmaison, *c.* 1802–20, by Léon de Wailly.

des Plantes remained influential throughout Europe. Its landscaped setting was soon adopted in the Madrid of Ferdinand VII (1808–33): at one of the extremeties of Buen Retiro, an artificial mountain was created as a home for animals, along with herbivore enclosures and a building housing felines. The Jardin's dispersion of exotic animals and edifices throughout a park of English design was reprised in 1822 at Peacock Island, an estate of the King of Prussia at Potsdam, and at Regent's Park in London in 1828. This arrangement became common during the nineteenth century, with the relationship being inverted in menageries that were conceived as a whole rather than installed in pre-existing parks; at Bristol, Rotterdam and Hanover, for example, plants and trees adorned the animal enclosures rather than vice versa.[20]

This tendency was at the root of the term 'zoological garden', which originated in England at the time of the establishment of the menagerie at Regent's Park, but did not truly spread to the Continent until the second half of the century.[21] This expression found itself in competition with the abbreviation 'zoo', which arose in nineteenth-century England, but did not catch on until the early twentieth century (appearing in France, for example, on the occasion of the *Exposition Coloniale* of 1931);[22] 'zoo' put the accent on the contents of the space (zoology) rather than the space itself, doubtless to distinguish this type of park more clearly from other ones.

The other important element of the Jardin des Plantes was its dedication to the good of the nation, in both its goals and its accessibility to a wider public. This aspiration aroused enthusiasm among the peoples of Europe at a time of mounting nationalism and demand for democracy. It lay behind the creation of a great number of establishments that appeared across nineteenth-century Europe in successive waves.

The first of these occurred in the UK, beginning with London (1828), Dublin (1831) and Bristol (1835), then the heavily populated and industrialized north of England (Manchester, 1836; Leeds, 1840), with Southport (1906), Halifax (1909) and Birmingham (1910) filling out the numbers at the turn of the century.

A second wave covered the Netherlands and Belgium between the 1830s and the 1860s: the capitals (Amsterdam, 1838; Brussels, 1851) and the large maritime, trading and industrial towns (Antwerp, 1843; Ghent, 1851; Rotterdam, 1857; Liège, 1861; The Hague, 1863). Then, in the middle of the century, came a few French towns with similar characteristics, at the time of the urban transformations of the Second Empire: Marseilles (1854), Lyon (1858), Paris again (the gardens in the Bois du Boulogne, 1860) and Mulhouse (1868).

The fourth wave, and by far the most significant one, developed in the German states which formed themselves into a federation in 1870. After the capitals of Prussia (Berlin, 1844) and the German Confederation (the free town of Frankfurt-am-Main, 1858), there was a proliferation of inaugurations, in particular during the years 1860–80, and especially in two regions: along the axis of the Rhine, the principal industrial zone, from Cologne (1860) to Aachen (1886) via Karlsruhe (1864), Stuttgart (1870), Düsseldorf (1874) and elsewhere; and in the larger towns of eastern Prussia (Breslau, 1865; Posen, 1875; Stettin, 1882; Jena, 1901) and Saxony (Dresden, 1861; Leipzig, 1876), the other great economic zone. To these can be added a few more isolated industrial or trading towns (Hamburg, 1863; Hannover, 1864; Munich, 1910).

Openings took place throughout the century in other European capitals – Copenhagen, 1859;

An elephant in Regent's Park, London, 1835, by George Scharf.

Aviary, London Zoo, 1830.

Ostrich enclosure, Amsterdam Zoo, 1875.

Brussels Zoo, 1851.

The Menagerie Deer Enclosure on Peacock Island, 1830,
by C. W. Pohlke.

Antwerp Zoo, *c.* 1843.

Moscow, 1863; Budapest, 1865; Stockholm and Lisbon,
1883; Rome, 1910 – and major cities – Basel, 1874;
Barcelona; 1892; Warsaw, 1911; Riga, 1912.[23]

The spread of the zoological garden was so rapid and
extensive because of the added political dimension of
competition between nations. Vienna, although it still
possessed its eighteenth-century princely menagerie, saw
another established in 1863. This was also a case of urban
élites emulating one another, a zoological garden being
seen as an indispensable tool in the confirmation or
maintenance of a city's status much like other features
that blossomed in the nineteenth (theatres, museums,
universities, chambers of commerce and exchanges) and
twentieth centuries (sporting facilities).[24] It was also part
of a pan-European movement involving the foundation of
museums, natural-history museums, literary academies
and so on. The spread of such institutions followed the
wave of the Industrial Revolution quite faithfully and
affected its principal sites, for increased wealth was a
prerequisite, and establishments were often sponsored by
a scholarly and enterprising bourgeoisie.

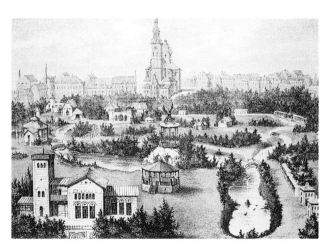

Ghent Zoo, *c.* 1850s.

Above: Aquarium entrance, Hamburg Zoo, 1868. Below: Parrot avenue, Hamburg Zoo, 1868.

Bear pit and waterfall-grotto, Hamburg Zoo, *c*. 1865.

Paris. **Le jardin d'acclimatation.** Le Chalet des Cerfs.

Deer hut, Jardin d'Acclimatation, Paris, 1905.

Camel house, Dresden Zoo, 1863.

Ape house, Dresden Zoo, 1863.

Flamingoes in front of the monkey house, Dresden Zoo, *c.* 1905.

Interior of the bird house, Breslau Zoo, 1890.

Bird-of-prey house, Breslau Zoo, 1890.

First main gate, Moscow Zoo.

Monkey house, Budapest Zoo, *c.* 1886.

Bactrian camel, Riga Zoo.

Main entrance, Rome Zoo, 2001.

Ornamental cage surrounds, Rome Zoo, 2001.

This is a corner of the Zoological Gardens. It is a lovely place but it is rather cold to visit just now! We are going to Carlsruhe tomorrow ...

Above: Long-legged-bird aviary, Hamburg Zoo, *c.* 1910. Below: Outdoor restaurant, Hannover Zoo, *c.* 1910.

Feeding the seals, Buffalo Zoo.

Bird cages, Cincinnati Zoo, c. 1910.

In the US, zoological parks began to appear following the Civil War. Philadelphia's long-planned zoo opened its doors in 1874; Cincinatti, New York's Central Park and Lincoln Park in Chicago (1868) – all conceived in the late 1860s – formed, with Washington, DC's national zoo, part of a prestigious series in major cities. These could be described as 'Atlantic, industrial and Northern': Baltimore (1876–86), Pittsburgh (1898), Buffalo (1875–95), St Paul (1895–8) and so on.[25] Atlanta (1889–92) represented the only zoo in a Southern state, San Francisco (1889–92) heralded the arrival of zoos in California's favourable climate, and Denver's zoo was to become Colorado's tourist showcase. Some twenty zoos opened between 1885 and 1900, all enjoying a healthy influx of visitors, and growth continued until 1940 at a rate of around two a year.

Pachyderm house, San Francisco Zoological Gardens, perhaps 1930s.

Polar bear, San Francisco Zoo.

Bear enclosure, New York Zoo.

Seal Grotto, Chicago Zoo (Lincoln Park).

John Shedd Aquarium, Chicago, *c.* 1930.

Bronze doors of John Shedd Aquarium, Chicago, *c.* 1930.

The inauguration of Vincennes zoological gardens, Paris, 1934.

HIGH SOCIETY

Scientists continued to occupy an important place in the creation of menageries. Returning to London in 1817, Stamford Raffles, Lieutenant-governor of Java and an amateur botanist, persuaded the naturalists of the Royal Society to participate in the creation of a zoological society for the assembly of a live collection similar to Paris'. The Zoological Club of the Linnean Society, founded in 1822, gathered together all of the materials necessary for the pursuit of science and opened its menagerie in 1828. Following its example, other zoological societies were formed, completing the gardens of Dublin, Amsterdam, Rotterdam and The Hague. The involvement of scholars, whether professionals or amateurs, remained marked until the early twentieth century. Several high-ranking professors, the director of the University Institute of Zoology among them, were members of the founding committee of the society of

Rome's gardens in 1909. In Paris, the Muséum's professors designed and managed the zoological gardens at Vincennes (1934).[26]

However, the greatest influence gradually reverted to the ruling bourgeoisie, politicians, administrators and business-men. In Lyon, it was the Prefect, Claude-Marius Vaïsse, who persuaded the municipal council to create an ornamental park and animal garden. In Marseilles, the instigators of the zoological society and gardens were a civil engineer (the creator of the Durance Canal), an architect and two prop-erty owners. The committee of subscribing members brought together a good portion of the local élite, including a chief engineer of bridges and highways and a tax collector-general. In Cologne, the idea for a zoological garden came from an innkeeper who exhibited a few beasts on his own premises, but the real work was done by a former professor of the local college, and the founding committee boasted the greatest names in culture (J. H. Richartz, founder of the

View from the bear pit towards the emu house, London Zoo, 1831, by James Hakewill.

Museum of Fine Art), science, banking and industry (Eduard Oppenheim, director of the famous bank), as well as members of the aristocracy, such as the King of Württemburg and Duke of Saxe-Coburg.[27]

When it came to the make-up of these élites, diversity was the rule – even when one category was dominant – and the nobility played a significant role. This diversity ensured that such enterprises would be well represented within both local administrations and fashionable society, and thus be granted a fuller hearing than they might otherwise have been, something that would prove particularly useful for fundraising. In Brussels, the first board of directors included two counts, two members of the House of Representatives, a deputy burgomaster, a director at the Ministry of Justice and a secretary of the Society of Flora. The first supervising committee was composed of a President of the Court of Appeals, an architect and a government commissioner to the national bank. Direction of the enterprise was entrusted to

Baron Muller, a doctor of letters and philosophy. In London, the Zoological Society recruited from colonial entrepreneurs (travellers, hunters and merchants), the cream of industry and business, and the nobility. The latter occupied the most prestigious offices, notably the presidency, held by Lord Derby in 1831, Prince Albert (who donated all the animals he received as gifts) in 1851, and the Duke of Bedford in 1899. However, a superintendent, chosen from the middle class, was appointed in 1847 to oversee the day-to-day management of the gardens. The same was true at Madrid, Turin, Rome and elsewhere. It was in France that the nobility was least in evidence, except in the society of the zoological gardens of the Bois de Boulogne (1860). Another subdued presence, this time right across Europe, was that of women. The example of Joséphine de Beauharnais was seldom followed, and women could only be found on the margins, among the members of the zoological societies – the London society was opened to them in 1827 – and as donors.[28]

Above: View from the emu house, London Zoo, 1831, by James Hakewill.

Below: Entrance terrace looking towards the bear pit, London Zoo, 1831, by James Hakewill.

Llama house and macaw cage, London Zoo, 1831, by James Hakewill.

Except in the case of the Jardin des Plantes, local governments never participated directly in the development of these gardens. Municipal establishments were therefore rare (Barcelona, Cardiff, Lyon and Ipswich) and of modest size, in order to avoid excessive investment or due to mistrust of public interventionism. With one large state garden and three small-scale menageries deep in the provinces, one of them municipal, France represents an exception that is indicative of the country's centralized bureaucracy.[29]

Outside France, the establishment of the first menageries was achieved by societies whose capital derived from donations and, above all, from the annual subscriptions of their members. London's Zoological Society comprised life fellows, annual fellows, corresponding members and outside fellows, all making different contributions. It was led by a council – elected yearly and consisting of a president, a treasurer and a secretary – that had executive powers and directed the gardens. This formula was repeated in Dublin, the Netherlands (Amsterdam and Rotterdam), Scandinavia and the US at the turn of the century. In Amsterdam, the Natura Artis Magistra comprised active members, donors and outside members (the latter living at least 3 kilometres from the town). It was managed by a board that retained a salaried director. This solution presupposed the formation of a fairly homogeneous group, united by acquaintance and objectives, and through social recruitment organized around a nucleus of scientists. The group resembled a British club or French *cercle* in social terms, and a limited partnership, of the kind that was catching on in the West at the same time, in economic ones.[30]

The advent of modernity was even more evident in the 1835 opening, in Bristol, of the first-ever zoological garden

Parrots at Clifton Zoo, Bristol, 1900s.

In the Zoological Gardens, 1942, by Otto Dill.

to be founded and managed by a joint-stock company: The Bristol and West of England Zoological Society. This new kind of economic structure, still quite rare in the West, would go on to enjoy marked success among zoological gardens, which thus served as a proving ground for capitalism. The model was appropriated at mid-century at Antwerp, Berlin, Brussels, Ghent, Marseilles and Mulhouse, despite continuing suspicion from governments and public alike, and began to spread further in the 1860s as it took advantage of the liberalization of the legal regulations governing business enterprises. It was used for the majority of establishments in Germany and also in Switzerland (Geneva), Portugal (Lisbon) and Italy (Rome). This type of structure made it possible to widen the pool of subscribers, both numerically and socially (the Brussels society offered twelve hundred shares in 1850); to obtain more substantial financing, which would then be renewable by the issuing of securities or loans; and to embark on major projects. In 1905, the society of the Cologne gardens had no less than 1,500 shareholders represented by an administrative board of sixteen, invested capital of 700,000 marks, and 49 salaried staff.[31] This formula also had the (theoretical) advantage of combining pleasure with profit while minimizing risk.

The different societies' objectives followed, to varying degrees, the example of the Jardin des Plantes: contribution to the advancement of science; experiments in acclimatization and domestication; access to nature; popularization of science in a refined, light and pleasurable way; support for the control of the wild; and creation of a trade in animals. Even if one of these objectives was selected as a priority – as, for example, science was in Paris and London, or acclimatization at the Bois du Boulogne – there was no specialization, for first the founders and then the directors needed to diversify the arguments and purposes that justified their creations in order to find support and attract members, shareholders and visitors. This eclecticism also happened to fit the bourgeois mentality of the time, which sought to combine the advancement of knowledge, good deeds and productivity.

Such gardens also had social functions to fulfil. In London, Amsterdam and elsewhere, the subscription societies offered not only the opportunity to contemplate living animals but also a museum of national history and a library where one could pass a few hours in study or conversation. In the gardens of the shareholding societies, which had to turn investment into profit in order to pay dividends, the tendency was to develop the venue's appeal as widely as possible. In Brussels, the garden's promoters wanted to transform Leopold Park into a vast conference and entertainment complex that would include the picturesque garden with its zoological elements, a lecture theatre, salons and other reception areas, exhibitions, scientific or literary gatherings, a restaurant, a bandstand, a pond for swimming or skating, and a farm selling butter, vegetables and fruit. At the Bois du Boulogne, the society built a huge edifice containing aviaries, greenhouses for exotic plants, a restaurant, salons, a 5,000-seat hall for conferences or concerts, and a planetarium. The society at Cologne staged multiple attractions (concerts, fireworks, electrical illuminations in 1889) and developed the breeding of homing pigeons, which proved very popular. In Leipzig, at the beginning of the twentieth century, the society erected a planetarium that also served as a cinema; made microscopes available so that the public could examine the bacteria famously discovered by Louis Pasteur; opened a museum; organized ethnographical exhibitions; and benefited from the neighbouring presence of a large hotel that functioned as a conference

Top: *A Concert in the Zoological Gardens*, 1872, by Knut Ekvall.
Above: *A Public Holiday in the Zoological Gardens*, 1878, by Knut Ekvall.

century, thanks to the progress made in employing iron and glass as building materials. The winter gardens of the Champs-Elysées in Paris were inaugurated in 1846. There, one could buy flowers out of season, have a meal or read a newspaper, or organize social gatherings among the exotic plants. Success was immediate, with 40,000 visitors a month.[33]

Promenading was the other aspect of social life that filtered into zoological gardens, for urban expansion, fed by an exodus from rural areas, had reduced the number of available open spaces during the first half of the century. Promenades were considered an indispensable activity by the working classes, who would walk every Sunday as the day of rest became more commonplace, as well as by the bourgeoisie and the aristocracy, who enjoyed them daily and saw them as recreation, as an opportunity to meet people and be on display. In Brussels, the author of a stroller's guide wrote in 1856 that 'the zoological gardens have today passed so completely into public habit that one must ask oneself what, three years ago, the inhabitants of Brussels did between coffee time and tea.'[34]

Pleasure parks, which were first established in London and were created throughout Europe at mid-century, and zoological gardens, whether independent of or integrated into the former, also responded to a growing desire among worthy citizens to escape, just for a moment, from urban noise, dirt and crowds. This had to do with increasing concerns about hygiene, a desire for clearer social distinctions and a new-found will to distinguish private and working life. The same writer from Brussels noted that there

centre on a regular basis.[32]

This trend was also at work in the royal gardens that were open to the public (in Madrid, the big cat house, built in 1830, included a discussion room) and in the municipal parks. This concentration on various aspects of the gardens' appeal, which had precedents in the aristocratic use of menageries in the early modern period, had its parallel in the winter gardens that opened almost everywhere at mid-

had previously been nowhere else 'one could go to breathe freely the warm air of summer'. Parks were therefore thought of as the antithesis of cramped, crowded and filthy towns, and the widespread choice of the picturesque garden was intended to introduce calm, clean air, open space and varied scenery, and to create an escape route away from civilization and into nature. The provision of such an opportunity doubtless explains the success of zoological gardens in Germanic countries, where a Romantic vision of the universe had been expounded since the late 1700s, one that insisted on the necessity of rediscovering unity between humanity and nature. Finally, the picturesque garden was a great encouragement to promenading, with its avenues for meeting or walking in company, and its shaded, winding, eventful paths that offered multiple views and endless invitations for the eye to fall on some item of novelty or curiosity, be it plant or animal.[35]

For this reason, zoological gardens often formed part of the urban renovation programmes being implemented all over Europe and characterized by the creation of broader streets, boulevards, squares and embankments to ease the movement of people and goods, to open out horizons, to encourage people to wander a little and look at monuments, and to improve air circulation and the general quality of life. Established on the immediate periphery of a town – or sometimes even right in the centre, as at Hamburg and Antwerp – and thus easily accessible, pleasure parks and zoological gardens were thought of in the context of contemporary hygiene theory as the green lungs which would regenerate urban spaces by introducing a recreated, domesticated and idealized nature, pumped directly into town centres along tree-lined boulevards, squares and embankments. In Marseilles, for example, a city enriched by trade but saturated by a growing population, the

creation of new avenues, embankments and squares, and the construction of middle-class housing and great public buildings (exchange, prefecture, law courts, cathedral) were carried out during the final days of the July Monarchy and (mostly) the Second Empire, on the initiative of the local prefect. The Durance Canal was dug to bring fresh water and irrigate the surrounding countryside. It was at the canal's mouth that its developer and others installed the zoological gardens and built the Palais Longchamp (1862–9) to disguise the water tower and house the museum of natural history. Located at the meeting point of the countryside and the town they overlooked, the gardens became a favoured place for promenades. A good many other zoological parks contributed to urban renovation schemes, for example at Lyon, Mulhouse, Paris (at the Bois du Boulogne) and Cologne.[36]

The importance of zoological gardens in fashionable society explains their foundation in parks in wealthy areas (Regent's Park in London, the Villa Borghese at Rome) and the fact that, when set up on the outskirts of towns, they accelerated, sometimes even directly provoked, the transformation of surrounding land into residential sectors for the aristocracy and bourgeoisie, who were increasingly unsettled by the social promiscuity and miasma of the cities. The opening of Leopold Park in Brussels energized the new quarter of the same name. Intended for the town's élite, this area was the first to be set up outside the city walls. Construction began in 1837 under the aegis of the Civil Society for the Enlargement and Development of the Capital, among whose number could be found ministers, bankers, the burgomaster and his deputies, and other notables. Zoological gardens were thus the vectors of property developments which furthered the geographical and social redistribution of urban populations, a characteristic of nineteenth-century urban history.

The investment in these gardens by the social élite was accompanied by entry restrictions in the first half of the nineteenth century. In 1797, access to the Jardin des Plantes was regulated because the Muséum's professors had to justify the menagerie's purpose. No-one was admitted without the written agreement of a scholar, which could only be obtained if one's interests were scientific in nature. This principle allowed for some play in social relations, however. In the face of overwhelming demand, it was decided in 1804 to allocate four days of the week to artists and the Muséum's scholars, and three days to the public. In London, the zoological gardens were well separated from the rest of the park, and access was limited to the members of the Zoological Society for the first two decades. 'Strangers' were admitted during the week, not on Sundays, and only on presentation of a letter of recommendation signed by a society member and at the cost of a shilling. This measure caused animosity towards the society, accused of encouraging social distinctions. But there was no question of allowing the lower classes to invade the gardens. For Harriet Pitvo, this limitation also had a symbolic element, the garden being a means of justifying the social dominance of the élite by demonstrating their active role in the establishment of the British Empire, and their *savoir-faire* in the mastery and appropriation of nature. Similar restrictions were adopted in Dublin, Leeds and Birmingham.[37]

In the US, a tremendous enthusiasm for the natural sciences from the late 1700s on had brought with it an interest in collections of stuffed specimens. The Natural Science Establishment founded by Henry A. Ward trained taxidermists, among them William T. Hornaday,[38] later to become director of the Bronx Zoo in New York. Naturalists remained a presence throughout the century – for example,

John Alden Loring, the first director at Denver, or Edmund Heller, who accompanied Theodore Roosevelt to Africa in 1909. As in England, zoological societies were the instigators of numerous and important zoos. The Smithsonian Institution had 4,000 naturalist correspondents (1879); it offered 160 acres in Rock Creek, on the edge of Washington, DC, for the creation of a national zoo.

The concept of the redemptive value of nature as a divine work, as well as the pastoralist utopianism of such influential personalities as Thomas Jefferson, who advocated regeneration through nature, favoured the establishment of public parks in countryside settings, with buildings dispersed throughout them. The landscape gardener Frederick Law Olmsted thought that the location of a zoo in New York's Central Park (1860) would detract from the contemplation of nature, even though that nature

Rock Creek, National Geographical Park, Washington, DC.

Bear cages, Forest Park, Springfield, MA, 1914.

New York Menagerie, Central Park, c. 1910.

Bronx River, Bronx Zoo, Bronx Park, NY, 1900s.

had been extensively remodelled by human hands into a sort of 'groomed nature' or 'middle landscape'. Hornaday felt that the Bronx Zoo's architect should use 'artistically and sensibly ... the work of nature', to which animals would add their wildness. The parks in which American zoos were set up were relatively wild and vast: 77 acres for Forest Park Zoo at St Louis (1913), 140 for San Diego Zoo in Balboa Park. Mrs Edith Rockefeller McCormick donated 83 acres near Chicago for Brookfield Zoo; by comparison, the zoo at Stellingen in Germany only occupied 25 acres. American zoos subjugated and classified animals just as parks imposed order on nature, but they also gave structure to sometimes insalubrious suburban areas. The Bronx, for example, was a 'jungle of ragged forest trees' infested with mosquitoes whose immigrant inhabitants were thought to be uncontrollable.[39] Some architects specialized in such projects; Adolphe Strach, designer of the suburb of Clifton, became superintendent of Cincinnati's parks. On some occasions, zoos followed international fairs in such districts; Audubon Park (New Orleans) profited from the *World's Industrial and Cotton Centennial Exposition* (1884–5). Having become a tool of town planning, zoos were considered to be 'the most distinctive marks of culture a city has to offer'.

FORCED DEMOCRATIZATION

The spread of joint-stock zoological societies brought with it the first liberalization of access – even if shareholders retained certain privileges (in Geneva, for example, they enjoyed free entry for a while) – because their attractions and pricing policy aimed to enlarge their middle-class clientele and thus ensure profitability. Ongoing financial challenges arising from the mounting costs of renewing livestock, renovating buildings and creating new attractions, as well as the limits placed on membership (thanks to social selection) and low attendance levels among the paying public, obliged them to change even further. Many of these stockholding societies failed. In Brussels, where the distribution of dividends had been promised from the first year even though the capital was not entirely subscribed, lack of funds led (from the 1860s on) to a reduction in the number of attractions, neglect of the buildings and animals, and, finally, dissolution in 1878. In Rome, the outbreak of the First World War sent takings tumbling, ruining the society there by 1917. In Geneva, in spite of corporate sponsorship from 1935 on (Pelikan, the manufacturer of inks, provided – appropriately enough – two pelicans), receipts barely covered maintenance costs, and liquidation beckoned the following year. The entrepreneurs, who had not been paid, took over the business, abandoning it in 1940.[40]

All of this brought about a process of democratization in the second half of the nineteenth century. The stockholding societies opened restaurants, sold rides on elephants, camels or ponies, and sold their surplus animals. Antwerp's position as the European centre of trade was thus strengthened. The subscription societies broadened the social recruitment of members, whose ranks swelled to greater sizes than those of the shareholders. In 1906, London had 3,700 members, Amsterdam 5,000 and Antwerp 7,800. Finally, the societies opened their gardens to the public. In London – the most significant example – the waning interest of the upper classes forced a change in policy after 1846 if liquidation was to be avoided. The general public was admitted during the week, while Sundays and holidays remained the preserve of members and those carrying recommendations. In 1908, the management obtained the right to expand into the park on the condition that they allowed certain animals to be observed free of charge.

Development followed a similar course in Dublin and Birmingham.[41]

A few European establishments – Marseilles (1861), Mulhouse (1893), Düsseldorf (1905), Budapest (1907), Rome (1917) – were purchased by local municipalities. It was a question of maintaining good social relations by wiping out their debts (Marseilles) or of avoiding the closure of what had come to be considered essential facilities. But in these cases as elsewhere (Lyon, Madrid), local authorities wavered between direct control, thought to be too expensive, and concession to private enterprise, which had the drawback of relinquishing a public asset while continuing to subsidize it.

This latter aspect took on political overtones towards the end of the nineteenth century due to the rise of right-wing parties, and is why most German and Scandinavian towns chose to grant subsidies to the stockholding societies to ensure their survival.[42] In exchange, they won certain concessions. In Berlin, primary-school children were admitted for free, and students at half-price. The same was true in Copenhagen, where free entry was extended to soldiers in uniform. Other municipalities pressed their franchise holders to establish pricing policies that would favour the greatest number of people. To further the education of the working classes, some communes upheld (Lyon, 1881) or introduced (Marseilles, 1898) totally free entry. The Jardin des Plantes in Paris had paved the way thanks to the indifference of the Muséum's professors towards its scientific function. From the end of the 1830s, the general public enjoyed free admission every day of the week.[43]

Democratization was justified and reinforced by a school of thought that surfaced in the second half of the century just as difficulties were beginning to accumulate. Through a slow reversal in social geography, and due to the popularization of exotic creatures and the declining interest of the élite, zoological gardens were proposed as venues for the entertainment and moral improvement of the working classes, an idea that would not really make itself felt until the early 1900s. In France, it germinated at Marseilles in 1869 and at Lyon in 1873, while in Mulhouse, it was at the very heart of the enterprise. The project of a zoological garden was suggested there in 1860 during a session of the Société Industrielle, a philanthropic institution devoted to improving the lot of the working class and behind the foundation of refuges, schools, libraries, orphanages, housing estates and savings banks. A people's park in the image of Manchester's Peel Park and Halifax's People's Park in the UK was deemed necessary for physical and mental health. In 1868, the Mulhouse Zoological Society's statutes dictated that the working class should find 'an honest and instructive diversion' there on Sundays. This idea was shared by another philanthropic association which acquired the gardens in 1875 to preserve them for its members and make them available for the recreation and education of working people, craftsmen and employees. In Düsseldorf, the municipality purchased the zoo in 1905 to lure working-class youths away from the taverns and offer them somewhere more healthy to relax.[44]

American zoos learned from their European elders. The physicist William Camac visited European zoos around 1850 to perfect plans for Philadelphia. In 1873, Herman Schwartzmann, with a group of naturalists in tow, studied Regent's Park for his designs for Fairmount Park. Many others followed them: Hornady (1896), Frederick Law Olmsted Jr, the Chicago Zoological Society (1927).[45] German influence seems to have predominated. Andrew Erkenbrecher, a German factory director, gathered Cincinnati's 'civic leaders' into a zoological society (1873, joint-stock company) based on the Frankfurt model and

The old bear pit, Mulhouse Zoo.

linked to the American Philosophical Society. This zoo, built on an old pilgrimage site, became the hub of a rich residential suburb.[46] Sol Stephan, trained by Carl Hagenbeck, was named its director, while Lee Williams, its secretary, was a broker for Hagenbeck, often responsible for warehousing his stock. Many German hunters who had established themselves in the US – the Reiches, Paul Ruhe, H. Bartels, Henry Trefflich, Julius Mohr and Arthur Foehl – supplied Cincinnati and maintained exclusive control on the importation of animals from Africa, South Asia and the East Indies. The loss of Germany's colonies in 1918, and especially of their specialized transport ships, undermined this hegemony. From 1872, Hagenbeck supplied the Barnum, Adam Forepaugh and Ringling circuses, creating his own circus in the US to take the spillover from Stellingen. His efficiency impressed and inspired his American rivals.

OTHER TRANSFORMATIONS

The requisition of the princely menageries which benefited the Jardin des Plantes in Paris at the time of the Revolution had, as we have seen, sounded a symbolic death knell for such places. Napoleon I, who wished to revive the splendour of the *Ancien Régime*, helped Empress Josephine to assemble a menagerie at Malmaison. His brother Louis, King of Holland since 1805, imitated this establishment. But the divorce of Josephine in 1809 and Louis' abdication in 1810 led to the closure of both establishments and an end to this particular princely tradition in France.

After 1815, the fashion for picturesque parks provoked the further transformation of French-style gardens and the abandoning of exotic menageries, almost as if the one sensibility went hand in hand with the other. At Weimar and Schwetzingen, menageries were eliminated or replaced by tree nurseries or arboretums. Other establishments were caught up in the surge of nationalism and democratization in the new century. The formation of zoological gardens by notable individuals active in the scientific, economic and colonial worlds, and their subsequent opening to the public, raised them to the status of symbols of national power and imperialism. Princely menageries gradually disappeared or were nationalized, for example in the cases of the menageries of the kings of Saxony and Bavaria and of the Landgrave of Hesse. In 1831, William IV gave his collection at the Tower of London to the new zoological gardens of Regent's Park and Dublin. In 1844, Frederick William IV of Prussia offered his animals on Peacock Island to the Berlin gardens, which had just been installed in the Tiergarten, also ceded by the sovereign. In Madrid, in 1869, the royal menagerie was granted to the municipality, which had been dreaming of a zoo of its own to compete with those in other capitals. [47]

There were some exceptions to these trends, however. In Austria, where absolute monarchy survived while a

Lake at Dublin Zoo.

multinational state was being established, the Schönbrunn menagerie enjoyed continued growth while taking on the attributes of a contemporary zoological garden. The kings of Piedmont and Sardinia, hoping to make their kingdom the most powerful on the Italian peninsula and then unify the latter to their profit, created an exotic menagerie at Stupinigi between 1815 and 1826 to proclaim the prestige of the court and the state. But, in tune with the times, it was built according to the model of the Jardin des Plantes and then turned into a stud farm in 1852–3, when the statesman Count Cavour was trying to modernize the kingdom. In 1864, Victor Emmanuel II decided to build a zoological garden in the park of his palace at Turin, and it too submitted to the prevailing mentality. It was meant less for the King himself than as an emblem of the new Italian state (proclaimed in 1861) and its capital. This zoo also formed part of the renovation of the town. In the end, it became a pleasure park for fashionable society with restricted access. In 1872, the King's move to Rome caused the symbolism surrounding the Turin zoo to be superseded. Umberto I, who lost interest in it, wanted to transfer its management to the municipality (another contemporary trend, as we have seen), but the failure of negotiations brought about its closure and the sale of the animals in 1889.[48]

Smaller-scale aristocratic menageries did survive on the peninsula, at least during the first half of the nineteenth century, such as those of the Prince of Savoy-Carignan at Racconigi or the Duke of Sartinara near Turin. The Duke, a painter, bibliophile, ornithologist and sometime president of the Entomological Society of France, perpetuated the

ways of the *Ancien Régime* with his natural-history collection, his garden of rare plants and his enclosures containing deer, gazelles and Sardinian mouflons. Another area where customs were upheld was the UK, which had remained sheltered from the revolutionary storms that had overtaken parts of Europe. The aristocracy maintained a great many hunting parks (395 in 1892) with thousands of deer and stags, but also a few private menageries, hidden deep within their estates. In 1804–5, the Duke of Bedford installed a large aviary and a kangaroo park at Woburn Abbey. Lord Stanley, the third president of London's Zoological Society, did the same on his own lands, while Baron Francis Rothschild erected an iron-and-glass aviary in 1889 for 340 species of bird. Decline was more evident elsewhere. French nobles were on the lookout for deer, swans and fowl to purchase from zoological gardens and place in the grounds of their châteaux or other houses on the outskirts of towns, a fashion that caught on with the bourgeoisie after having long been the exclusive preserve of the aristocracy. This desire ran parallel to the introduction of greenhouses for exotic plants from mid-century, as the garden became a fundamental element of bourgeois life, a symbol of familial tranquillity. A few well-to-do individuals attempted to resuscitate the splendour of the *Ancien Régime*: at the turn of

The Zoological Society of London's aquarium, c. 1853.

Aquarium, sea-grotto and bird house, Aquarium unter den Linden, Berlin, 1879, by Emil Schmidt.

the century, Amédée de Broglie installed an elephant presented by a Maharajah in the grounds of the Château de Chaumont-sur-Loire.[49]

The custom of keeping wild animals inside residences survived into this period. Birdcages became rare in upper-class homes just as they began to appear, perhaps as early as the 1700s and on a smaller scale, in the windows of labour-ers and artisans. They were replaced in well-to-do households by small aquariums, which proliferated in the wake of the success of the zoos' vivariums and aquariums, the first of which opened at Regent's Park in 1853. The growth of tourism in the second half of the nineteenth century, as well as the journeys to the colonies undertaken by soldiers, administrators, merchants and engineers, reinforced the habit of bringing a live animal home, just as travellers might have returned with exotic carpets or archaeological artefacts. Most of these were 'peaceful' animals (monkeys, parrots), and certainly the vogue for big cats that slept at the foot of one's bed was restricted to marginal aristocrats, nostalgic colonials and artists (Sarah Bernhardt, for example, kept a puma around 1895). In short order, these animals were considered an embarrassment and offered to zoological gardens.[50]

Imitating the Parisian decision of 1793, many towns gradually forbade the exhibition of wild animals in the streets, which provoked the slow disappearance of the small-time showmen. The only ones to survive were bear trainers, those beasts having vanished almost entirely, except for some in the Pyrenees and Eastern Europe, by the twentieth century.[51] In the same way, the fight against cruelty to animals led to a ban (in 1822 in the UK, in 1833 in Paris) on fights between dogs, bears, wolves and even tigers and lions provided by merchants and fairground entertainers, though this movement encountered resistance in Britain, France and, of course, Spain. But showmen remained a presence at fairs, which kept their old-world feel until the mid-1800s. At the Hamburg fair, the father of Carl Hagenbeck, the future founder of the Stellingen gardens, exhibited six seals in

Frank Bostock with animals from the Bostock & Wombwell Menagerie, in Hull for the 1931 Hull Fair.

1848, a bear, a hyena and various birds in 1852, and six trained bears in 1863.[52]

Travelling menageries, which first appeared in the second half of the eighteenth century, became numerous. Most possessed between five and ten animals, but a few took on considerable proportions. The menagerie of the Englishman George Wombwell was founded in 1805 and ten years later consisted of fourteen carriages pulled by 60 horses. Such menageries reached their peak during the years 1870–1900, the age of the great fairground festivals, and then suffered a decline during the first half of the twentieth century. The largest of them became so enormous that they were forced to set themselves up in one place before they collapsed under their own weight or were swallowed up by circuses. Others returned to their original modest dimensions. Simultaneously, while the earliest sedentary menageries closed their doors in the eighteenth and nine-teenth centuries (Blaauw Jan in 1784, Exeter 'Change in 1829), others were developing in Germany and England. In Manchester in 1836, John Jennison founded Bellevue Gardens, which assembled animal and all sorts of other attractions (restaurant, ballroom, museum, mechanical games, sports and, later, a cinematograph) over an area of 32 hectares. Similar establishments prospered in London (Covent Garden, Crystal Palace), Halifax and such seaside resorts as Southport and Blackpool.[53]

These menageries maintained close links with the zoological gardens, selling them animals and sometimes even creating them. The zoological society of Rotterdam appealed to the famous Henry Martin to help found their own gardens in 1857. The merchant Carl Hagenbeck, who had already opened his warehouse to the public, built his gardens at Stellingen in 1907 and oversaw the creation of several others. Menageries also dealt with circuses, whose

Exeter 'Change, London, 1812.

customary format – circular rings, equestrian spectacles and acrobatics – had been invented by Philip Astley in London around 1770. In Paris, the Franconis used wild animals in their shows from the 1820s, but it was the English Sanger Circus which popularized the fusion with menageries between 1856 and 1870, a time when its exotic animals formed the greatest itinerant collection in the UK. American circuses took on considerable proportions from 1880 on, possessing between fifteen and 30 elephants on average. When the Barnum Circus visited Europe in 1897–1902, having joined forces with its rival Bailey, 67 wagons and twenty heavy crates transported more than 500 horses, over twenty elephants and some rare specimens (rhinoceroses, hippopotami, a chimpanzee) that many zoological gardens did not possess. Carl Hagenbeck created one of the biggest circuses in Europe in 1887 to keep his beasts and employees busy, and profitable, between exhibitions.[54]

The presentation of these animals differed from that employed at the zoological gardens and recalls the hotchpotch of the old-world seraglios. In Herman and Wilhelm Van Aaken's travelling menagerie, painted by Paul Meyerheim in 1864, barred carriages were the permanent home of the big cats. Elephants were chained, bears

Carl Hagenbeck's 'Zoological Paradise', 1898.

The Menagerie of Herman Van Aaken, 1864, by Paul Meyerheim.

attached to wheels, and snakes placed in wooden cases, while birds and monkeys perched on poles. Spectators moved along a corridor, looking at the showmen's exhibits. Great success was achieved throughout Europe, with a more socially heterogeneous public in attendance thanks to more modest prices. In the many regions that lacked their own zoological gardens, itinerant menageries and circuses served to acquaint the public with exotic creatures, even – thanks to parades – people who did not attend their shows.

In the US, beginning in the late eighteenth century, menageries had begun to exhibit trained horses and the more or less wild animals that would later be shown in circuses;

from 1820 on, these menageries became itinerant, using portable tents. Barnum and Bailey competed against theatres – which were considered to be immoral at the time – by presenting honest family entertainment, with victorious results.[55] P. T. Barnum progressed from his own museum (with added attractions) to international fame, from his circus to shows that were at once playful and enlightening. Pleasure parks, known as Elysian Fields, had included animals since the 1700s: at Coney Island's Luna Park, counting horses preceded the twenty elephants provided by Hagenbeck in 1904. Sensational displays were mounted at the international exhibitions: a hundred cages of big cats were

Alligator farm, Arkansas, late 19th century.

shown in 1901 at the *Buffalo Pan America Exhibition*, while
30,000 animals (1,000 rhesus monkeys among them)
appeared at Frank Buck's Jungleland in 1939. These spectacular enterprises were complemented by more modest affairs
for travellers and immigrants – roadside zoos of a sort – as
well as innumerable ranches and game and hunting farms.
Zoos integrated themselves into this pre-existing network of
animal shows, and there was a constant exchange of knowledge, personnel and animals. There was also surely an
exchange of audiences that had become accustomed to seeing
wild animals as one element of a stunning theatrical universe.

6 IMPERIAL GLORY

At the time when Europe was amassing its immense colonial empire, four methods for the appropriation of exotic animals presented themselves. The first and most extreme, hunting, often took on a heroic dimension, especially for colonial servicemen who would add to their personal prestige by purging a country of its wildlife. The imposition of spatial limitations on animals – housing them in zoos – was often combined with the third method, acclimatization. Finally, psychological appropriation, especially in the taming of big cats, was such a perfect match for the colonial process that anti-establishment cartoonists used it as an allegory for slavery, and indeed it was to a lion-tamer that Maréchal Lyautey entrusted the zoo of the *Exposition Coloniale*, the showcase of triumphant imperialism. Hunting, zoos, acclimatization and taming – in constant interaction – stimulated demand that fuelled the growing success of the exhibition of wild animals, but also decimated their populations. Renowned importers maintained world-wide networks of huntsmen, who added ever more sophisticated rifles to the traditional methods of capture. Impressive convoys of animals wiped the wholesale slaughter from memory; it was not thought to be of any importance anyway. To heighten their prestige, animal dealers would mount ethnographical exhibitions in European zoos, featuring strange men, women and beasts, lumped together under the term savages.

TAKE THEM ALIVE!

The hunter was omnipresent in the European zoological garden. Lutz Heck, son of the director of Berlin's zoo, gave his hunting memoirs the title *Aus der Wildnis in den Zoo auf Tierfang in Ostafrica*,[1] and the zoo historian Gustave Loisel applied for an off-season hunting permit.[2] Jules Janin described with gentle humour the man, disabled in a hunt, who came to the menagerie every day just to verify that 'there is still something left to kill in this world'.[3] Whether he went under the name of Bombonnel or Tartarin (as Alphonse Daudet called his character), the hunter of lions was the king of hunters, vanquishing the king of animals. Trophies perpetuated their glory.[4] The 28 May 1881 issue of *Caricature* transformed the dead lion lying motionless behind *Pertuiset the Lion Hunter*, as painted by Edouard Manet, into a bedside rug. In England, the game hunter was most closely associated with the colonial enterprise, the hunter emerging 'as both the ideal and definitive type of Empire builder'. For example, Rovaleyn Gordon Cumming joined the cavalry of the East India Company in 1838 and began his career as an explorer of Africa (1840) as well as a big-game hunter. Towards the middle of the century, he returned to London with an enormous cargo of trophies and stuffed animals, causing a sensation. Frederick Courteney Selous, who served as a soldier in Rhodesia, was also an intrepid hunter. He was praised for having 'advanced the cause of civilization and helped extend the British Empire'. Another generation succeeded these men, remaining active until after the First World War.

Trophies from colonial hunts, like the animals of a zoo, bore witness to the 'conquest of lands that had been discovered and colonized'. From the early nineteenth century on, William Bullock's India Museum (1801), attracted between ten and twenty thousand visitors a year. Dealers in wild animals accumulated the trophies and animal remains (turtle shells, seashells, teeth, horns) so appreciated by eighteenth-century collectors, as well as objects that would today be called ethnological (weapons, ornaments, clothing, jewellery); the Hagenbecks, for example, possessed a superb collection of horns and stags' antlers.[5] Advances in taxidermy (the art of stuffing animals) led collectors to have large specimens killed to complete their collections. Walter Lionel de Rothschild gave a precise order to Coryndon to

Eugene Pertuiset, The Lion Hunter, 1881, by Edouard Manet.

find and kill a rhinoceros for this purpose. Exotic animals that had died in zoos were disparaged, enthusiasts considering them to have been deformed by captivity. The most sought-after specimens were the rarest beasts, or the hardest to kill. The Earl of Derby's museum collected some 25,000 specimens.[6]

In his lecture 'La Lutte de l'homme contre les animaux', Pierre-Amédée Pichot (son of the romantic Anglophile from Arles) declared: 'Animal species disappear when they cannot peacefully orbit the centre of gravity that is man.'[7]

The old idea of a limitless, inexhaustible nature allowed the massive destruction of the penguins on the islands near Cape Town to take place around 1787.[8] Only the weapons used, more efficient than the muskets of old, distinguished the colonial period from the past. After 1875, 26 men could kill 56 elephants in a day.[9] The only way to capture a living animal was to kill the suckling females or the herd's leaders. The account of the Tornblad expedition to Kenya tells of the slaughter of adult giraffes that enabled the capture of a calf, who was immediately welcomed into the group, cared for and given a name, Rosalie. Hagenbeck found himself 'too often obliged to kill' elephants who were protecting their young by using their own bodies as shields.

Every explorer became a hunter to finance his travels. Around 1830, Dixon Deham returned from Chad with a menagerie in tow, as did Stanford and Natterer, selling the animals to Carl Hagenbeck. The influence hunters had on the public went far beyond stuffed animals and living examples in zoos, since many published their memoirs. This literary genre enjoyed great success, especially in England. In 1820, S. and W. Daniel published *Sketches Representing the Nature, Tribes, Animals and Scenery of Southern Africa*, which demonstrated a documentary interest going beyond animal life. Later generations of hunters imbued their memoirs with all the thrills and suspense of a novel. *Five Years of a Hunter's Life in the Far Interior of South Africa* was published by Gordon Cumming on his return to London in 1850, when he opened his exhibition of trophies. Some passages of this book were reprinted in popular journals such as *The Illustrated London News*. These publications made a major contribution to the success of zoos, readers wishing to see the actual animal protagonists in the tales they printed. The success of hunting books continued to grow: Samuel White Baker's *Rifle and Hound in Ceylon*, first published in 1850, saw six editions. Courteney Selous used his collection of large stuffed animals, brought back from Africa in 1874, as a backdrop for his exhibitions and lectures. He published *A Hunter's Wanderings in Africa* (1881); less of a braggart than Gordon Cumming, his impact on the scientific world was greater. These books awoke in adolescents of the late nineteenth century the desire to become hunters, adventurers and explorers, accomplishing this all the more easily because the major publications that published them, from the distinguished *Oriental Sporting Magazine* to the most populist newspapers, reached all social classes.

Some professional European huntsmen learned the traditional methods of capture from native inhabitants of the areas they visited; accounts magnified the 'exceptional bonds' created 'between the European hunter and his native counterpart'. Europeans claimed to be civilizing people at the same time as beasts; Carl Hagenbeck boasted of having taught the Mongols to tame wild horses. One of his 50 huntsmen – Casanova, an Italian, in Hagenbeck's service since 1865 and a *habitué* of Ethiopia and the Sudan – taught the local hunters how to handle the taka sword. Many of the traditional methods of capture, such as fire or the felling of trees, were damaging to the environment. Traps of all kinds, such as hidden pits or small huts (3 by 2 metres) with lures for monkeys, required great delicacy in their use.[10] Accidents were common, mostly broken limbs, and carnivores often devoured ensnared animals. The shock of being captured was such that, according to tamers, 'a big cat [would] be almost mad on arrival.' A recent veterinary manual confirms the dangers inherent in the most common forms of capture.[11] When reservations are restocked by the physical movement of animals, deaths are inevitable in even the most careful operations.[12] Stress can be measured by the level of plasmatic cortisol; when restrained, a rhesus monkey's level rises by 52 per cent; if the trauma of immobilization is avoided, this figure falls to 13 per cent.[13] The hypodermic rifle, a more recent invention, lets the quarry be put to sleep at a distance, but not without danger for the fleeing animal. Many creatures apparently never recover from being captured.

Immediately after the First World War, the Paris Muséum, its stock depleted, financed a hunting campaign in the colonies. The minister of public education granted it the patriotic stamp of freedom from export duty, and the governors of the French colonies were requested to assemble 'as great a number of specimens as possible'. Many colonists obtained permits for capture and free travel under the pretext of making donations to the menagerie, which also allowed them to seek postings in France. Trafficking began.[14] Rich private individuals went hunting in Africa with the help of agencies that were encouraged by the government. Les Voyages et Grandes Chasses de Sainte-Adresse (Le Havre) obtained an exemption for their entire cargo of living animals in May 1925.

The devastation of colonial wildlife triggered controversy about hunting, defended by Paul Bourdelle[15] and M. Pochard, director of the Compagnie Française du Continent Africain, who proposed to classify lions and tigers as pests.[16] A crisis of conscience developed, especially after a conference in London in 1900 and under the influence of W. Schoenichen, among others. England (like Germany, Belgium and Portugal) made efforts to apply and prolong existing measures: the protection of species threatened with extinction, the creation of reserves where hunting was banned, and the introduction of hunting permits (which turned out to be extremely lucrative). In turn, the English Agencies were founded, aiming for a wealthy clientele who were enthusiastic about large-scale hunting. These 'sportsmen' were furnished with all that was necessary (equipment and native helpers) for hunting in British East Africa.

Many regulations succeeded one another, such as the British decrees of 1889 that protected gazelles and Egyptian wildlife.[17] In 1931, Bourdelle deplored the 'pointless slaughter that, sadly, is characteristic of present-day collections of living animals' and proposed centres of acclimatization that did in fact develop. A trade association of French zoos was formed to compete with the hunters. Much local legislation was proposed in the French colonies:[18] in Cochin China in 1925, Indochina in 1927, French Equatorial Africa in 1929 and Cameroon in 1930. Preservation zones (French West Africa in 1925; French Equatorial Africa in 1927) and nature reserves were created, and although the effect was barely perceptible, at least the necessity of putting a stop to the waste was being recognized.

Members of scientific expeditions, every one of which returned with live animals, educated themselves by reading *Instructions pour les voyageurs et les employés dans les colonies*, in print until 1860. These scientific missions collected great quantities of samples, but also living animals like the camels, lions, gazelles and ostriches brought back from Tunis by Félix Cassal in 1798. In 1804, 18,414 mineral samples and preserved animal remains, and about 70 live animals donated by the Governor of the Cape of Good Hope or purchased in the Île-de-France (a renowned black panther among them), were unloaded from Captain Beaudin's *Géographe* and *Naturaliste*. From 1815 on, expeditions proliferated, led by illustrious scientists or seafarers like Louis-Isidore Duperrey, Léon-Louis Vaillant or Louis-Marie Dupetit-Thouars; Jacques Gérard Milbert brought 49 mammals and 70 birds, all alive, from Hudson Bay. At the Jardin des Plantes, India was represented by a part of the Sultan of Mysore's collection, purchased in London, and

North America by Milbert's animals. The *Buffon* and the *Georges-Cuvier*, fitted out by the Bordeaux trader Dussumier, brought large animals back from the Indian and Pacific oceans; J.-S.C. Dumont d'Urville journeyed to the South Pole aboard the *Astrolabe* (he discovered the brown kiwi).[19] The biggest menageries organized their own expeditions. A. Vekeman, for the Antwerp gardens, hunted in Africa and bought a monkey (which soon died) from a caravan, and then another from a merchant called Headle, whom he encountered near Sierra Leone. On their return, rare surviving animals were purchased from expedition members by zoological gardens.[20] In the early 1900s, the Muséum sent numerous missions to the French colonies, including French West Africa, Madagascar (Bocteau, 1939–40) and Shanghai (Imbert, 1926). Jean Delacour, ornithologist and founder of the zoo at Clères, led seven expeditions to Indochina between 1932 and 1940, and one to Madagascar in collaboration with the American Museum of Natural History, in New York, on behalf of the London Zoo and Paris Muséum.

While accounts of such voyages were highly successful, other relevant books also made their mark at this time. It is difficult to measure the impact of *Expression of the Emotions in Man and Animals* (1872) by Charles Darwin, other than to state that it confirmed the convergence of human and animal that had previously only been hinted at. The author of the bestseller *La Vie d'amour dans la nature*, W. Bölsche, was a friend of Ludwig Heck and, like him, a fervent Darwinist. *The Life of Trees*, published in the US by Henry David Thoreau, and many other books contemporary with Rudyard Kipling's work, were at once documentary and poetic in style, and were distributed throughout Western Europe, often in English. While they more or less overtly proposed a new attitude towards nature and wildlife, they did not incite open criticism of zoos. Grey Owl, the figure-

Left: Gorillas, Jersey Zoo. Right: The dodo, symbol of extinction, on the gate of Jersey Zoo.

head of this movement, gave his last lecture in London, shortly before his death, in 1938.

Reportage of heroic hunts was internationally popular, both in print and on film. *Bring 'em Back Alive* was written by Frank Buck, a Texas hunter and salesman of orang-utans from Borneo and 'man-eating tigers'. The work of Bengt Berg, a Swedish writer, was translated into German and Russian. *Les Aventures d'Abu Markub, Mon ami le pluvier, Le Tigre et l'Homme* all depicted a superman, the hero of many films. In 1941, Paul Eiper published a book on the circus in Paris, soon followed by the celebrated *Les Bêtes vous regardent*.[21] In 1946, Lorenz Hagenbeck's memoirs *Ces bêtes que j'aimais* appeared in French, followed by Carl Hagenbeck's *Cages sans barreaux* and *Danneh, tigre royal* by John Hagenbeck in 1953. It was in this environment that young zoo directors like H. Hediger were made. Curiously, there was renewed interest in hunting tales (especially those from Germany!) in France after the Second World War, as if the slaughter of animals could erase that of people. This trend receded in the face of the development of documentary films (especially on television). Gerald Durrell, made wealthy by tales of his collecting expeditions (filmed by the BBC in Sierra Leone in 1961), opened a zoo in Jersey that he described in his later works.[22] This zoo (1959) was a sort of Noah's Ark dedicated to the survival of endangered species. Durrell founded the Jersey Wildlife Preservation Trust in 1963; its 6,000 members came from 38 different countries. Even though this zoo did not escape criticism, Durrell later

opened an avenue for the voice of opposition. André Mercier, a member of a scientific expedition who became a hunting entrepreneur in Africa, and then Peter Scott, author of *The Eye of the Wind*, and finally Jean-Yves Domalain, all abandoned and then denounced hunting and capture, thus joining the postcolonial voice of dissent.[23]

A DELICATE COLONIAL COMMODITY

African wildlife was generally classified as a 'colonial commodity' and, like all other 'commercial resources', was exploited without much care and at terrible expense, for the animals at least. Carl Hagenbeck told of a caravan's progress as, laden with animals, it crossed the burning deserts of the Sudan at night over the course of several weeks. A hippopotamus, wrapped in a stretcher made of hide, was carried by two dromedaries, and the water for his bath by two others. Goats followed; they suckled the younger creatures, and were then killed by the big cats. J.V. Domalain described such practices in twentieth-century Laos as quite usual: wounded cats were not given anything to drink and then abandoned to the sun, their gangrenous legs tied together. Hagenbeck related that a sea elephant weighing 1,410 kilos, sent from the Cape of Georgia to Stellingen, held out for 40 days without a bath or food.[24] This was at a time when travel was still very stressful. In 1810, according to Frédéric Cuvier, it took three months to get from Borneo to Spain, then two more to get to Paris across the snow-covered Pyrenees. In 1824, an Indian elephant would travel for six months to reach Paris; in 1850, five months; in 1870, 62 days. It would often arrive exhausted with sea-sickness. In 1928, the month's journey from Cameroon or Madagascar to the zoo at Lyon was still long enough for animals to arrive emaciated and wounded.[25]

The 'packaging for this material', according to the term used by Lyon's zoo in 1934, was the sabot, a small cage reinforced only at the front, as animals did not try to escape from the back. Tossed about without protection for their claws, big cats tore themselves to ribbons and bled to death, or put their own eyes out. The movements of the great circuses taught many lessons, and ships began to specialize in the transport of wild animals. Around 1923, the Congo's riverboat services and several others were offering the attractive price of 50 francs per cubic metre.[26] A surcharge for large animals cost one first-class ticket, for reasons of food: for an Indian elephant, two thousand kilos of hay, twelve hundred of bananas, five hundred of sugar-cane and four hundred of green cabbage had to be taken on board.[27] Aboard ship, gorillas were given food that had been poorly preserved in refrigerators of inadequate size, and the water was unsuited to the aquariums.[28] Delivery of animals by air began in 1948, the zoos of Copenhagen and Antwerp being pioneers in this area.

The tonnage of animals transported was enormous. *Le Petit Marseillais* of 18 November 1894 reported a turnover in this category of 566,000 francs for the port of Marseilles alone. Between 1866 and 1886, Carl Hagenbeck exported around seven hundred leopards, a thousand lions and four hundred tigers, a thousand bears, eight hundred hyenas, three hundred elephants, 70 rhinoceroses from India, Java and Sumatra and nine from Africa, three hundred camels, 150 giraffes, six hundred antelopes, tens of thousands of monkeys, thousands of crocodiles, boas and pythons (in which his firm specialized) and substantially more than a hundred thousand birds. Loisel enumerated precisely the six consignments expected in early 1910 from western Africa, Djibouti, Ceylon, central and western Siberia and India, reaching a total of around 150 animals identified as large mammals, without counting other mammals, birds (40 ostriches) and six hundred monkeys.[29]

These figures do not take account of the losses suffered en route. All merchants estimated losses in transit at around 50 per cent of animals embarked; Hagenbeck's 'tens of thousands' of monkeys or the 350 gibbons captured by Domalain must therefore be doubled. Five or six very big traders, a good ten or so smaller merchants, and innumerable amateurs, colonists and seamen imported monkeys, as did zoos like Antwerp which had their own huntsmen. Deaths before embarkation cannot even be guessed at. For most monkeys and for some other animals, the destruction of mothers and, effectively, of their descendants must also be counted. James Fisher, an assistant manager of London Zoo, estimated that one captured orang-utan eliminates four in the wild, of which three would be potential mothers.[30] Domalain reckoned the number of animals killed for every one visible at a zoo to be ten. Even in the late twentieth century, mortality rates for legitimate air transport continued to be high: between 1988 and 1991, they were between 10 and 37 per cent for baboons and long-tailed monkeys from Africa; around 10 per cent from the Philippines; and 18–54 per cent from Indonesia. Ornithological importation was on a massive scale: every August, the aviaries of exotic birds at Antwerp would contain between 50,000 and 60,000 birds.[31]

Antwerp – one of the oldest focal points for the sale of wild animals – was where Jacques Kets, founder of its

Die Girafe in Schönbrunn
im August 1828. 18. Monathe alt, 9½ Schuh hoch, kommt von Darfur in Afrika 700 Meilen von Wien, mit dem arabischen Wärter GAGI ALLI SCIOBARI.

The giraffe sent from the Sudan to Schönbrunn in 1828, with keeper Gagi Alli Sciobari.

Unloading zoo animals after the voyage to Europe, *c.* 1870.

Feeding zoo animals at sea, early 20th century.

zoological gardens, organized a 'genuine annual market-place', something of a rendezvous for zoo directors.[32] Hamburg, with links to Djibouti through coal trading, was the Hagenbecks' fiefdom. The trade in animals profited from new colonial ports (Dakar in 1857) and the opening of the Suez Canal. The British controlled most of the market in Australia, the Indies and South Africa. There was not, however, an exact correspondence between captors' nationality and colonial possessions. The local situations in Africa were complex; France often granted exploitation rights around Brazzaville to British or German companies. Somalia and the Sudan were supposed to have inexhaustible

reserves of elephants, black rhinoceroses – Hagenbeck was the first to import one of these, in 1868 – giraffes and big cats (tigers included). Brindisi was reached via Djibouti after a pause for acclimatization on the island of Briani in the Adriatic. Some accounts mention sites in the Gobi Desert, in Nubia, on the Gach or at the foot of Mount Sahaney, where Abdullah Okoutt caught 26 large male baboons. From his base in Khartoum, Vice-Consul Petherick supplied various European societies with animals.

Charles Jamrach of London, originally from Hamburg and allied to the Hagen-becks, established his firm in London at the beginning of the nineteenth century, the date 1799 appearing on his animal ware-house. Together with a captain, he traded and sold zoological bric-a-brac, and was later employed by London Zoo. He supplied wild animals to zoos and to circuses such as those of Van Amburgh; soon, he was amassing and selling animal trophies and ethnological objects. Charles Jamrach traded between 1840 and 1891, supplying some of the biggest zoos in the world. The animal were stacked in cramped sabots, and the stench was appalling. Albert Edward Jamrach (180 St George's Street, London) took over the business around 1894.[33] Edward Cross initially set up at the wild-animal dock in Liverpool,[34] then at Exeter Change. Even better known than his rival Jamrach, he crammed in similar merchandise: exotic animal trophies, living creatures and ethnological objects, described as 'life-sized fragments of the Empire'. Other English merchants are recorded in various archives.

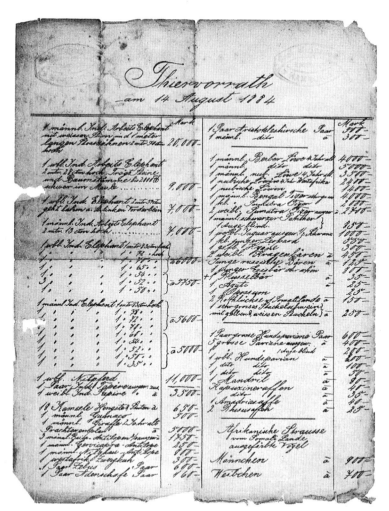

Hagenbeck wild-animal price list, 1884.

Around 1900, one finds Fred Shaw Meyer and Wilfred Frost;[35] in 1920, J. D. Hamlyn of London and Palmer's of Camden Town. French archives show traces of Edgar Bell of London (49 Delaford Street), seller of rare animals, and Chapman (London, 1926).[36]

Having risen from modest beginnings as the son of a fish merchant in Hamburg's Sankt-Pauli quarter, from 1866 Carl Hagenbeck supplied the zoos of Berlin and then Hamburg, managed by the celebrated Alfred Brehm. A prodigious businessman, Hagenbeck set up shop in the US in 1883 and founded a circus in 1887. His huntsmen travelled the entire globe; his own zoo at Stellingen was the crowning glory of his career. The Reiche brothers, Germans who settled in New York in 1844, specialized in the canaries carried by miners in the Gold Rush. M. Ruhe, a one-time associate of theirs in Alfeld (Hannover) and later their rival, and his son received consignments from the hunter Mynheer Van Goens. At Cros-de-Cagnes, where G. von

Wild-animal shop, c. 1900.

Basilevski acclimatized animals that had come via Marseilles for him, Ruhe wrote *Wilde Tiere, frei Haus*. He supplied the trainer Auguste Mölker around 1935, as well as his compatriot, the famous Franz Kraml, lion-tamer of the Sarasini Circus and the Circus of a Hundred Lions, featured in the Italian film *Quo Vadis?* After 1960, Ruhe's son, Hermann, exported animals from Russia and Africa across the world; his descendants became managers of the children's zoo in San Jose, California, in 1991.[37] Among many others, the merchant Otto Hebron (Hebrophon, Hebronia and Haka) and Franz Katzenstein of Berlin, who around 1925 put together 'the biggest convoy ever seen' for the Muséum in Paris, are noteworthy.

Nothing of this sort was to be found in France. Circuses, tamers, the organizers of animal fights, game breeders and bird catchers occasionally sold wild animals. One could also buy marmosets at the Samaritaine. Around 1920, the director of the Muséum suspected 'English and German touts of buying animals under the cover of foreign zoos which are no more than commercial private enterprises'.[38]

The prices of wild animals varied considerably according to rarity, age and, later, their amenability to training. The risk of death was borne by the purchaser, as in the case of a monkey acquired by the Paris menagerie from Jamrach in April 1831 which was dead by June. A panther was worth ten louis in 1809, and the first white rhinoceros to arrive in Europe was priced at 60 livres in 1850. Lions were abundant and inexpensive, costing between 5,000 and 10,000 francs at the turn of the century; a professor of the Beaux-Arts at Lyons, earning 3,000 francs a year, could have afforded a crocodile, a camel or a bear (around 800 francs), or even a reasonably handsome tiger (1,000–4,000 francs). The most spectacular animals were the most expensive. On the eve of the First World War, an acclimatized hippopotamus was worth 8,000 francs, an elephant between 4,000 and 25,000 francs depending on age, a polar bear a little less than a zebra at 15,000 francs, but a giraffe was valued at 25,000 francs. Finally, a rhinoceros at 30,000 francs would have cost a labourer twenty years' salary! In 1965, a Siberian tiger, a black rhinoceros or an orang-utan cost as much as an inexpensive car (around 10,000 francs), a chimpanzee barely a third of that, but a giant panda was worth as much as a luxury automobile (75,000 francs).

REPLACING THE DEAD WITH THE DEAD

The attempts at protective legislation at the turn of the century sought to moderate the supply of animals rather than the demand for them, which was ceaselessly fuelled by the mortality rates that people tried in vain to check while still considering those losses to be 'more or less immaterial'.[39] In Turin, the finger of blame was pointed at the cold and humidity that laid waste to the aviary. In Brussels in 1853, a quarter of the animals were struck down, 140 out of 567. In Madrid, animals died of hunger and disease, and yet there was no vet until 1869.[40] Philip Street observed about London that

> P. Chalmers Mitchell's first move was to examine the records of all deaths occurring at the zoo between the years of 1870 and 1902 ... the results were convincing; it was quite clear that under existing methods an animal's expectation of life once it arrived at Regent's Park was very poor.

In 1879, a report on the lions' cage described an intolerable odour of ammonia that was affecting the eyes, brains and nasal passages of the big cats. In 1891, Alphonse Milne-Edwards, director of the Paris menagerie, protested against the lack of personnel; the monkey house resembled a hospital, with its dark cages and contaminated air, where 'consumption reigns in perpetuity.' There was devastation that winter, and the pachyderms suffered from cracked and suppurating skin.[41] L'Éclair published an article entitled 'La Misère du Muséum': 'Death, especially during this season, is decimating its inhabitants.'[42] In 1913, under pressure from the public, the Muséum's director questioned the menagerie's director Trouessard, who replied: 'I have never been officially informed when an animal has been ill.' After an autopsy report on a flying lemur, the belatedly consulted professor of pathology declared that the animal should not have been purchased in the first place.[43] The animals brought back by twentieth-century missions fared just as badly. Fifteen from the Bertholet expedition that arrived in June 1932 did not make it to 1933; the three flying lemurs survived for one year, and the gorilla for a few weeks. All the animals from the Bruntchi-Brandes mission that ended in 1932 died after five months.[44]

The Paris menagerie's records allow the case of 3,780 monkeys to be studied. The distribution of their population between 1830 and 1959[45] shows an explosion in the fashion for monkeys from 1835, its subsequent fluctuations, and (between 1850 and 1899) the most harmful seasons for them: January was worse than December, March was difficult, while May and June remained the best months.[46] Between 1830 and 1959, the length of stay for each monkey was an average of 18.6 months. Longevity was at its highest in the menagerie's early days, and then again at the end of the period. The methods used to catch monkeys suggest that they arrived young in Paris, and their stay at the zoo therefore represented most of their lifespans.

After 1945, nearly half the monkeys survived twenty months in captivity. A few of these managed to hang on for ten years, and one of them spent eleven at the menagerie. According to G. Bomsel, African long-tailed monkeys and some macaques have an apparent lifespan of about twenty years in the wild. It is therefore almost certain that only a few rare exceptions reached maturity. The official reports made by the vet at Antwerp Zoo corroborate and explain this assertion: pulmonary infections, despite the use of vaccination from 1926[47] and antibiotics, were devastating. The monkeys' birth rate was far from able to offset losses. Anthropoid apes have great difficulty reaching adult age in captivity;[48] their average survival at the menagerie was 17.7 months. Nearly 75 of the 96 did not reach twenty months. A few exceptions spent twelve or thirteen years at the zoo; there was the case of Solange, who apparently lived there for 28 years. A few American zoos – Philadelphia, New York and Chicago – have kept gorillas successfully for 50 years.

It is true that anthropoid apes arrive old in zoos much more frequently than other primates, after being resold several times. Their life expectancy in the wild, grouping all the species together, is 30 years or so; chimpanzees, who reach puberty at around ten, live for between 40 and 50 years, orang-utans for 50.[49] There are many testimonies to the brevity of their survival in captivity: H. Hediger confessed to his constant failures with orang-utans between 1924 and 1934, and the one purchased by Bourdelle in Amsterdam in 1927 died in the menagerie soon after. Eiper[50] wrote that the chimpanzee at Berlin reached the age of eleven 'thanks to man', and that Bobby the orang-utan reached the age of seven – this is why he was filmed before being stuffed. The passionate interest aroused by this species led to its ruin, despite a total ban on exportation in 1933 from which zoos were exempted as scientific establishments.

It is possible to evaluate the survival rate of mammals

and birds at the Paris menagerie in the years 1859, 1863, 1890, 1904, 1906, 1920, 1930, 1939 and 1947. The figures show an extremely high mortality rate during the first six months at the zoo, and again by the third six-month period, the animals therefore seldom completing a two-year stay. In 1859, more than 80 per cent did not live beyond two- and-a-half years; by 1930, 52 per cent were surviving beyond this mark. A few veterans appear in the records for 1930: two bears (one polar, one black), a dromedary, a mouflon, a stag who arrived in 1911 and five birds all spent about twenty years at the menagerie.

In the face of international rivalry, the asset of longevity among its animals could make a zoo's reputation. This is without a doubt why, in 1930, Bourdelle prepared and published an article on the longevity of the animals at the menagerie he directed,[51] basing his average on exceptions, which he presented as everyday cases. In 1931, Captain S. Flower published a study limited to cases that were rare among primates; he was soon imitated by Crandall, then Hediger and, finally, Jones for ungulates. Average lifespan interested none of these zoologists.[52] The longevity claimed for all inhabitants of zoos in direct contradiction with the statistics, has been widely broadcast by the media. W. and W. Dolder expressed it as follows: 'The life expectancy of zoo animals is three to four times greater than those of crea- tures in wild, who have to fight day after day to survive.'[53] A controversy exploded in the press in August 1979, when a reader of *Télé* expressed indignation about the reduced life- span of orang-utans in zoos. This was denied by a professor at the Muséum, who stated: 'It is absolutely normal for orang-utans in zoological gardens to be kept for fifteen or twenty years.'[54] In actual fact, the extreme mortality of wild animals in zoos has always been the driving force behind the enormous scale of importations.

THE ZOO AS IMPERIAL SHOWCASE

In Paris, diplomatic gifts arrived one after another at the menagerie; a gift from the American Embassy in 1797 preceded others from the Bey of Algiers in 1800, Napoleon Bonaparte and the Bey of Tunis (1825). Notable were a she-wolf from the famous statesman Chateaubriand and a macaque monkey from Alexandre Dumas around 1848. As one writer put it, 'Once, the navy, travellers – either by taste or by profession – and missionaries were our principal agents … since the extension of the colonies, it is mostly colonial officials, or any person living in the colonies.'[55]

Officials, colonial travellers, soldiers and policemen, doctors, engineers, missionaries and a member of the Conseil d'Etat brought Algerian gazelles, macaques, cranes and herons. In 1859, approximately 50 identifiable gifts came from individual Parisians or zoological societies. At the turn of the century, aristocratic donors began to fade from view.[56] Women remained firmly in the minority. Lions from the painter Rosa Bonheur and Cécile Sorel and Sarah Bernhardt's puma joined gifts from Mmes Carnot and Paul Bert and Baroness Rothschild. In Antwerp, the journal *Zoo* regularly made mention of gifts from vacationing colonials between 1945 and 1960. At the Berlin zoo, the donors whose names appeared on plaques on the cages in 1903 constituted a who's who of senior colonial personnel: a bear from 'our old friend, the indefatigable … consul general W. Schön-lank'; an African ass from the colonial attaché at the Paris embassy; a panther from Edward VII.[57]

The British aristocracy was quick to involve itself with exotic animals in London, especially those from India. Sir George Pigot, Governor of Madras (1755–63, 1775–7), sent a cheetah (adorned with red hood and belt) to England with two servants; George Stubbs painted its portrait around

1765 (*Cheetah with Two Indian Attendants and a Stag*). Raffles of India undertook to bring his collection of Sumatran animals back to London in 1824, but they were destroyed when his ship caught fire. The wealthiest English aristocrats possessed private reserves of exotic animals, often brought back from the Empire. Edward Smith Stanley, 13th Earl of Derby, sought to introduce Sinhalese animals to England. The London zoo effectively became the national zoo, having originated as a lease of land in Regent's Park by the sovereign. Queen Victoria followed the tradition established by William IV by depositing a 'stream of barbaric offerings ... (lions, tigers, leopards) ... flowing from the tropical princes'. She was present at the zoo to witness the arrival of lions and zebras from Emperor Menelik of Abyssinia, and again for the 'wild beast train' offered by Jung Bahadour, ennobled for his loyalty to the Empire. The sale of the African elephant Jumbo to the Barnum Circus was felt by the newspapers to be a treasonable act because he came from India; a fund was started to buy him back, because 'Jumbo loves England and the good old Union Jack.'[58]

English zoological gardens exhibited animals from Canada, Australia, and African and Asian colonies. The London zoo's acquisition of giant pandas witness to its economic power in Asia. Imperial Britain also established zoological gardens in its possessions: in Australia, that at Melbourne opened in 1857, after the fruitless attempts at acclimatization made by E. Wilson. Zoos created in India under English influence were of varying design. Calcutta's 21-hectare zoo (1875–6), funded by the government of Bengal, included many animals, local or otherwise (such as tapirs), left at relative liberty around a large lake with many birds. The large enclosure at Jaipur was more reminiscent of the aristocratic or princely menageries of England, with its

horde of antelopes grazing freely across its fourteen hectares, but there were also cages and chained monkeys. Bangalore was a beautiful, predominantly botanical public park. The 1862 zoo at Bombay was transformed in 1889 into 'Victoria Gardens', though its cages remained intact. The tiger enclosure at Alwar, a circle 28 metres in diameter and surrounded by a ditch, was a prefect illusion. Some zoos were private and princely. At Mysore, the elephant enclosure was also home to a mahout; there were tigers there too, as well as polar bears. The ruins of a reservoir at Sarkey, dating from the fifteenth–sixteenth centuries, accommodated monkeys in total liberty, but could this truly be called a zoo?

Captain S. Flower, an English soldier, naturalist, curator at Giza and official representative on several missions, visited the zoological gardens[59] of British India. The ordered European approach to nature was directly opposed to the Indian conception of life as global and non-hierarchical. This concept shocked Flower when he visited the religious refuge of Pinjrapol, belonging to the Jain sect, where animals were crowded together and left uncared for. In Egypt, the English zoological gardens at Giza included African wildlife, although, in 1912, mortality rates reached a third of the population. This zoo received approximately two hundred thousand visitors; its donors were local, English or foreign, sometimes Indian. The establishment founded by the British at Khartoum after their conquest of the Sudan at the turn of the century resembled a reserve. The British founded a zoological garden in Pretoria at the end of the Boer War, and again in Johannesburg in 1903. Private collections survived everywhere, and every colonial had a cage in his bungalow.

Other countries created zoological gardens ostensibly to represent their colonial empires, such as those of Lisbon,

311. PARIS — Jardin des Plantes — La Girafe Ménélik
Don de S. M. le Roi d'Abyssinie au Président de la République

Ménélik the giraffe, gift of the King of Abyssinia to France, c. 1910.

established in 1884, and, above all, Antwerp, which in the twentieth century became an 'embassy for our protected colonial wildlife'. From 1945, 'edifying living testimonies donated by the Governor-General of the Congo' arrived at the Antwerp zoo, which had been devastated by the Second World War, but which benefited from the patronage of successive royals, Leopold III having personally intervened to the advantage of the zoo's huntsmen, Jean de Médina (1894–1971), stalker of elephants in the Congo from 1912, and Charles Cordier. This zoo also housed the acclimatization and expedition centre maintained by Brother Hymelin of the Norbertine Catholic mission at Buta, similar to the one at Epulu.[60]

The purchase in 1930 of a polar bear by a Moroccan zoo shows the extent to which Europe was influencing other parts of the world just as it had itself imported curiosities from elsewhere. The ethnographical exhibitions of the late nineteenth century revived an ancient tradition, linking it firmly to the zoological garden. Back around 1800 Verniquet planned an ethnographical-zoological park where 'each man would be costumed in the manner of his country and placed in an environment appropriate to his way of life.' A company of Oneida Indians from America appeared in London in 1817, then some Egyptians; in 1822, Bullock's Laplanders attracted huge crowds.[61] In America around 1840, the painter George Catlin toured his paintings of Native Americans with an entourage of living 'extras'. P. T. Barnum's circus exhibited the bizarre and deformed alongside ethnic 'types'; fairground stalls showed so-called savages and cannibals; international exhibitions like the one at Crystal Palace in 1851 developed them into organized spectacles. The American writer James Fenimore Cooper started a short-lived fashion for Mohicans. After 1870, the pursuit of rare animals was coupled with a quest for spectacular tribesmen. Buffalo Bill performed in England on the occasion of Queen Victoria's jubilee and at the Chicago international exhibition of 1893. Sarassani staged supposedly artistic and exotic numbers with Moroccan, Chinese and Indian performers. Between 1878 and 1926, approximately 50 ethnological exhibitions took place in Germany and travelled to Copenhagen (Laplanders, 1887) as well as to the zoos of Vienna (Ashantis, 1897 and 1898), Berlin and Basel, and the Berlin colonial exhibition (Africans, 1907).

When Carl Hagenbeck's animal trade suffered a downturn due to the closure of Sudan's borders after the Mahdi revolt, he was able to turn to Hazelius' ethnographical museum in Sweden for inspiration.[62] Between 1874 and his death in 1913, Hagenbeck organized 54 ethnological shows. This number fell to fifteen in the years up to 1931, although the Hagenbecks' polar panorama was featured as late as 1937 at the Paris World's Fair alongside Doctor Mennerat's 'civilized monkeys'.[63] All Hagenbeck shows began in Hamburg, where Heinrich Umlauff, the creator of their scenarios, founded an ethnological museum in 1889. The companies travelled extensively. For example, a group of Nubians surfaced in Paris (1876), where their show returned on five occasions (1876–90); Sinhalese were exhibited at the Jardin d'Acclimatation in 1883, and Eskimos and Greenlanders at Brussels (1877, 1879); companies visited Prague (1880), Switzerland, (1881), Vienna (1884) and London (1886, 1894), accompanying the Hagenbecks' circus (1887, 1926). More

Monkey brook at the Chiffa gorges, Blida, Algeria.

than half of these tribal peoples came from areas that commonly exported animals – fifteen or so from Ceylon and the Sudan thanks to the hunter John Hagenbeck, married to a Sinhalese, who shot documentary films beginning in 1924.

The explorer Johan Adrian Jacobsen and some huntsmen-turned-recruiters encountered many religious, linguistic, financial and hygienic difficulties in the course of their interminable negotiations regarding these human exhibitions. The diary (translated into German) of Abraham the Eskimo, who arrived in Germany in 1880, expressed immense fatigue in the face of the crowds. Some 'savages' became popular personalities and hired themselves out at great cost. Animals participated in these exhibitions, which were sometimes called 'anthropo-zoological'; Nubians performed a hunting demonstration in 1878. The title of one show – 'Around the World for 50 Pfennigs' –

Wooden 'American' bison house, Berlin Zoo.

The recently restored 'Egyptian temple' for ostriches, Berlin Zoo.

indicates that their educational qualities were used to justify the power exerted by these marvels. Spectators sought to communicate with the actors and, as at the zoo, to touch them and attract them with food. While a powerful erotic fascination was awakened on both sides, the scientific value of these shows was deceptive, the scenarios and supporting cast were German, and communication with the ethnic 'performers' remained elusive; only the importance of certain artefacts donated to museums and the Berlin Anthropological Society was indisputable.

The appropriation of these tribal peoples was theoretically reversible, but five adult Eskimos from Labrador and their children, visitors in 1880–81, died of smallpox on their return. Hagenbeck wrote to Jacobsen: 'You know to what extent I am a friend to all men, and you can imagine how this tragedy affects me,' but he did not suspend his shows. Shortly thereafter, despite vaccination, five of the twelve members of a group from Tierra del Fuego died of tuberculosis. Few of these tribes came from German colonies, apart from the Doualas from Cameroon in 1886, because from 1901 the German authorities forbade the immigration of indigenous peoples for health reasons. Some shows attracted half a million spectators (Paris); the men from Tierra del Fuego arrived at a time when marine mammals and glacial zones were of great popular interest. Ceylon also

Illustration of Eskimos exhibited at the Berlin Zoo, 1878, by Paul Meyerheim.

captivated the attention of the European public; in London, in 1908, a group of Sinhalese pulled in five million spectators. The press made no objection; however, there was indignation that the burial of the Indians who died in Germany was exploited as a publicity stunt, and, in 1885, a cartoon in *Feuilles volantes* depicted an inversion of the situation, often applied to the zoo: 'savages' were shown paying to attend a Bavarian caravan feast (as at the zoo, meals were considered to be attractions in their own right). Ethnological displays favoured the installation of fixed 'sets' in zoos, but they developed into theatrical fictions, opening the way for the scenography of Stellingen.

In the twentieth century, live wild animals were put on display at the great international exhibitions.[64] Usually, these were everyday or domestic animals accompanying tribal people grouped into villages (for example, the Laplanders' reindeer, or the animals of an African farm): after the exhibitions, the animals were given to local zoos. The 1931 *Exposition Coloniale* in Paris was the high point of the zoo as colonial showcase, for three almost symbolic reasons. First, it was organized by Maréchal Lyautey, an emblematic figure, the conqueror of Morocco. Second, Lyautey had the idea of including a temporary zoo at the exhibition to reveal to Parisians 'the splendours of their colonies ... wildlife

presented for the first time in a setting evoking those exotic countries'. Third, the organization of this temporary zoo was entrusted not to the veterinarians of the Paris menagerie, but to a journalist and sometime lion-tamer.[65]

Subsequently, the director of the Paris menagerie, Bourdelle, sought to ensure that the empire was represented in its entirety at the exposition: 51 animals from North Africa, 365 from French Equatorial Africa and French West Africa, 48 from Madagascar, 106 from Indochina, 68 from Guyana.[66] When, in April 1931, H. Thétard became the colonial zoo's figurehead, it was in fact as a friend of the real organizer, Hagenbeck. With more than five million visitors, the colonial zoo was an unhoped-for success. Thétard's *Petit Parisien* welcomed a definitive zoo, 'great school of our hunters and importers of exotic beasts'. Both the colonial milieux and the general public were enthused by a display that was dramatically opposed to the menagerie's old cages. Germany had a strong presence: the animals came from Stellingen, as did their keepers, their trainer, the writer Eiper and the design of the fake rocks, constructed of 250 tonnes of cement poured over wooden frames. These were quickly destroyed by a fire that also claimed the sheds and five chained elephants. The *Exposition Coloniale* zoo nonetheless became the model for the zoo at Vincennes,

Mixed human and animal exhibits, Renberget Skansen, Stockholm.

built not far away a few years later.

Colonialism, triumphing over the wild, was flaunted everywhere. P. Boulineau, a specialist in colonial agronomy, wrote in 1934: 'Captive wildlife brings to man, its king, the tribute of its subjection.' A rare discordant note was heard from an anti-colonial exhibition in Aragon: 'The confinement of free and proud animals to cages ... is ... one of the most abominable practices of colonisation.'[67]

7 THE EXPLOITATION OF NATURE

The creation of the menagerie at the Jardin des Plantes in Paris realized the utopias of Bacon and Leibniz, and the aspirations of many eighteenth-century scholars. This was the first such enterprise to be formed by and for scientists: its precedents at Schönbrunn and Madrid – which had already integrated their menageries to some degree with botanical gardens and natural-history museums – were controlled by the aristocracy. From 1801, the Muséum benefited from the stability of Napoleon's government and enjoyed rapid growth with the expansion of its collections and zoological laboratories, the completion of a greenhouse, and the development of botanical beds. It quickly rose to the highest level of scientific institutions in both the number of its chairs and the renown of its professors. They developed ambitious programmes in the fields of anatomy, physiology, classification, behavioural studies and acclimatization, thus reflecting the priorities of the period.

Private zoological societies, and even municipal gardens, displayed identical objectives. At Berlin and Frankfurt, for example, collaborations were initiated with scientific institutes. In 1877, the municipal authorities of Amsterdam granted a plot of land to the zoological gardens for the construction of an aquarium, on the condition that it should include a lecture hall and laboratories for the university. Scientific research was given priority even at gardens that lacked adequate expertise or equipment, in order to implement the programme of triumphant capitalism: to classify, acclimatize and domesticate nature, in order to exploit it.[1]

A CONTRIBUTION TO CLASSIFICATION

When the idea of installing a menagerie at the Jardin des Plantes had first taken shape in 1792, its advocates had been hoping to continue Buffon's work by creating a place where animal behaviour could be studied. Bernardin de Saint-Pierre had opposed most scholars of his time by arguing that the study of skins and other remains and the determination of genus and species were not enough to know an animal; its development had to be observed. Study in the wild could usefully be replaced by research in a good menagerie.[2]

In reality, this programme was barely implemented. Only Frédéric Cuvier, warden of the menagerie from 1804 on, headed up original studies on the behaviour, intelligence, sociability and domesticity of animals to determine, as if in a laboratory, not 'what takes place in nature, but what can take place there'. These studies, however, earned him the enmity of another professor, Etienne Geoffroy Saint-Hilaire, a more traditional zoologist, who prevented Cuvier from creating a chair in 'the nature and education of animals' in 1837, and who, after Cuvier's death in 1838, did away with the chair in animal physiology which he had occupied.[3] This setback ruined the chances for behavioural analysis at the menagerie for many years. Some, but not much, work was done in London (for example, on a chimpanzee in 1835) and in Berlin (on a gorilla in 1876).[4] This lack of progress was caused by the belief that an individual could not represent a species, by the high mortality rates that prevented long-term study, and by the inherited conviction that captivity distorted behaviour.

Chimpanzee or African Orang-Utan, Zoological Gardens, Regent's Park, 1835, by George Scharf.

A fine example of this conviction is to be found in R. Hartmann's famous study devoted to anthropoid monkeys (1886), which gives only limited space to the study of their habits (two chapters out of twelve) and which distinguishes between observation in the wild and that practised within a zoo. The first, which in reality amounted to no more than a critical analysis of travellers' accounts, referred to areas of population, movements, diet and the structure and functioning of groups, a fashionable theme since Victor Espinas' work *Des sociétés animales* (1878). Examination in captivity, notably of a gorilla and a chimpanzee in Berlin and another chimpanzee in Dresden, concerned individual deportment, especially the capacity for imitation of human gestures and behaviour (bipedal movement, eating at table, games and various other tasks), and indications of intelligence. It was concerned less with the desire to understand a species than with an assessment of how that species was transformed by contact with civilization. The dream of domestication, encouraged by transformist principles after 1865, was present in the background. Hartmann's work was precisely in keeping with the research of Charles Darwin (*Descent of Man*, 1871) and his disciples (e.g., George John Romanes, author of *Animal Intelligence*, 1882), which aimed to show the continuity between the minds of animals and humans, and therefore the possibility of a genealogical link. But this form of study attracted harsh criticism in the early twentieth century and was accused by some scholars of promoting a naïve anthropomorphism. Such anthropomorphism discredited research performed in zoological gardens in favour of work in laboratories or at zoological stations in the wild.[5]

Buffon's plan for behavioural studies had been marginal even in his own time, and the gardens were placed in the service of a descriptive kind of zoology, just like the princely menageries of earlier eras. In 1800, Cuvier published an inventory of animals at the Jardin des Plantes. Descriptions of species were entered into the proceedings and transactions of London's Zoological Society, and similar work was done in Amsterdam and Berlin.[6] On each occasion, observation centred on external characteristics and the fundamental aspects of life that captivity did not seem to influence: posture, movement, calls, way of feeding, reproduction and education of offspring. It allowed errors to be rectified, gaps to be filled, closely related species to be differentiated and, above all, integration into an improved system of classification. So it was that listening to the cry of a jaguar convinced Saint-Hilaire that it was an animal distinct from the panther. The presence of a chimpanzee at the London zoo in 1835 and of an orang-utan in Paris gave him an opportunity to separate the two species. At Amsterdam, the aviary and aquarium

Hippopotami, 1853, by Joseph Wolf.

gave rise to work on the structure of birds and the reproduction and development of fish.

The increase in the number of animals in zoological
gardens also allowed more accurate drawings to be made of
them. In fact, it was while examining an 'excellent illustration' of London's chimpanzee that Saint-Hilaire made his
distinction between it and the orang-utan in his own
menagerie. Made from life, but showing creatures posed
quietly enough to be sketched accurately, these drawings
(and the photographs that followed them beginning in the
late nineteenth century) reasserted the role of pictorial
rendering in the distribution and preservation of knowledge. At the Jardin des Plantes, the collection was enlarged
by such painters as the Redouté brothers for plants or Nicolas Maréchal for animals. They also illustrated literary
works: *La Ménagerie du Muséum* (1801) by E. de Lacépède
and Georges Cuvier, and *Histoire naturelle des mammifères*
(1819) by Saint-Hilaire with Frédéric Cuvier. In London, the
Zoological Society took on the services of such young litho-
graphic artists as Edward Lear (whose drawings graced
Gleanings from the Menagerie, about Lord Derby's private
collection at Knowsley) and John Gould, both specialists in
the drawing of birds. From 1848 to 1880, Joseph Wolf

supplied the society's journal with numerous lithographs
and produced plates for *Zoological Sketches* (1861–7). Like
the menageries of the early modern period, zoological
gardens contributed to the twin goals that zoology had been
pursuing since the eighteenth century, and would continue
to pursue until the early 1900s: the inventory and classification of wildlife. Although only 10 per cent of the species of
mammal known in 1993 were recognized in 1800, that
figure rose to 50 per cent in 1890 and 84 per cent in 1930.[7]

Gardens that hosted true scientific activity were few in
number, however. Many confined themselves to expressions of intent without any real results, or to popularization
and entertainment. In Rotterdam, the library and small
museum were there mostly for appearances. In Antwerp,
the library envisaged in 1843 had still not been realized by
the beginning of the twentieth century, and study, if it
occurred, never resulted in publication. The more or less
established links with natural-history museums and universities bore little fruit. In Lyon, for example, it was the
scholars who, in the person of Charles Lortet (director of
the natural-history museum, professor of zoology and dean
of the faculty of medicine), secured the scientific direction
of the park from the municipality in 1880 in order to create

a synergy between the museum, the faculty of sciences, and the veterinary and medical schools: the zoological garden was seen as the ideal terrain for such a fusion. But the proposed laboratories were never built, and *Archives du Muséum*, launched in 1872, did not publish a single article on the subject of the zoo's livestock.[8]

Even among gardens dedicated to scientific research, the part played by the observation of live animals was minor. In the *Annales du Muséum*, there were only seven articles on the subject between 1803 and 1810, although between 50 and 100 essays were published each year. In the famous *Rapport historique sur les progrès des sciences naturelles depuis 1789* (1810), Georges Cuvier was credited only indirectly, and solely with regard to his drawings. Saint-Hilaire, despite being the most deeply involved, published only a few texts and quickly abandoned his column 'Mouvements de la ménagerie', while his *Histoire naturelle des mammifères* barely made reference to the available livestock. While professors devoted endless pages to the disastrous consequences of the shelling of 1870 on the Muséum's collections, they dispatched its effect on the menagerie in two lines![9] Live animals hardly fared any better at Regent's Park in London. The first guide to the London zoo (1829–30) featured descriptions based on observations made in the cabinet and not of live specimens.[10]

The situation was identical in Amsterdam, Berlin and Hamburg and did not change in the 1900s. Alfred Brehm, despite being director of the Hamburg gardens and a great advocate of descriptive zoology, based little of his famous *Vie des animaux* (1864–9) on specimens in zoos. The garden at Vincennes, opened in 1934 at the instigation of the Muséum's professors, was not mentioned in that institution's publications. It was often the same in Rome. Scientific results were therefore scarcely more significant than in the eighteenth century.

Many naturalists still preferred to work on animal remains. Frédéric Cuvier, for example, was delighted to dissect any that died at the Jardin des Plantes. In the mid-nineteenth century, laboratories of anatomy and physiology were installed behind the carnivore house so that operations could begin as soon as possible after death. The Muséum's professors argued over the right to dissect and preserve animals' remains to such an extent that a 'commission for the distribution of animals that die at the menagerie' had to be organized in 1840–41. Further 'statutory clauses relative to menageries' were decreed in 1906.[11]

This focus on the dead was to be found everywhere, and relevant links between learned institutions were active. In Madrid and Turin, the remains of animals were systematically sent to the natural-history museums. The gardens in Copenhagen had to do the same in exchange for their state subsidy. There was a great deal of work on comparative anatomy at Berlin's Tiergarten and Regent's Park, where the animals were dissected by Richard Owen and C. T. Buckland and findings published in the society's journal.[12] Zoological gardens thus played an important role, but they did not become fully fledged laboratories. In fact, they were no more than annexes, maintaining biological reserves waiting to be used (hence the scholars' scant concern at the creatures' high mortality rates), since they had failed to find a legitimate place between study in the laboratory and in the wild. The nineteenth century confirmed the division that had emerged in the early modern period: to the layman the enjoyment of the living, to the scholar the use of the dead.

This situation was accentuated by the evolution of zoology. Buffon's death in 1788 triggered a reaction against his despotic authority: Linnaean classification, which he had fought, was almost immediately considered worthy of more detailed study, while Buffon's horror of systems and his questionable descriptions of behaviour were stigmatized as having slowed the progress of science. But naturalists, who often performed only external examinations, leaving dissection to doctors versed in natural history, did not think of using the latter process to classify animals, despite the idea's having been suggested by Linnaeus. It was Georges Cuvier, trained in the Germanic lands, who on arriving at the Muséum in 1795 developed the comparative examination of internal organs as a method of and rigorous criteria for systematic analysis, and who brought anatomy and zoology, dissection and classification, together. By 1800, his colleagues were coming round to his point of view, and dissection became the principal tool of systematic study across Europe. Interest was thus diminished in external observation of live animals, and the intentions of the original advocates of the Muséum's menagerie were sabotaged.[13]

The fields of study that emerged in the 1840s and afterwards, such as physiology and evolutionary classification, reaffirmed the marginal status of zoological gardens, because these disciplines were less concerned with differences between living species than in the function and development of organs. The menagerie created for experimentation at the Jardin des Plantes in 1840, and run first by P.-J.-M. Flourens and then by Claude Bernard, used dogs and pigs. The decline of systematic analysis, which began at the end of the century, and the growth of laboratory zoopsychology in the early 1900s, accentuated the estrangement of science from zoos.[14] The latter provoked criticism in London and Paris in the late nineteenth century, some scholars retaining their belief in the possibility of transforming them into genuine instruments of science. In Paris, Gustave Loisel reproached zoos for having neglected experimentation, behavioural observation (which was returning to prominence) and the study of evolution, and for having left experimental centres to be established elsewhere. In 1904, he proposed the conversion of the Jardin des Plantes into a zoological centre devoted to transformism, using as a model an establishment on Long Island, near New York. The project failed because the Muséum had been expanding and maintaining its collections and examining colonial wildlife since 1892, in an attempt to preserve its identity in the face of competition from universities and laboratories.[15]

Zoological gardens were an instrument of power and prestige for the discipline of natural history, even of its survival in the late nineteenth and early twentieth centuries as scientists pursued other paths. This explains why the scientific utility of zoos was trumpeted well into the 1900s despite an often contradictory reality. When Milne-Edwards defended the Jardin des Plantes' menagerie in 1891, he could only cite the work of Frédéric Cuvier and the institution's progress in dissection and taxidermy. In 1961, a retrospective assessment of research at Leipzig since the late 1800s interspersed histories of and guides to the zoo (such as one by a cycling club) with learned publications that were often only one or two pages in length and that tackled such topics as the features of a domestic cat's tail! It is easy to understand the pressure from the Muséum's professors to reject a plan for a private research zoo and instead to assume responsibility for the development and management of the Vincennes gardens, even though the latter were of little use to them.[16]

This argument of scientific utility was accepted by other sectors of society because, in its strict pursuit of knowledge and rationality, it theorized and justified their ambition to make an inventory of the world, to appropriate it. Zoological gardens were considered to be both showcases for and instruments of this domination, at once symbolic and practical. Visiting the Paris zoo, Citizen Jauffret wrote in 1798 that 'some of those animals that man has subjugated and whose character he is changing' could be seen there. At the Antwerp gardens, a fresco depicted the inhabitants of various lands offering their wildlife to the city. In London, the association of scholars with empire builders (soldiers, administrators, explorers) in the Zoological Society was ahead of its time and resulted in an interest in acclimatization, training, reproduction and crossbreeding – that is, in exploitation that might legitimize colonization and make it profitable. This agenda remained theoretical for a long time at the Jardin des Plantes. The alliance between the Muséum's professors and military supporters of colonization did not begin to form until the Second Empire and only truly developed under the Third Republic. In Rome, in the 1830s, the management chose to highlight the zoo's scientific character at the very moment when Italy launched itself on the colonial adventure.[17]

AN ILLUSTRATED ENCYCLOPAEDIA

In 1792, Bernardin de Saint-Pierre had argued that close observation of animals' behaviour presupposed their physical integrity and their location in natural surroundings. Consequently, he proposed to recreate their original environments. In 1795, Lacépède had suggested the creation of a landscaped park with enclosures for herbivores, areas supplied with 'cavernous rocks' for foxes, badgers or big cats, ponds for marine mammals, large trees for monkeys to play in, and pastoral plateaus covered with rocks for birds of prey. Each enclosure would contain flora from the country of origin, and the animals would enjoy a measure of free-

dom. Elephants, hippopotami and rhinoceroses would bathe on the banks of canals, and 'one would be able to study, in Europe, the habits of those roving colossi in a state of independence a little closer to that which they enjoyed in the lands that witnessed their birth.' These concepts were given form in plans by the architects J. Molinos (1798) and C. Verniquet (1801) and adopted by the assembled professors of the Muséum: liberty would provide

> an accurate idea of [the animals'] forms, their agilities and their habits ... there is so little difference, for the purposes of study, between stuffed animals and those who are imprisoned in cramped pens, that the latter are not worth the cost of their upkeep.[18]

This programme was partly realized for docile herbivores with the creation of adapted enclosures, but it was abandoned for other animals in favour of pits and conventional buildings. The great cave-riddled rock designed by Molinos for felines was judged to be too expensive by the government and too humid by the Muséum's professors. It was replaced by a rotunda composed of a circular hall and five radiating lodges, which in the end was allocated to the large herbivores (elephants, camels and so on). Ferocious animals were installed in a rectilinear building of neo-Classical style, where approximately twenty cages were lined up next to each other. The same design was used for the aviary of birds of prey; the pheasantry boasted an exterior circular cage half surrounded by a neo-Classical monkey house.[19]

Surviving documents do not explain the reasons for this gulf between intention and realization. Beyond the government's desire to spend as little as possible and the habitual autonomy of the architects, who rarely presented plans that answered the needs of the zoo's directors, two further factors seem to have intervened.

First came the political context. The rotunda project had imperial support during the reorganization of France and the revival of courtly society. The abandoning of the open park in favour of a radical design could therefore be read as a symbolic re-assertion of control over nature parallel with control over society.

Illustration of the monkey cage, Zoological Gardens, Regent's Park, London, 1835, by George Scharf.

The second factor was a scientific one. Frédéric Cuvier supported the project because the architectural forms corresponded to the ways in which the animals were being used. The alignment of the cages implicitly reproduced the layout of natural-history cabinets, giving its occupants the status of the constituent parts of a collection, and lending the ensemble feel of an inventory. It thus expressed the predominant interest in systematic analysis. Isidore Geoffroy Saint-Hilaire, Étienne's son and the menagerie's director from 1841, wanted his establishment to be consistent with the general design of the Muséum and represent a living display cabinet with a number of well-laid-out and correctly classified species. The cages were showcases, display shelves or even tableaux, rather than habitats, allowing naturalists and artists to examine often immobile animals closely as if they were models. Milne-Edwards described the aviary of 1825 as follows:

> The large birds of prey can never spread their wings, and all these birds, hungry for air and light, are permanently relegated to the back of a sort of dark cupboard; their plumage, never washed in the rain, cannot have that sharp cleanliness that is one of the beauties of wild birds, and they are always covered in huge numbers of parasites.[20]

In fact, this style was adopted in all nineteenth-century gardens. In London, enclosures for fowl and herbivores were situated alongside the bear pit and large buildings like the western aviary (52 metres long and containing two hundred species of bird), the monkey 'palace', a lion house made up of a double row of cages, and so on. Arrangements were similar in Turin, Lyon, Brussels and elsewhere and were consistent with only the most basic kind of zoology. For the bareness and meagre size of the cages (50 square metres for a bear plus a den of 3 square metres; between 13 and 22 square metres and 20 to 35 square metres for internal and external cages for big cats; 53 and 50 square metres for those of the elephant at Lyon early in the 1900s) clearly show the reduction of animals to their vegetative functions and the neglecting of links with their natural environments.[21]

This tendency was also perceptible in the gardens' large aquariums. The first of these, which opened in Regent's Park in 1853, was soon imitated elsewhere in the UK and

Interior of the hummingbird house, Gardens of the Zoological Society, London, 1852.

Crocodiles, Parc de la Tête d'Or, Lyon, 1900s.

'Aquatic vivarium', Gardens of the Zoological Society, London, 1853.

then in Europe, for example at the Bois de Boulogne's acclimatization gardens in 1860. Aquariums were often rectangular buildings with visitors' galleries overlooking a series of portholes and pools in lines, where exotic fish and marine mammals were kept. The bottoms were generally decorated with sand, rocks and plants.[22]

Various modifications to these installations in the second half of the nineteenth century hinted at their naturalization. Aviaries – the first of this kind was set up in Rotterdam around 1880 – were provided with floors of soil or turf, trees, bushes, nests and shelters, and their dimensions grew to permit some flight or, for birds of prey, the opportunity to spread their wings. Monkey, feline and even bear houses were augmented by adjoining exterior cages adorned with trees, logs and rocks, thus giving an illusion of nature and allowing a little physical exercise and exposure to the open air, even in winter. The use of rocks to disguise dens or encourage climbing was extended to small rodents, llamas, chamois and sea-lions. While the Jardin des Plantes, deprived of an adequate subsidy, seemed outdated in its ageing equipment and limited reconstruction, the gardens of Berlin and London led by example. Berlin was one of the

first to boast outdoor enclosures for lions (1870) and monkeys (1883). Regent's Park upgraded its buildings with the construction of a new 'lions' palace' (1876) that was also equipped with exterior cages, a similar monkey house where sociable species were mixed together, another for felines (1904) with rocks and tree-trunks, enclosures for otters, sea-lions and seals (1905–6) with pools, islets and rocks, and, finally, aviaries containing a bit of greenery (1903–7).[23]

These modifications may have been influenced by the ideas of contemporary zoo-technicians regarding the benefits of breeding in the open air. Above all, they were concomitant with the renewed interest among scientists – especially English and German scholars – in the study of animal behaviour and society. The zoos had to give the impression of a more natural life, even though the environments they provided amounted to no more than a handful of the most essential aids to basic biological functions, symbolizing environments more than reproducing them. They certainly did not challenge the encyclopaedic perspective that had found its way into the choice and presentation of the animals.

Gardens sought the greatest possible diversity of

Monkey house, Berlin Zoo, c. 1884.

Lion house, Berlin Zoo, c. 1905.

species with an eye to forming the richest possible collections. They often worked together complement with local-natural history museums by leaving to them the species that were more difficult to exhibit (insects, molluscs, large marine mammals), although some – Cologne, Frankfurt – created insectariums. The gardens favoured rarity and zoological curiosity, often satisfying themselves with a single specimen or a pair; made use of every opportunity (reproduction, purchase, gift, exchange) to obtain them; and disposed of surplus by the same routes. The principal aim of London's Zoological Society was to illustrate the multiple variations of the animal world, and the interest that greeted each new arrival signalled the taxonomic void it filled. Gardens with lofty scientific ambitions also adopted systematic presentation. Such was the case in London, at least in the zoo's first few decades, and in Berlin, which equally used geographical classification in the late nineteenth century to show the influence of environment on the varieties of a species or on the species of a particular genus.[24]

The presence of scholars around zoos of course contributed to the development of this museological approach, but it was to be observed everywhere, because the enumeration of nature was a symbolic assertion of its seizure by modern humanity. It was therefore not by chance that it could also be found applied to the exotic flora in zoos and botanical gardens. Lyon's collection of trees, composed of one or two examples of each species, was dotted along the paths that led to the animal enclosures. Not only did the gardens incarnate the victory of civilization over the presumed ferocity of the animal world; they substituted rational order for nature's apparent disorder.

Entrance and insectarium, Riga Zoo.

ACCLIMATIZE AND DOMESTICATE

In 1861, Saint-Hilaire set a third, practical objective for natural history alongside observation and theory: the acclimatization (i.e., the adaptation to a new bioclimate) and domestication of exotic species with the aim of introducing new resources to society at large. This idea had already existed in ancient Egypt, where shepherds had kept herds of gazelles and antelopes from the Fourth Dynasty, and in Greece and Rome, where villas had had parks filled with gazelles, peacocks or guinea fowl for hunting and food. In fifteenth- and sixteenth-century Europe, certain nobles had acclimatized American turkeys, Chinese pheasants, guinea fowl and Indian hens for both game and table; we have already noted the success of pheasantries near aristocratic houses. In the 1500s, the Spanish introduced the llama and alpaca from the Americas for transport. A century later, the Grand Duke of Tuscany set up a stud farm near Pisa to raise dromedaries, which he used and sold as beasts of burden more efficient and robust than horses. The dukes of Richmond and Portland and the King of Portugal tried to domesticate the zebra in their parks and at the Queluz menagerie, in the hope of harnessing them to carriages. The Spanish had imported rams from the Barbary Coast already in the 1300s, thus creating the race of merinos that would spread across Europe, while the Dutch invented the *flandrin* sheep by using rams from the East Indies. In France, Daubenton began experimenting with various crossbreeds of merino and English and Flemish sheep in 1776, hoping to improve wool production.[25]

Having thus been practised long before it was named, acclimatization became the subject of much thought for some eighteenth-century naturalists and physiocrats. Buffon, for example, who seems to have been the first to use the verb *acclimatize*, in 1776, congratulated himself on the introduction of the llama; championed the introduction of species from South Africa, which would yield good meat and thick hides; and hoped for the same for reindeer. He noted that nature 'still has species in reserve which could make up for the shortcomings [of indigenous species]; it is entirely up to us to subjugate them and make them serve our needs'. In the Netherlands, Nélis published *Mémoires sur la possibilité et les avantages de naturaliser dans nos provinces différentes espèces d'animaux étrangers* (1777). Arthur Young, who attacked the nobility's pointless game parks, felt that to gather all of the world's domestic species was the highest possible goal of a menagerie, because it was of use to agriculture. Acclimatization occupied a growing place in the debates and studies of early nineteenth-century naturalists and agronomists. In France, it gave rise to Frédéric Cuvier's studies on the domestication of mammals and in particular to the propagandistic texts of Saint-Hilaire, who wrote the famous *Acclimatation et domestication des animaux utiles* (final version, 1861).[26]

Acclimatization had of course been one of the objectives of the original instigators of the Jardin des Plantes' menagerie. Bernardin de Saint-Pierre believed that it would enable wild animals to be tamed, domesticated and put to work, or crossed with indigenous beasts to create larger, more robust creatures.[27] The capacity for the taming and breeding of certain animals, especially fowl, was studied carefully. From 1829, Saint-Hilaire proceeded to more sustained tests on a few useful creatures (stags, llamas, wild asses, Egyptian geese) and worked on breeding. Acclimatization and domestication figured among the priorities of most zoological societies – London, Dublin, Antwerp, Marseilles, Turin – until the 1870s.[28]

The success of this field within and around zoological gardens rested on the conviction that the value of captivity lay in the breeding of wild animals. When A. Déclémy campaigned for the construction of an aviary at the Jardin des Plantes in 1841, he recognized that it would mostly be used to acclimatize species and achieve their reproduction in captivity, a facet which he considered to be essential, and which was often substituted for simple description as an objective for scholars from the 1830s and '40s.[29]

Another reason for acclimatization's success lay in the utilitarian discourse that accompanied it. From a strictly biological point of view, acclimatization could concern any species introduced in sufficient numbers that was capable of reproduction, be it tame or wild, and could just as easily have domestication in mind as release into a forest or hunting park. But in the eighteenth and especially the nineteenth centuries, the term's sense narrowed, usually underpinning as it did a desire to domesticate and breed for commercial ends (transport, meat and wool). It was not by chance that Saint-Hilaire – who popularized the use of the term *acclimatization*, coined in 1832, in Europe – distinguished two possibilities: naturalization, or adaptation to a new environment while remaining in a wild state, and domestication, a term used in Britain from 1825 and France from 1832, which interested him more because it better answered a need for meat and wool. Unlike preceding centuries, acclimatization at this time involved wild animals as much as tame ones. Saint-Hilaire believed that there were only 34 domesticated species in Europe and that there was a lot to be done if the use of animals was to keep pace with plant domestication. To this end, he proposed the introduction and domestication of the tapir, antelope, gazelle, kangaroo, rhea and other species.

Acclimatization was thus consistent – and this was another cause of its popularity – with contemporary ideology of progress and world conquest. Saint-Hilaire wrote that 'through the perfection of navigation, the multiplicity of international communications, and the establishment of European colonies in every corner of the globe, the natural riches of the entire world' were there for the taking. Humanity had to appropriate wildlife for its own ends, 'either with the help of conquests of nature as yet unachieved, or by taking possession of species already in the power of other peoples'. Acclimatization had its roots in a rhetoric, awakened in the 1800s by the Industrial Revolution and the optimism inspired by contemporary progress, of human grandeur.[30]

This context justified the creation in Paris in 1854 of the Société Zoologique d'Acclimatation, which brought together naturalists (among them Saint-Hilaire, who assumed the presidency), politicians, administrators – especially from the colonies or abroad – and above all a great many landowners, including aristocrats motivated by a kind of agro-mania that drove them to invest capital and create agricultural associations, journals, exhibitions and confer-

Entrance to the Jardin d'Acclimatation, Paris, 1891.

Herd of blackbuck, Jardin d'Acclimatation, Paris, 1903.

ences. It was in this spirit that the Société d'Acclimatation organized meetings, published findings, exhibited, made awards and imported useful animals and plants, which it entrusted to volunteers for experimentation. Other societies were established in France and elsewhere, including in

Reindeer in the wilderness park, Leipzig.

Berlin and Moscow. The one in London, founded in 1860, co-ordinated the introduction of species from Britain's overseas possessions, through its many links with colonial administrators and officers.[31]

In France, the unsuitability of the Jardin des Plantes, organized as it was in collections, and the dispersion of the Société d'Acclimatation's herds and therefore its efforts, made the creation of a specialized centre a priority. This idea, championed by Saint-Hilaire since 1838, was initially put into practice with the formation of the acclimatizing stud farm at Versailles, but this only functioned for a few months in 1849. In 1858, the Société d'Acclimatation founded a limited company with the aim of establishing a garden in a part of the Bois de Boulogne set aside by the City of Paris. The subscription was popular and won the support of seventeen princes and eleven European sovereigns, Napoleon III among them. Implementation was entrusted to D. W. Mitchell, secretary of London's zoological gardens, and, after his death in 1859, to Albert Geoffroy Saint-Hilaire, Isidore's son. The society was inaugurated in 1860 in the presence of the Emperor and a distinguished crowd, its objective being to acclimatize and ensure the reproduction of useful animal (yaks, goats, sheep, llamas, kangaroos, stags, rheas, fowl) and plant species, to popular-

ize them through exhibition, to sell them, and to advertise the riches of the colonies and thereby justify the politics of conquest. The necessity of making the enterprise profitable prompted its expansion into species intended for ornamental purposes (flowers), pleasure or hunting, which were sought after for the gardens of notable villas or the reserves of châteaux.[32]

Similar establishments were created in Madrid, by the natural-history museum there, in 1860, and in Moscow and Lisbon, by acclimatization societies, in 1863 and 1883. These institutions complemented the efforts of major landowners, who had formed acclimatization parks or adapted their own hunting parks to the purpose, in the UK (Knowsley, in the case of the Earl of Derby; Woburn Abbey, in that of the Duke of Bedford), Germany, Austria, Italy (the royal park of la Mandria near Turin, in 1860) and Russia (Askania-Nova, in 1889; Pilawin, in 1901).[33]

This movement produced only meagre results, however, as is illustrated by the trials and tribulations of the acclimatization gardens in Paris. The attention focused at the Emperor's behest on the wider distribution of regional and European species diverted the society's efforts somewhat during the first few years. The destruction of 1870, the cost of reconstruction, and the loss of the society's links with the

'Grande Exposition "India"', Jardin d'Acclimatation, Paris, c. 1910.

Muséum through staff turnover exacerbated the situation and led the management to turn to the staging of various attractions (for example, ethnographical exhibitions), not that these warded off financial difficulties and general deterioration after 1914. Intentions similarly ran aground at Madrid, which closed in 1868, and at Marseilles, while the research that did take place in London barely came to anything beyond the adaptation of the grey squirrel and the golden hamster. Work was similarly fruitless at the Jardin des Plantes, which abandoned it in 1900. There as elsewhere, scholars were losing interest in acclimatization proper in favour of experiments in hybridization to delimit and define species, measure their variability, improve those that were already domesticated and create new ones.[34]

These developments occurred in part due to the inherent difficulties of the undertaking. Isidore Geoffroy Saint-Hilaire had himself reduced the scope of investigation by limiting practical tests to two species (llama and alpaca) and initial experimentation to four others, while exhibiting caution with regard to wild species. Moreover, there was still no clear idea about how acclimatized animals might be

used, and without this the entire enterprise verged on the puerile. An assessment of the achievements of the gardens at the Bois de Boulogne recognized in 1873 that the llama, camel, buffalo and yak all reproduced without great difficulty, but the first was vicious, the next two only worked well on certain terrain, and the latter lost its coat. As for the zebu, the South African zebra and the Indian elephant, they were only good for giving rides to small children![35] Scepticism, perceptible from the 1870s, became an admission of defeat in the 1900s. Emile Trouessard, then Director of the Jardin des Plantes' menagerie, reported that hybridization had stumbled on the problem of the sterility of offspring, and that animals acclimatized in gardens did not adapt to liberty: those that had been released into the forests of the Île-de-France in 1891 had vanished by 1911. Some hope of success survived until the 1930s, with a few individuals continuing to attempt domestication, but this was *in situ* in the colonies, while acclimatization in the West was henceforth restricted to reproduction in captivity. This trend was accelerated by the policies of wildlife preservation that emerged between the 1900s and the 1930s, and by the fact

Zebras and Galla tribesmen, Jardin d'Acclimatation, Paris, c. 1910.

that the initial goals of increasing locomotive power and the production of wool and meat were gradually attained thanks to mechanical advances and the improvement of indigenous livestock.[36]

This failure sounded the death knell for the scientific ambitions of zoological gardens, which in the twentieth century would in many cases stray far from the path of science. The minor scale, both quantitatively and qualitatively, of the work that took place in the menageries of the early modern period and the zoological gardens of the 1800s is apparent if it is compared to the studies made in botanical gardens. The latter played a fundamental role in the development of vegetal physiology and systematic analysis, from John Ray in the seventeenth century via Linnaeus to Alexander Braun, director of Berlin's botanical gardens and, in 1864, the first person to propose a phylogenic system of classification. Furthermore, those gardens and greenhouses, in use since the 1500s and widespread in the 1800s, took the lead in the acclimatization of plants, fruit and exotic flowers

with the valuable help of horticultural societies (London, 1805; Ghent, 1808; Paris, 1827), which increased the number of exhibitions in order to disseminate their methods. It is doubtless because botany had occupied the central role in natural history since the seventeenth century that zoologists had been keen to apply its methods and copy its institutions, forgetting the complexity and fragility of animal life.[37] The disappointment of the zoological gardens' scientific ambitions thus brought another of their functions to the forefront: the entertainment and education of the masses.

8 THE THRILL OF THE WILD

Growing public interest was quick to influence the history and aims of zoological gardens. In London, for example, the decline in admissions noticed around 1845, one result of the zoo's diminishing stocks, led in 1847 to the appointment of an administrator who modernized the place, thus rekindling visitor interest. At the turn of the century, the inertia of management in place since 1859 provoked a fresh drop in admissions which endangered the gardens' survival and forced the renovations of the 1900s.[1] When the acclimatization gardens opened in Paris in 1860, worldly preoccupations were as important as scientific concerns – a sign of the times. Their founders hoped to combine functionalism and pleasure, fuelling the public's curiosity with incessant acquisitions and face-lifts, all in 'picturesque surroundings that would appeal to passers-by when they were not attracted by more serious interests'. The importance of paying admissions to the income of stockholding establishments explains this focus, but it was just as significant in subscription-run gardens, which had to please their members, and in municipal parks, which were determined to justify public expenditure. Above and beyond their declared scientific pretensions, then, most nineteenth-century gardens assigned great importance to recreation, a function that was already present, if secondary, at the time of the foundations of the menageries at Regent's Park and the Jardin des Plantes.[2]

THE RULE OF RECREATION

Animals attracted promenaders. At the Jardin des Plantes, the menagerie had more visitors than the botanical gardens or the Muséum. Zoological gardens often played host to substantial crowds, especially on days when entry fees were reduced (twelve thousand people in Cologne in 1888) or on public holidays (37,000 in Hamburg at Whitsuntide 1876, 35–45,000 at the Bellevue menagerie in Manchester at the beginning of the 1900s). These figures should be taken with a pinch of salt, however. Loisel's estimate of 80,000 visitors per summer's day in Berlin at the turn of the century is equivalent to 111 admissions a minute over twelve hours, a figure that seems incompatible with the realities of the time. Nevertheless, the success of such places remains undeniable, and failures seem to have been a consequence of higher than expected running costs rather than of shortfalls in attendance.[3]

The first visitors to zoological gardens were the aristocracy – a significant presence at Regent's Park (visited frequently by Queen Victoria and the Prince of Wales), Madrid, Turin, the Bois de Boulogne and elsewhere – and the members of the wealthy bourgeoisie who were behind their foundation. Members of the middle class also began to visit in the second half of the nineteenth century, depending on when entry was free or, conversely, restricted to subscribers, and on whether the management adopted promotional pricing policies on certain days. The bourgeoisie and working classes were gradually, depending on the country in question, benefiting from regulated working hours, the general acceptance of Sunday as a day off, and the establishing of public holidays (starting in Britain in 1870), which they would use in part to promenade in the parks in imitation of the upper classes.[4] From this shift came a division in visiting times. Gardens controlled by subscription

The crowded gardens of the Zoological Society, London, on Whit Monday, 1865.

Crowds around the elephants at the 1931 Exposition at the Bois de Vincennes, Paris.

Princess Mary and a king penguin, with George V, P. Chalmers Mitchell (secretary of the Zoological Society) and others, London Zoo, 1911.

societies were usually frequented by the wealthy on Sundays, but at free, public establishments like the Jardin des Plantes and Lyon, and in a number of the gardens of stockholding societies, they visited on weekdays instead, leaving Sundays and other public holidays to their inferiors.

The importance of satisfying visitors was paramount. At the Jardin des Plantes, for example, popular success and what was essentially a *post-mortem* use of animals led to the erection of buildings with spectacle rather than science in mind. The human field of vision became the standard measure for installations everywhere. Small enclosures and cages may have robbed animals of a normal physiological and psychological life and provoked stress and high mortality rates, but they ensured spectators a quick and certain sight-

ing, a further reason for the development of the encyclopaedic zoo discussed earlier. In the same way, the circular or hexagonal designs which became popular in the course of the nineteenth century for outdoor cages and enclosures (the Jardin des Plantes' aviaries and monkey house, the lion house in London) alarmed the animals by giving them the sensation of being surrounded and exposed them to draughts, but meant that more people could see them, and from every angle.[5]

Zoo directors increased their efforts in the area of display. An amphitheatre was installed at the Bellevue menagerie in Manchester for observation of the sea-lions, effectively a primitive version of modern-day marine parks. The mid-nineteenth century was marked by the progressive

41. — *Paris. - Au Jardin des Plantes. - Palais des Singes.*

'Monkey Palace' and circular aviary, Jardin des Plantes, Paris.

abandonment of wooden palisades, instituted in the early modern period and still present at the Jardin des Plantes and Schönbrunn, in favour of wire fences which obscured less. In Brussels, in 1856, a guidebook presented as a wonderful novelty the covering of the otter enclosure in a 'tracery of iron that is so thin it is almost invisible'.[6] At the end of the century, glass began to replace bars in the public rooms of gardens in Germany and the European capitals. Glass allowed reptiles to be approached more closely (Jardin des Plantes, 1874), animals to be protected from illness (gorillas in London, early 1900s), and visitors to avoid disagreeable odours (Berlin in the same period) at a time when such things were increasingly being remarked upon in public. These trends emphasized the transformation of zoo animals into living tableaux, and gave exhibition rooms the appearance of fine-art museums.[7]

In all cases, buildings containing the most highly prized specimens were placed at the centre of the gardens, and settings were contrived to exploit them to the full. In Lyon, for example, the bear cages (1865, 1882) were placed at a point were several avenues converged, and were surrounded by vast lawns filled with smaller animals, the aim being to make the bears seem gigantic. This arrangement undermined the pretence that the animalstock was being classified scientifically and was no more favourable to the animals' well-being than any other. In fact, none of the construction criteria adopted in the second half of the century improved their living conditions: the use of stone or cement floors – sloping towards channels and sewers to allow the rapid cleaning of cages and easy disposal of excrement – was intended to help keepers in their work and meet the public's new demand for hygiene, but prevented activities that were vital to the animals (digging, burying, rolling in the dust) and caused deformation of their bones if they thumped their limbs or stamped their feet. The director of the Marseilles gardens noted openly in 1861 that such adjustments were intended to benefit spectators, not animals.[8]

THE HUNGER FOR EXOTICISM

The crowds that flocked to zoos did not do so to see familiar animals, wild or otherwise, as was demonstrated by the unhappy experience of the Basel gardens, which opened in 1874 with the aim of collecting Alpine species, and which were forced to convert to exotic animals in an effort to attract a dissatisfied public. Neither did visitors want to see domesticated exotic animals, as was proved by the decline of acclimatization gardens.[9] Thus the Bois de Boulogne gardens had quickly to introduce more exciting animals, especially monkeys and elephants, to increase the number of paid admissions. The public wanted creatures that were curious, wild, ferocious and very different from European animals, to provide a change of scene and a chance to

65 — NIMES — Muséum d'Histoire Naturelle. Galerie du 1er étage, Lion de l'Atlas, tué par Gérard, dit le « Tueur de Lions » — ND

A stuffed lion shot by Gérard, 'the Lion Killer', in the Museum d'Histoire Naturelle, Nîmes.

dream of distant lands. This had already been a common sentiment when the Jardin des Plantes had first opened. To visit it, wrote Citizen Toscan around 1800, was to travel by means of thought alone.[10] Until the 1950s, zoological gardens continued to act as a substitute for travel, and to satisfy the craving for exoticism and escape which intensified in the West with the advent of Romanticism and colonial adventure. A passion for the wild was apparent in other related areas such as public sculpture, as witness the innumerable statues of lions scattered throughout London's public spaces, including Trafalgar Square, lions being a symbol of the Empire, and therefore of national mastery.

This same attraction was apparent in the literature of the period. In France, well studied by Emile Revel, the term *exotisme* was coined around 1845 to describe Europe's passion for other worlds. Never, Revel wrote, 'had literature suffered such an invasion of animals' as writers dreamed of an elsewhere often symbolized by exotic wildlife: 'I have passed whole days by my fireside hunting tigers', wrote Gustave Flaubert in a letter of 1846, 'and have heard the sound of the bamboo breaking under the feet of my elephant, which would bray in terror when it sensed the ferocious beasts nearby.' Chateaubriand filled his *Voyage en Amérique* and *Atala* with prodigious descriptions of bison, snakes and, especially, dragon-like crocodiles. Victor Hugo portrayed colourful jungle fauna in *Les Orientales*, bringing tigers, lions, boa constrictors, hippopotami and hyenas together in one place. This interest was not the sole preserve of the Romantics, however: Flaubert, in *Salammbô*, and the Parnassian poet Leconte de Lisle evoked exotic wildlife which aroused intense public interest. This fashion explains the success of hunting accounts such as those by the famous Jules Gérard, *La Chasse aux lions* (1855) and *Le Tueur de lions* (1858), which inspired Alphonse Daudet's *Tartarin de Tarascon* (1869).

Animals embodied the desire for escape, and their powerful instincts and mingled beauty and violence made them natural adjuncts of the tortured heroes of Romanticism. Hugo walked in the Jardin des Plantes with his grandchildren and published the 'Poème du Jardin des plantes' in *L'Art d'être grand-père* (1877). The Jardin – a 'perfect miniature' of the universe – allowed one to go to Assyria or Timbuktu without leaving Paris, to contemplate God as the inventor of beauties and monsters. The latter attracted Hugo because they posed questions about the mysterious nature of beasts. They also answered an 'immense need for astonishment', enabling the poet – as he compared them to the children who came to see them and meditated on that meeting of innocence and ferocity – to construct a symbolic vision contrasting unblemished souls with the damned, who roared in their torments.

The same tastes extended into the visual arts. Animal sculpture became a distinct genre in the sculptures of Antoine-Louis Barye, which were influenced by the realistic equestrian paintings of Antoine-Jean Gros or Théodore Géricault and the fantastical battles depicted by Peter-Paul Rubens. From 1831 (*Tiger Devouring a Crocodile*) and 1833 (*Lion and Snake*), Barye's scenes of struggle between exotic beasts displayed a savage realism, mixing a determined anatomical and postural accuracy in anatomy and movement with a Romantic sense of the tragic grandeur of violence: big cats pouncing or tearing each others' throats out, transformed by hunger and irresistible instinct, or reptiles and saurians twisted around their dying prey. Barye visited the fairground menageries and Jardin des Plantes to do research. He attended courses in zoology, observed animals closely, worked on their remains, and measured their hides, their skinned corpses and their skeletons, which he drew in vast numbers. These activities were furthered by his appointment as the Muséum's lecturer in zoological drawing in 1857. But his anatomical realism went hand in hand with unrealistic situations. By bringing together animals that would never have met or fought in their natural habitats, Barye was delivering a fantasized vision of nature, which was thus perceived as an never-ending tempest of base instinct and violent fury, a perpetual act of cruelty linking life and death. This notion was close to the Romantic perception of life and the soul, and must be thought of in parallel with the idea of the fight for survival outlined by Charles Darwin in the same period.

A whole school of animal sculpture (C. Fratin, P. J. Mène, A. N. Cain) soon formed itself in the master's wake, reprising his methods and themes, and contributing to the public's growing familiarity with zoology, since part of its output occupied public spaces in the tradition of the elephant at the Bastille, erected at Napoleon's orders in 1813. Barye's *Lion and Snake* and Cain's *Tiger Crushing a Crocodile* and *Rhinoceros* were installed at the Tuileries. Painters mined the same material, notably Eugène Delacroix, a friend of Barye and his companion when observing animals at the Jardin des Plantes. Delacroix created several scenes of combat (*Lion and Crocodile*) and portraits of felines, beginning in 1831. This taste for exotic animals and furious contests existed in other European countries as well: in the eighteenth century, the British painter Stubbs drew several fights between a horse and a lion, while E. Meister painted a mêlée of lions in 1833 in Cologne.[11]

This fascination with exoticism did not manifest itself solely in the omnipresence of ferocious and exotic animals in zoological gardens; it also found expression in a growing trend for ethnographical architecture in the second half of the nineteenth century. The latter replaced the fabrications in wood, brick and thatch that had been inspired by the buildings in eighteenth-century landscaped gardens; once having spread to all zoos, it heralded a fashion for the theatrical and picturesque, but also a desire to integrate foreign wildlife into a European domestic setting and make it subservent to human requirements. One of the first examples of exotic architecture was to be found on Peacock Island near Potsdam, a summer residence of the kings of Prussia. Buildings were erected there during the 1820s that rather fancifully evoked the countries of origin of kangaroos (Asia!) and buffaloes (North America). This style became widespread during the second half of the century in Belgium, the Netherlands and Germany, thanks both to artists being allowed to work on a grand scale and to the policies of the stockholding societies, who needed spectacular fixtures and fittings to attract their publics.[12]

It was thus that, in 1856, an Egyptian temple for

elephants, giraffes and camels was unveiled in Antwerp, decorated with frescoes and bas-reliefs depicting scenes from Egyptian art. Brussels imitated this, while Ghent constructed housing for its camels in the shape of a nomad's tent, an idea that received a second iteration at Rotterdam. At Berlin's Tiergarten, which took this style to its peak, an Indian pagoda was built for the rhinoceroses and elephants (1873), an oriental home for the camels (1897), a Japanese dwelling for the wading birds (1897), an Egyptian temple for the ostriches, and a wooden house in Native American style for the bison. The Egyptian temple, Moorish residence and Asian pagoda were to be found everywhere, functioning as stereotyped images of countries or even continents, but they were not always used to house the same creatures: the first contained elephants in Düsseldorf and flamingos in Hamburg; the second, monkeys in Breslau, elephants in Cologne, and ruminants in Hanover. Thus the exotic dream took some liberties with geography. This style was used in other cities (Marseilles, Basel and Turin) and, to an extent, survived into the twentieth century: African huts were built in Rome in 1925 and in Geneva in 1935. The public was seduced by such evocations, which while not always realistic did transform the gardens into fragments of foreign lands at a time when literature, newspapers, guidebooks and the first trips by train or steamboat to Switzerland, Greece and the Near East were fortifying the popular interest in exoticism.[13]

Painting of the water-bird enclosure, Peacock Island, Berlin, 1830, by Carl Wilhelm Pohlke.

'Egyptian Temple', Antwerp Zoo.

'Egyptian Temple', Antwerp Zoo, after the 1980s restoration.

'Antelope Mosque', Antwerp Zoo.

'Oriental' entrance from the Ku'damm, Berlin Zoo.

'Indian pagoda' for pachyderms, Berlin Zoo, *c.* 1873.

'Oriental' giraffe house, Berlin Zoo, *c.* 1910.

'Siamese' buffalo house, Berlin Zoo.

Ape and palm house, Berlin Zoo.

Drawing of deer in front of their sleeping quarters, Berlin Zoo, c. 1879, by Mickow.

'African huts', Rome Zoo, 2001.

'Egyptian' doorway, Rome Zoo, 2001.

Entrance, Budapest Zoo, 2001.

Building in traditional church style, Budapest Zoo, 2001.

Elephant house, Budapest Zoo, 2001.

Detail of the elephant house, Budapest Zoo, 2001.

Interior of the elephant house, Budapest Zoo, 2001.

Pheasant house, Budapest Zoo, *c.* 1886.

Hoofed-animal house, Moscow Zoo, 1884.

Bear pit with castellated surrounds, Cologne Zoo.

Elephant house, Basel Zoo, *c.* 1910.

Monkey temple, Clifton Zoo, Bristol.

Belvederes, Lisbon Zoo, c. 1905.

A tiger in front of exotic architecture, Miami Metro Zoo.

Orientalizing gateway, Berlin Zoo.

Rotterdam Zoo, 1992, by Candida Höfer.

Bear castle, Helsinki Zoo, 1890s.

The aim of educating visitors, initially proclaimed by the Jardin des Plantes and, later, by all gardens, took on greater importance as scientific use declined and attendance became more democratic. It was strengthened by the interest in science, particularly natural history, that characterized the literate European public from the second half of the eighteenth century, resulting in the publication of numerous books, journals, dictionaries and encyclopaedias. Scientists responded to this new demand by writing more popular works, including Cuvier's *Le Règne animal* (1817), *Histoire naturelle des mammifères* by Geoffroy Saint-Hilaire and Frédéric Cuvier (1820–42), Alexander von Humboldt's *Tableaux de la nature* (1847–51), Alfred Brehm's *Tierleben* (1864–9), Francis Buckland's *Curiosities of Natural History* (1857–72) and so on.[14]

Most zoos adopted this mantra of popularization; for example, Amsterdam's society proposed to 'improve understanding of natural history in an agreeable and attractive manner'. They were aided by guidebooks and visitors' accounts published by scholars or advertisers with an interest in natural history. H. Perron d'Arc noted in 1860 that many visitors arrived with little scientific knowledge and that they left barely the wiser if they were not taught in the meantime, thus justifying the presence of explanatory plaques. Such texts rarely *described* animals, however. They were, rather, manuals of natural history, presenting in a systematic manner the geographical origin, anatomy, diet, habits and reproduction of each species, with material drawn from the work of the most famous naturalists of the eighteenth and nineteenth centuries. The animal in a cage – the 'specimen', to use Perron's word – often served only as an illustrative tag, fulfilling the function of modern colour photographs in books and magazines.[15] Only the arrival of a little-known creature, like the giraffe that turned up in Paris in 1827, demanded special attention, and it was not until the end of the century that guidebooks took an interest in animal behaviour in captivity, especially that of anthropoid apes.[16]

Thus these documents provided a learned, rather than a popular, vision of zoological gardens. The two did have a common starting point in the love of novelty, however. In public gardens managed by scientists like the Jardin des Plantes, there was a tacit accord between scholars preoccupied with the enlargement or completion of their collections, and the crowds drawn by new arrivals. In gardens that were private or charged admission, managers soon understood that novelty was the perfect means by which to entice new visitors. In London, for example, after 1849, the Zoological Society introced new arrivals to help resolve its various difficulties, including an Asiatic elephant (1831), a giraffe (1836), a mandrill (1849), a hippopotamus (1850), a porpoise (1862), an African elephant (1865), a chimpanzee (1883), a gorilla (1887) and an okapi (1935).

In each instance, success was considerable, especially when a specimen was the first such animal to arrive in Europe, or entailed a new installation at the zoo, as was the case with an orang-utan in Paris (1836), a vivarium-aquarium in London (1853) and a gorilla in Berlin (1876). The number of visitors to London's gardens doubled in the year the hippopotamus arrived (1850). Collections were thus broadened gradually, and species became more and more common, as a result of which the public's anatomical knowledge grew. The elephant, still exceptional in the 1700s, was now almost ubiquitous in its Indian variety. Gorillas became more common from the 1890s. Giraffes, unseen between the sixteenth century and 1827, grew in number. They were

An elephant in his bath in the Zoological Gardens, London.

| Cabas | Omar | ZAIDA | MABROUCK | SELIM | GUIB ALLAH | Abdalah | M Thibaut |

The GIRAFFES with the ARABS who brought them over to this Country.

ZOOLOGICAL GARDENS.
Regent's Park.

'The Giraffes with the Arabs who brought them over to this Country', Zoological Gardens, London, 1835, by George Scharf.

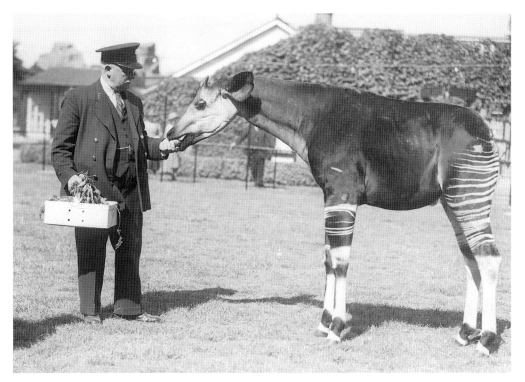

The first London Zoo okapi with keeper, 1935.

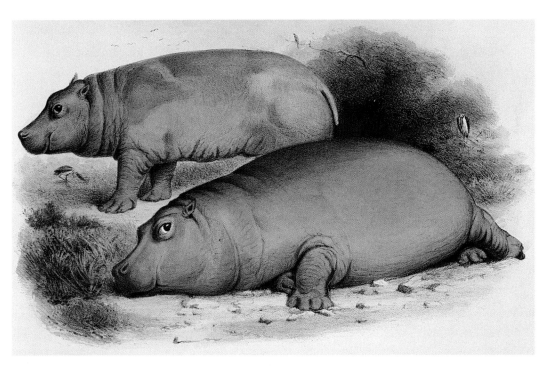

'Obaysch', the first London zoo hippo, 1849, by Joseph Wolf.

guests in London in 1829, from 1836 to 1892, and without interruption from 1895.[17]

Some arrivals triggered crazes and fashions. London's hippopotamus was welcomed by an immense crowd, becoming the hero of *Punch* cartoons and a multitude of engravings, which were distributed throughout the country. Small silver reproductions of him were sold in the Strand, while the 'Hippopotamus Polka' was a hit in London's salons. The arrival of an elephant at Stupinigi in 1826 also inspired artistic outpourings.

The most significant example is that of the three giraffes offered by the Viceroy of Egypt in a quest for rapprochement with the European powers; they arrived in 1827–9 in Paris, London and Vienna. The French animal disembarked at Marseilles at night, in November 1826, for fear that a rumour describing the arrival of a gigantic monster might spread through the town. She spent the winter in the courtyard of the prefecture, where receptions were held in her honour. Every day, from noon to three o'clock, she was walked through the town with a good deal of ceremony, amid sizeable crowds. In May 1827, she set off for Paris, travelling in short stages under the direction of no other than Etienne Geoffroy Saint-Hilaire, who entered towns and villages on foot, in front of her, preceded by an escort of gendarmes and followed by wagons of supplies. The crowds, who arrived in entire communes from neighbouring districts, got larger and larger, the press published daily accounts, and Charles X was kept regularly informed. In Lyon, the army's help was required to install the animal in the Place Bellecour, but she escaped, scared the horses and triggered panic among the spectators. The next day, newspapers printed the names of 'children lost in the pandemonium caused by the giraffe'; they had been waiting to be collected at the police station. Arriving in Paris in

June, the animal was presented to the King at Saint-Cloud in the presence of generals and professors from the Muséum and university – in other words, the principal protagonists in the conquest of exotic wildlife. Once she arrived at the Jardin des Plantes, 600,000 visitors from all corners of the country jostled to see the giraffe's afternoon strolls between June and December 1827.

The animal inspired the publication of almanacs and calendars bearing her image, and the sale of engravings in fairgrounds, markets and elsewhere; she was the subject of plays, pamphlets satirical ('La Girafe ou le Gouvernement des bêtes', 1827) and humorous ('Dame girafe à Paris: Aventures et voyage … racontés à l'ours Martin', 1827), songs and music ('La Girafe', a waltz for piano by Singer). Great quantities of crockery were produced, carrying often fantastical drawings of her, while feminine fashion went wild: dyes, gloves, trimmings, necklaces, ribbons, parasols and hairstyles, all *à la girafe*. Without reaching quite the same heights, there were noticeable echoes in London and particularly in Vienna, where a dance (the giraffe gallopade), an operetta (*La Girafe à Vienne*) and an opera (*La Muette de Portici*) were created. A few animals continued to arouse intense interest after 1850, such as the gorilla which appeared in Berlin around 1936 – the first to survive in a zoo for a reasonable length of time – or the pandas which arrived in Paris in 1973, but they did so without sparking off fashions comparable to those of the years 1750–1850, years that correspond, not by accident, to the period when public interest in the natural sciences was at its greatest.[18]

All sources agree that the public made its preferences clear by flocking to the cages of certain animals, always the same ones, which therefore possessed greater 'show' value than the others. These were the large mammals (elephant, giraffe, rhinoceros, hippopotamus) whose proportions, bulk

Cover for the music to 'Jumbo's March', by George Barnham.

THE THRILL OF THE WILD

Monday-afternoon
elephant ride,
Zoological Society's
Gardens, London,
1871.

730 THE ZOO (London).
The Elephant Ride. — LL.

The elephant ride, London Zoo, c. 1910.

Lion enclosure, Dresden Zoo, 1863.

and strength seemed astonishing feats of nature. The elephant was the most appreciated because its domesticated status meant that visitors could establish some contact with it, even ride on it. Big cats were also the focus of great interest, because they symbolized wildness and cruelty (they were always suspected of being man-eaters) and encapsulated both the fear of nature and the satisfaction of having overcome it. Reptiles appealed because their appearance, apparent remoteness and genuine threat were fascinating and terrifying in equal measure. Finally among these popular creatures were any animals that were still little known or thought to be strange in shape (kangaroo, sea-lion, okapi), or those who stood upright and therefore seemed to imitate humans: bears, penguins and, above all, monkeys.[19]

Some animals became mascots in the UK and Germany. The death in 1826 of Chunee, an elephant domiciled at Exeter 'Change, provoked a commotion; the sale of his congener Jumbo, of Regent's Park, to Barnum's Circus of America in 1882 triggered a national outcry. At mid-century,

Obaysch, a hippopotamus, and, in the 1880s and '90s, the chimpanzees Sally in London and Consul in Manchester, were the objects of similar affection. In Germany, one can cite the gorilla who in the late 1930s became the symbol of Berlin's zoo, even appearing on its seal. These mascots were the fruit of subtle selection and the tacit accord between the gardens' management (hoping to attract spectators), a fast-growing press in quest of timely topics, and the public. Novelty was not enough. Dangerous animals such as big cats or reptiles could not be exploited in this way, nor those, like the giraffe, that seemed indifferent. As Harriet Ritvo has noted, while the lion became the symbol of Britain triumphant, it was not adopted as a national mascot because it inspired neither affection nor imagination. Mascots were mostly herbivorous mammals remarkable for their size (Jumbo was the biggest pachyderm living in captivity) that were considered to be docile, 'good creatures', could connect with the public, and inspired hope for a harmonious existence at a time of popular belief in the

Löwe Brigant — Löwin Manda

The lion and lioness Brigant and Manda, Dresden Zoo.

302 PARIS – Jardin des Plantes
Lion et Lionne – Félis leo (Linné) – Afrique
Don de Mme Cécile Sorel de la Comédie-Française

Lions in a cage, Jardin des Plantes, Paris.

Lions in a Cage, 1907, by Adolf Oberländer.

Kangaroos, Hamburg Zoo, 1865.

Feeding the elephant seal, Jardin des Plantes, Paris.

Syrian brown bear, Münster Zoo, 1994, by Britta Jaschinski.

Queen Mary at the Lubetkin/Tecton penguin pool, London Zoo, c. 1934.

Rhesus monkeys, Antwerp Zoo.

Consul, the Manchester Zoo chimpanzee.

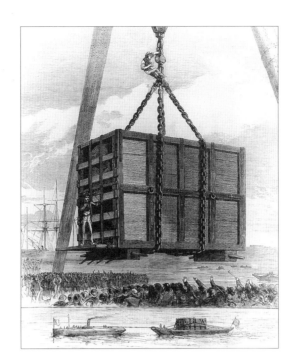

'The Departure of Jumbo: Hoisting his Box from the Barge to the Quay at Millwall Docks', 1862.

Jumbo the elephant, dead in Canada, 1865.

virtues of domestication. The anthropoid apes were loved because they made an effort, so to speak, to Europeanize themselves (Sally and Consul were both dressed, raised and fed in the English manner) and because they thus supported the general intention to Westernize other populations and impose 'true' civilization on them.[20]

Every inquiry and study indicates that the public's preferences did not change in the twentieth century. Surveys of children in London and Basel in the 1960s and '70s produced results identical to those of earlier decades. Even the progressive arrival of wild elephants from Africa did not disturb the pachyderm's popularity, because it came to symbolize the untamed, undaunted nature that was so much in demand.[21] Here was a profound trend in humanity's relationship with the animal world which zoos had to take account of in order to satisfy their visitors.

Since the nineteenth century, the spectrum of wildlife kept in zoos had undermined the scientific ideal (if it had ever been genuine) of systematic collections of live animals. A typical example of the more popular approach is a 1933 report from the Jardin des Plantes by a journalist and regular zoo visitor. It lingers over the animals' forms, the beauty of their coats, focusing on creatures that are pleasing to the eye or reassuringly reminiscent of more familiar species. The author shows an interest in diet, habits, character and offspring, and especially in animals that seem to conform to human habits, such as agouties, of whom she offers a remarkable anthropomorphic description:

> Nothing could be more amusing than to watch them eat: delicately taking the fruit I offer them, they sit down and use their front paws like hands to hold the titbits and bring them to their mouths; they nibble them with the tips of their teeth, taking visible care

not to dirty themselves. Then they stand up in an expressive gesture to ask for another piece of the nice, sweet fruit.

She also favours creatures that seek out contact with humans, even co-operating in their own captivity: she describes the elephant and anteater as happy to live in the gardens, the hippopotamus as a 'sociable character who approaches willingly'.[22]

In the context of this everyday zoology, anatomy, especially of new arrivals, continued to be analyzed with reference to more mundane animals, an attitude that did not begin to fade until the end of the nineteenth century, when photography, the growth in the popular press and, later, television caused a proliferation of animal images.[23] The appearance and character of an animal were at the root of a simple, Manichean classification (quite different from the scholarly version) based on dichotomies of bad and good, vicious and gentle. Reptiles, big cats and carnivores in general fell into the first category because a fondness for meat had long been considered the sign of a barbaric and violent nature. Monkeys, thought of as mischievous and lustful, were often similarly categorized. Herbivores, especially domesticated ones, were in the second category. This system was primarily applied to mammals, the closest creatures to humans, but not really to birds or fish, which were thought of as objects of beauty or as food.[24] The system was a vehicle for ideas that had been firmly rooted since ancient times, often in direct contradiction with reality: bears, thought to be good-natured, are in fact dangerous, and the antelope one might have wanted to stroke could kill a man, while the allegedly ferocious jaguar would seldom attack a human being.

Face-to-face confrontation did little to overturn these

2.
AVENTURES
D'UNE TIGRESSE
A MARSEILLE

— Pouah ! ! ! ça sent l'ail

Adventures of a Tigress in Marseilles: 'ATTENTION! – HONEST DOGS POISONED BAIT' – 'Ugh!!! this stinks of garlic'.

saw in the wild in order to justify their own attitudes, or to convey the thrill of the wild to their armchair readers. The example of the gorilla is significant. P. du Chaillu, perhaps the first person to observe living gorillas and describe them (before killing a few), in 1861 imposed his vision of a ferocious animal on the world, a vision that would resurface much later in the myth of King Kong. Despite being challenged by some scholars in the late 1800s, the heyday of Darwinism, it went largely unchanged until the 1960s, when field study began to develop.[25] Its persistence can be explained by its symbolic function, since it purports to document a firm divide between cruel nature and peaceful civilization, and because it allows the former to be set up as an example to be avoided in the struggle to build a better world, a concept long expounded by Christian writers and, more recently, by some philosophers.[26]

The public's relationship with the animals in a zoological garden was therefore based on attraction and repulsion, curiosity and fear. This ambivalence left its mark in the use of railings through which, wrote one visitor in 1798, one could watch without fear. Pictures, books, designs, plans and archives constantly call to mind the strong wooden joists, and the bars and fences, doubled and tripled as the decades passed in response to demands for greater security. Progress in metallurgy brought ever more reassuring solutions: bars of 17 millimetres for a tiger's cage in Marseilles in 1898 became 35 millimetres for that of an elephant in Lyon in 1927. In some less affluent gardens, security was the only motive for renovation. Fear deepened when escapes occurred; they bred rumours and fantasies and, usually, even if it was only a monkey, ended in death for the animal guilty of breaching the frontier and invading the spaces of civilization. Fear also ran high during wars, leading to big cats being locked in their dens, or even put down.[27]

notions; on the contrary, caged animals encouraged them. A 1850 guidebook for Brussels describes hyenas as 'villains in body and spirit' and disparages those who swore that their appearance was deceptive. These beliefs were not actively contradicted by scientists, whose ideas continued to be based on travellers' accounts. Indeed, a fair number of explorers, often hunters, applied these beliefs to what they

THE THRILL OF THE WILD

181

Bear pits, Manchester Zoo, 1903.

MÜNSTER, ZOOLOGISCHER GARTEN, RAUBTIERHAUS.

Beast-of-prey cage, Münster Zoo.

A dead elephant in the bombed elephant house, Berlin Zoo, 1943.

The contrast was sharp between the cages allocated to ferocious animals that were still wild or barely tamed, and those assigned to 'peaceful' herbivores that were quite often fully domesticated. This symbolism was not lost on visitors like Jules Huret, who declared of the big cats:

> Staring into their cruel eyes I experience a violent emotion which inflames my fighting spirit ... I dream of being well armed and armoured, of going before these old enemies of the human race and cutting their throats or suffocating them in hand-to-hand combat, just as the legends tell it. I envy the lion-tamer who whips them.[28]

This is why the public's attitude swung between a desire for contact and the temptation of violence. The former was made concrete in the offer of food, a trend notable since the early days of zoological gardens which mostly involved children, and which reached considerable proportions as people became wealthier. On a single day in Brussels in 1855, a bear was given five hundred bread rolls, and on 19 June 1959 in Antwerp, an elephant wolfed down 1,706 peanuts, 1,089 pieces of bread, 1,330 sweets, 811 biscuits, 198 orange segments, seventeen apples, seven ice creams and one hamburger! The meaning of these gifts was, and is, ambivalent: they reinforce the sense of superiority over a captive, reduced to receiving food according the whims of its captors; they are a more or less conscious way of inducing the surrender of the wild. In 1850, a guide to the Jardin

The Lion-Tamer, 1927, by René Auberjonois.

des Plantes noted that the elephant that solicits food has lost its wild nature through contact with civilized life. Gifts, of course, also have a symbolic function; they establish contact, act as signs of peace and the desire for exchange, and maintain friendship.[29]

Twentieth-century work in zoo-psychology has confirmed what a number of nineteenth-century texts suggested: that animals accustomed to captivity adapt to crowds, and, if many are indifferent, others (monkeys, big cats, large and marine mammals, deer, bears) are stimulated by a presence that relieves their boredom and makes them more lively. A relationship develops based on assimilation (the human treated as a congener, the animal analyzed in anthropomorphic terms) and mutual exhibitionism whereby the human seeks to attract the animal's attention, reacting badly if ignored, and the latter responds by begging. Animals beg to ensure a constant supply of food (in the case of bears) or to amuse themselves by abandoning stereotyped behaviour. They use their tongues (giraffes, deer), trunks (elephants), hands (monkeys) and paws (felines, bears) and learn profitable expressions and gestures from experience, which are then borrowed by their congeners. These gestures please the public, who gather around the cages, pass favourable judgement on the creatures in question and feed them even more, while deciding that the other animals are stupid or lazy and occasionally throwing objects to make them react.[30] This anthropomorphic reading of animal behaviour has caused accidents, mostly with bears, for whom the discrepancy between their presumed and real natures has always been the greatest: spectators climb over fences or down into pits to feed them, doubtless believing that the bears would react well; in fact, they are attacked immediately.[31]

In the nineteenth century, feeding by the public was tolerated and even encouraged by zoo directors because it reduced their own costs; its drawbacks (force-feeding, obesity and death) were little recognized or thought unimportant at a time when wildlife was being liberally wasted. The first bans on feeding by visitors appeared in the early 1900s (Dresden, Manchester), becoming common after 1950 thanks to developments in the understanding of diet and the increasing difficulty of removing specimens from the wild. Such bans encountered strong resistance from the public.[32]

Zoological gardens could also be the scene of violent attacks: a rhinoceros died from a sword wound in 1793, and efforts on behalf of the Muséum's professors to avoid poisonings can be seen in the very earliest building plans at the Jardin des Plantes. This phenomenon seemed to increase with the democratization of gardens, which introduced a less sophisticated public, used to violence in social settings and accustomed to brutality towards animals, an attitude common in town and country alike.[33] In 1891, the director of the Jardin des Plantes noted, on the subject of free admissions, that the growth in the number of visitors multiplied the number of incidents: birds' wings were burned or pulled off; animals were hurt by blows from canes and stones, or food poisoned with phosphorus, alcohol or tobacco or laced with fish hooks or razor blades. A zebra was attacked with a needle attached to a walking stick. Locks were changed constantly and patrols mounted to counter raids at night. Theft of edible poultry was sometimes perpetrated by staff and became more common during wars. Along with poisonings and killings, it formed part of the general misuse by the masses of any park that was open to all and poorly guarded. The same abuses occurred in private, paid-entry gardens like London, Madrid and Turin, but their extent is difficult to gauge. An

'The Sick Elephant', 1874.

account by a supervisor at the Moscow zoo in the early 1900s may explain the thinking behind them:

> All day long, an immense crowd, rowdy and bother-some, filed past the cages. This multitude, which would have been seized by mortal panic at the distant sight of any one of these animals at liberty, took great delight in seeing them thus disarmed, humiliated and debased. They took revenge for their own cowardice by deriding them, heckling them in loud voices, and shaking their chains, and the keepers' remonstrations would come up against an unanswerable argument: 'I've paid.'

This taste for brutality was also apparent in the great success of large snakes' feeding times – opened to the public in London from 1849, and also in Moscow – in attracting visitors, who were fascinated to see them swallow their living prey.[34]

Most zoo managers, however, attempted to curb this behaviour through regulations. In this, they were supported by members of the upper classes, who shared a growing distaste for violence towards animals, prompting them to organize press campaigns, progressively forbid animal fighting and support legislative crack-downs (Germany, 1871; Great Britain, 1900; Italy, 1913; Belgium and Spain, 1929; France, 1976). There were also attempts to control working-class behaviour and model the uses of public spaces on those of the upper classes: promenade, contemplation and instruction. In London, a press campaign and change of administration ended in the abandoning of public access to reptile feeding in the early 1900s.[35]

The popular approach to zoos was reinforced by the practices of travelling menageries and their sedentary counterparts, which continued to promote their exhibitions under the banner of the extraordinary. In Hamburg, around 1850, seals were dubbed 'sea nymphs' or 'marine horses'. Such fantastical patter diminished at the end of the century, due to advances in primary-school education and zoological knowledge generally.[36]

The door was left open, however, to displays of trained animals – which, having been arranged by showmen in earlier times, were adopted by circuses in the 1820s – and to the lion-taming acts which were invented in the same period. In 1819, the Frenchman Henri Martin managed to tame a tiger of the Van Aaken menagerie in Bavaria, having devised a method (combining violence and kindness) by which he was able to enter the cages of big cats and make them obey his commands. The results he achieved astonished his contemporaries: bringing a lion and a tiger together, snatching away a cat's quarry to replace it with his own arm. The other founder of lion-taming was an American, Isaac Van Amburgh, who trained all the animals of the Titus menagerie from 1832, using the same techniques as Martin. Van Amburgh would place his head or arm, streaming with blood, into the open maw of a big cat (whose lips would be drawn over its fangs to stop them from biting), or group a lion, a lamb and a little girl together in picturesque composition. From 1887, Carl Hagenbeck had his circus abandon the red-hot irons they had used to tame animals, developing instead the so-called art of gentle taming, based on the use of a whip and administration of rewards in the form of food.

The success of these acts was considerable. Martin, who toured the Germanic lands and the Low Countries between 1823 and 1829, drew audiences that included the grandest princes. Van Amburgh, having arrived in Britain in 1838, performed for the aristocracy, including the Duke of Wellington, and organized a special soirée for Queen Victoria. The enthusiastic response led to even greater spectaculars. In 1831, the management of the Olympic Circus in Paris created the pantomime *Les Lions de Mysore* (the story of a dethroned nabob being chased through the jungle) with Martin and his lions in the leading roles. Having enjoyed success there, it was performed in London and throughout Britain before returning to France. The idea was borrowed by Van Amburgh, who presented *Charlemagne* (1838) in London and then *La Fille de l'émir* (1839) in Paris.[37]

Martin and Van Amburgh's techniques and showmanship were copied by all other animal-tamers in the second half of the century, in travelling menageries as well as in circuses, where wild animals were eclipsing equestrian acts and taking pride of place alongside the clowns. But it was the cinema that, from the 1900s, brought these acts to public attention (*En pâture aux lions*, 1912; *Le Cirque à domicile*, 1913). The taming of big cats, which effectively replaced the animal fights that were in the process of being banned everywhere but in Spain, and which developed in parallel with the process of international colonization, communicated clearly the conscious or unconscious but (in view of its success) universally shared resolution to enslave the wildest of wildlife. At the same time, the taming of cats expressed a willingness to civilize them. For the journalist P. A. Pichot, it marked a 'rebirth of the ancient fellowship' between wild animal and human.

This explains the popularity of acts where a trained animal, more often than not an elephant or a monkey, would imitate humans to comic effect. At Franconi's Circus

Inside a Menagerie, 1835, by Johann Geyer.

In the Menagerie, 1891, by Paul Meyerheim.

Eduard Deyerling ('Karl Hagenbeck's newest lion-trainer'), 1889.

in Restoration Paris, Baba the elephant would place a napkin around its neck and sit at table. At Barnum's, the little elephant Tom Thumb feigned drunkenness. In 1886, another pachyderm danced the *Ballet des éléphants, fantaisie zoologique* to the music of Saint-Saëns' *Carnaval des animaux*. As Robert Delort has noted, circuses contributed to a change in the image of such animals, replacing their status as ferocious or curious beasts with that of clowns that were applauded by their audiences, who felt some sort of kinship with them.[38]

Success was such that training and taming were adopted by zoological gardens as a way of attracting the public. In the early years of the Jardin des Plantes, a keeper called Felix, former owner of a requisitioned menagerie, would enter cages, stroke lions and open their mouths at the request of spellbound audiences. But it was in the final third of the nineteenth century that such acts began to spread among zoos run by fairground entertainers (Belle Vue in Manchester, Stellingen, the zoo of the *Exposition Coloniale* in 1931) and a few others, for example the gardens in the Bois de Boulogne. In 1935, a trained chimpanzee was presented in Geneva who ate and drank like a human: 'He takes his breakfast on arrival, his lunch at two in the afternoon and his dinner at half past six. His meals consist of sweetened chocolate mixed with oatmeal.' The distinction made by Paul Bouissac between the zoo, which confirms in its use of barriers a radical break between human and animal, and the circus, which fosters confusion by humanizing the latter, did not truly come into play until the mid-1900s.[39]

The introduction of such showmanship to the zoo environment was in keeping with a policy that saw attractions develop as the public's involvement broadened: the staging of animals' meals; rides on ponies, dromedaries

Carl Hagenbeck with a performing tiger, c. 1907.

Performing animals at Carl Hagenbeck's zoo, 1903.

YOUNG CHIMPANZEES AT TEA

'Young chimpanzees at tea', London Zoo, perhaps c. 1930.

416, B.—EDUCATED ORANGS DINING.
NEW YORK ZOOLOGICAL PARK.

Educated orangs eating, New York Zoo, c. 1905.

Dinosaurs, Tierpark Hagenbeck, Hamburg-Stellingen.

A dinosaur, Barcelona Zoo.

and elephants; animal parades in town centres; animal fights and so on. Gardens in Amsterdam, Berlin and Antwerp created open-air museums devoted to contemporary animal sculpture to appeal to the cultured élite. Taking advantage of a growing fascination with prehistory, already exploited by the recreation of an iguanodon and other dinosaurs at London's Crystal Palace in 1851, Carl Hagenbeck installed life-size reconstructions of prehistoric animals at Stellingen around 1910. This idea was revisited in the inter-war period at Berlin and Schönbrunn, where the region's extinct species were presented, and at Vincennes in 1984, Cologne in 1993 (resulting in a 27-percent increase in admissions) and in special prehistoric parks. It was as if the abandoning of the fantastical approach to exotic animals required extraordinary and fearsome creatures to be summoned from the past in order to maintain public interest and involvement.[40]

A NEW EDEN

The keeping of animals in captivity provoked no condemnation in the sixteenth and seventeenth centuries because it seemed natural in a society founded on inequality and on the concept of the subject, even the serf – a society that practised slavery. Criticism surfaced in the eighteenth century as we have seen. 'I allow aviaries in a garden', wrote the Prince de Ligne in 1781, 'but do not let them create unhappiness … I would prefer [gardens] to contain trees, and to be extensive enough that the birds may cause a joyous chorus to be heard there, for I have heard nothing but whining up till now.'[41] The liberation of animals followed that of human subjects, including slaves and the mentally ill. P. Pinel, who in 1792 approved Bernardin de Saint-Pierre's plans to move the Versailles menagerie and create a park for the study of

animal behaviour, freed the mental patients at Bicêtre from their chains around 1794 in order to transform that facility into a home for medical observation and experiment. This solidarity with the oppressed was undoubtedly influenced by the philosophers of the Enlightenment, especially their ideas regarding the kinship between violence towards humanity and towards animals. It explains the numerous diatribes of the 1790s and 1800s against the Jardin des Plantes' temporary cages, thought by some to be miserable prisons, as well as the high hopes pinned on the various plans for that park. But there was no question of condemning of the act of enclosure itself, and the Revolution was just as fundamental to the creation of psychiatric asylums as zoological gardens in France.[42]

Complaints about the Jardin des Plantes resurfaced under the more liberal July Monarchy, and again under the Second Empire thanks to comparisons with more modern European zoos and to disputes, by the government and in the newspapers in 1849 and 1858, about the purpose of the Muséum, 'that necropolis whose contents are known to no-one' (La Presse, 30 August 1858). They became louder between 1880 and 1914 as the Jardin's installations fell into dilapidation and obsolescence through lack of funds (during the same period, Regent's Park in London was restored twice). As Paul Escudié put it in the Journal of 21 March 1911, 'There is in Paris a cursed place: there, harmless animals as well as magnificent big cats, torn from the desert, rot slowly in ridiculously cramped gaols, in the damp and mud and in revolting filthiness.'[43]

Even so, in this as in other things the status quo prevailed. Throughout Europe, each new zoo was met with admiration. Significantly, the term palace was used in Madrid to describe the feline house (1830), at the Jardin des Plantes for the monkey house (1837), and in London and

'Monkey Palace', Jardin des Plantes, Paris, 1860s.

Berlin. To begin with, cages seemed spacious and well-organized (though decades later, they were judged to be quite the reverse, thanks to an increase in public awareness) because they echoed the urban norms of the time. In Lyon, for example, the bear cages of 50 square metres, with a den of three square metres and a pool, were thought by Loisel to be beautiful in 1912. Despite barely paying lip service to the animals' ethology, they corresponded to the everyday experiences of contemporary people. In 1896, 71 per cent of accommodation in Lyon was composed of one to three rooms of around ten square metres, and only 55 per cent of buildings had running water. This application of the norm of the human universe to the world of animals illustrates an ignorance of the latter's needs. It acted as a curb on criticism for quite some time.[44]

Gardens were often thought of as new Edens where the cruelty of nature was abolished and peace reigned under the benign influence of culture. The public had a passion for stories of friendship between animals, a lion and a dog in 1794–6, an eagle and a rooster in 1807. 'Without diminishing his courage', wrote G. Toscan of the lion, '[civilization] ... has awakened affections in him that perhaps would have been forever denied him in his solitude.'[45]

These philosophical currents explain the longevity of the accord between supporters of the animal kingdom and the objectives of zoological gardens. In France, for example, the Société Protectrice des Animaux, founded in Paris in 1845, had 'the goal of improving ... the lot of animals, with an eye to justice, moral standards, a proper understanding of economy and public hygiene'. Until the end of the century, the SPA's struggles concerned the transport and slaughter of animals destined for the butcher's, poor treatment of horses and beasts of burden, bullfights, defence of countryside birds and so on, but never exotic animals. This difference is explained by the group's social profile: for a long time, it was dominated by members of the medical profession – active in matters of philanthropy, hygiene and public morals, and inclined to stop violence against domestic animals – as well as by agronomists and landowners, supporters of the modernization of agriculture and therefore of breeding methods which should take animal's well-being into account in order to be more productive.

The relations maintained by the SPA with agricultural societies and, especially, the Parisian Société d'Acclimation, were close. Isidore Geoffroy Saint-Hilaire, the latter's President and director of the Jardin de Plantes' menagerie, was a member of the SPA's board of directors. Auguste Duméril, lecturer at the Muséum, director of the reptile menagerie and secretary of the Société d'Acclimatation, became the SPA's secretary-general in 1856. Their headquarters were moved the following year to the premises of the Société d'Acclimatation, and communal committees were set up, notably for the defence of insectivorous birds. In 1861, five members (out of twelve) of the committee of the Société d'Acclimatation were members of the SPA.

This alliance stemmed from the interest of the agricultural and acclimatization societies in improving breeding. Geoffroy Saint-Hilaire's ideas were disseminated in the SPA's bulletin and met with a favourable response, because he gave them a moral dimension in line with contemporary ideals of animal protection (all animals were meant to dedicate themselves to human welfare, by subjugating themselves to human control, working for human beings, even giving their lives; in return, they were owed respect, justice and compassion). This is why the SPA was circumspect when it came to conditions in the gardens, and exotic animals were not mentioned except when discussing the acclimatization of species that had already been domesticated and, sometimes, domestication.[46] Criticism of animal enslavement took refuge in satirical poetry and literature in this period. In *Scènes de la vie privée et publique des animaux* (1842), by P. J. Stahl, with illustrations by J. J. Grandville, a group of animals meets to decide how best to free themselves from human control.

In England, the Society for the Prevention of Cruelty to Animals (SPCA) took the same position as the French SPA – that is to say, they approved of zoos – but for different reasons, because the SPCA existed in a different cultural context. First, the English associations for the animal protection came into being at roughly the same time as zoos themselves, unlike the French ones, which developed much later. The SPCA, whose goal was to create legislation, was not the only group of its kind. The Society of Animal Friends, founded by Lewis Gompertz in the 1820s, and the Quaker Rational Humanity Group worked to modify attitudes towards animals. These movements were more clearly consistent than their French counterparts with a global effort to 'civilize' the lower classes. Cruelty towards animals seems to have been more widespread and visible in England than in France, in town and country alike.

In the US after the Civil War, the savage world of the Wild West declined in interest, while the continent of Africa became a popular symbol of wilderness and a theatre of adventure. Some hunters, however, including Hornaday, Theodore Roosevelt and the members of the upper-crust Boone and Crockett Club, became aware of the pillaging of wildlife and advocated moderation. Roosevelt, who had been President since William McKinley's death in 1901, declared some sites 'sanctuaries for birds alone'.[47] And in an amazing *volte face*, the exterminator of bison Buffalo Jones (Charles Jessie Jones) became the curator of Yellowstone National Park. These changes did not prevent the immense success, as in Europe, of hunting tales in which heroic men would kill malevolent creatures. To these were added books by trappers of live animals, who, however, covered up the sordid details of what they were doing: the disastrous mortality rates, the slaughter of mothers protecting their young. In this context, the zoo seemed a peaceful haven. Animals were not wounded, beaten or hunted there.

Zoos also made observation possible. Qualities were discovered in animals and given as examples, mostly to children, for whom numerous books were published, especially after 1850, with illustrations by talented artists. *The History of British Birds*, illustrated by Thomas Bewick, is mentioned in Charlotte Brontë's *Jane Eyre* (1847). *Domestic Pets: Their Habits and Management* began the long series of children's books by Jane Loudon. Specialist journals (such as *Animal's Friend*) and popular publications like *Penny Magazine* (with a circulation of 200,000), printed images of wild animals alongside information and advice. The zoo animal thus appeared more privileged guest than captive; the time had not yet come to venture beyond appearances to question what lay behind them.[48]

THE YEARNING FOR NATURE (1900s)

9 A PUBLIC QUEST

The democratization of zoos in the twentieth century is effectively summarized by the example of Regent's Park, simultaneously one of the first to begin liberalizing its admissions and one of the last to abandon all restrictions: it opened to non-members during the week in 1847, on Sunday afternoons only in 1940 and on Sunday mornings in 1957.[1] This same process occurred in most gardens in the years 1880–1910, although regular access for all members of the public did not become possible until the 1950s with the general rise in living standards in the West. The weight of public opinion on the development of zoos is rarely discussed, but in fact demands close examination.

cial and other difficulties experienced by the Rome zoo resulted in see-sawing attendance figures. Those of Berlin doubled between 1900 and 1940 (from one to two million), fell after 1945 due to economic ruin and partition, and did not regain pre-war levels until 1952. In the first third of the century, the strongest advances (doubled or tripled admissions) were made by zoos in European capitals and major cities such as Antwerp, Berlin, Lisbon, London and Stockholm, which experienced solid demographic growth with a 'captive' audience on Sundays. Some (Lisbon, Stockholm) continued to expand until mid-century, but it was largely the gardens of lesser towns that grew fastest at this stage, for example those of Frankfurt-am-Main or Basel, the latter

A POPULAR SUCCESS

All estimates reveal a sharp increase in the number of zoo visitors during the first half of the twentieth century, from four million in 1900 to six million in 1920, eight million in 1930 and 18.5 million in 1950. Statistics from individual zoos corroborate this development, influenced, of course, by local factors. Regent's Park, which tripled its admissions between 1900 and 1930 (from 0.7 million to approximately two million), saw them fall by a third in the 1950s under the effect of competition from Whipsnade, which opened in 1931 and was larger and more modern. The finan-

An evening concert at Artis Zoo, Amsterdam, by Nicolaas van der Waay.

The Playground in the Zoological Gardens, 1914, by Erich Büttner.

having been renovated by Heini Hediger.

Although reliable estimates for the last third of the century are hard to come by, it remains clear that overall expansion was even greater: by the beginning of the 1990s, approximately 150 million visitors across the whole of Europe. However, the disparities between establishments were accentuated by their increased number and localization, as well as their multiple new forms. Many urban zoos saw a slowdown in growth, perhaps due in part to the growth in car ownership. Admissions in Zurich grew by 68 per cent between 1950 and 1960, and just 15 per cent in the years up to 1974. The Basel zoo multiplied its admissions by four between 1950 and 1956, and by just 1.4 up to 1979. Zoos in capitals and major cities suffered declines. From 1968 to 1984, admissions to the Jardin des Plantes and Vincennes fell respectively from seven hundred thousand to a little over five hundred thousand and from 1.5 to one million. At Regent's Park, they dropped from three million in 1950 to 1.3 million in 1990, Londoners preferring parks on the outskirts. The trend of overall growth seems primarily to

Snowflake, the only known albino gorilla, a major attraction at Barcelona Zoo since 1966.

have benefited new establishments in rural areas.

Today, visitor numbers are still considerable, making zoos some of the biggest leisure businesses in the world: around one million a year in Basel or Copenhagen, three million in Barcelona and so on.[2] This increase is a result of the removal of social restrictions, the general adoption of pricing policies designed to attract the widest possible public and, above all, the sustained interest in exoticism. The inter-war period, for example, was distinguished by the success of colonial exhibitions. Possession of wild animals was popularized by the middle classes from the 1960s on, having mostly been an aristocratic pursuit during the early modern period.

A novel phenomenon was a growing interest in the wild stripped of romanticism, instead displaying respect and a desire for communion. A detailed study of this change in outlook would be extremely welcome. It began in the years 1890–1900, at the same time as the first measures for the protection of colonial wildlife, manifesting itself in, for example, the success of the Boy Scout movement, which began in England in 1909. An understanding of it, if not a complete explanation, can be reached through study of the prolific literature that emerged in the Anglo-Saxon and Germanic worlds at the time, including such best-sellers as *The Jungle Book* (1894) and *Kim* (1901) by Rudyard Kipling and *Mon livre vert* (1901) by Hermann Löns. In Jack London's *The Call of the Wild* (1903), the dog Buck follows a path opposite to that of the one in *White Fang* (1906), who abandons human company to rejoin his ancestors, the wolves. In *Nomads of the North* (1919), James Oliver Curwood relates the friendship between a dog and a bear. The spokesperson for wildlife Grey Owl relinquished his work as a trapper in Canada because the First World War convinced him of the need to protect rather than destroy life. Having become a warden at a zoological reserve, he transformed himself into an advocate of the Native American perception of nature with the publication of *Pilgrims of the Wild* and *Tales of an Empty Cabin*, both translated throughout Europe during the 1930s. After 1945, continued interest inspired a number of wildlife films, such as those produced by Walt Disney in the US (*Seal Island, In Beaver Valley*) after 1947, *The Great Adventure* made by the Swede Arne Sucksdorff, *Les Animaux* (1963) and *La Fête Sauvage* (1975) by Frédéric Rossif, and Jacques Cousteau's many films. The recent populist science of practical ethologists like Jane Goodall and Cynthia Moss is also widely read.

European demographic growth and the rise in living standards resulted in new social patterns and the expansion of free time, the latter accelerating after the First World War with the introduction of paid vacations, from Austria (1919) to Sweden and the UK (1937–9) via Italy, Poland and France (1936). Until the 1950s, most people spent Sundays and holidays at home, walking every other day, finding green spaces and a change of scene in the surrounding countryside or at zoos. The 1950s and '60s, marked by economic growth and the spread of the automobile, constituted a watershed, because a proportion of the population began to travel for pleasure. This trend was accentuated during the second half of the century by the extension of paid vacations and the institution of the two-day weekend. Excursions to the countryside, holidays by the sea and, later, in the mountains, and the further growth of sport and leisure activities undoubtedly contributed to the high attendance rates at establishments set up in holiday resorts, as opposed to the slight downturn among urban zoos, which occurred despite the fact that automobiles allowed more people to visit them.[3]

The proliferation of surveys after 1960 enables a more thorough understanding of the zoo-going public in recent decades. Most urban establishments fostered loyalty among their clientele: 25 per cent of admissions to Mulhouse in 1974 were season ticket-holders; 58 per cent of visitors to Vincennes in the early 1980s came at least twice a year. A study made at the Jardin des Plantes and Vincennes between 1968 and 1984 found large crowds during the spring and summer holidays, as well as in May and June on account of school outings and fine weather. Outlying zoos, meanwhile, seem to attract the public in a constant stream. At Sigean safari park on the coast, 87 per cent of visitors – schoolchildren and tourists – come between May and October. The rest of the year sees a steady flow of people from neighbouring regions. School groups and especially families (three-quarters of admissions to the Frankfurt zoo in 1969) dominate everywhere, making the majority of visitors children and adults aged between 25 and 40.

Attendance does seem to differ among countries: for example, it is higher in Germany than in France, and in France than in Spain, as confirmed by the unequal number of gardens, but there is insufficient published data to determine whether this is a constant state of affairs or if there have been progressive changes. These discrepancies are attributed by the administration of Barcelona's zoo to varying levels of education and interest, to which we would add differences in living standards. A 1964 study revealed marked disparities within countries. In what was then West Germany, for example, the attendance ratio was an average of four visits per inhabitant of the town per year in Karlsruhe, three in Frankfurt, one in Berlin and one-half in Hamburg. Such discrepancies can be explained by the size of regional populations, the capacities of individual establishments, the strength of their reputations, their pricing structures, and competition from other forms of entertainment.[4]

The social composition of attendees seems to be similar across establishments, however. In France, surveys of the 1970s found similar proportions everywhere of middle managers (around 20 per cent) to white-collar workers (15–30 per cent), craftspeople (5–10 per cent) and labourers (5–15 per cent). The situation was similar in Frankfurt in 1969, where 40 per cent of adult visitors were white-collar workers or officials. These figures confirm that the zoo is an especially popular diversion for the lower middle class. It is impossible to pinpoint the moment at which this pattern began to appear, although the inter-war period seems most likely. The proportion of labourers perhaps grew later; in 1935–40, in Geneva, for example, a visit to the zoo remained a luxury (admission was 1 Swiss franc per person, 50 centimes for children). This zoo guaranteed free entry to any child accompanied by an adult on Thursdays, and organized half-price 'people's days'. But working-class people from the zoo's neighbourhood who were children at this time recall visiting it only rarely, entry representing quite an expense for families whose monthly income was 200 francs at best.[5]

It is children who more often than not decide on visits to the zoo. The first guide to Regent's Park to be addressed to children was published as early as 1829 (*Henry and Emma's Visit to the Zoological Gardens*). The archives show that children attracted the attention of zoo management from the late 1800s, especially in the choice of attractions and animals. Their importance grew in the twentieth century thanks to improved schooling, which multiplied the number of organized visits, and the increasingly privileged

'The Squirrel Cage' and 'The Bear-Pit' at London Zoo, from an 1832 children's book.

Illustration of children's ride, Berlin Zoo, 1878, by Knut Ekvall.

Young Lions in the Zoo by Otto Dill.

place they enjoyed in families.[6] Children's imaginations began to be ruled by animals. Studies of this phenomenon are in short supply; some date its beginnings to the 1800s (although Charles Perrault's fairy tales from the previous century come to mind), and it certainly grew in scope in the twentieth century with the widespread popularity of plush toys (including wild beasts of all sorts), illustrated books and comic strips (for example, Jean de Brunhoff's *Babar*, 1931), and animated films (Disney, whose success in Europe was immediate, from 1928–32). These media either presented animals in their natural milieus but with anthropomorphized behaviour (*The Jungle Book*, *The Lion King*, *Winnie the Pooh*) or set them in a humanized environment (Babar, Mickey Mouse, Dumbo, Teenage Ninja Turtles). By transforming real creatures into imaginary ones, these books and films inverted the process that had taken place in the early modern era of enhancing the reality of animals that had seemed fantastical.

Children's attention at the zoo is at its most focused when they are between the ages of four and ten. When younger, they tend to see only smaller animals (pigeons, sparrows); when older, they lose interest in the subject to some extent. Between four and ten, however, they project their own imaginary bestiaries onto the animals they see, who thus serve as illustrations of a sort of virtual reality. Children begin by examining animals' morphologies, remarking on their characteristic traits (trunk, neck, hump) and using their own experience to identify them. They ask their names or give them names of their own. The youngest children (four to six years) speak to animals and assign them places in a human universe (house, daddy, mummy), preferring species that look like their plush toys. Older children choose those that correspond to the heroes of their books and films, and attribute similar characteristics to them. Some writers discern in this process a dulling of animal imagery and a failure to appreciate the reality of nature, which is in fact cruel and entirely focused on the fight for survival. But this perception is just as false; children are merely amplifying the anthropomorphic vision of adults.[7]

The idea that the public could be educated at zoos reached the height of its popularity between the wars. In 1933, the management of the Jardin des Plantes declared that it was necessary to provide 'French democracy' with educational pastimes. The conviction was such that the *20th Century Larousse* (1931) gave no further definition of the zoological garden than this: 'where either indigenous or exotic animals are raised and bred for the education of visitors'. Such ideas survived everywhere until the 1950s. In 1957, for example, the Czech Erich Tylinek defined the zoo as the 'best of all schools for children' and a 'complementary school for adults'. In England, interest in the educative role of zoos resulted, in the mid-1900s, in the creation of

Düsseldorf Zoo, *c.* 1930s.

courses for children, which were hugely successful. At Regent's Park, Whipsnade and Paignton, such courses dealt with biology, movement, diet, the social behaviour of big cats, reptiles, monkeys and other subjects.[8]

An intense effort to educate the public at this time is indicated by the development of middle schools and more inclusive secondary education. In Weimar Germany, schools established annexes in the countryside for nature studies. These developments were in line with a desire to organize the leisure activities of the working class. Local worthies established urban fêtes and associations for gardening, music, sports and rambling, a return to nature being associated in inter-war France and Germany with the idea of physical regeneration. The clergy multiplied its youth clubs, its gymnastic and musical unions. Trade unions founded associations to promote healthy pastimes. In 1930s France, for example, political, economic, religious and union leaders agreed that people's free time should be devoted to carefully chosen and supervised educational activities.[9]

The division was thus deepened between the culture of social élites, centred on intellectual activities and dedicated to the development of individual talents, and a more concretely based popular culture. This development was accompanied by the steady distancing of the great and the good from the world of zoos, which seems to have increased after the First World War. Other factors may have contributed to this trend, among them the increasing scarcity of notable naturalists and the aversion to unpleasant smell mentioned earlier. (Seeing ladies enter his zoo with handkerchiefs over their noses, the exasperated director of Geneva's gardens posted the following notice: 'You are visiting a zoo, not a perfumery.') In some places, the élite actively encouraged the popular appropriation of their zoological gardens. In inter-war Marseilles, the socialist municipality campaigned for teachers to take children to the zoo, and even contemplated organizing visits for adults. In 1924, the mayor decided to alter the name of the zoo's recently arrived fourth Indian elephant. Rather than Frazor, thought to be too snobbish on account of its English origin, this pachyderm was christened Poupoule, while other animals were given the name Fanny![10]

It is difficult to estimate the impact of this educational project on visitors themselves. It reached its height just as their numbers were rising dramatically, so it may have played a part in that development. In Geneva, it was adopted by the families of craftspeople, the lower middle and middle classes, and, occasionally, labourers who were hoping to improve themselves socially. Parents would take their children to the zoo as a reward for good school reports or to round off their lessons. But the élite's educational rhetoric crumbled in the 1960s in the face of less state intervention in social and cultural matters and demands from various groups for self-determination under the influence of protest movements of the time. A study of observation periods at Regent's Park in 1985 revealed that spectators stood in front of the monkey enclosure for an average of 46 seconds, and spent 32 minutes in a pavilion containing a hundred cages. Rather than indicating thor-ough examination, this is reminiscent of the speed at which television programmes, and even works of art in museums, are 'consumed'. What we do not know is whether rates of observation have changed since the advent of zoos.[11] In any case, recent studies have determined that educational aims do not feature strongly among the public's motivations for visiting them today.

In the US, zoos were recognized as cultural institutions in the same way as museums and libraries (by a bill of September 1888, for one), but with the added status conferred by high visitor numbers. In 1909, the Bronx Zoo in New York received 1.6 million visitors and $110 million in subsidies, while the Metropolitan Museum of Art in the same city received only 938,000 visitors and $8.5 million. The élite effectively considered the zoo to be a public and social necessity for the education and recreation of the lower classes, the burden of which should fall on the taxpayer. Interminable discussions of this subject appeared in the press and in political debates at both state and federal level. For example, between 1870 and 1900 the zoos of Philadelphia and Cincinnati, both in debt, passed from private to public ownership, after trials of a 'cheap day'. Chicago's Lincoln Park 'exemplified the dilemma of municipal zoological gardens in the late nineteenth century'.[12] The Bronx Zoo's forceful founder, William Temple Hornaday was a champion of patriotic regeneration by means of the zoo, 'the truest expression of American ideals'.[13] In 1899, *Science Magazine* celebrated 'the awaking genius of American Science which artificially intervened to check the destruction [of animals]'. And in 1921, Alfred Brooks went so far as to write: 'No child with access to animals would become a professional criminal.'[14]

Reality struggled to confirm such optimism. Zoos' neighbours complained not about the animals, but about

Ostriches from the 1931 *Exposition*, Jardin des Plantes, Paris.

Markhor sheep, Tierpark Hagenbeck, Hamburg-Stellingen.

the overindulgence in alcohol encouraged by the profitable, and therefore permanent, refreshment stalls. Zoos that did not admit black people were rare, but chimpanzees were often referred to as 'Uncle Remus', and Hornaday loved to underline the superiority of the white race, ensuring as it did the survival of wild animals left unprotected by Africans on their own continent. In 1904,[15] he agreed to put Ota Benga, or 'Batwa-pygmies', that had appeared at the *Universal Exhibition* on show near (and even in) the primates' cage; this experiment was halted following complaints, however, and remains an isolated case. Black people gathered in zoos to 'roll eggs' every Easter Monday, until after 1960, due to the fact that black children were excluded from the annual egg-rolling ceremony in the gardens of the White House in Washington, DC. The 'Colored Only' crowds numbered as many as 6,000 people at Washington Zoo in 1900, and 30,000 in 1905 with almost 60,000 in Phildaelphia around 1940. While zoo personnel tried to ensure the protection of the animals and to clean up and repair any damage that might occur on these occasions, Hornaday vented his impotent anger.

Despite his racial prejudices, Hornaday's contribution to the conservation of wild species is still recognized today.[16] Around 1889, he was sent on a mission by the Smithsonian Institution, under Spencer Fullerton Baird's direction, to search for the survivors of the bison massacred by pioneers travelling out to the Far West and by such famous hunters as Buffalo Bill, who effectively collaborated with the military in its avowed goal of eliminating the Native Americans who lived off these herds. After months of searching, Hornaday found 25 survivors, kept by chance in enclosures. Haunted by visions of fields of bone, he made plans for a bison farm at the Bronx Zoo.[17] Sadly, his enthusiasm was not shared by the zoo's visitors.

GLIMPSING ANIMALS' LIVES

Between the end of the 1800s and the mid-twentieth century, the simple display of form, colour and limited movement ceased to satisfy the public, which greeted the zoos without bars which started to appear from 1907 onwards with enthusiasm. At the 1931 *Exposition Coloniale* in Paris, the press marvelled at the chance to see various herbivores side by side in the 'African savannah' or to watch monkeys move in groups around their rock. Reactions were similar at Stellingen, Rome and Vincennes and in the semi-free parks which began to develop between the wars, and which were popular because they gave an impression of life in the wild.[18] In England, the public's interest in animal life manifested itself in the success of safari parks, which were well attended right from the opening of Whipsnade in 1931, and also by the success of works meant to popularize ethnology from the 1950s on.

It is difficult to say whether zoos instigated this new approach, pioneered as it was by a handful of founders such as Hagenbeck at Stellingen, or if it formed part of a growing popular fascination with nature, identifiable in the mounting criticism of zoos as they had existed until then. In any event, zoos relinquished individual, encyclopaedic exhibits as far as possible in favour of presentations in groups that attempted to recreate social structures and ways of life. Trained acts and lion-taming displays were largely abandoned after 1960 in an attempt to distance zoos from circuses, themselves increasingly under fire. Training today is often left to marine parks or sanctuaries for birds of prey.[19]

From 1910 on, important technical innovations, marked a decisive turning point in the life of American zoos, whose status was elevated thanks to developments in the cinema.

Feeding a sea-elephant, Antwerp Zoo, 1980s.

Feeding penguins, 'Polar World', Montreal Biodome, 2000.

Aquatic display, Barcelona Zoo.

Following the First World War, automobiles overflowed zoo parking lots (4,000 cars at Washington in 1918, 8,000 in 1924, 12,000 on one Sunday in November 1926). Zoos outside towns began to find their way onto tourist itineraries; San Diego, for example, was conceived in 1916 as the tourist showcase for an entire region.

Perhaps it was such pressures, unfamiliar to the directors of traditional zoos, that prompted them to renew their focus on animals in October 1924 via the formation of the American Association of Zoological Parks and Aquariums (AAZPA). This self-run scientific association held annual, often thematic conferences with regularly published proceedings. Technical treatises appeared, such as the comprehensive manual on equipment and planning by L. H. Weir. New advertising techniques found perfect clients in zoos. Hired professionals sought animal stars above all; bison were thought to be boring, so St Louis disposed of them.[20] Australia furnished unknown specimens: the first duck-billed platypus, on display for one hour every day, died after 47 days at Bronx Zoo. The elephant Toto Tembo, the first animal to arrive at St Louis in 1934 by aircraft (thus causing a sensation), met a similar fate. A giant panda brought to Brookfield in 1937 at the cost of $20,000 was followed by those of the Bronx, Chicago (1938) and St Louis (1939), which took merchandising to a new level with toys, cards and decorations. Curator William M. Mann's expedition to Tanganyika aimed more to publicize Washington Zoo (which it did thanks to his wife, Quarry Mann, a well-known journalist) than to supply it with animals.[21]

The presentation of animals was intended more than ever to captivate spectators. Denver Zoo went so far as to make on-site moulds of Dinosaur Mountain in the Colorado Rockies, so that it could be reproduced in concrete, colours and vegetation included. Kansas's Independence Zoo presented a faithful reproduction of the town at a scale of 1:3. The force-feeding of large snakes took place in ten-thousand-seat stadia (San Diego and St Louis), and zoos had trained animal 'shows' identical to those of the circus, with lions on tricycles or chimpanzees playing jazz. Concerts, business banquets, fairground rides: they all helped to sell hot dogs. Publicity professionals worked at zoos full-time, especially under the three 'show-oriented directors' – Ger Vierheller (St Louis, 1922–62), Clyde Hill (Denver, 1924-59) and William Mann (Washington, 1925–56) – as well as the sole woman director, Belle Benchley (San Diego). This second generation succeeded the first group of great directors, who disappeared around 1930: Hornaday, Madison Grant and Henry Fairfield Osborn.

Alligators in a pool, New York Zoo (Central Park).

Feeding a snake, Central Park menagerie, New York.

Indian elephants, San Diego Zoo.

Cascade Canyon, San Diego Zoo.

They showed a talent for expanding zoo coverage on the radio; Mann presented nature programmes himself. Joint promotions and unofficial partnerships were established – for example, a collaboration on plush toys between San Diego Zoo and Marston's Department Store – as did sponsorship – Firestone financed Washington Zoo's expedition to Liberia, where it had rubber plantations, and participated in the acquisition of the rhinoceros. Denver Zoo's twin polar bears, named Klondike and Snow, starred in the video *Saving Klondike and Snow*.[22] Dr Roderick MacDonald, a former Harvard professor of zoology, was forced to resign the directorship of Philadelphia's zoo in 1935. As he said: 'I didn't come here to run a menagerie or a circus'.[23]

Giant panda, Chicago Zoo (Brookfield), 1938.

Raja the elephant, St Louis Zoo.

At the start of the Great Depression (1929–33), the wealth of American zoos fell by 30 per cent, with many municipalities reducing their subsidies (Philadelphia had 400,000 visitors in 1929, and 150,000 in 1932; $50,000 in 1931 and $25,000 in 1933), but they went on to find federal backing as they were felt to be the only source of entertainment left to the unemployed. Some zoos even expanded. San Diego's attendance figures grew by half a million visitors, while Toledo Zoo constructed a reptile building, a museum, an amphitheatre, an aviary and an aquarium. Federal support confirmed the social value of zoos to such an extent that, paradoxically, the crisis of 1929 and the Second World War revived the fashion for zoos as amusement parks.

In Europe, meanwhile, individualization of animals emerged between the 1930s and '50s in parallel with the desire to know more about their lives. Suzanne Pairault, one of many authors of the time to describe her pleasure at going to the zoo, argued in 1951 that it was not just an animated tableau of exotic forms to be recognized and classified. Rather, it was like a town where the personality, character, quirks, loves and hates of each inhabitant were brought to light: '... the zoo is filled with faces.' Pairault's descriptions pay attention to animals' 'familial' relationships and to psychological portraits indicative of the popularization of Darwinian ethology. This personalization of animals was expressed through intensified anthropomorphism, a desire for physical contact and, finally, a growing appetite for the details of day-to-day life like feeding, care and reproduction. The latter had already aroused great interest during the nineteenth century; the birth of pythons in 1862 and of a hippopotamus in 1871 in Regent's Park drew large crowds. More recently, though, births have often been the only information about zoo life to be conveyed by the

The baby giraffe born at Antwerp Zoo in 1871, by Joseph Ratinckx.

media and have also inspired extensive literature for children.[24]

Public interest inspired a rash of writing describing life at the zoo by those close to management or visitors with a passion for wildlife. This genre first appeared in England at the end of the nineteenth century (C. J. Cornish, *Life at the Zoo*, 1899), following the lead of more scientifically minded visitors' accounts. Especially popular in Germany, it developed all over Europe, where it reached its peak between the 1930s and '50s before fading from view.[25] The memoirs of individuals directly involved in zoo life, on the other hand, are still popular today. A. D. Bartlett, a superintendent of the London zoo, paved the way with his *Life Among Wild Beasts in the Zoo* in 1900. Other directors imitated him, for example Hagenbeck of Stellingen and Heck of Berlin, beginning in Germany during the first half of the century. A few zookeepers did the same at mid-century before giving way to open veterinarians in the 1960s, whose role as carers enhanced their public appeal. These works, widely distrib-

uted and often translated, portray life behind the scenes, a life rich in anecdotes and always centred around a few carefully chosen animals. They let their readers duck under the barriers, enter enclosures and cages, and stand in the wings of the theatre of the wild, thus giving an impression of an intimate and individual relationship with animals.[26] Such literature presents the zoo as a way to learn to love and respect animals. Diversity was no longer enough; visitors wanted to be able to develop a sense of friendship with them.[27]

From the 1950s, under the influence of print journalism, the cinema and writing on animals that raised doubts about their presumed ferocity, their image improved. Field ethologists supported this trend with well-received studies, at first in England and Germany and, later, thanks to translations, in

Hippopotami, London Zoo, 1903.

Zoologischer Garten Leipzig

„Aufzug eines jungen Eisbären"

Rearing a young polar bear, Leipzig Zoo, c. 1900.

the rest of Europe. Ingeborg von Einsiedlen published *Mutter-liebe bei Tieren*, six editions of which were published between 1956 and 1960. George Schaller began the reappraisal of the gorilla with *The Mountain Gorilla* (1963). In fact, zoo directors had been contributing to this movement since the beginning of the century. Carl Hagenbeck, inventor of 'gentle' training and the zoo without bars, wrote in his memoirs:

> We do animals a disservice by systematically ascribing a vicious character to them, big cats especially, who as a rule deserve much better than their reputation. You can believe me when I say that I have had lions, tigers and panthers who were great friends to me, and that I was able to behave with them exactly as I would with a domestic dog, and with as much confidence.

Whereupon he related his memories of friendship among wild animals and with (tamed) big cats, furthering the idea of universal harmony that was adopted by colleagues, writers and the broader public at mid-century.[28]

Many sources indicate a decrease in violence in zoological gardens beginning in the inter-war period. Tylinek, in Czechoslovakia, wrote that people were no longer seeking attractions but friends, and that the time when zookeepers had to protect the animals was long past, the public being unwilling to tolerate aggression. Without having necessarily disappeared altogether, violence remained marginal throughout the second half of the twentieth century.[29] The new zoos without bars played a part in this change. A guide to Vincennes reported in 1957 that there had been a decline in vandalism compared to the Jardin des Plantes because the newer park had changed the status of the animals and the behaviour of the spectators. While caged animals, imprisoned and diminished, provoke mockery, species in semi-liberty retain their dignity and arouse interest.

In the US, humanization of the zoo animal had first manifested itself in 1885 with W. H. Beard's book *Humor in Animals*. According to the Bronx Zoo's first guide, bears were ferocious, but the 1913 edition describes them as being gentle and amusing. Theodore Roosevelt's adventures may have had something to do with this change in attitude. On his return empty-handed from hunting in Mississippi and Louisiana in 1907, he refused to kill a stray and orphaned bear cub. The confectioner Mitchton made a fabric figure of the spared cub; shortly thereafter, the Ideal Toy Company launched the Teddy Bear. In 1943, Walt Disney's bear ranger, dressed in jeans, replaced Bambi as the logo of the Forest Service. Another bear was fortuitously incarnated as Smokey, a cub saved from a forest fire. Adopted as the mascot of the fire brigade, he was displayed on the side of fire extinguishers.[30]

This triumph of fiction over science reached its apogee with the transformation of the elephant, the most irreducible of captive animals into a 'pet'. The elephant's strength could in fact only be mastered if it was starved, beaten, electrocuted, isolated or chained for life, with the frequent consequence of infected feet ('foot scald'). A report by Jane Frisch[31] lists these violent acts, which zoo directors described as inevitable rather than giving up animals that were capable of boosting admissions by 40 per cent.[32] The popularity of pachyderms was such that, in 1914, 75,000 donors from all walks of life responded to the *Boston Post*'s monumental publicity campaign for the acquisition of 'an elephant for civic unity' with the slogan 'People who love kids buy them an elephant'.[33]

In all cases, children were the favoured clientele of zoos, under an educational pretext that conferred a philanthropic value on them. In Philadelphia, around 1933, Baby Zoos had immense success in the US. The commercial targeting of children also ensured the perennial success of zoos: the generation brought up with them took their offspring there in turn. The American press has been extravagant in its exploitation of the subject, as is evidenced by accounts of an accident on 16 August 1996 at Chicago's Brookfield Zoo, where a child who had fallen into the gorilla compound, was saved by the female Binti Jua. The gorilla received a thousand letters of congratulation and a medal from the

American Legion, but no offer of reintegration into a suitable forest. Without entering the imaginary domain, Frans de Waal reminded us that compassion exists in the animal world too.[34]

Here, then, was a new opinion of zoos. For many, the zoological garden had become a peaceful place to which humans came to see tame animals (taming was still a requirement) relieved of the presumed ferocity of nature, individualized and humanized animals with whom bonds of respect and friendship could be established. An illustration of this tendency can be found in the serene sculptures, devoid of the Romantic violence of examples by Barye and his followers, made from life by Rembrandt Bugatti at the

The famous Chicago Zoo gorilla Binti Jua.

Walking Jaguar, c. 1904, by Rembrandt Bugatti.

beginning of the century in the Antwerp zoo.[35]

At this time too, societies of friends of zoos succeeded the zoological societies of the 1800s, with similar objectives but less exalted memberships. In France, the biggest of these was formed in Mulhouse in 1949 by members of the middle classes, precisely those to whom zoos and their educative role appealed the most. Its first committee included a shopkeeper, a teacher, an office worker, a technician and an orthopaedist.[36]

Enthusiasm for zoos also found expression in the wildlife magazines which proliferated in Europe after 1945. The French journal *Zoo Ami des bêtes*, launched in 1951, centred around domestic animals, but it did run a column on the zoo at Vincennes which announced births and new arrivals, illustrating in anthropomorphic style their individual characteristics and integration into human society. The journal's tone became more naturalistic in the 1960s, but reports from the zoo – presented as a haven of peace and plenty – remained the only coverage of non-domestic animals.[37]

Protective associations shared this approach.[38] In the nineteenth century, the SPA investigated massacres of elephants, and in 1906 it participated in the creation of a society dedicated to their protection. Its position on zoos, more or less indifferent up to that point, became more favourable between the wars. It monitored living conditions – for example, the transport of animals to the *Exposition Coloniale* in 1931 – but without questioning the principle of captivity. It inspected Vincennes in 1934 and declared itself satisfied. Changes occurred over the years within the organization; between 1890 and 1925, for example, tensions ran high between supporters of 'noble' animals (the horse in particular), mostly members of the aristocracy and upper middle class, and those who advocated priority action on behalf of domestic animals (dogs and cats), mostly members of the lower middle class. The latter group won the upper hand in the 1920s and the emphasis was transferred to the development of homes for dogs or the fight against vivisection, while an anthropomorphic and individualized understanding of animals was adopted. This was also applied to zoos.[39]

MOUNTING CRITICISM

Visitors' displeasure was expressed as early as 1880–1900 in donors' demands for better conditions in zoos. It was overtly expressed in the inter-war period by 'a group of regular visitors' to one park, and by 'an animal lover and her friends' (women were a significant new voice), who deplored – again without questioning the propriety of zoos themselves – the insufficient care, dirty enclosures, confined animals, brutal keepers and tiny cages.[40] In Mulhouse, in the 1960s, visitors and even Friends of the zoo made pointed remarks about the size of the cages. A survey carried out in 1969 indicated a clear majority opinion: 67 per cent of respondents felt that the animals had to be rehoused before new acquisitions could be considered.[41]

From this fertile ground grew a more radical kind of criticism. In Geneva, readers of one newspaper rebelled in 1929 against a projected zoo, arguing that God had made animals to give life to nature and not to fall into 'slavery'. The French writer Colette announced in 1953 that she would never again visit a zoological garden, not even to see animals that she had watched and loved for many years: 'There is no beautiful, human face, no snowy coat of fur, no sky-blue feather that can enchant me, if it is striped by the intolerable parallel shadows of bars.' Societies for the protection of animals made a few early attacks: on Helsingfors in Finland at the beginning of the century, and on Geneva in 1935, denouncing the 'cruel curiosities' there in the name of respect and freedom for, and preservation of, wildlife.[42]

The killing in 1958 of a two-year-old child, Julia Ann Vogt, by a lion at Washington Zoo acted as a catalyst for latent disquiet in the US,[43] even among some zoo directors; Theodore Reed, for example, accused zoos of humiliating animals. His criticism of children's zoos prefigured P. Batten's: reproduction was induced to provide young animals for sale to petting zoos, animals that could not survive the maltreatment inflicted by children, who were unable to distinguish between playmate and plaything. The educational value of such establishments was nil. Stephen Kellert extended these investigations to adults in a 1979

inquiry initiated by the Zoological Parks in American Society. It ended in the same admission of public disinterest as in Europe; visitors were engaged only in the anecdotal or the extraordinary. The book *The Human Zoo* (1969) by the zoo director Desmond Morris supported Henry Bergh's line of thought: animals were never considered in their own right. Batten felt that the 1973 Animal Welfare Act (US Department of Agriculture) offered no protection for animals outside the zoo.[44]

Batten's revelations were all the more damning because, as a former zoo director, he detested the 'vociferous defenders of the Humane Society of the USA'. Possessing animals from Africa and Indonesia himself, he spent five years searching America for a zoo to house them. Beginning in March 1974, he visited several hundred zoos and accumulated three thousand photographs. *Living Trophies* contains 104 notes and telling technical evidence of overpopulation, unsuitable conditions, groupings of antipathetic animals, mutilation and illness. Batten demonstrated that high mortality was disguised with rigged figures; only animals that had survived for more than three months were included, this artifice giving credence to the myth of increased longevity.[45] In 1995, an American Zoological Association conference paper stated: 'It is still the rule rather than the exception for most zoo animals to spend the greater part of each day in concrete cubes or cages ...'.

This position gathered support in the 1960s. In England, the Captive Animals' Protection Society had been founded in 1957 to oppose the brutal training and poor conditions of animals kept by travelling menageries and circuses; its members fought for tighter control of these enterprises to the point of their suppression. From the 1970s on, it extended its attacks to Greek and Romanian bear-baiters and circuses in the Eastern Bloc, whose shows revolved around animal acts, and pressed European institutions for harmonized legislation. The Society opposed the dolphinariums that first appeared in the US in 1938, in England in 1964 (Morecambe) and then throughout Europe, being adopted by zoos (Barcelona, Nürnberg) and amusement parks (Parc Astérix). It joined an international movement led by organizations promoting the protection of ocean life, such as Greenpeace, marine-life enthusiasts such as Cousteau, and scientists. It participated in the reintroduction of captive dolphins to the sea, as well as in campaigns that cut the number of dolphinariums in England from roughly 70 at the beginning of the 1970s to two twenty years later.

In 1984, the actress Virginia McKenna, who had appeared in wildlife films (*Born Free*, 1964) and written *On Playing with Lions* (1966), was outraged, as were the general public, by the accidental death at Regent's Park of the elephant Pole-Pole, with whom she had filmed. McKenna founded an association called Born Free Zoo Check to inspect zoos and finance the creation of African reserves to protect animals in the wild. In the 1980s, small underground groups mounted liberation operations and demanded the abolition of zoos, which they considered to be 'concentration camps'. Zoo Check videos, filmed in a hundred zoos world-wide, showed a great many animals whose behaviour indicated serious psychological distress; these were studied by specialists such as Roger Mugfort. 'Polar bears pacing aimlessly up and down, a concrete travesty of their natural environment': the British *Daily Mail* newspaper gave an article of March 1993 on the subject the headline 'Do zoo animals go mad?'[46]

Criticism became louder and more radical elsewhere, especially during the 1970s. In Italy, newspaper articles, books and television programmes (*La zoo folle* on RAI in 1974) denounced animal captivity and the pointlessness of zoos. An association called Ambiente e Fauna opposed plans for a large zoo in Rome. Germany saw the publication of critical studies and the foundation of groups such as Menschen für Tiere or the Internationale Zoo-Initiative, which argued that only one zoo should be maintained in Europe.[47] In France, dissent flourished among groups – scientists in the first instance – alive to the need for the preservation of nature. In 1965, Jean Dorst, a professor of the Paris Muséum, published *Avant que nature ne meure*, which predicted the inevitable destruction of wildlife and saw no hope beyond nature reserves and breeding in captivity. This is why he criticized zoos which plundered wildlife, kept animals in the 'worst conditions' and did not encourage reproduction. Examples of British opposition to zoos included publications by Desmond Morris (*Abnormal Behaviour in Animals*; *The Human Zoo*, 1969) and John Berger (*Why Look at Animals?*, 1981).

From the 1970s on, opposition to zoos was constant in the US. The Society for the Prevention of Cruelty to Animals and the animal-rights movements fought against poor treatment; People for the Ethical Treatment of Animals (PETA) based its position on recent discoveries in ethology and animal psychology that proved animals' closeness to humans.[48] The Ark Trust militated against the detention of primates.[49] Debra Jordan, a former wild-animal handler, stated: 'In fact it appears that zoos are more interested in promoting human recreation and their commercial image than they are in promoting the welfare of the animal they ostensibly claim to protect.'[50] Sadly, the 143 zoos accredited by the AAZPA have spent more than a billion dollars since 1980 without improving the conditions of captivity.[51] The video cassette *Born Free* (1993), showing the madness suffered by captive animals as revealed by the *Pittsburgh Post-Gazette*, was criticized by some, but its verdict was confirmed by *Behavioral Therapy*, a study made of the bears in New York's Central Park Zoo by T. Desmond. The Navajo Nation demanded the liberation of the animals of Window Rock Zoo in Arizona, their capital city, because maintaining these creatures in captivity disturbed the natural order of things.[52] Peter Singer and Animal Rights supporters expressed the view that 'both humans and animals will be better off when (zoos) are abolished.'[53] Their position on scientific research in zoos was in accord with that of the American Association of Zoo Veterinarians: 76 per cent of zoos claimed to participate in research, but the results were never published.[54] (The exceptional work of the ethnologist Frans De Waal had been conducted in establishments that were themselves exceptional in the US and Europe: San Diego, Arnhem.) United Action for Animals aimed 'to promote public awareness of vivisection on zoo animals', zoos having worked with laboratories for a long time: Hagenbeck had supplied 8,000 rhesus monkeys in 1920, and 12,000 a year between 1936 and 1938. According to Batten, 'experimental euthanasia is not uncommon in zoos.' Artificial fertilization and the freezing of sperm, the 'frozen zoos' beloved of journalists,[55] were for the most part achieved in laboratories specializing in human infertility treatment. [56] As for the cloning of rare animals, it is very much in the news to this day.

The ground was thus prepared for more militant opposition. Some European associations, the Jeunes Amis des Animaux among them, demonstrated against the dilapidation and lack of space at the Jardin des Plantes in April 1973, and against Parisian bird-sellers in December of the same year. The following January, a group led by the explorer Paul-Emile Victor, the lecturer in medicine Jean-Claude Noüet (who went on to co-found the Ligue des Droits de l'Animal in 1977) and representatives of the World Wildlife

Fund occupied the grounds of the Tropicanim Society, specialists in the importation of exotic animals, and found a charnel house among the minuscule cages. There were loud reverberations in the press and among the public as the extent of this disaster came to light. They were amplified by the death that same month of the male panda which had just arrived at Vincennes. The coincidence provoked severe criticism of zoos' failure to adapt and their part in the general waste of wildlife, thus forcing the French government to announce new regulations on the importation of animals and the establishments that kept them. That same year, Philippe Diolé, an explorer of deserts and oceans and a companion of Cousteau, published *Les Animaux malades de l'homme*, a successful work that condemned animal deaths caused by smuggling, confinement, exhibition stress, inactivity and overcrowding.[57]

Although there were some late conversions to the cause (Diolé had taken part in the inauguration of the marine park at Antibes), opposition mostly came from the young and from new associations who were developing a global understanding of the animal world and who were principally interested in wild animals, emphasizing previously neglected aspects of their welfare (mortality rates, psychological damage, conservation). Some observers advocated the transformation of zoos into farms for the education of children and the conservation of wildlife in its original habitat, while others simply wished to separate good establishments from bad ones because they considered zoos to be a useful way to maintain a link between people and nature and encourage an interest in preservation.[58]

In this climate, the old protection associations really had to rethink their commitment to the idea of everyday contact with animals. The Lyon SPA took note of Diolé's book and in 1975 decided to organize an investigation by its youth branch into living conditions in zoos. The annual zoo visit, however, was successfully extended to all members in 1976, proof that conditions met with their approval, while the Society's journal continued to publish favourable reports until 1980. The zoo was felt to be necessary for the conservation of threatened species and animals born in captivity, whose release was impossible. It was thought to be acceptable if the animals were clean, well fed and provided with enough space. The creation of zoos without bars in the same area, and the similar renovation of Lyon's zoo itself, were well received on the grounds that the animals would have a better life there than if they were at liberty. In the end, it fell to readers, especially the younger members, to voice criticism. The results were catastrophic. In 1982, a letter written by one of the Society's groups following a visit to the zoo at Saint-Martin near Lyon, an establishment still reminiscent of nineteenth-century gardens, shook the entire association:

> Is this really a wolf, this animal that no longer hunts, no longer runs, no longer lives ... What, in this kind of place, can children learn that is of value? They see the animal life-size, in the flesh, but they also experience the despair and degradation of slavery, the madness even! Is this what zoos are for?

To those who approached wild animals as if they were pets and who thought of the zoo as a friendly place of domestication and individualized contact, teenagers brought up on adventure books were expressing a more ecological point of view.[59]

The democratization of television during the 1960s and the broadcasting of a great number of wildlife programmes let European viewers see animals at liberty: biotopes became the touchstones which invalidated zoos. Parks where animals enjoyed semi-freedom appeared to many, even to some zoo opponents, to be an acceptable compromise.[60] In addition, the understanding of animals was changing. New disciplines such as ethology and animal psychiatry, popularized in books and wildlife magazines, brought with them an enhanced awareness of the complexity of animal behaviour and psychology and the problems created by confinement. The evolution of ecological sensibility as a reaction to urban living made people more sensitive to the preservation of wildlife. The principle of domination was itself challenged, for example by the animal liberation philosophy popularized by the Australian Peter Singer in 1975, which was disseminated with some success in Germany and the Anglo-Saxon world, though less so in Italy and France, and which resulted in the creation of national movements. The Universal Declaration of Animal Rights by UNESCO in 1978 was another result of these shifts in consciousness.[61]

In 1969, Desmond Morris had identified the zoo as a product and symbol of the alienation of urban life: overcrowding, anxiety, aggression and nervous disorders characterized both. The town was a human zoo, the zoo a reproduction of the modern city. Other commentators included zoos in a critique of social institutions. The Canadian psychoanalyst Henri Ellenberger compared them in 1960 to psychiatric hospitals, describing the similarity between their keeper-patient-visitor relationships and psycho-pathological syndromes. This concept developed in a more politicized way in Britain and Italy, where the zoo was included among the various forms of capitalist alienation (along with hospitals, old people's homes, prisons and factories). Emilio Sanna, a journalist specializing in prisons, Sardinian crime, ecology and ethology, all unorthodox subjects at the time, described the zoo in 1976 as belonging (along with prisons and asylums) to the concentration-

Giraffe house, London Zoo, 1992, by Britta Jaschinski.

Llama and Malayan tapir in cages, London Zoo, 1992, by Britta Jaschinski.

Washington, DC, Zoo, 1992, by Candida Höfer.

Bronx Zoo, NY, 1999, by Candida Höfer.

Empty Tank, 1974, by Gilles Aillaud.

camp ethos created by modern societies. He drew parallels between the changes in these institutions in light of public protest: greater openness, less segregation and reintroduction to a natural milieu were all occurring in safari parks, outpatient hospitals and the prison system. In France, these issues were seldom aired. Michel Foucault, writing on prisons, clinical institutions and insanity, did not raise the question of zoos, an indication of the French intellectual's lack of practice in thinking of humans and animals together.[62]

During the 1980s and '90s, the controversy became more intermittent, reflecting larger trends in social protest. In France, most wildlife magazines and programmes claimed the middle ground once more, advocating the selective screening of establishments, persuading themselves of the benefits for the preservation of certain species, and concentrating their criticism on smuggling. Associations abandoned their zoo visits and discarded their educational arguments, both increasingly rejected by their memberships; zoos never became a hobbyhorse for them, unlike

Snake in Water, 1967, by Gilles Aillaud.

Lion, 1971, by Gilles Aillaud.

circuses and travelling menageries, which were attacked unanimously from the 1970s on. Instead, they continued to be treated as poor relations by animal-protection societies, doubtless because it was difficult to question the legitimacy of domestication.[63]

Surveys show, however, that a proportion of the European population remained opposed to animal captivity (81 per cent in England during the 1980s) and refused to go to the zoo. The imprint of this sensibility can be found in a number of literary and artistic works. At Vincennes, the photographer P. Reverdot found not exoticism but a world of concrete. In his *Figures de l'enfermement*, the painter Gilles Aillaud presented animals reduced to decorative elements: the *Serpent* (1972) became a mosaic, the *Lion* (1971) became a rock, and in *Piscine vide* (1974) the formless mass of a hippopotamus is absent, only its designation remaining on a placard.[64] This critical attitude forced all zoos to adapt.

THE ADAPTATION OF ZOOS

The long-term growth in attendance levels was reflected in an increase in the number of zoos in Europe (50 in 1912, 180 in 1965, 302 in 1995, excluding Russia), which was in turn consistent with their spread world-wide (1,165 in 1993, of which 545 were in Asia). These statistics provide no more than an estimate, however, because a great many small establishments are not listed in guidebooks or international journals like the *International Zoo Yearbook*. Until the early 1960s, this expansion was driven by the desires of a 'captive' urban population. In Germany (twenty zoos in 1912, 45 in 1965 including East Germany) and the UK (eight, 35), new establishments spilled out into new regions from the inter-war period on. Southern European countries gradually began to make up ground. Italy, which had three zoos in

1912, boasted eleven by 1965 in its northern and central cities. France (five, twelve) saw expansion mostly in its northern, most heavily populated and wealthiest half, while its coastal cities opened aquariums (eleven by 1959) devoted to either local or exotic marine life. After 1950, there was a noticeable increase in Eastern European countries (ten in Yugoslavia, nine in Poland, and fourteen in Czechoslovakia in 1965).[65]

From the 1960s to the present, growth accelerated in response to further increases in attendance, while distribution of zoos nationally and across Europe adapted to the rise in weekend tourism and annual vacations. Some new zoos were created on the outskirts of towns, within a radius of between 20 and 50 kilometres, and thus were a feasible day-trip on Sundays and during the week for school groups. This trend was accentuated by the fashion for safari parks and amusement parks combining fairground attractions and the exhibition of dolphins, such as Europa-Park near Rust in Austria and Parc Astérix in France, which required large tracts of cheap land. Other establishments were created in tourist areas, to capture the summer trade. This new positioning occurred in all countries, but particularly in southern Europe, especially France (twelve zoos in 1965, 35 in 1995), Italy (eleven, 25) and Spain (three, ten). While development stagnated in the Eastern Bloc for economic reasons, which also came into play in the former East Germany, the rich countries of the north-east saw marked growth, especially Great Britain (34, 72).[66]

Faced with increasing competition, zoological gardens began to specialize. After aquariums came marine parks, vivariums, ornithological reserves and parks for local wildlife or farm animals. Most zoos established after 1950 were founded not by zoological societies but by individuals, in the mould of Hagenbeck at Stellingen. A few of these

Octopus, Monaco aquarium.

were former big-game hunters or former zookeepers; many
had worked at ordinary jobs before setting off on a more
adventurous path, and their social backgrounds appear
modest in comparison with those of nineteenth-century zoo
founders. They often managed their own enterprises and
were, with their families, the sole proprietors, building and
buying land and animals over the years as profits rolled in
and further opportunities presented themselves. Many
claimed to have loved animals since childhood and
expressed a wish to establish relationships with them that
would destroy the myth of their ferocity once and for all.
The interest shown in these establishments by protection
societies and wildlife magazines in the years 1950–70 is

Aerial view of Ljubljana Zoo.

Nikolaev Zoo, Ukraine.

quite understandable, as they were participating in the trends towards personalization and anthropomorphism exhibited by older gardens, just as they shared their personnel.[67]

But this way of looking at animals (which ignores the ecological dimension), a lack of capital and, for many, the desire to make a quick profit often led these new owners to neglect habitat and environment: they built small zoos resembling the nineteenth-century Jardin des Plantes, with rows of cramped cages, grilles, bars, haphazard lodgings, chains or even fenced-off caves. Later on, the inappropriateness of this situation was recognized by some of them; it was condemned at the time by the directors of more established gardens. The spread of this type of zoo, common in eastern and southern Europe, notably in France, was a significant factor in the explosion of protest in the 1970s, because it took place in direct opposition to the long-term trend towards larger cages and enclosures.[68]

It was in order to put a stop to this deteriorating state of affairs that the opponents of these small zoos, along with the directors of a few well-established ones, successfully lobbied for legislation to be passed in some countries. In the UK, the Zoo Licensing Act (1981) placed restraints on methods of acquisition of animals and imposed minimum

standards with respect to the environments in which they were kept. In Switzerland, an edict of 1981 set minimum surface areas for cages and enclosures. In France, a 1976 law confirmed the right to keep and use wild animals while at the same time recognizing their status as sentient beings, which presupposes living conditions compatible with biological imperatives. This law requires any person responsible for an establishment to hold a certificate vouching for his or her ability to look after animals, keep the public informed and assure their safety. It also makes prior authorization compulsory for any public opening.[69]

Circuses were also the object of regulation. A British act passed as early as 1925 had had as its purpose the control of training and taming methods. In 1959, Scandinavian countries adopted a law forbidding the use of rare and protected animals, a measure also taken by Finland in 1989. In France, circus directors, protection societies and the ministers concerned signed an agreement in 1981 that forbade violent training methods and the presentation of idle animals in the ring, limited the number of species to be used and required animals' native characteristics to be taken into consideration when performances were being designed.[70] But these measures did not produce the desired effects, because they expressed only minimum requirements that were rarely checked in any case. A 1992 Swiss enquiry found that regulations remained imprecise and insufficient.

In an attempt to forestall the development of a debate on the very principle of confinement, a number of venerable public and private establishments denounced circuses, travelling menageries and hastily erected zoos, arguing for selective grading. In France, Jean Richard, owner of the zoo at Ermenonville, founded the National Association of Private Parks and Zoological Gardens in 1970. It awarded seals of approval to 'good' establishments to put a stop to the 'carnage' Richard perceived – and, of course, to the fierce competition and damage to zoos' collective image. In 1975, the director at Vincennes created the Syndicat National des Directeurs Français de Parcs Zoologique, which went on to organize such conferences as the 1977 colloquium on zoos' role in education. These initiatives were modelled on the precedents of the International Association of Directors of Zoological Gardens, founded in 1962 in Anglo-Saxon countries to promote their educational and scientific aspects at international conferences, and the Ibero-American Federation of Zoological Parks, established in the same year and with similar aims.[71]

Justification of zoological gardens, based on the reiteration of nineteenth-century arguments, continued until the 1950s, perpetuating the idea that a zoo is a 'pleasant and familiar refuge' (as the zookeeper R. Riedtmann put it).[72] This argument carried weight with the protection societies, at least until the 1960s, and above all with the public.

The promotion of the educational dimension of zoos continued as well, their recreational value seeming insufficient to 'justify putting wild animals in cages', as the director of Paignton put it in the 1970s. Numerous educational initiatives, aimed principally at children, were devised across northern Europe. Antwerp developed educational designs after 1945: taxonomic information beside the enclosures; signs explaining ethology, zoo-geography or ecology; guidebooks, films, exhibitions and conferences; and a natural-history museum. Beginning in the 1960s, the larger establishments in the Benelux countries, the UK, the two Germanys, the USSR and elsewhere employed educators who worked with associations and schools, organized expeditions, made films, ran in-house newspapers like those of Antwerp (created in 1949) and Barcelona (1962), and gave lectures and courses for children (Cologne, London), students and teachers (Frankfurt, Paignton). At Regent's Park and Whipsnade in the 1970s, 80 per cent of participants were primary-school children. In France, the educational role of the zoo was not really encouraged until 1976, at which point it followed the example of northern Europe.[73]

Younger children were the object of particular attention. At Stellingen, they were allowed to ride ponies, giraffes and elephants. This initiative was reprised at Paignton in the 1960s, but mostly it inspired the creation of petting zoos, which appeared in Berlin and London between the wars before spreading throughout Europe in the form of annexes to mainstream establishments, as at Basel and Peaugres. These used domestic dwarf species chosen for their docility, or the young of wild animals (monkeys, elephants, felines), thus reinforcing children's anthropomorphic imaginations. At the park at Thionne, a guinea pigs' village complete with church, school, town hall and houses made cartoons a reality. This policy undoubtedly contributed to healthy attendance figures.[74]

By 1962, the US possessed a quarter of the world's zoos, and by 1974 it had 305. The 75,000 children of the 'baby boom' contributed to a revolution in their appearance, or at least served as a pretext for it. Following the success of the animated film *Bambi* (1942), Walt Disney opened Disneyland in Anaheim, California (1955), complete with exotic animals. Attractions diversified according to changes in fashion, developments in information technology being particularly important.[75] In 1949, television penetrated this world. The director of Chicago Zoo, R. Marlin Perkins, instigator of 'Zooparade', reached an annual audience of 90 million viewers. The broadcasting rights, going for as much as $1 million to the national network station NBC, saved zoos yet again, and their attendance figures shot up between 1940 and 1960 (41 per cent in Philadelphia, 240 per cent in San Diego), as did those of competing leisure parks that included animals. In 1991, fifteen million visitors converged on West Edmonton Mall in Alberta, Canada, which had a petting zoo.[76] Partners such as supermarkets entered the picture. Thus the zoo bowed before the altar of American finance and consumer culture.

The desire to restore a credible scientific impetus to European zoological establishments in the 1950s and '60s manifested itself at the Barcelona zoo, which transformed its newsletter into a journal for the popularization of ethology in 1970. This example was followed in France by the scientifically trained directors of public parks (who were not satisfied to settle for mere recreation, nor even education), before being adopted by a few private zoos during the 1970s. Once again, Mulhouse played a pioneering role, co-ordinating a small-scale collaboration with the University of Strasbourg in 1965–7 on the study of the social behaviour of macaque monkeys.

In fact, the earliest such work dated back to the beginning of the century and the development of the statistical study of the behaviour of small rodents, the scientific world's reaction to Darwinian ethology. A form of primatology based on flexible observation methods and empathy

with animals appeared in some zoos, the only places to possess anthropoid apes, which were still very rare in Europe. The Englishman R. Garner studied the artistic endeavours of a chimpanzee in Manchester around 1896; Alexander Sokolowsky did the same in the 1920s in Hamburg, where he was co-director, as did Desmond Morris in London in 1956, subsequently publishing *The Biology of Art* (1962). From the inter-war period on, however, the most important studies of intelligence and language were made in laboratories, as the survival rates of anthropoid apes in captivity began to improve. From the 1960s on, zoos found the analysis of group behaviour to be most

Desmond Morris with a young chimpanzee.

Hothouse section of the monkey house, Darmstadt Zoo.

An open enclosure within a glasshouse: monkey house, Darmstadt Zoo.

tempting. For this, too, there were precedents: in London, where Solly Zuckerman observed a group of baboons in the inter-war period (*The Social Life of Monkeys and Apes*, 1932), and in Zurich, where Hans Kummer worked during the 1950s. Some zoos specialized in this field, notably Arnhem in the Netherlands, whose research centre enabled the famous studies by Frans De Waal on the social behaviour of chimpanzees; these were made from a colony that was carefully isolated from humans and whose make-up closely reflected that of groups in the wild to allow a complex social life to develop.[77]

These, however, were exceptions, insofar as there was a fundamental contradiction between the requirements for space and isolation made by science and the criteria of public satisfaction, namely for smaller enclosures providing better views and for smaller, less expensive groups that ensured a diversity of species. Most work undertaken in zoos was less concerned with this kind of fundamental research than with a kind of applied ethology, the zoo-psychology founded by Hediger between the wars to rationalize the conditions under which animals were kept. This avenue had been opened with the appointment of veterinarians as directors at a number of gardens (Lyon in 1910, Paris in 1917), because their work in traumatology, parasitology and zoo-psychol-ogy was less focused on improving knowledge of species in and of themselves, and more on keeping captive animals in good health.[78]

The one true scientific dimension zoos could claim as their own was the preservation of species, which, it appears, did not require special installations of any kind. Discussion of this idea began in the inter-war period as governments and scholars became aware of the scope of destruction in the colonies. It was supported initially by scientifically trained zoo directors, who found in it a task in keeping with their own sensibilities, and by acclimatization societies, for which it represented a valuable application for their work (which, since the turn of the century, had been limited to captive reproduction). It was then universally adopted, becoming the principal argument in the face of criticism of zoos, insofar as it constituted a justification of captivity. From the 1960s on, the argument was strengthened by projects of reintroduction of some species into the wild. This was an inversion of the utopia of acclimatization: the new dream of a humankind with delusions of godhood.[79]

The four functions of recreation, education, research and conservation which from the 1960s on formed the central credo in the justification of zoos were well received by the public. Surveys, readers' correspondence and press articles show that educational efforts and the conservation of species were perceived by visitors, journalists and even animal protectionists as essential and justifiable functions of any zoo.[80] And yet they were far from being effective. A vet at the Paris Muséum entrusted with the supervision of these initiatives estimated in 1991 that only 10 per cent of establishments had taken them on board in any real sense. Moreover, even if activities with schoolchildren were consistent with a move towards education, the same cannot be said with any certainty about families. Surveys from Frankfurt to Mulhouse have shown that 80 per cent of visitors questioned claimed to have learned something, but one 1979 investigation noted that they were less sensitive to the need to respect nature than hikers, even after their visits.[81]

So it seems that zoos' necessary adaptation to change was restricted to superficial transformations of setting and presentation.[82] This process of adaptation accelerated during the twentieth century as the shift towards a demand for more space and a more natural environment devalued existing installations with ever greater speed and obliged their swift replacement.

○ 10 THE ILLUSION OF LIBERTY

In replacing the image of a confined animal with that of one at liberty, the new style of presentation at Stellingen appears to have been responding to what may have been an unconscious repulsion against any symbols of captivity at all. The sensational inauguration in May 1907 of this zoo, which sprang as if by some miracle from a potato field, marked a definitive break with the past and was feted as a liberation of zoo animals. The Frenchmen J. Huret and P. Morand saw in its German founder, Carl Hagenbeck, the 'benefactor who was first to open the cages'.[1] In England, Peter Chalmers Mitchell wrote the introduction to Hagenbeck's memoirs from 1909 published under the title *On Animals and Men*; Jouan, in 1951, changed it to *Cages sans barreaux*.

The animals' apparent freedom at Stellingen was attractive to visitors, who found themselves in an imaginary realm that simulated, and stimulated, the illusion of their own escape. The scenography of illusionistic zoos rests implicitly on the belief that civilized human beings can rediscover a life of freedom through contact with the wild. From being a passive captive behind bars, the animal, on Stellingen's fake rocks, came to play the part of the wild creature it no longer really was, developing an illusory freedom that would be modified, and justified, later.

CAGES WITHOUT BARS

Stellingen was built at the same time as Stuttgart, shortly after Halle and just before Munich, in the midst of fierce competition in Germany. As a supplier, Hagenbeck was attempting to revive his own market by introducing a new style of exhibition that contrasted with the architectural exoticism that the Berlin zoo had taken to its peak. Between 1847 and 1911, 25 architectural firms had created approximately 40 projects for Berlin, projects that Stellingen's rocks, needing no architects, radically rendered obsolete.[2]

When, in 1902, he purchased a few hectares near Hamburg, Hagenbeck, at the pinnacle of his fame, had

Carl Hagenbeck, *c.* 1903.

Building the artificial mountain at Stellingen, c. 1911.

barely more than ten years to live – he died on 14 April 1913. Two years after Stellingen's memorable inauguration, he collaborated in Buenos Aires's centenary celebrations. He was trying to realize one of his earliest dreams, inspired by the bucolic attitude of the 1700s:[3] to make all apparatus, all attempts at classification – indeed, any trace of human intervention – vanish in favour of the animals themselves, presented in groups in an environment that simulated nature, sometimes called the 'geozoo'. Hagenbeck intended to turn the animals in his warehouse to a profitable purpose by acclimatizing them at Stellingen and exhibiting them – for example, the 28 elephants destined for the Ringling Circus and the Luna Park on Coney Island in New York, which he assembled into a memorable convoy. At Stellingen, he also created a permanent circus theatre and ethnographical exhibitions and had his own lion-tamers. As an effective warehouse, the zoo could exhibit sizeable groups of animals, competing with one of its own clients, Hamburg's urban zoo.

Ever since the Berlin exhibition in 1896, Hagenbeck had been putting the finishing touches to a kind of ditch inspired by the architectural ditches (or ha-has) employed in eighteenth-century landscaped gardens to visually annex neighbouring territory; the landscape gardener Insch, whom Hagebeck hired at Stellingen, was a master of this technique. First made to measure and then tested, from 5 to 6 metres wide and steeply sloped, they amounted to impassable obstacles, replacing cages, grilles and bars. Later, it would be discovered that the zebras and kangaroos at Hannover would not try to leave a plot of land if it was surrounded by even a shallow dip.[4] When these ditches were filled with water – around monkeys, for example – the enclosure became an island (a favoured motif of Baroque scenography), recalling Potsdam's Peacock Island (1795) – a sort of animal Cythera of the kind that had been organized around 1888 by a syndicate of eau-de-vie merchants on a small island off Helsinki.[5] In 1896, Hagenbeck, with the help of the Swiss sculptor Urs Eggenschwyler, had taken out a patent on a 'Panorama of Natural Sciences' whose plateaus, separated by this type of ditch, could support numerous animals, as well as a group of Eskimos, at which visitors could look down from overhead. This zoo-theatre was reminiscent of that created by the Russian actress Sophie Gebhardt, to be seen in St Petersburg until 1909, as well as the zoo at Skansen, near Stockholm, founded by Dr Hazelius, an open-air museum of rural habitats and plant life. Animals moved freely in natural surroundings, with wolves, for example, living in a cave.[6]

Seen from over 50 metres away,[7] fake rocks dominated Stellingen's drab site, bringing to mind the geological improbability beloved of earlier painters of flat Nordic countries such as Hieronymous Bosch, who depicted imaginary Dolomites in blue, a microcosm of the wonders of the universe. Springing from some chthonic domain, mysteri-

View of Carl Hagenbeck's Tierpark from the 'Russian Tower'.

The artificial mountain, Stellingen.

ZOOLOGISCHER GARTEN, LEIPZIG   Berganlage (Aufstieg zur Alm)

The artificial mountain, Leipzig Zoo, *c.* 1905.

Köln a. Rh. Zoologischer Garten. Eisbärenklippe

Polar-bear crag, Cologne Zoo, *c.* 1910.

Illustration of the rocky enclosure, Hannover Zoo, 1870, by Oskar Friedrich Schmidt.

ous and inviolate, rockeries were used to decorate Baroque parks as well as fairground fêtes and the gardens of Catholic convents. Advances in mountaineering made the silhouette of the Matterhorn fashionable, and it was reproduced in the goat enclosure at Rome, while Stellingen's Algerian mouflons gambolled on the slopes of the Atlas Mountains. Rocks had, of course, been used in zoos for many years. J. Molinos' cave project at the Paris Muséum had found its way to Boulogne in 1860, Berlin's aquarium in 1869, Hanover in 1870 and Leipzig in 1899, augmented by a water-fall.[8] In Cologne, the zoo designers imitated the basalt of a Neanderthal valley. On one side, the 40,000 cubic metres of Stellingen's hill accommodated a polar landscape – polar bears and penguins moving around the whitewashed concrete – and, on the other, an equatorial garden overlooking a pond containing 500 aquatic birds, placed near the enclosure of a large herd of herbivores. Joseph Pallenberg, in

his guise as a specialist in prehistoric wildlife, brought huge saurians to life, rising out of the water; the elephant, housed with no physiological plausibility in a cavern (they live in forests and on the savannah), must have emerged from the concrete, grey on grey, like a mammoth in an animated wall-painting. This scenography was deployed in a restricted space, estimated by Loisel at 22 hectares. However, Boulin-eau's plan[9] (1/2250 scale) shows just 4 hectares arranged into two climates, with the longest side at 180 metres in 1907. A small zoo but an immense theatre, Stellingen's space was unified by its ditches and made to seem larger by means of all kinds of artifice. Display areas made from verti-cal rocks compensated in height for the lack of surface area. Viewers watched animals from below, like actors on a stage, a common arrangement from then on. From the entrance, gigantic beasts sculpted by Eggenschwyller lent the zoo colossal scale in the German style, dwarfing visitors. As at a

Main entrance, Hagenbeck Tierpark, Hamburg-Stellingen, *c.* 1908.

circus, everything was done to captivate, and contemporary accounts hailed the place's genuine success: 'One has the impression of something extraordinary ... something rare ... something unprecedented.'[10]

Did the animals at Stellingen appear genuinely 'free and in all their splendour'? Movement, characteristic of animals in the wild, was encouraged by some of the presentations: monkeys frolicked unfettered on the rocks, for example. The prairie visibly accorded the herbivores a certain ease, but J. Huret pointed out that the carnivores remained in cages, and panes of glass still separated visitors from the snakes; Loisel reported birds of prey chained to the rocks, and the birds on the pond had clipped wings. The animals could scarcely turn around in their minuscule shelters. Their behaviour was modified by the constant endeavours of a trainer, who persuaded them to tolerate each other with varying degrees of success: fighting broke out between the lions loaned to the Parisian *Exposition Coloniale*. In addition,

Loisel emphasized the failure of acclimatization efforts at Stellingen, estimating 100-per-cent mortality among the flamingos and gazelles.

Hagenbeck, trusting in the results of earlier tests, refused to install heating, which in any case would have been impossible in the wooden stables and ineffective for animals in transit. Zoo directors like Ludwig Heck of Berlin and William T. Hornaday of the Bronx Zoo in New York were violently opposed to Stellingen as representing an affront to the scientific and educational role of zoos, which required clear visibility and careful classification. It is true that the width of the ditches made the enclosures seem small, depending on the spectator's point of view. Bourdelle of the Vincennes zoo dismissed the 'mystique' of Stellingen's rocks, imposed even on animals from the steppes. He attempted to limit the use of concrete, but in vain, as the architects plastered it over everything, down to the least significant outbuilding and a good proportion of the ground

Polar-bear enclosure, Hamburg Zoo, 1994, by Britta Jaschinski.

as well; he could not even avoid it in the giraffe house. Although he did not condemn Hagenbeck's ditches, around 1934 he perfected a glass partition that offered animals better protection than bars from a public that fed them poorly and passed infections to them.[11] The 'rock' at Nürnberg, again made of concrete poured over a wooden structure, collapsed in 1930. Pachyderms, attracted by visitors' offerings, would injure themselves on the spikes marking the ditches' edges; the latter also caused animals to fall, often with lethal consequences, as at Lyon as recently as 1998, when many monkeys drowned. The predominantly

Germanic Union of Zoo Directors, at their international conference in Basel in 1935, were explicit in their disapproval of Stellingen: 'Journalists do not understand that instead of just contemplating animals ... [on] various artistically arranged rocks, [it is important to] pay attention to ventilation, to work on the walls as well as the working spaces.' A preoccupation with hygiene developed, hidden, as at Vincennes, behind the rocks. The rhinoceroses' concrete stables had clean corners and light-coloured ceramic tiling to facilitate cleaning. In the end, the naturalistic approach revealed its limits: Frankfurt's rocks, modelled

Constructing the artificial mountain at Nürnberg Zoo.

Outside zoos, naturalistic effects were used in dioramas, which also benefited from the contemporary revolution in dermoplasty. This technique for stuffing animals began with the skeleton, which was then bulked out with muscles and skin, with astoundingly realistic results. In Stockholm, G. Kolthoff created a 'biological museum with panoramas of animal life' in 1893. The zoo at Schönbrunn presented, in its octagonal pavilion, dioramas of local wildlife past and present in its natural habitat, as did the Frankfurt natural-history museum. In Bern, around 1930, the painter H. Würgler collaborated with the naturalist G. Ruprecht in an impressive series of reconstructions. The Paris Muséum abandoned its 'Eden of dust and factory of classification', replacing it with a spectacular installation, the Gallery of Evolution.[14]

in the form of a mountainous island on the Serengeti plain, jarred noticeably with their surroundings.[12]

The real limitations of the animals' apparent freedom were even suggested by the vocabulary used to describe these zoos. The Germans devised the term *Freianlage* – a free enclosure or enclosure of freedom – which they defined as the 'restoration of real territory [to the animal] in all senses of the word'. In France, the term *semi-liberté* implies the existence of a complementary semi-captivity. At Mulhouse, an 'impression de vie en liberté' was preferred, and they even used – surely this was a slip of the tongue? – the term *simili-liberté*: imitation freedom![13] After Stellingen opened, Huret's guide used the word *paradis*; Zukowsky made it the title of his book on Stellingen, *Paradis allemand des animaux*, and in Rome the herbivore enclosure was named Paradise, perhaps a reference to the wooded gardens of ancient times.

Carl Hagenbeck in the 'Northern Lands' diorama, Tierpark Hagenbeck.

Diorama of the Arctic regions, Jardin des Plantes, Paris.

Diorama of the Anglo-Egyptian Sudan, Jardin des Plantes, Paris.

A comparable quest for realism was expressed in early German animal photography. From 1863 on, Ottomar Anchütz published snapshots taken at the Breslau zoo that might have been taken in Africa and elsewhere. The renowned hunter C. G. Schilling was sent there on a mission by a Berlin photographic firm. In 1905, a *Guide du photographe animalier* appeared. The famous Zeiss factory at Jena sponsored the Leipzig planetarium in 1925. Close-ups and snapshots were particularly useful in making a zoo animal appear to be free. Lutz Heck published *Zoo en images*, an album of photographs taken at Berlin. Of 176 shots, 61 were close-ups of animals that had actually been photographed at the zoo, 88 appeared to have been taken in the wild, and only a few showed discreet signs of captivity; these were mostly rustic fences or old walls, shown with such domesticated animals as a Swedish calf. This tome formed part of a long series of books on zoological gardens that intermingled, with no indication that they were doing so, the wild world with the world of zoos. The Dolders, for example, lent their renown as African wildlife photographers to *Le Grand Livre du zoo*, many of whose photographs seem in fact to have been taken in the wild.[15]

The cinema went even further, film turning its gaze on wild animals from its very beginning. Bengt Berg wrote the screenplay for *Derniers unicornes*, filmed at Stellingen, whose inauguration was also captured on film. Carl-Heinrich Hagenbeck recorded the soundtrack to *Jungle à tigres* there. The Leipzig zoo was saved from bankruptcy by

A tiger in a *Freianlage*, Antwerp Zoo.

becoming, in 1920, a film studio. Its 18-metre-high rock and its waterfall served as scenery, and its lions, bred in-house, as actors: the tiger Michel appeared in *Samson and Delilah*, but, during the filming of *Lucretia Borgia* (1923), pounced on the cameraman on seven occasions, while Caesar (another wild animal) escaped. Film became a more powerful promotional tool for zoos than posters, which vied for attention with those of circuses: always in pursuit of the sensational, fearsome tiger followed gigantic elephant drawn by Gustave Soury or Rosa Bonheur. These posters avoided any hint of captivity. Ludwig Hohlwein juxtaposed the pelt of a spotted feline with that of a black panther, the two big cats, with piercing eyes, seeming ready to pounce; the 1929 poster by O. Baumberger for the Zurich zoo contrasted an elephant's static mass with the fluid lines of pink flamingos. Images of felines became symbols of power and freedom during this period. They lent their strength to spirits, German beers and, around 1930, to Chauvet rum, helping to evoke a now-dead 'colonial' nature, suggested by a pith helmet forgotten in the jungle.[16]

'THE MYSTIQUE OF THE ROCK'

At one blow, Stellingen had left every other zoo looking outdated. While, as we have seen, a great many of them adopted its rocky landscape, at least in part, everyone wanted a *Freianlage*, a free enclosure, at the very least: Antwerp in 1909; Milan simultaneously with Rome; Nürnberg in 1912; Leipzig in 1927. Budapest became entirely rocky, while Hellabrunn, whose director, Heinz Heck, was Hagenbeck's son-in-law, had a free enclosure, as did Berlin in 1932, even before Ludwig Heck's departure, and again under his son and successor Lutz. John Hagenbeck founded the zoo of Ceylon in 1928. Hagenbeck dispatched Schroeder to America, where he became a zookeeper in Detroit; San Francisco, St Louis and Cincinnati all adapted to contemporary tastes. In 1956, the new Indian national zoo at New Delhi was designed from scratch by Carl-Heinrich Hagenbeck; 80 years after Carl Hagenbeck's death, the whole of Romanèche-Thorins in France continues to bear witness to his influence.[17]

A few spectacularly successful examples stood out. The site of Rome's zoo, on a hill near the Borghese and Medici villas, was well suited

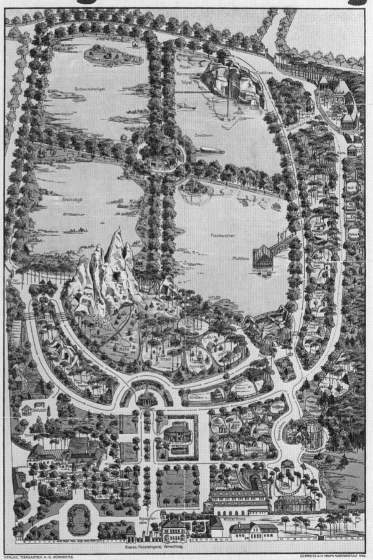

Poster of Nürnberg Zoo, 1911.

The artificial mountain, Budapest Zoo, 2001.

View from the artificial mountain, Budapest Zoo, 2001.

An old tomb in the grounds of the National Zoological Park, New Delhi.

to theatrical effects. Twisting footpaths, rocks and islands surrounded by water crowded its grounds. This zoo was produced, 'ready to visit', by Carl Hagenbeck, who provided everything from plans to construction, from animals (282 mammals, 682 birds and 56 reptiles) to the director, Theodor Knottnerus-Meyer, his scientific adviser. The Italian climate allowed zoology and botany to be combined. The elephant was housed in a ruin to provide an archaeological reminder of its location. When Rome's zoo was renovated in 1933, the use of contemporary materials – steel and glass – was intended to glorify technology.

Hagenbeck's links with England were complex, the German drawing some of his inspiration for the layout of Stellingen, as we have seen, from the English countryside. Animals were presented naturalistically in Manchester, one of the canals at which was bordered by a panorama populated with them. And it was in England that Hagenbeck found one of his most enthusiastic disciples in the person of Peter Chalmers Mitchell, who was convinced of the virtues of acclimatization: animals from tropical regions could be made to adapt to the cold, he believed, while confinement increased mortality rates. These ideas were also being put forward by the hygienists of the time; Chalmers Mitchell was in touch with Leonard Hill, an advocate of open-air living.

During the 1920s Chalmers Mitchell began the construction of London Zoo's Monkey Hill, which accommodated baboons without heating, in an area around which they could move freely. Revised several times, Monkey Hill included rocks from 1925. In 1909, Hagenbeck's book *Von Tier und Menschen*, was published in London under the title *Beasts and Men*. The famous Mappin Terraces were built in 1913 on Chalmers Mitchell's instigation, with the entrepreneur Mappin's generous help (generous because it yielded him no financial reward). The Terraces displayed a judicious adaptation of the principles behind Stellingen; their designers borrowed from Antwerp the idea of exploiting the vertical potential of limited terrain by constructing overlapping levels. The Terraces' complex, interlocking structure, almost frightening in its daring, differentiated them from Stellingen. Deer on the ground were overlooked by bears, themselves overlooked by the inevitable restaurant. The hidden flow of visitors poured along an 87-metre curve constructed from reinforced concrete in imitation of a limestone outcrop. A spectacular sight, this vertically organized space was something of a technical event, hailed by specialist journals. A little later, the National Park of Scotland, first planned in 1908, was set up as a wildlife reserve in the grounds of a stately home. A donation from the Carnegie UK trustees enabled the construction of a tropical birdhouse (1925), an island for baboons, and rocky enclosures surrounded by ditches that were used for polar bears in particular.[18]

The most prestigious descendant of Stellingen remains the zoo at Vincennes. The Paris menagerie, by this point, was cutting a sorry figure. *L'Illustration* of 18 August 1923,

Elephant house at the old Rome Zoo, 2001.

Aviary in the post-restoration Rome Zoo, 2001.

Monkey house in the post-restoration Rome Zoo, 2001.

African rhinoceros, Bois de Vincennes, Paris.

comparing it to the Sydney zoo, called it a 'humiliation for the capital of France'. After the closure in December 1932 of the zoo of the *Exposition Coloniale*, the creation of Vincennes' future zoo by a private society fell through, but the Muséum successfully intervened with its architect, Benjamin Chaussemiche, soon replaced by the architect of civic buildings and national monuments Charles Letrosne, and with help from the Ville de Paris. Visits were made to the major European zoos such as Munich, Budapest and Berlin; Rome stunned Bourdelle, and Stellingen enchanted Achille Urbain, a professor in the ethology of wild animals at the time. Bourdelle wanted to

> give [the animals] the maximum number of outdoor activities, to put them back in a natural setting and the surroundings of their original habitat as completely as possible, [and to give it] a spectacular character within the boundaries of good taste.

Beginning in 1932, he saw to the proper orientation of the enclosures, sheltering them from the wind behind the highest of the rocks bordering the site. The kangaroos' terrain was extended to give them room to jump; the monkeys had space to move about among the trees on their island.[19] The town's chlorinated water, fatal to animals, necessitated the

digging of a separate well.

Scenography was harder to maintain across Vincennes' 14 hectares than across the 2 hectares of the original Stellingen. The technical services were ingeniously hidden away, the bears' rock serving as cover for the electrical transformer and the administrative buildings. A major network of paths offered a variety of routes, where twists, steep alleys and viewpoints followed one after another, just like the new tourist roads with their panoramas and overlooks. The marine animals' glazed underground gallery inside the rock allowed viewers to follow the seals' underwater movements. The entire ensemble was crowned by a tall rock whose double spiral staircase, as at Chambord, separated streams of visitors ascending, gazing at the view of Paris and then descending once more.

What satisfied the crowds at Vincennes, which was immensely popular? Were they completely taken in, as if they had been at the theatre?

The 'difficult problem of giving prisoners the appearance of liberty' was not lost on the press. In fact, the architects spelled it out: 'It is a kind of theatrical scenery in cement, a stylized wild landscape, sometimes soothing, sometimes severe and impressive, but always and openly artificial.' As at Stellingen, scientific classification was abandoned in favour of spectacle; everything became an invitation to escape, perhaps more so than a convincing illusion, something that had become difficult to achieve in the cinematic age. More engineers than vets visited the zoo's building site. The rocks' framework of concrete beams supported a series of rails and, on the surface, a fine metallic mesh, all of which was more suitable than wood for the imitation of crystalline stone. Inaugurated on 2 June 1934, Vincennes was without contemporary rival, due to its rapid construction and costs that remained relatively under control (23 million francs).[20] The great central rock, 67 metres high, advertised itself as an Eiffel Tower for eastern Paris: its function as a symbol, as part of the identity of an entire *quartier*, exceeded any of a zoo's real needs. Facing the real Eiffel Tower, a hymn to metal construction, Vincennes displayed a tower of concrete disguised as rock, whose message was: 'Here cling the vestiges of a life of freedom, in untamed nature.' In 1993, the zoo was renovated, as befit its position as an 'emblem of the 12th *arrondissement* ... many Parisians would see its destruction as a violation of their heritage'.[21]

Vincennes indirectly relayed the ghost of Stellingen to Mulhouse, which was visited by Urbain in 1950 as adviser on an extension featuring rocks and perimeter ditches. In 1973, plans were laid to assemble a geozoo of polar wildlife; a new bear enclosure offered spectators two views of the platform, built entirely of concrete. Hagenbeck's name was mentioned in the guidebooks. Lyon, too, modernized its old installations in 1971.

During the same period, Barcelona expanded and modified its rocky enclosures, which dated from 1931. In 1962, its new scenography added three levels of interlocking, super-

Crowds by the lion enclosure, Bois de Vincennes, Paris.

View of the 'Grand Rocher' from a cave, Bois de Vincennes, Paris.

imposed circles; as at Stellingen, visitors were able to take in all of the African fauna at a single glance. Despite a few trees, however, the zoo retained its reputation for boiling heat.[22] Although a great number of these revisions were born of technical artifice, fashion or ostentation, they were nevertheless evidence of a desire to see wild animals in appropriate settings. This desire persisted at a time when

Flamingo pool, Barcelona Zoo.

Budapest Zoo, 2001.

Budapest Zoo, 2001.

Rome Zoo, 2001.

geometric concrete forms, the result of contemporary innovations in architectural design, were becoming omnipresent in urban settings, and created an aesthetic in opposition to the naturalism of Stellingen.

ABSTRACT ANIMALS

Stellingen opened just as Picasso was unveiling his revolutionary painting *Les Demoiselles d'Avignon* in 1906–7. A few years later, as the architect Berthold Lubetkin crossed Europe from east to west, fleeing the Russian Revolution, he visited every bastion of abstraction. Trained in the radical thinking of Russian Constructivism, he studied reinforced concrete with A. Perret, joined Konstantin Melnikov in Paris to build the USSR's pavilion for the 1925 *Exhibition* and, finally, founded the Tecton Group in London. Lubetkin was to become the only architect of the twentieth century whose most significant work would be done for zoos. An heir and disciple of Russian Suprematism, at once mystical and poetic, Lubetkin believed that it was the artist's duty to replace the real world, ruined by technique and thus ripe for destruction, with his own creations. In 1933, in the beautiful countryside at Whipsnade, Lubetkin built a villa for himself whose rigorous geometry signified 'humanity

taking control of nature'. This was the concept that would be expressed by the enclosures created by the Tecton Group for a handful of zoos, enclosures that made the group's name.

The circular gorilla house at London Zoo, completed in 1933, was an aesthetic arrangement of curved, interlocking volumes; blessed with technical perfection, it both provided for the animals' care and handling and gave them an environment of sterile, harmoniously proportioned surfaces and flooring of varied texture that became more comfortable the nearer they were to those observing them. In short, this was a perfect setting. The open-air penguin pool at London Zoo unfurled its spiralling shapes in which the black and white birds circulated, appearing to the spectators, envious of such accommodation, like dancers in a choreographed routine. This enclosure became the symbol of the British architectural avant-garde of the time. Dudley Zoo, conceived as a whole and set in the grounds of a medieval castle, called in the Tecton Group to provide a tourist development with animals and a restaurant. Lubetkin created sculptural settings for the animals and a striking ravine for the bears around a natural cavern. Animals served to animate his mathematically precise volumes connected by harmonious curves of concrete, a substance he mastered to perfection. Sanitation, plumbing and visitor circulation were all as well thought out as they would have been for a hospital. Lubetkin favoured animals that enhanced his aesthetic: the black and white of the penguins put the finishing touch to his dramatic composition, described by Paul Morand as a 'concrete island decorated with penguins'. The cries of the gibbons were

Exterior of the Lubetkin/Tecton gorilla house, London Zoo.

Interior of the Lubetkin/Tecton gorilla house, London Zoo.

Black-footed jackass penguins, London Zoo, 1993, by Britta Jaschinski.

Lubetkin/Tecton penguin pool, London Zoo, 1979.

London Zoo, 1992, by Candida Höfer.

Lubetkin/Tecton penguin pool, London Zoo, 1977.

amplified by a vault to attract crowds. Whipsnade's elephant shelters were justly called silos, whose cylindrical form and blind walls they shared. The unit of measurement on which they were based was the movement of elephants who, when deprived of space, walk endlessly in circles: German research suggested that there was no point in building large enclosures for pachyderms, because their movement always fell into small, repetitive patterns. Thus Lubetkin moulded his concrete around the animals' behaviour in captivity.[23]

Lubetkin had his disciples. The zoo built in Warsaw in 1936–7, a former animal warehouse, was designed by Van Zabinski, who aspired to create settings that would highlight each animal's distinctive features. It had 'artistically stylized' rocks, a curving, domed elephant house in concrete, and raised enclosures. At Mulhouse, Roger Holl inclined 'towards an original architectural work that both respects the animal's living conditions and gives it an ideal setting for the visitor. The structure built at Mulhouse retains nothing of rock but its name'. It was in fact a kind of abstract sculpture in concrete, rising out of a pit, whose close-fitting blocks allowed primates to climb up to the visitors' level and then retreat again. For the zoo's centenary (1968), multicoloured cubic habitats were conceived for the monkeys, enlivened by plastic and metal and with ceramic

Lubetkin/Tecton bird house/aviary, Dudley Zoo.

partitions, where they could move around in a totally abstract setting. Many vets appreciated a genre that encouraged hygiene, but felt that such installations would date within a decade.[24]

In 1937, the architect Fredrick J. Kiesler, commenting on Lubetkin's models on display at the Museum of Modern Art in New York, had doubts about the functionality of his shel-

Lubetkin/Tecton elephant house, Dudley Zoo.

Lubetkin/Tecton polar-bear pit, Dudley Zoo.

Madrid Zoo, 1995, by Candida Höfer.

Polar-bear enclosure, Bremerhaven Zoo, 1993, by Britta Jaschinski.

ters. Indeed, Regent's Park's elephant houses, designed shortly afterwards and in similar style by Hugh Casson, were imposing in their brutalism, but when an elephant died in 1980 she had to be dissected on the spot because it was impossible to remove her body. The smell threw her neighbour, the famous Pole-Pole of the film *An Elephant Called Slowly*, into a blind panic, and she started to spin round in circles, dying six weeks later.[25] Kiesler mounted a war cry to the effect that zoos were obsolete, instead advocating naturalistic animal parks, for which, he believed, the way had been paved by Stellingen.

'TERRITORY IS A NATURAL CAGE'

The directors of Stellingen-style zoos sought ways to conserve wild animals within them, as well as arguments to justify their existence. Heini Hediger, a German-Swiss zoologist, began his career shortly after 1930 as an herpetologist in New England, before travelling to Morocco on an expedition. He was a contemporary, roughly speaking, of Achille Urbain, who, through Flammarion in 1940, published *Psychologie des animaux sauvages*, a summary of Anglophone research, but who disappeared after the war without having produced much work. Hediger, having read Konrad Lorenz, especially on the subject of domestication (1940), took an interest in human-animal relationships. Shortly before the Second World War, he published work in Basel, Bern, Berlin and Stuttgart on captivity and the psychology of trained animals. The first edition of his *Wild Animals in Captivity* appeared in Basel in 1942, as well as his *Studies of the Psychology and Behaviour of Captive Animals in Zoos and Circuses*, in German and then in English. Hediger led an expedition to the Belgian Congo alongside Verschuren in 1948.[26] He was interested in how animals occupied space, in their territories and their reference points, as well as the distances they fled when confronted by humans, which varied according to species and circumstances. Though he was open to the new field of comparative psychology, Hediger seldom, if ever, applied it outside the bounds of circuses and zoos, which he directed in Bern, Basel (1944–53) and Zurich.

Hediger's book *Wild Animals in Captivity*, translated into French after the war and followed by several others, became bedside reading for zoo directors hungry for practical advice. His innovative approach consisted of using the principal tenets of the new ethology to modify the conditions of animals in captivity, which up to that point had been determined purely by practical considerations. He proposed the reconstitution of social groups, the enhancement of enclosures, and the use of training as a distraction from boredom.[27] He calculated the dimensions of cages according to each animal's distance of flight, so that beasts would not feel permanently terrorized by spectators; other Hediger designs prevented animals from killing themselves by throwing themselves against the bars. He did not deny the pathologies created by zoo life, which he studied in detail – stereotyped movement, for example – but accorded them minimal importance. Having seen zebras in the Congo rubbing themselves against termite mounds, Hediger had the idea of installing a concrete mound in their zoo enclosure. They had hardly seen the thing before they flung themselves on it, destroying it in the process. When it was rebuilt, they strained with such force to get to it that it took several men to hold them back. This powerful impulse was interpreted by Hediger as an excellent response to his invention, which was essentially true, but an ethologist might also have considered that such an explosion of energy was typical of an intense frustration which had previously found no outlet. The recurring story of escaped animals spontaneously returning to their cages was used to evade suggestions that zoo animals should be set free in their original habitats.

To justify captivity, Hediger referred to the physiological beliefs of the time: 'The animal who lives in freedom does not live freely, no more so in space than in its behaviour towards other animals.'[28] This statement ignores migratory animals, of course, be they herbivores or anthropoids, as well as those who, like the Siberian tiger, wander over immense territories of between 100 and 1,000 square kilometres. The argument met with great success nonetheless. Gerald Durrell responded that 'By caging an animal, one deprives it of the possibility of making organized journeys.' In 1992, a scientist, I. Debyser, gave Hediger's notion the following succinct formulation: 'Territory is a natural cage.'[29]

Hediger's linking of the notion of freedom with spatiality was very much in keeping with trends in German scientific thought in the 1930s. The philosopher Martin Heidegger gave courses on animality at the University of Freiburg im Breisgau in 1929–30; his aim was to define the existence of inanimate and animate objects through the nature of their relationships with space, the way in which, in his words, they 'access what is available to them'. An animal, not very different in this respect from a stone, is almost entirely at one with where it lives. Heidegger shared this point of view with Max Scheler, author of *Die Sonderstellung des Menschen im Kosmos* (1928): 'The organism ... is in an environment within which its behaviour is never elaborated.' The German term *Benommenheit*, chosen by Heidegger to describe animal behaviour, means 'numbness': it can also be translated as 'absorption', 'engrossment' or 'stupor', but M. Richir has proposed the more accurate expression 'behavioural captivity'. Freedom is impossible

for an animal, consumed as it is by its biological functions. This is how a zoo, which fulfils these functions (food, water, shelter), can be said to entirely replace a wild animal's territory. Hediger was evidently well versed in contemporary research into the nature of time, since he entitled the second chapter of *Wild Animals in Captivity* 'Space-time', an expression used by Erwin Strauss, from a different perspective, in *Du sens des sens* (1935). Hediger, considered a pioneer of comparative psychology, studied animal behaviour almost exclusively in zoos and circuses. This observational method brought him closer to the behaviourists, who were experimenting in artificial settings themselves, a practice which ethologists would soon judge to be entirely inappropriate.

Hediger's world, then, was that of the behaviourists J. B. Watson and Ivan Pavlov. Their works, well known in Germany in 1926, were refuted by the German pioneers of animal ethology, Erwin Strauss, Lorenz (whose 1935 article on the territory of birds Hediger cited), Niko Tinbergen and Jakob von Uexküll. All of these writers developed the theory of an active environment in which intentionality had its place, even among animals.[30] A 'perspective taking the evolution of species and ecosystems into account' provided the (now classic) basis for their ethological textbooks.[31] Writing about animal territory no longer mentioned mechanistic theories, incompatible as they were with the extremely diverse utilization of territory by its animal owners.[32] As for birds, being deprived of flight might, according to Hediger, seem drastic to visitors, but not to the birds themselves:

> The need to fly, as a physiologically necessary activity, is non-existent among birds of prey ... The need to fly is the most striking form assumed by the need to move, which is felt most keenly by man himself. Man

is projecting this need in typically anthropocentric
fashion onto the captive animal.

In fact, Hediger was ignoring what any physiological hand-
book would have taught him: 'The originality of the
anatomy and physiology of a bird stems from its ability to
fly. Its whole organism is modified for the purpose.'[33]

Hediger's practical input contributed to the extended
success of Hagenbeck's zoos, while improving, if only
slightly, the survival of the animals in them. All construction of illusionist zoos in the early twentieth century centred
around settings that benefited humans and not animals,
who cannot have been fooled by the concrete that enclosed
them. Hediger's theories, grounded in Cartesianism, were in
fact anthropocentrist. And, despite its shortcomings,
geological illusionism would lead to the botanical illusionism of fake savannahs, implanted, at great expense, in zoos
graced with exotic names, in the course of the next generation.

○ 11 THE IMITATION OF NATURE

From the end of the 1960s, the increasingly perfect imitation of nature became the major concern of many zoos. Tropical and polar climates were recreated at Montreal's Biodome. Its commercial success incited Disney to bring its vast means to bear on the creation of a little corner of Africa in Florida, sealing the union of the zoo and the theme park. These famous achievements became reference points for Europe. Even so, the perfection of the illusion was not enough to mask the concern caused by the vertiginous disappearance of wild species. Zoos therefore endeavoured to become wildlife conservatories. Despite real progress, however, they were unable to avoid high mortality rates. Genetic decline remained the immutable physiological law in captive populations, the documented example of

Przewalski's horse adding further proof if proof was needed. Comparison with biotopes discredited *ex situ* conservation, while changes in attitude and developments in the natural sciences made it difficult to accept the idea that 'captivity should be taken as a reference point for freedom.'[1]

NATURE, A HARD TASKMASTER

The 'wildlife park', a formula offering animals 'almost natural freedom' in Europe, appeared around 1930, inspired by the vast territories of preserved wildlife that were being created at the time, especially in Africa.[2] Located far from towns in large, open spaces – 60 hectares at Nürnberg, 50 at Hellabrunn (1928) – these parks were sometimes set in the surroundings of historic castles (Branféré) and became destinations for the weekend expeditions favoured by the advent of the automobile.

Among the first wildlife parks, Whipsnade occupied 200 hectares in Bedfordshire, to the north-west of London, and was accessible by train. Illustrious benefactors like the Duke of Bedford, Alfred Ezra and Lady Yule offered animals; an Indian elephant was sent from London Zoo. The collection of deer presented an opportunity for observation, and captive birds attracted free migrators under the watchful eyes of ornithologists. In the face of unhoped-for crowds beginning with its opening in May 1931, Whipsnade was expanded. Unlike at

Views of the Montreal Biodome.

Washington, DC, Zoo, 1992, by Candida Höfer.

London Zoo, where enclosures were slotted like specimens into a hierarchically organized space, the animals' own territory seemed paramount and offered viewers the pleasure of intruding within it. (At Clères Park, before Whipsnade, it was said that 'the master ... aspire[d] only to acclimatize and breed exotic species, keeping segregation to a minimum.'[3]) Even so, the fairly restricted enclosures and elephant silos at Whipsnade symbolized the limits of a system that would never be able free itself entirely from constraint.

The desire to approach animals that was evoked by wildlife parks had been expressed by European artists since the beginning of the twentieth century. The German painter August Macke, trained in Cologne, used zoo animals as models around 1911, to express the communion between humans and other creatures in a single brightly coloured space, unhindered by barriers. Macke was killed in the First World War before he had time to complete a décor for a zoo's restaurant, but he did finish *Le Petit Zoo* (1912), *Le Grand Zoo* (Munich) and a 1913 triptych.[4] The Swiss artist

Paul Klee, in his canvas entitled *Zoo*, juxtaposed fields of colour which were given meaning by animal hieroglyphs. For the heirs of Surrealism like the Cobra group, just after the war, wild animals represented not just anticulture, but the reverse of rationalism. In his *Discours aux pingouins*, the Danish artist Asger Jørn connected with the absolute otherness of wild animals, covering similar ground to the German Conceptual artist Joseph Beuys, known for his astonishing meditations on the inter-penetration of human and animal territories. In 1974, Beuys lived for several days in the René Block Gallery in New York in a glass-walled space which he shared with a coyote (the totemic fox of some Native American peoples).[5] Reaching for a new organization of the living world that would put an end to humanity's destructive supremacy, Beuys opposed the 'new playthings of the consumer society'; dangerous wild animals were now being kept by people in their homes.

The permeable barrier between human and animal that was highlighted by Beuys's work, and the exchange of their territories, began to be used as a selling point for safari

Wolves in 'Wolf Wood', Whipsnade, 1934.

Lions at Whipsnade, 1934.

Zoological Gardens I, 1912, by August Macke.

parks, which advised visitors to 'Get in touch with your instinct!' Going one step further, the Marquenterre Park in France proclaimed itself to be 'the opposite of a zoo; here the humans are caged and the animals are free'.[6] This system – what Lorenz called the inverted cage – became widespread: at Bellewaerde, near Ypres, boats moved through a recreated jungle. Visits to parks in the visitors' (or sometimes the park's) own cars were reminiscent of African explorations, so this type of establishment assumed the name safari park. Such establishments opened at Saint-Vrain (near Paris), Gelsenkirche and Tüdderen (Germany), Arnhem (Netherlands) and Tamazoo (Japan).

In fact, the imitation of nature that so many visitors found so pleasing was achieved at the cost of a good deal of artifice. The traditional cages and enclosures survived (usually hidden, but occasionally quite visible), even at the

African Sigean Reserve in the midst of genuine freedom, where the big cats were kept inside at night during the winter and, occasionally, during the day as well. Adjoining the open African expanses where ostriches and rhinoceroses roamed was a traditional zoo, with lines of cement-floored enclosures that were not always spacious. The Fota Wild-park in Ireland raised two leopards taken from Namibia around 1986 along with others, in enclosures of between 1,442 and 2,613 square metres. Those responsible for maintaining safari parks came up against even tougher constraints than zoos in the renewal of their stock: a feline older than ten years was no longer fit for exhibition (the Panthera association of Geneva welcomed a few veterans); monkeys in regular contact with the public would become dangerous as they grew older and had to be replaced frequently. In 1979, Estérel Safari Park had about 60 young monkeys captured in Senegal to replace its stock.[7] Visitors meanwhile would not tolerate the provision of living prey for the carnivores, even at a time when the public was captivated by the carnage in the film *La Griffe et la dent*. The administration of Panaewa Zoo in Hawaii solved this problem by installing clay figures in the tiger enclosure that were operated by a computer accessible to the public, so that they could, on demand, see the tiger 'hunting' a rabbit or squirrel (in clay) that could then be 'saved' by a computer![8]

Herons in the Zoological Gardens, 1913, by August Macke.

Safari parks were growing in popularity in Europe just as the creation and rebuilding of traditional zoos was drawing to a close in East Germany. Safari parks were forbidden there, considered dangerous, artificial and unhygienic – although it should be noted that the East's low level of car ownership made them unworkable in any case. A few forests were transformed into reserves, most commonly for bison, for example at Moritzburg near Dresden. As the venerable

Entrance, Dresden Zoo.

Tiergarten stood in the western half of Berlin, in July 1954 the citizens of East Berlin decided to create their own zoo in the grounds of Friedrichsfelder Castle, conceived by the landscape architect P. Lenné. Contemporary photographs show volunteers digging in line; schoolchildren broke open their piggy-banks, and donations from individuals and businesses made the 1955 opening possible.

The success of zoos was immense in East Germany. Approximately 40 local ones, 30 large zoological gardens, a few nature museums, twenty-odd aquariums (mostly in the south) and the four prestigious, historic zoos – Leipzig, Dresden, Halle and East Berlin – received six million visitors annually between them. Approximately 30 zoos opened during the 1950s alone, of which twelve were renovations; fifteen or so were inaugurated around 1960, around eight in the following decade, and another one around 1980. They employed a sizeable workforce, doubling the number of members of the Association of European Zoos (ECAZA). All of these zoos had areas for children, and many displayed miniaturized ethnological installations and traditional crafts – mills and forges. The animals were exotic for the most part, except in approximately twenty zoos specializing in indigenous species, which could also be found in many public gardens and along the routes of botanical tours.

Bernhard Grzimek in 1958 and Heinrich Dathe at the time of the inauguration of the zoo at Leipzig both stressed the zoo's educational importance and its social role in the recreation and congregation of workers. According to Grzimek, the traditional zoo was a 'model of a people's state', as well as a sign of their profound humanity; Latin countries, where bullfights were staged and the cruel captivity of singing birds was practised, had very few zoos.[9] Zoos 'founded on the concept of dialectical materialism' demonstrated the truth of Darwinism and the theories of Pavlov. Ostankino, near Moscow, was a living laboratory, a worthy contributor to the 'material and intellectual progress of the entire Soviet Union'; it included a museum dedicated to transformist doctrine and a scientific cinema, built in grandiose neo-Classical style.[10]

Faced with commercial competition in the form of safari parks, some traditional zoos adapted, eliminating visual obstacles between visitors and animals and allowing the latter a bit more comfort and freedom. During the 1960s, glass panels became standard around the pools containing marine mammals, as did infrared lighting that could change day into night (thus creating what were called nocturamas), a process that gave viewers access to the lives of nocturnal animals. Naturalistic zoos installed glazed observation

Glassed-in tiger enclosure, Hannover Zoo.

boxes above enclosures planted with moderate amounts of vegetation. The chimpanzee enclosure in Detroit attracted something of a following in Europe. Over a hectare in size, its eight viewpoints allowed the animals to be seen from just 6.5 metres away, the carefully chosen plants permitting unobstructed views.[11]

Additional activities were developed by many zoos. Some safari parks attempted to revive the past, situated as they were around castles or stately homes whose grounds they enhanced and populated with animals. In England, Woburn Abbey, home of the Duke and Duchess of Bedford, was revived in this way. This installation distinguished itself by gathering together the last surviving examples of the species of stag known as Père David. The National Park of Scotland revisited this idea, installing the zoo's restaurant 'in an old mansion', whose picturesque nature was emphasized with fitting décor. Activities from earlier times were often staged in these parks, including displays of falconry, putting (trained) wild animals in more direct contact with humans, particularly with children. Many parks – for example, Disneyland and Parc Astérix – began to exhibit trained

European bison, Woburn Abbey.

animals, usually dolphins, or semi-domesticated animals like reindeer. Even commercial breeders of wild animals such as ostriches and crocodiles opened their doors to the public.[12] Finally, so many wild animals were being used in advertising that specialized training centres, again open to the public, sprang up. Responding to the cinema's ongoing need for animal 'actors', Frank Inn founded the American Happy Valley in 1969 and was the supplier to innumerable famous films, including Claude Zidi's *L'Animal* (1976). The polar bear hero of *Alaska*, far from being a product of nature, was one of Mark Weiner's star pupils.[13] At their pinnacle, films succeeded in achieving perfect illusions of nature.

The greenhouses of earlier times, adapted to serve as tropical aviaries, have been succeeded by zoo-botanical installations. East Berlin Zoo's Alfred Brehm House marked a significant step in this direction; in the 11,000 square metres of its tropical hall, a reconstruction was attempted of a jungle's vegetation and bird life. Many such attempts, the most spectacular of which are outside Europe, have proved that, while a simulation can be achieved, an exact replica remains impossible. The vegetation provided for the enclosure of Melbourne Zoo's 'rainforest gorillas' suffered such difficulties that it eventually had to be replaced by artificial trees.[14]

Montreal's Biodome, set in the former velodrome of the 1976 Olympic Games, remains a prototype of great renown in Europe. Visitors pass from the tropics to the poles (without actually entering the refrigerated display, which, for the first time, mixes species from both poles) via the local St Lawrence region. The plants in the Biodome were acclimatized, some coming from Montreal's botanical gardens. Imported specimens were selected for their aesthetic qualities, their lack of toxicity and their resistance to assault by animals. To these were added artificial tree-trunks and foreign species. The hot, humid air through which visitors move, exacerbating the pollution they bring with them, affects the animals and plants very differently than in the wild; the animals seem visually well integrated with their environment.[15] In Europe, botanical reconstructions have been limited to the (usually meagre) enrichment of cages and enclosures, and the model of the wildlife park has prevailed.

The idea of observation parks took shape between 1960 and 1970, aiming at a clientele that would be willing to accept certain constraints; at Amboseli National Park, visitors spent 45 per cent of their time seeking out and observing a single animal, while they would have seen dozens if they spent the same amount of time looking into cages.[16] Branféré Park in southern Brittany, bequeathed to the Fondation de France by P. Jourde, a writer converted to

Buddhism, imported animals, many of whom roam freely. Today, it emphasizes its dedication to education in an environment close to its natural state. Such enterprises aim to introduce visitors to active wildlife protection. Insofar as is possible, human protection in observation parks only produces slight alterations in animals' natural states. Can the same be said for zoo animals?

NOAH'S IMPOSSIBLE ARK

In 1863, Père David, a French missionary, discovered in an impenetrable imperial estate to the south of Peking a species of deer that had been thought extinct. After 1894, a few specimens were gathered together by the Duke of Bedford, and some zoos helped to save the remaining survivors. Friedrich Falz-Fein, like several other Russian aristocrats, devoted his vast territory of Askania Nova to species under threat in 1863. Austin Corbin, the railroad king, did the same on Long Island in New York in 1886, a year in which the extermination of bison prompted the Smithsonian Institution to dedicate itself to their preservation. Washington's Zoological Park was created for this purpose.[17] Yellowstone Park in the western US was a model that inspired numerous initiatives, among which the 1933 London convention on wildlife parks stands out. The colonial authorities in Africa founded wildlife reserves that were either open to tourists (Kagera, 1934) or entirely closed, like Garamba National Park (1938).

As J. N. Hyson has put it, 'What turned many [American] zoo leaders into ardent conservationists was not the beginning of environmentalism in the US but the end of colonialism in Africa.' From 1962 on, breeding farms and the international co-ordination of efforts (conferences in London in 1964 and San Diego in 1966) were an attempt to move towards reduced importation.[18] Interest in the environment diminished the influence of London's Tecton Group, represented in the US by Charles Coe among others, with its aseptic 'maternity suite' style, for example at Philadelphia. Desmond Morris denounced 'the shame of the naked cage'. Naturalist presentations, sometimes called 'living dioramas', appeared in 1958 at Fort Worth Zoo in the guise of apparatus that could produce rain and thunder. The Sonora Desert Museum in Arizona recreated the desert habitat of the animals on display; Disney filmed *Living Desert* there. In 1999, the Congo Gorilla Forest at Bronx Zoo was described as an 'appeal to [visitors'] emotions and sense of discovery'.[19] A book by Robert Sommer whose title effectively denounced this deception – *Homocentric Environmental Ethics in Zoos* – nonetheless enjoyed great success.

The image of Noah's Ark became, after 1945, the new inspiration for zoos, not without encountering a number of obstacles along the way, the most obvious of which was the damage suffered by animals in captivity. Birds had their wings amputated, while the overtaxed feet of wading birds such as pink flamingos fractured easily, and their beaks, used as supports, became deformed.[20] Elephants were also affected by being deprived of movement; a recent development at Zurich Zoo has permitted their chains to be removed, even at night.[21]

The major obstacle to the eventual reintroduction of zoo animals to the wild was the reduction in their life expectancy. The high mortality rate outlined earlier continued to be reflected in the rapid turnover of animal stocks in zoos. A chart drawn from data in the *International Zoo Yearbook* showed stock turnover of about one-fifth at London's traditional zoo and Whipsnade wildlife park alike. At Vincennes,[22] a similar but more elaborate calculation placed annual stock turnover at around 17 per cent of the total population. After a detailed investigation in American zoos between January and May 1974, supported by three thousand photographs, P. Batten estimated that stock turnover was nearer the quarter mark. Theoretically, zoos could be closed just by calling a halt to their supply of animals for four to six years; at the end of that time, only a few veterans would remain in their care.

Interestingly, an assessment of the number of six-month periods spent at Vincennes by all its animals for the years 1951, 1960, 1970, 1975 and 1980 shows that the situation there remained largely unchanged across this range of dates. The curve for 1985 in our graph (see p. 395) closely follows that plotted for the Paris menagerie of 1839. In all instances, mortality remained high during the first eighteen months, the principal difference being the presence of a few veterans among twentieth-century animals. Only 21 per cent of pandas produced by artificial insemination in Chinese zoos reach the age of three.[23] The reduction of life expectancy in marine mammals has been the subject of official study: porpoises live for fourteen years against nearly 30 in the wild, while dolphins' life-spans are reduced by 30 years.[24] These estimates do not take epizootic diseases into account, such as the meliodiosis that was identified in 1976 at the Paris menagerie, too late to prevent the death of two keepers on top of the total destruction of the animals.

Opinions regarding compensatory reproduction in captivity have varied. Darwin believed that captive animals refused to procreate; Loisel found examples of mating in the unsanitary lodgings of sixteenth-century menageries and at the Tower of London, thus clearly demonstrating that reproduction among captive animals does not amount to proof that they have adapted well. This idea runs contrary to the claims made not just by present-day media but also by

scientists like James Fisher – 'Tigers learn to accept cage life, and reproduce there' – and the zoologists of Fota Wildlife Park.[25] Not all animals achieve high birth rates, but lions, whose reproduction is limited by responsible zoos, are very prolific. According to statistics given by the ISIS database for Vincennes (1991–2), roughly 20 per cent of birds and 48 per cent of mammals achieve healthy reproduction in zoos, but roughly 61 per cent of birds, 41 per cent of mammals and 100 per cent of reptiles fall into the category of difficult or even impossible reproduction. The sexual over-activity of certain species is evidence of the behavioural aberrations caused by boredom and the disruption of social order. Births in captivity cease to be seasonal: 60 per cent of captive Przewalski mares foal in September and nearly 20 per cent in December, while free mares only ever gave birth in the early summer, survival being impossible for any foal born in early winter. Mating also becomes increasingly precocious.

Breeding by humans can hardly avoid creeping domestication, favouring as it does any aptitude for captivity; this condition is characterized in ungulate mammals by low adrenaline emissions, which, in the wild, would leave them exposed to predators by reducing the muscular power available for flight. Genetic decline is also commonly observed in zoos. Crandall mentioned a leopard with a bulldog's 'pushed-in face' and shortened paws; many studies have investigated juvenile mortality in consanguineous populations.[26] Deformations in birds occur from the first generation, mostly due to their not being able to fly, which affects the entire organism; fattening causes modifications to the skeleton, organs and plumage, which change so much that, 'with exceptions, the captive form has no more than a passing likeness to the wild form.' Changes to the nervous system have been brought to light in storks, disrupting their migratory habits. If migration is suspended for just one season, it becomes very difficult; half-tamed storks return from migration increasingly early, nest at the wrong time of year in adverse conditions and develop changes in their sexual behaviour.[27] Defence instincts are the first to be subdued or eliminated by captivity. The nenes, or Hawaiian geese, successfully bred at Slimbridge were massacred by predators on their release.

It has long been established that many captive animals are affected by mental pathologies. In *Salammbô*, Flaubert describes the 'continual oscillation of captive animals', as did Rainer Maria Rilke in his poem 'La Panthère'. Stereotyped movements – leaps, pounces, greetings, indefinitely retrodden paths – evident in zoos to the point that they deform limbs, were studied as symptoms of mental illness by François Bourlière, then a gerontologist, in the primates and polar bears at Stuttgart, and by Roger Mugford, who established their frequency and development (76 per cent of time spent in stereotyped movement in 1989, 67 per cent in 1992). The hypothesis has been ventured that this ersatz

Caged panther and lion, Lyons Zoo.

Storks, Budapest Zoo, 2001.

Lionesses Pacing in a Cage, 1901, by Max Slevogt.

occupation, common to any confined being, might facilitate the production of a hormonal secretion that reduces anxiety.[28] Henri Ellenberger, while calling for qualification of this comparison, noted that 'psychopathologies attributable to a prolonged stay in a closed environment' had been observed in all places of confinement, including zoological gardens.[29] Doctors have been able to back this statement up with comparative statistical studies of the frequency and nature of pathologies observed in prison populations and in captive animals.[30]

To stereotyped movement the list of pathologies observed in captive animals[31] adds sexual disorders, auto-aggression and auto-mutilation, and consumption of faeces and the paintwork of cages, most of which make it impossible to exhibit the animals. Some causes have been studied experimentally – for example, the dimensions of cages – but exploration of this vast field of psychiatric study is still too fragmentary to permit any assessment of the how reversible these effects might be in captive animals – animals that too often become, to use Henry Vercors' term, 'denatured'. Trans-location is therefore the chosen method for the reintroduction of species to the wild. For example, bears captured in a Slovakian forest were transported to the Pyrenees, to which a translocated she-bear had adjusted well before being killed by a hunter.

THE DREAM OF ECOLOGY

In the face of the difficulties inherent in captivity, difficulties that well-run zoos tried their best to overcome, other solutions for the preservation of endangered species began to suggest themselves. There were attempts to influence the soaring rate of extinction among wild species (a third in 50 years) by legislative means. The ban on exportation of the species listed in three appendixes to the 1973–5 Washington convention known as CITES (Convention on International Trade of Endangered Species of Fauna and Flora), while only relatively effective, marked an important step. The French legislation of 1974 (*Journal officiel*, 23 November) was judged unworkable by J. V. Domalain,[32] because it legalized removal from habitat by zoos and laboratories, the principal predators of snakes. Zoo directors were quick to commit themselves to associations for the conservation of wild populations. In 1967, the International Union of Zoo Directors (IUDZG) allied itself to the International Union for the Conservation of Nature and its Resources (IUCN), publisher of *Red Databooks*, *Studbooks* and assessments of and monographs on endangered species (the bison in 1932, the Père David deer in 1957). The IUCN concerned itself with legislation and the acquisition of reserves. Its programme for captive breeding (Captive Breeding Specialist Group, or CBSG) was led by a zoo director. The IUCN also co-ordinated the TRAFFIC (Trade Record Analysis of Fauna and Flora in Commerce) network and, after 1973, ensured the application of the Washington convention, funded by the United Nations environmental programme (PNUE).[33]

Various zoo associations the world over created their own plans for survival of endangered species.[34] Zoo chiefs presented plans for preservation, and many edited *Studbooks* (including H. G. Klös, on the white and black rhinoceroses). Their role was so prominent that wildlife conservation has been essentially, if not exclusively, seen in terms of captivity. The European and Anglo-Saxon conservation plans (EEP and SSP) in particular tend in this direction. They make it a rule that the more a species is endangered in the short term, the larger the captive population should be and the faster it should be removed from the wild, in order to preserve '90 per cent of the average heterozygocity [genetic potential] of the wild genetic pool over 100 years'.[35] Removal from the wild on such a large scale, performed on a population already at a critical level, evidently risks causing that population to disappear entirely, simultaneously condemning the captive population, which, without input from the wild, cannot escape genetic decline. Some have wondered if the solution is not worse than the problem.

Wildlife conservation has also come up against a problem of feasibility. In 1967, the *Studbooks* contained four species; in 1980, there were twenty; in 1996, 130. How many of the ten thousand endangered species can zoos possibly save when 70 to 80 per cent of mammals are not even represented? It has been estimated that they could preserve 3 per cent of the 172 species in immediate danger of extinction, that is to say 0.00017 per cent of all life forms currently known on earth.[36] When it comes to subspecies, the choices become impossible: for example, of the five hundred tigers in North American zoos, 40 per cent are identifiable as subspecies and the others are mongrels – which should be saved? Looking at the evaluation in spatial terms, US Seal calculated in 1991[37] that the available space in all zoos (ISIS database), if it was dedicated to conservation in its entirety for two hundred years, would manage to save a maximum of two thousand endangered species. Finally, the cost of conservation through captivity is exorbitant:

> If we were to select [on invitation] 2,000 species of which we wished to keep 500 specimens each for 30 years with lower feeding costs than a herbivore (625 pounds per okapi), it would cost 25 billion dollars, which is roughly the same investment needed to put a man on the moon.[38]

Of 418 endangered species mentioned in *Action Plans*, only nineteen have reintroduction plans. Zhang Hemin, a Chinese researcher at the Wolong reserve, declared in the *China Daily* that 'it is not desirable to artificially breed so many pandas' that one does not know what to do with them afterwards.

Some successful reintroductions might help zoos find new solutions. Two European bison calves have been released with success, but near the Polish farm where they were raised, and on 80 hectares of land. Of 39 condors bred in captivity, eight were released in 1992, and seven of them were still alive in 1993.[39] An initially disastrous experience with golden tamarins eventually succeeded in 1976–84 with the animals being trained progressively for life in the wild. The conservation of the Arabian oryx, in decline since 1950 due to overhunting, shows the importance of political support. In 1962, subjects were distributed between three and, later, twelve zoos and private collections, before reintroduction in 1980 in the Jiddat al-Harassis (25,000 square kilometres), where the animals, protected by legislation and the local population, thrived.[40]

After these successful (but still exceptional) attempts, the UICN suggested that captive breeding, away from the site of origin, should be no more than a short-term stage if genetic decline was to be avoided, and that all breeding should take reintroduction into account. More and more biologists came to feel that preservation was impossible outside the guiding principle of Fauna-Flora-Habita (FFH), according to which the species in question should form part of a biological system with interactive elements. Protecting parcels of wild land almost certainly saves large quantities of plant and animal species, particularly insects, which are not included among endangered species.[41] Several institutions and a small handful of zoos have understood that, rather than bailing out a Noah's Ark that is as expensive and exigu-

Empty Cage, 1971, by Gilles Aillaud.

ous as a spacecraft, it would be better to try to hold back the flood. The World Wide Fund for Nature (WWF) works to preserve Madagascan lemurs *in situ*, alongside the Paris Muséum and J.-J. Petter. Frankfurt Zoo, in caring for a monkey for the Pointe-Noire reintroduction centre,[42] opened up an innovative, if still rarely followed, path. It seems that zoos are feeling the need for a new direction, 'the need to be more than a zoo',[43] to take a more prominent role in education and forge stronger links with systems of reintroduction that are still too rare and mostly the result of private initiative. For monkeys, many enterprises follow the way cleared by Jane Goodall.[44] D. and S. Siddle in Zambia and the Avelings in Sumatra care for and release wounded animals from cages or laboratories. The association Habitat Ecologique et Liberté des Primates (HELP) succeeded for the first time in 1996 in the reintroduction of seven young chimpanzees, former captives taken by the Congolese forestry commission. Released on the Conkouati Islands to the south of the Congo, they are tracked by means of radio collars. The females have integrated with the native population better than the males.

The veterinary doctor M. Ancrenaz[45] wrote that the enterprise of reintroduction was a remarkable 'tool for the awareness of the local population and the wider public', very useful in 'stopping destructive human activity (poaching, deforestation)'. The case of the tiger alone speaks eloquently of the change in attitudes to wildlife. Arjan Singh, a conservationist at Dudhwa National Park in India, is releasing tigers that, scarcely half a century ago, were being hunted down as man-eaters.

Out of the many such projects discussed in the US, three plans for the breeding of endangered species reached fruition: San Diego's Wild Animal Park (1,800 acres, 1972, $6 million from the zoological society), which would be the only one open to visitors; the National Zoo Conservation and Research Center in the Shenandoah Valley in Front Royal, Virginia (Washington Zoo); and St Catherine's Island off the coast of Georgia (New York Zoo). A great many private 'sanctuaries' succeeded the 22,000-acre one established by Austin Corbin on Long Island in 1886.[46] Today, 156 such facilities are approved by an association of not-for-profit sanctuaries. The breeding and sale of endangered species are forbidden in all cases, but the reality of the situation was exposed in 1999 by a *Mercury News* investigation[47] into zoo directors. This study compared the ISIS database (the International Species Information System, dependant on the AAZPA, not publicly owned, but opened under State Public Records Law) and the eighteen annual editions of the *Finders Guide Catalogue of Exotic Animals for Sale*. These documents revealed that 19,361 mammals left accredited zoos between 1992 and mid-1998, 38 per cent going to merchants, auctions, hunting ranches, unidentified individuals or unaccredited zoos or game farms, as well as to trophy collectors. On the subject of hunting, P. Batten recalled that the safari organizer Curtis Prock, of Donnelly, Iowa, used the same plane (from the TACA) to transport hunters and (in crates in the luggage hold) the lions they were going to kill!

The *Mercury News* further denounced collusion between commerce and so-called conservationism. For example, the director of Fort Worth Zoo is the businessman Ron Surrat, owner of the Premier Wildlife Ranch. The newspaper also cited numerous illegal sales made by private sanctuaries: chimpanzees sold by Martina Colette (photographed posing with a baby chimpanzee); wolf cubs sold by the Soul of the Wolf Wildlife Sanctuary (Santa Barbara, California). The case of the English entrepreneur Henry Wallace is typically ambiguous. The press lauded the 'non-

Black macaques, Chessington Zoo, 1994, by Britta Jaschinski.

profit private zoo Henry's Ark on his 600-acre farm in Prospect, Kentucky' for assembling '26 animals left homeless', but the *Mercury News* quoted the City of Birmingham's audit: Wallace was claiming sold animals as deaths.[48] Many zoos and several of the 24 organizations affiliated with the AAZPA were practising illegal sales on a large scale. The studbook for giraffes, edited by Laurie Bigaman Lackey, mentions six hundred animals that disappeared from view after sale (1997). The 'best zoo in the world', San Diego, numbers among the three biggest black marketeers, with a rate of 79 per cent. Endangered species have not escaped the inflated market created by snobbism and speculation. The *Mercury News'* conclusion: 'AAZPA-accredited zoos claim that they actively work to propose reintroduction when they purposely breed animals in order to exploit their commer-cial appeal and then cast them into ignominious conditions.'[49] The environmentalist Aldo Leopold expanded on this idea, placing the institution of the zoo in its commercial context: 'Zoo-goers still [see] nature less as a community to be conserved than as a commodity to be consumed.'

Yet, just as exhibitions of clothed primates playing jazz were drawing huge crowds to American zoos, Robert M. Yerkes was working on a comparative study of the psychology of apes, in which he discovered a similarity to humans that was not so much diverting as disconcerting. The ambiguity of zoological gardens is still more marked in the US than elsewhere: among their visitors, some laugh while others find themselves questioning their true nature.

○ EPILOGUE

The aim of this history of zoos has been to reveal the diversity of, and changes in, the motives that have led Westerners to keep animals in zoological gardens and to treat them as proof of the existence of the Other, as hostages from a conquered world, as survivors of a universe on the road to extinction. Until the twentieth century, zoos clearly reflected the will of a triumphant Europe to classify and dominate. Their creation contributed to the plundering of wildlife and, devoted as they were to the exhibition of exotic animals, fit perfectly within the context of colonial era that began in the fifteenth century. Of course, zoos also participated in the long process of understanding wild animals, despite the fact that the specimens they offered for observation were more often virtual than natural.

In the 1900s, shifting intentions towards nature charged zoological gardens with contradictory objectives. Western society was increasingly torn between the persistent drive to exploit and a new desire to preserve and respect. It simultaneously expressed, accepted and attempted to disguise the inconsistency of these impulses through the intermediary of the zoo, transforming it into an ersatz natural, open space. Zoos no longer expressed genuine aims, but rather wished-for ideals, and their adaptation was achieved through illusion and in spite of a contrary truth, because the plunder of natural habitats only intensified. The zoo made concrete, in an enclosed space, what society wanted to do in nature, as, with the advance of urbanization, people felt an increasing need to preserve the wild. But the desire remained unrealized, because Western society did not want its methods called into question, and because, in the final analysis, it preferred to transplant, delimit, cultivate and arrange nature however and wherever it liked, rather than leave places truly free of human influence. Here again, a parallel can be drawn with the processes of decolonization and neo-colonialism, which expressed, and continue to express, the same dialectic between sentiment and reality. Thus the zoological garden has shared, and continues to share, all of the doubts and contradictions of Western society's relationship with the rest of the world.

Fraut   Ralf   Lisar   Sascha
                                                              Nero

Previous page: Klara Huth with her lions at Leipzig Zoo, before 1900.

LONDON

First proposed in 1817 by Stamford Raffles, a British administrator in the East Indies and the founder of Singapore, a zoological garden opened in London in 1826, thanks to support from the Zoological Society and a lease of land in Regent's Park from the King. Certain of this zoo's denizens are remembered to this day: the giraffe offered by Muhammad Ali of Egypt in 1827, the hippopotamus (1850), the short-lived gorilla (1869) and Jumbo (at the zoo 1865–82), who gave his eponym to elephants throughout the world.

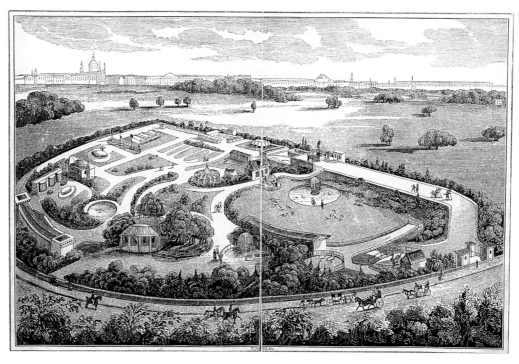

'The Gardens of the Zoological Society, Regent's Park', 1830.

Above: Brahmin–bull house, *c*. 1830. Below: Monkey houses, *c*. 1830.

Illustration of the camel house, 1835, by George Scharf.

Illustration of pelicans and other birds, 1835, by George Scharf.

Above: 'The Zoological Gardens, Regent's Park', 1837. Below: New reptile house, 1883.

Polar-bear enclosure, *c.* 1905.

The Snowdon Aviary, 1986.

⟩ SAN DIEGO

Since its foundation in 1916, San Diego Zoo has become southern California's gateway for tourism. The zoo's attractions have multiplied over the years to include such features as exotic forests, rivers and canyons, as well as underwater displays, thus making it one of the most visited zoos in the US.

Main street entrance, c. 1930.

Main entrance, 1940s.

A lion transporter, 1920s.

The 'Flight Cage' aviary, 1937.

The wolf house, c.1916.

Completed lion grotto with benefactor Ellen Browning Scripps, 1923.

Crane Canyon, 1964.

◔ MOSCOW

It was a long-time practice of Russian princes and aristocrats to maintain large private reserves of wild animals. The Russian Imperial Acclimatization Society founded a garden based on the Parisian model, with Asian deer and an aquarium containing indigenous species.

Imperial bust, 1878.

Moscow Zoo, 1878.

Apiary and bird department, 1878.

Keeper with a lion cub, 1920s.

Moose yard, 1903.

Mamlyuk.

Above: Main gate, early 1910s. Below: The war-damaged Moscow Zoo.

Above: Main gate, 1949. Below: Moscow Zoo, 1950s.

A celebrity visit to Moscow Zoo.

Bear enclosure, 2001.

Wall decoration, 2001.

● AMSTERDAM

Dedicated to research from its earliest beginnings, the Amsterdam zoo 'natura artis magistra' was founded in 1837 close to an ethnographic museum. In 1877, it became part of the university. An insectarium for nocturnal butterflies and an aquarium based on the Parisian model both attracted specialists to the zoo, while monkeys and lions drew members of the general public.

Top left: Main entrance, 1860. Top right: The ferry and museum building, 1853.
Bottom left: Giraffe enclosure, 1861. Bottom right: Elephant enclosure, c. 1870.

General view.

ZOO

308

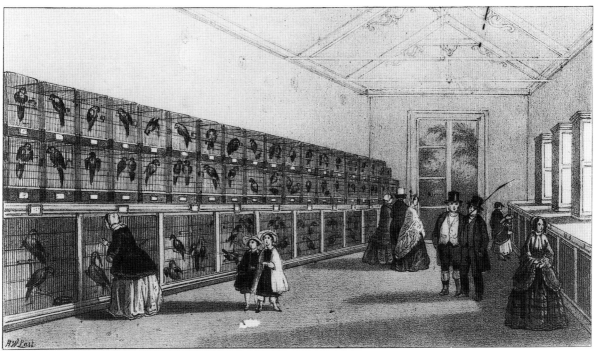

Two views of the aviary's interior, 1856.

Amsterdam Zoo, 1928.

Bactrian camels and camel house, 1931.

ZOOS THROUGH THE AGES

Monkey cages.

Amsterdam Zoo, 2001.

Above: Deer, 2001. Below: Amsterdam Zoo, 2001.

Amsterdam Zoo, 2001.

Above: Giraffe house, 2001. Below: Elephant house, 2001.

⊙ ANTWERP

From 1843 on, the French Royal Zoological Society directed a zoological
garden in the heart of this port city with direct links to Africa. The zoo, a
showcase for the Belgian colonies and a sophisticated cultural centre, was
also the site of an annual exotic-animal fair. The Egyptian temple housing the
elephants and the zoo's other exotic buildings have all been restored.

JARDIN ZOOLOGIQUE D'ANVERS
Otarie.

A sea-lion.

The old hippopotamus building.

1, JARDIN ZOOLOGIQUE D'ANVERS.
Aquarium (Entrée).

Aquarium entrance, 1905.

Monkey house, *c.* 1905.

Stereoscopic view of the bird pond in the gardens, 1905.

A painting of Antwerp Zoo, *The Yak Park around 1880*, by L. Dierckx.

Animal pits and caves (above) replaced by terraces and bars (below) in the 1890s.

Poster for Antwerp Zoo and Aquarium, 1932, by F. de Smet.

▷ ROTTERDAM

Founded by a society of shareholders in 1857, the Rotterdam zoological garden was accompanied by a library, a museum and a botanical garden, and was directed by a specialist in African fauna and long-time colonial administrator. A picturesque garden, large glasshouse and several animal houses, including one for monkeys and another for reptiles, ensured the zoo's success.

Main entrance, before the Second World War.

Sea-lion basin, before the Second World War.

Crocodiles, before the Second World War.

Flamingos, 2001.

Top: Bactrian camels and aviary, 2001. Bottom: Rotterdam Zoo, 2001.

Gorillas, 2001.

JARDIN DES PLANTES, PARIS

In 1793, on the heels of the Revolution, an exhibit of live animals was organized by the scientists affiliated with the new Muséum. The animal enclosures were located in a picturesque garden called the Swiss Valley. The success of this menagerie enhanced the Muséum's reputation throughout Europe.

13. — PARIS — Jardin des Plantes. Lion d'Afrique
Don du Capitaine Boutieq.   G. Bouchetal, édit., 72, Boul. de l'Hopital, Paris.

An African lion given to the Jardin des Plantes, c. 1930.

Paris. - Au Jardin des Plantes. - Fosse aux Ours.

Above: Polar-bear pit, *c.* 1906. Below: Kako the hippopotamus.

343. PARIS — Jardin des Plantes — L'Hippopotame Kako

Monkey palace, 1930s.

A lion.

FRANKFURT am Main

A stockholding society remodelled the old zoo around a function room and restaurant. A large salt-water aquarium was installed in 1877, as well as a terrarium for reptiles in a spectacular glasshouse. The journal published by the Frankfurt zoo became an important link with Germanophone zoos elsewhere.

Top: Tower and lake, 1903.
Left: Giraffe house, 1950s.

Frankfurt Zoo, 2001.

Frankfurt Zoo, 2001.

Previous page: *The Lion-Trainers*, 1985, by José Garcia y Màs.

○ ARTISTS AND THE ZOO

The eighteenth-century Italian painter
Tiepolo and his contemporaries were
fascinated by the arrival of a rhinoceros
in Europe. Artists of earlier centuries,
from the English painter Sir Edwin
Landseer to the Frenchman Eugène
Delacroix, like those of the present day,
attempted to break down barriers in
order to restore caged animals to freedom or at least to the life they had
known before captivity. Of all of the
Impressionists and Post-Impressionists,
the German painter Max Liebermann
was the most successful at rendering the
light and movement he observed during
visits to the zoo.

Few visual artists have posed serious
questions about the nature of zoos,
however. In his observations of monkeys, the French painter
and graphic artist Gustave Doré, like the naturalist Charles
Darwin, questioned the nature of humanity. In the twentieth century, zoos inspired the German painter August
Macke with a poetic vision of the mystical connections
among all living creatures. In *The Tamer*, Fujita illustrated
an ambiguous female figure dominating a wild beast, while
José Garcia y Màs transposed the contemporary political
scene in Germany into a cage of wild animals.

Punchinello and the Elephant, 18th century, by Giovanni Tiepolo.

Artists today tend to explore zoos by means of more
sombre imagery. The photographers Candida Höfer and
Britta Jaschinski depict difficult confrontations between
wild animals and human beings in urban settings. For the
painter Gilles Aillaud, an empty cage is sufficient to evoke
the human appropriation of animals and the essential
incompatibility of the human and animal worlds.

Herman Van Aaken's Travelling Menagerie, 1833, by Johann Nepomuk Höchle.

In the Monkey House, 1872, by Gustave Doré.

Study of a Lion, c. 1862, by Edwin Landseer.

The Parrot Man, 1902, by Max Liebermann.

Alley of Parrots, 1902, by Max Liebermann.

The Zebra House in the Berlin Zoological Gardens, c. 1909, by Victor Freudemann.

Small Zoological Gardens in Brown and Yellow, 1912, by August Macke.

In the Zoological Gardens, 1914, by Erich Büttner.

Tiger in a Cage, 1925, by Otto Dill.

Vulture Cage, c. 1930, by Josef Hegenbarth.

The Lion-Tamer and the Lion, 1930, by Tsugouharu T. Leonard Foujita.

Guy the Gorilla, 1982, by William Tymym.

Hannover Zoo, 1997, by Candida Höfer.

Antwerp Zoo, 1992, by Candida Höfer.

Hamburg Zoo, 1990, by Candida Höfer.

London Zoo, 1992, by Candida Höfer.

Basel Zoo, 1992, by Candida Höfer.

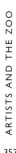

Hamburg Zoo, 1992, by Candida Höfer.

Stuttgart Zoo, 1991, by Candida Höfer.

Amsterdam Zoo, 1992, by Candida Höfer.

Berlin Zoo, 1991, by Candida Höfer.

Washington, DC, Zoo, 1992, by Candida Höfer.

Leipzig Zoo, 1994, by Candida Höfer.

Lion, Los Angeles Zoo, 1995, by Britta Jaschinski.

Common seal, Berlin Zoo, 1992, by Britta Jaschinski.

Indian rhinoceros, Los Angeles Zoo, 1995, by Britta Jaschinski.

Walrus, San Diego Zoo, 1995, by Britta Jaschinski.

Bactrian camel, London Zoo, 1992, by Britta Jaschinski.

Beluga whale, New York Zoo, 1995, by Britta Jaschinski.

Asian elephant, Hamburg Zoo, 1994, by Britta Jaschinski.

REFERENCES

INTRODUCTION: THE CALL OF THE WILD

1 J. M. Bradburne, 'Où sont les bêtes sauvages? Du rôle des jardins zoologiques', *Alliage*, VII–VIII (1991), p. 139; G. Mermet, *Tendances 1995, le nouveau consommateur* (Paris, 1996), p. 215.

2 F. Poplin, 'Que l'homme cultive aussi bien le sauvage que le domestique', in J. Desse and F. Audoin-Rouzeau, eds, *Exploitation des animaux sauvages à travers le temps* (Juan-les-Pins, 1993), pp. 527–39.

3 R. Delort, 'Rapport introductif', in *L'Homme, l'animal domestique et l'environnement du Moyen Age au XVIIIᵉ siècle* (Nantes, 1993), p. 13.

I ANCIENT TROPHIES

1 G. Maschietti *et al.*, *Serragli e menagerie in Piemonte nell'ottocento sotto la real casa Savoia* (Turin, 1988), p. 15; A. Rey, ed., *Dictionnaire historique de la langue française* (Paris, 1992).

2 The only available summary is G. Loisel, *Histoire des ménageries de l'antiquité à nos jours* (Paris, 1912). See also J.-D. Vigne, 'Domestication ou appropriation pour la chasse: Histoire d'un choix socioculturel depuis le Néolithique', in *Exploitation des animaux sauvages à travers le temps* (Nice, 1993), pp. 203–4; M. Malaise, 'La Perception du monde animal dans l'Egypte ancienne', *Anthropozoologica*, VII (1987), pp. 28–48; *Les Animaux dans la culture chinoise, Anthropozoologica*, XVIII (special issue) (1993).

3 H. Limet, 'Les Animaux enjeux involontaires de la politique (au Proche-Orient ancien)', in L. Bodson, ed., *Les Animaux exotiques dans les relations internationales* (Liège, 1998), pp. 33–51; B. Lion, 'La Circulation des animaux exotiques au Proche-Orient antique', in D. Charpin and F. Joannes, eds, *La Circulation des biens, des personnes et des idées dans le Proche-Orient ancien* (Paris, 1992), pp. 357–65.

4 L. Bodson, 'Contribution à l'étude des critères d'appréciation de l'animal exotique dans la tradition grecque ancienne', in *idem*, ed., *Les Animaux exotiques*, pp. 139–212; G. Jennison, *Animals for Show and Pleasure in Ancient Rome* (Manchester, 1937), pp. 10–29; D. Goguey, 'Les Romains et les animaux: Regards sur les grands fauves, liens affectifs entre l'homme et l'animal', *Homme et animal dans l'Antiquité romaine* (Tours, 1995), pp. 51–66.

5 R. Delort, *Les Eléphants, piliers du monde* (Paris, 1990), pp. 81–8; C. Perez, 'La Symbolique de l'animal comme lieu et moyen d'expression de l'idéologie gentilice, personnelle et impérialiste de la Rome républicaine', in *Homme et animal dans l'Antiquité romaine*, pp. 259–75.

6 J. Aymard, *Essai sur les chasses romaines des origines à la fin des Antonins* (Paris, 1951), pp. 185–96, 391, 557; F. Bertrandy, 'Remarques sur le commerce des bêtes sauvages entre l'Afrique du Nord et l'Italie', *Mélanges de l'Ecole française de Rome, Antiquité*, LXXXIX/1 (1987), pp. 211–41; D. Bomgardner, 'The Trade in Wild Beasts for Roman Spectacles: A Green Perspective', *Anthropozoologica*, XVI (1992), pp. 161–6.

7 Loisel, *Histoire des ménageries*, vol. I, pp. 146–63, 247; Delort, *Les Eléphants*, p. 89; G. de Gislain, 'L'Evolution du droit de garenne au Moyen Âge', in *La Chasse au Moyen Âge* (Paris, 1980), pp. 37–58; B. and P. Beck, 'La Nature aménagée: Le Parc du château d'Aisey-sur-Seine', in M. Colardelle, ed., *L'Homme et la nature au Moyen Âge* (Paris, 1996), pp. 22–9; J. M. Gilbert, *Hunting and Hunting Reserves in Medieval Scotland* (Edinburgh, 1979); R. Delort and C. Beck, 'Wilde Tiere', *Lexikon des Mittelalters*, VIII (1998).

8 *Il Giardino zoologico di Roma* (Rome, 1935), pp. 17–19. For Florence, see F. Rabelais, *Pantagruel*, bk IV, chap. 11; De la Lande, *Voyage d'un Français en Italie fait dans les années 1765 et 1766* (Paris, 1769), p. 330.

9 Countess d'Aulnoy, *Relation du voyage d'Espagne* (Paris, 1926), p. 378; G. Toscan, *L'Ami de la nature* (Paris, an VIII), p. 280; L. Lambton, *Beastly Buildings: The National Trust Book of Architecture for Animals* (London, 1985), p. 9; L. Guicciardini, *Descriptions de tout le Païs-Bas* (Antwerp, 1567), p. 332.

10 C. Patin, *Relations historiques et curieuses de voyages en Alle-magne* (Lyon, 1767), pp. 216–17; B. Paust, *Studien zur barocken Menagerie in deutschsprachigen Raum* (Worms, 1996), pp. 44–5.

11 Loisel, *Histoire des ménageries*, vol. I, pp. 263–77.

12 P. Belon, *L'Histoire de la nature des oiseaux* (Paris, 1555), p. 191 (Francis I); Marquis de Sourches, *Mémoires* (Paris, 1882), vol. I, p. 77.

13 Lambton, *Beastly Buildings*, pp. 9, 130–36.

14 Loisel, *Histoire des ménageries*, vol. I, pp. 203, 266–8; E. Hamy, 'Les anciennes ménageries royales et la ménagerie nationale fondée le 14 brumaire, an II', *Nouvelles archives du Muséum*, 4th ser., V (1893), p. 19.

15 J. Mocquet, *Voyages en Afrique, Asie, Indes orientales et occiden-tales* (Rouen, 1645), pp. 123, 126; C. Luz, *Exotische Welten: Exotische Phantasien: Das exotische Tier in Europäischen Kunst* (Stuttgart, 1987), p. 15.

16 E. Hamy, 'Le Commerce des animaux exotiques à Marseille à la fin du XVIe siécle', *Bulletin du Muséum d'Histoire Naturelle*, VII (1903), pp. 316–18; P. de l'Estoile, *Journal de Henri III* (Paris, 1875), vol. I, p. 137; *Recueil des voyages qui ont servi à l'établisse-ment et aux progrès de la Compagnie des Indes orientales* (Amsterdam, 1702), p. 358; P. Camper, *Œuvres* (Paris, 1803).

17 J.-B. Lacroix, 'L'Approvisionnement des ménageries et les transports d'animaux sauvages par la Compagnie des Indes au XVIIIe siècle', *Revue française d'histoire d'outre-mer* (1978), pp. 153–79.

18 A. Thévet, *Cosmographie du Levant* (Lyon, 1556); M. de Laborde, *Compte des bâtiments du roi (1528–1571)* (Paris, 1880), vol. II, pp. 216, 269, 271; *Lettres, instructions et mémoires que le S. Mosnier fait porter à Paris* (Paris, 1861–82), vol. V, p. 437; P. Dahlgren, *Les Relations commerciales et maritimes entre la France et les côtes de l'océan Pacifique* (Paris, 1909). vol. I, p. 550.

19 Paust, *Studien zur barocken Menagerie*, p. 133.

20 *Gazette de France*, 16 July 1764.

21 *Lettres, instructions et mémoires*, vol. V, pp. 553–4; AN, AJ15 512, Ponchartrain to the Consuls, 21 January 1711; Lacroix, 'L'Ap-provisionnement des ménageries', pp. 158, 163, 166; AN, AJ15 512, no. 507, Letter from Rouillé, n.d.

22 Camper, *Œuvres*, vol. I, p. 48; AN, AJ15 512, Letter of 26 August

1715; A. Vosmaer, *Description d'un recueil exquis d'animaux rares* (Amsterdam, 1804), p. 3.

23 J. Guiffrey, ed., *Compte des bâtiments du roi sous le règne de Louis XIV* (Paris 1881–1901), vol. II, col. 6; Lacroix, 'L'Approvision-nement des ménageries', pp. 156, 169; X. Salmon, *Versailles: Les Chasses exotiques de Louis XV* (Paris, 1995).

24 Loisel, *Histoire des ménageries*, vol. I, pp. 203, 207, 234, 263, 272; Guicciardini, *Description de tout le Païs-Bas*, p. 332.

25 A. Franklin, *Dictionnaire historique des arts, métiers et profes-sions exercés à Paris depuis le treizième siècle* (Paris, 1906), p. 268; Luz, *Exotische Welten*, p. 15; L. Orsi, 'The Emblematic Elephant: A Preliminary Approach to the Elephant in Renaissance Thought and Art', *Anthropozoologica*, XX (1994), pp. 70–74.

26 Belon, *L'Histoire de la nature des oiseaux*, p. 191.

27 J. Calvette de Estrella, *Le Très Heureux Voyage fait par … (le) Prince Don Phillipe* (Brussels, 1876), p. 87; Loisel, *Histoire des ménageries*, vol. II, pp. 57, 98.

28 Loisel, *Histoire des ménageries*, vol. I, pp. 212, 274; De la Lande, *Voyage d'un Français en Italie*, pp. 330–31; J. Toland, *Relation des cours de Prusse et de Hanovre* (The Hague, 1706), p. 32; J. Heroart, *Journal* (Paris, 1868), vol. II, p. 81.

29 Loisel, *Histoire des ménageries*, vol. I, pp. 217–19.

30 *Mercure de France* (October–November 1719), p. 42.

31 L. Cimber and F. Danjou, *Archives curieuses de l'histoire de France* (Paris, 1834–40), vol. VII, p. 355 (Charles IX in 1572); *Mercure galant* (August 1682), p. 135.

32 Loisel, *Histoire des ménageries*, vol. I, p. 267.

33 C. Estienne, *L'Agriculture et maison rustique* (Paris, 1564), pp. 121–2; P. Salvadori, *La Chasse sous l'Ancien Régime* (Paris, 1996), pp. 17, 32.

34 Valmont de Bomare, *Dictionnaire raisonné universel d'histoire naturelle* (Paris: Lacombe, 1768), vol. IV, p. 389.

35 M. Moser and G. Teyssot, eds, *Histoire des jardins de la Renais-sance à nos jours* (Paris, 1991), pp. 87, 184; Salvadori, *La Chasse sous l'Ancien Régime*, pp. 166–7, 210–11; Countess d'Aulnoy, *Relation du voyage d'Espagne*, p. 378; A. Macgregor, 'Deer on the Move: Relocation of Stock between Game Parks in the Sixteenth and Seventeenth Centuries', *Anthropozoologica*, XVI (1992), pp. 167–79; M. Brown, *Richmond Park: The History of a*

Royal Deer Park (London, 1985); Maschietti, *Serragli e menagerie*, pp. 35–7.

36 Estienne, *L'Agriculture et maison rustique*, p. 135.

37 Paust, *Studien zur barocken Menagerie*, pp. 26–38; Moser and Teyssot, *Histoire des jardins de la Renaissance*, p. 55; Salvadori, *La Chasse sous l'Ancien Régime*, pp. 70, 80, 166, 229. An example of such a theorist is L. Savot, *L'Architecture française* (Paris, 1624), pp. 168–9.

38 Salvadori, *La Chasse sous l'Ancien Régime*, pp. 166–7, 207–9, 228; Loisel, *Histoire des ménageries*, vol. I, pp. 201, 234, 264; vol. II, p. 15; Patin, *Relations historiques et curieuses*, p. 216 (Dresden).

39 G. Coyer, *Voyages d'Italie et de Hollande* (Paris, 1775), vol. I, p. 115.

40 Coyer, *Voyages d'Italie et de Hollande*, I, p. 115; N. Elias, *La Société de cour* (Paris, 1985), pp. 240–42; Loisel, *Histoire des ménageries*, vol. II, pp. 11, 14, 22, 60, 65–6, 100; Salvadori, *La Chasse sous l'Ancien Régime*, pp. 187–8, 240–42.

2 THE ARISTOCRACY'S NEW-FOUND CURIOSITY

1 A. Rey, ed., *Dictionnaire historique de la langue française* (Paris, 1992); the word is borrowed from the Latin *exoticus*, itself taken from the Greek *exotikos* ('outside, exterior'): F. Rabelais, *Pantagruel. Quart Livre*, chap. 2, cited in L. Bodson, ed., *Les Animaux exotiques dans les relations internationales* (Liège, 1998), p. 145.

2 K. Pomian, *Collectionneurs, amateurs, et curieux, Paris, Venise: XVIᵉ–XVIIᵉ siècle* (Paris, 1986), pp. 16-52; H. Haupt *et al.*, *Le Bestiaire de Rodolphe II* (Paris, 1990), pp. 15, 31.

3 W. Blunt, *Linné, le prince des botanistes* (Paris and Berlin, 1986), pp. 130–31.

4 G. Bazin, *Le Temps des musées* (Brussels, 1967), pp. 57–8, 70–75; Pomian, *Collectionneurs*, pp. 61–5, 91–5.

5 G. Olmi, 'Science. Honour. Metaphor: Italian Cabinets of the Sixteenth and Seventeenth Centuries', in O. Impey and A. MacGregor, *The Origins of Museums: The Cabinet of Curiosities in Sixteenth and Seventeenth-century Europe* (New York, 1996), p. 5ff; Pomian, *Collectionneurs*, pp. 86, 118–24, 143–61.

6 L. V. Thiéry, *Le Voyageur à Paris* (Paris, 1761), vol. I, p. 124; Y. Laissus, 'Les Cabinets d'histoire naturelle', in R. Taton, ed., *Enseignement et diffusion des sciences en France au XVIIIᵉ siècle* (Paris, 1964), pp. 659–712; W. Blunt, *Linné* (Paris, 1986), pp. 278–81; Pomian, *Collectionneurs*, pp. 248–54.

7 A. Schnapper, *Le Géant, la licorne et la tulipe: Collectionneurs et collections dans la France du XVIIᵉ siècle* (Paris, 1988), pp. 10–13, 63–83, 309 (Thévet et Neikel); C. J. de Villers, *Catalogue raisonné d'histoire naturelle et de physique qui compose le cabinet de M. de Montribloud* (Paris, 1782), pp. 133–78.

8 G. Buffon, *Histoire naturelle* (Paris, 1749–83), pp. 133–78; A. Thouin, *Voyage dans la Belgique, la Hollande et l'Italie* (Paris, 1841), vol. II, p. 232; Blunt, *Linné*, p. 280; Pomian, *Collectionneurs*, pp. 266–7.

9 Haupt, *Le Bestiaire*, p. 32; C. Patin, *Relations historiques et curieuses de voyages en Allemagne* (Lyon, 1676), pp. 212–17.

10 J.-B. Lacroix, 'L'Approvisionnement des ménageries et les transport d'animaux sauvages par la Compagnie des Indes au XVIIIᵉ siècle', *Revue française d'histoire d'outre-mer* (1978), pp. 158–9; Blunt, *Linné*, p. 231.

11 Cited, without references (archives of the Musée Condé), in G. Loisel, *Histoire des ménageries de l'Antiquité à nos jours* (Paris, 1912), vol. II, p. 192.

12 P. Dan, *Le Trésor des merveilles de Fontainebleau* (Paris, 1642), pp. 156, 85; Loisel, *Histoire des ménageries*, vol. II, pp. 50, 215.

13 Haupt, *Le Bestiaire*, p. 9; Schnapper, *Le Géant*, p. 78.

14 L. Lambton, *Beastly Buildings: The National Trust Book of Architecture for Animals* (London, 1985), pp. 9, 130–36; Hervieux de Chanteloup, *Nouveau Traité des serins de canarie* (Paris, 1719), pp. 4–13; J. Boyceau de la Baraudière, *Traité du jardinage* (Paris, 1707), pp. 127–8.

15 S. Locatelli, *Voyage de France (1664–1665)* (Paris, 1905), p. 194.

16 Jean de la Fontaine, *Les Amours de Psyché et de Cupidon* (The Hague, 1700), p. 4.

17 F. Audouin-Rouzeau, 'Temoignages ostéoarchéologiques sur la place du dindon dans l'Europe des temps modernes', and J.-L. Flandrin, 'Le Dindon sur les tables européennes, XVIᵉ–XVIIIᵉ siècle', in *Ethnozootechnie*, XLIX (1972), pp. 63–70, 71–84; B. Paust, *Studien zur barocken Menagerie in deutschsprachigen*

Raum (Worms, 1996), p. 118.

18 G.-L. Le Rouge, *Jardins anglo-chinois à la mode* (Paris, 1770–88), vol. VIII, p. 28.

19 Marquis dc Dangeau, *Journal* (Paris, 1854–60), vol. I, pp. 28, 207; Paust, *Studien zur barocken Menagerie*, pp. 51–3.

20 A. Franklin, *Dictionnaire historique des arts, métiers et professions exercés à Paris depuis le treizième siècle* (Paris, 1906), pp. 14–15.

21 M. Jimenez de Cisneros, *El Parque zoologico de Madrid* (Madrid, 1994), pp. 14, 19.

22 List published in Loisel, *Histoire des ménageries*, vol. II, pp. 172–83. On the United Provinces of the Netherlands, see A. Vosmaer, *Description d'un recueil exquis d'animaux rares* (Amsterdam, 1804), p. 7.

23 J. Guiffrey, ed., *Comptes des bâtiments du roi sous le règne de Louis XIV* (Paris 1881–1901), vol. I, cols 915–21, vol. V, pp. 62, 418; Marquis d'Argenson, *Journal et mémoires* (Paris, 1859–67), vol. VI, p. 85; P. A. Lablaude, *Les Jardins de Versailles* (Paris, 1995), p. 155.

24 Buffon, *Histoire naturelle* (Paris: Imprimerie nationale, 1749–83), article 'Axis'.

25 Loisel, *Histoire des ménageries*, vol. II, p. 222; Duke de Luynes, *Mémoires, 1735–1758* (Paris, 1860–1986), vol. X, p. 317.

26 J. Rowe, 'Ethnography and Ethnology in the Sixteenth Century', *Kroeber Anthropological Society Papers*, XXX (Spring 1964), pp. 1–19, cited in Schnapper, *Le Géant*, p. 108; Haupt, *Le Bestiaire*, pp. 46, 92.

27 On this, see M. Moser and G. Teyssot, eds, *Histoire des jardins de la Renaissance à nos jours* (Paris, 1991), pp. 77–8; Schnapper, *Le Géant*, pp. 37–43; and contributions in S. Van Sprang, ed., *L'Empire de Flore: Histoire et représentations des fleurs en Europe du XVIe au XIX siècle* (Brussels, 1996).

28 A. Manesson-Mallet, *Description de l'univers* (Paris: Thierry, 1683), vol. V, p. 42.

29 Haupt, *Le Bestiaire*, p. 9; J. C. Calvette de Estrella, *Le Très Heureux Voyage fait par … Don Phillipe* (Brussels, 1876), vol. II, pp. 87, 92; Patin, *Relations historiques et curieuses*, pp. 216–17; Loisel, *Histoire des ménageries*, vol. II, p. 61.

30 Loisel, *Histoire des ménageries*, vol. II, pp. 24, 31.

31 AN, O^1 1889 B, Plan of Vincennes of 1778; A. Marie, *Naissance de Versailles* (Paris, 1968), pp. 41–2; Paust, *Studien zur barocken Menagerie*, pp. 132–3.

32 H. Scherren, *The Zoological Society of London* (London, 1906), p. 44.

33 Paust, *Studien zur barocken Menagerie*, pp. 86, 98–104, 133, 139; Cisneros, *El Parque zoologico*, pp. 14–16.

34 *Dictionnaire de l'Académie Française* (Paris, 1718). On the etymology of the word, see Rey, *Dictionnaire historique*.

35 Paust, *Studien zur barocken Menagerie*, pp. 19–21.

3 BAROQUE SCENOGRAPHY

1 G. Loisel, *Histoire des ménageries de l'antiquité à nos jours* (Paris, 1912), vol. II, p. 264; W. Kourist, *Vierhundert Jahre Zoo* (Bonn, 1976), pp. 15–16; H. Haupt *et al.*, *Le Bestiaire de Rodolphe II* (Paris, 1990), p. 44.

2 W. Blunt, *The Ark in the Park: The Zoo in the Nineteenth Century* (London, 1976), p. 16.

3 G. Bazin, *Le Temps des musées* (Brussels, 1967), pp. 51, 61; W. H. Adams, *Jardins en France, 1500–1800: Le Rêve et le pouvoir* (Paris, 1980), pp. 11–12, 32; M. Moser and G. Teyssot, eds, *Histoire des jardins de la Renaissance à nos jours* (Paris, 1991), pp. 33–55, 162, 181–2; description of Roman villas in C. Percier and P. Fontaine, *Choix des plus célèbres maisons de plaisance de Rome et de ses environs* (Paris, 1809).

4 H. Acton, *Villas toscanes* (Paris, 1984), p. 54; Moser and Teyssot, *Histoire des jardins de la Renaissance*, p. 55.

5 M. Laird, *Jardins à la française: L'Art et la nature* (Paris, 1992), p. 41.

6 Moser and Teyssot, *Histoire des jardins de la Renaissance*, pp. 87–91; C. Lazzaro, *The Italian Renaissance Garden* (London, 1990), pp. 13, 252.

7 F. Raguenet, *Les Monuments de Rome* (Paris, 1700), pp. 19–46; E. Wharton, *Villas et jardins d'Italie* (Paris, 1986), p. 59.

8 J. Manilli, *Villa Borghèse Fuori di porta Pinciana* (Rome, 1650), pp. 117–18, 161–75; B. Di Gaddo, *Villa Borghèse: Il giardino e le architetture* (Rome, 1985), pp. 15–26, 31, 51–8, 69–78, 93–9; *Il Giardino zoologico di Roma* (Rome, 1935), pp. 23–31 (Rome's zoo

is in the Borghese Gardens).

9   A. Palladio, *Les Quatre Livres de l'architecture* (Paris, 1650),
    pp. 113–29.

10 M. Murado and P. Marton, *Civilisation des villas vénitiennes*
    (Paris, 1987), pp. 84–5, 94–5, 215; K. Pomian, *Collectionneurs,
    amateurs, et curieux, Paris, Venise: XVIᵉ–XVIIᵉ siècle* (Paris,
    1986), pp. 89–91, 119.

11 Adams, *Jardins en France*, pp. 10, 13, 21–5, 30, 37; Moser and
    Teyssot, *Histoire des jardins de la Renaissance*, p. 58.

12 Kayser, *Stockholm*, chap. XI; see also J. Boyceau de la
    Baraudière, *Traité du jardinage* (Paris, 1707), pp. 107–28; A.
    Dézallier d'Argenville, *La Théorie et la pratique du jardinage*
    (Paris, 1713), pp. 85–95.

13 J. C. Nemeitz, *Séjour à Paris* (Leiden, 1727), p. 561; A. Dézallier
    d'Argenville, *Voyage pittoresque des environs de Paris* (Paris,
    1755), p. 260.

14 A. Manesson-Mallet, *Description de l'univers* (Paris, 1683), vol.
    IV, p. 296 (Madrid); J. Furttenbach, *Architectura Civilis* (Ulm,
    1628), and *Architectura Recreationis* (Augsburg, 1640), cited in
    B. Paust, *Studien zur barocken Menagerie in deutschsprachigen
    Raum* (Worms, 1996), pp. 33–6, 50; Moser and Teyssot,
    Histoire des jardins de la Renaissance, pp. 58, 188.

15 J.-F. Solnon, *La Cour de France* (Paris, 1987), pp. 231–5, 262–71,
    385; P. Verlet, *Le Château de Versailles* (Paris, 1985), pp. 125–6.

16 J. Guiffrey, ed., *Comptes des bâtiments du roi sous le règne de
    Louis XIV* (Paris 1881–1901), vol. I, col. 82; BN, Mss, 'Mélanges
    Colbert', vol. CXIX *bis*, fols 583, 1026; vol. CXXVII, fol. 11; vol.
    CXLIX, fol. 558; P. de Nolhac, *La Création de Versailles*
    (Versailles, 1901), p. 211.

17 Y. Bottineau, 'Essais sur Versailles de Louis XIV: La Distribu-
    tion du château et le plan du domaine et de la ville', *Gazette des
    beaux-arts* (September 1988), p. 84.

18 M. de Scudéry, *Célanine* (Paris, 1671), pp. 58–9; J. A. Piganiol
    de La Force, *Nouvelle description des châteaux et parcs de
    Versailles et de Marly* (Paris, 1717), vol. II, p. 190. For an inven-
    tory of the iconography, see Loisel, *Histoire des ménageries*, vol.
    II, pp. 358–67.

19 Based on perspective views, varying in detail but agreeing in
    the essentials, from Perelle, BN, Cabinet des Estampes (before

1668); d'Aveline in A. Manesson-Malet, *La Géometrie pratique*
    (Paris, 1702), pp. 149, 152; and from N. de Fer, BN, Cabinet des
    estampes (1705), which gives the names of the yards.

20 P. Salvadori, *La Chasse sous l'Ancien Régime* (Paris, 1996),
    pp. 213–14; L. Savot, *L'Architecture française des bâtiments parti-
    culiers* (Paris, 1624), pp. 168–9; plan of the château and of the
    gardens of Versailles by Pierre le Pautre (1710); C. Delfante,
    Grande Histoire de la ville (Paris, 1997), pp. 67, 129–57.

21 Solnon, *La Cour de France*, pp. 72, 110–11, 140, 272, 321,
    397–401.

22 Adams, *Jardins en France*, pp. 35, 63–73, 84.

23 A. Félibien, *Les Divertissements de Versailles donnés par le Roi à
    toute sa cour au retour de la conquête de la Franche-Comté* (Paris,
    1674), and *Description du château de Versailles* (Paris, 1696),
    p. 197; A. Marie, *Naissance de Versailles* (Paris, 1968), pp. 47–9.
    See also M.-C. Moine, *Les Fêtes à la cour du Roi-Soleil* (Paris,
    1984); S. Du Crest, *Des fêtes à Versailles: Les Divertissements de
    Louis XI*, (Paris, 1990).

24 G. Dumur, ed., *Histoire des spectacles* (Paris, 1965), pp. 230–34
    (ref.), 581–8, 632–3. On the diffusion of the Italian model in
    France, see J. Jacquot, ed., *Le Lieu théâtral à la Renaissance*
    (Paris, 1964).

25 *Mercure galant* (June 1686); Marquis de Dangeau, *Journal*
    (Paris, 1854–60), entries for 15 November 1696, 23 May 1698,
    28 August 1707; Guiffrey, *Comptes des bâtiments*, vol. IV, cols
    441–2; P. Narbonne, *Journal des règnes de Louis XIV et Louis XV*
    (Paris, 1866), pp. 142, 183.

26 *Gazette de France* (July 1664); Solnon, *La Cour de France*, p. 299;
    Duke de Croy, *Journal* (Paris, 1906), vol. IV, p. 16; Baron
    d'Oberkirch, *Mémoires* (Paris, 1853), vol. I, p. 209; Louis XIV,
    Manière de montrer les jardins (Paris, 1982), pp. 14, 34, 50.

27 Dézallier d'Argenville, *Voyage pittoresque*, pp. 123, 150, 260; M.
    de Scudéry, *La Promenade de Versailles* (Paris, 1669), p. 95;
    Nemeitz, *Séjour à Paris*, p. 507. On the decoration, see F.
    Kimball, 'Le Décor du château de la ménagerie', and G.
    Mabille, 'La Ménagerie de Versailles', *Gazette des Beaux-Arts*
    (1936), pp. 245–6; (1976), pp. 5–36.

28 P.-A. Lablaude, *Les Jardins de Versailles* (Paris, 1995), pp. 34–67.

29 Paust, *Studien zur barocken Menagerie*, pp. 82–136, 146–56,

162–8, 178; H. Hammeyer, 'Der Tiergarten des Prinzen Eugen', *Der Zoologische Garten* (1938–9), pp. 193–8; M. Jimenez de Cisneros, *El Parque zoologico de Madrid, 1774–1994* (Madrid, 1994), pp. 14, 19.

30 J.-F. Blondel, *Cours d'architecture* (Paris 1771–7), vol. IV, pp. 68–9; Paust, *Studien zur barocken Menagerie*, pp. 137–41, 168–72; Here, *Recueil des plans … des châteaux* (Paris, 1753), pl. 4; Dézallier d'Argenville, *Voyage pittoresque*, pp. 339, 344; L. Lambton, *Beastly Buildings: The National Trust Book of Architecture for Animals* (London, 1985), pp. 142, 152.

4 POPULAR PLEASURES

1 H. Haupt *et al.*, *Le Bestiaire de Rodolphe II* (Paris, 1990), p. 31; A. Félibien, *Les Divertissements de Versailles donnés par le Roi à toute sa cour au retour de la conquête de Franche-Comté* (Paris, 1674), and *Description du château de Versailles* (Paris, 1696); L. Thiéry, *Le Voyageur à Paris* (Paris, 1788).

2 L. Lambton, *Beastly Buildings: The National Trust Book of Architecture for Animals* (London, 1985), p. 152

3 M. de Montaigne, *Journal du voyage en Italie* (Paris, 1774); Jean de la Fontaine, *Les Amours de Psyché et de Cupidon* (The Hague, 1700); J.-F. Solnon, *La Cour de France* (Paris, 1987), p. 300; Marquis de Dangeau, *Journal* (Paris, 1854–60), entry for 30 May 1699.

4 B. Paust, *Studien zur barocken Menagerie in deutschsprachigen Raum* (Worms, 1996), p. 133; F. Pieters, 'Notes on the Menagerie and Zoological Cabinet of Stadholder William V of Holland, Directed by Aernout Vosmaer', *Journal of the Society for the Bibliography of Natural History*, IX/4 (1980), p. 540.

5 *Le Voyage de France dressé pour la commodité des Français et des étrangers* (Paris, 1687), p. 235 (Berne); G. Loisel, *Histoire des ménageries de l'antiquité à nos jours* (Paris, 1912), vol. I, pp. 201, 232; vol. II, p. 50.

6 V. Bourilly, ed., *Journal d'un bourgeois de Paris sous le règne de François Ier* (Paris, 1910), p. 49; A. Franklin, *La Vie privée d'autrefois: Les Animaux* (Paris, 1899), vol. II, p. 43.

7 G. Maschietti *et al.*, *Serragli e menagerie in Piemonte nell'ottocento sotto la real casa Savoia* (Turin, 1988), p. 22.

8 *Gazette de France*, 30 July 1633; *Il giardino zoologico di Rome* (Rome, 1935), p. 32; M. Jimenez de Cisneros, *El Parque zoologico de Madrid, 1774–1994* (Madrid, 1994), p. 18; *Discours apologétique en faveur de l'instinct et naturel admirable de l'éléphant* (Rouen, 1627), p. 30.

9 Advertisement of 1749 in E. Camparon, *Les Spectacles de la foire* (Geneva, 1970), vol. II, pp. 312–13; E. Barbier, *Journal historique et anecdotique du règne de Louis XV* (Paris, 1846–1956), vol. III, pp. 68–9.

10 R. Gandilhon, 'Saltimbanques et comédiens aux foires de Reims', *Mémoires de la Société d'Agriculture de la Marne* (1980), pp. 121–36; Campardon, *Les Spectacles*, vol. I, pp. 301, 316, 321, 391; vol. II, pp. 219, 230, 407–8 (this work is a collection of documents).

11 A. Vosmaer, *Description d'un recueil exquis d'animaux rares* (Amsterdam, 1804), p. 5; Lambton, *Beastly Buildings*; Campardon, *Les Spectacles*, vol. I, p. 380: vol. II, p. 107.

12 K. Thomas, *Dans le jardin de la nature* (Paris, 1985), p. 361; Campardon, *Les Spectacles*, vol. I, pp. 30, 321; Barbier, *Journal historique et anecdotique*, vol. II, pp. 68-9; Loisel, *Histoire des ménageries*, vol. I, p. 219; vol. II, p. 53.

13 J. B. Ladvocat, *Lettre sur le rhinocéros* (Paris, 1749); C. Temminck, *Histoire naturelle des pigeons et des gallinacés* (Amsterdam, 1813–15), vol. II, p. 458; A. Schnapper, *Le Géant, la licorne et la tulipe: Collectionneurs et collections dans la France du XVIIe siècle* (Paris, 1988), p. 79.

14 *Journal: Voyage en France (1783–1786)* (Paris, 1896), p. 69.

15 Barbier, *Journal historique et anecdotique*, vol. III, pp. 68–9.

16 Campardon, *Les Spectacles*, vol. I, pp. 151, 362; vol. II, pp. 76, 219, 312; Gandilhon, 'Saltimbanques et comédiens', p. 127–31.

17 Campardon, *Les Spectacles*; Gandilhon, 'Saltimbanques et comédiens', pp. 133–4; A. Kotzbue, *Souvenirs de Paris en 1804* (Paris, 1805), vol. I, p. 74; J. C. Nemeitz, *Séjour à Paris* (Leiden, 1727), p. 177; M. H. Winter, 'Le Spectacle forain', in G. Dumer, ed., *Histoire des spectacles* (Paris, 1965), pp. 1436–8.

18 H. Thetard, *La merveilleuse histoire du cirque* (Paris, 1978), p. 34.

19 C. Patin, *Relations historiques et curieuses de voyages en Allemagne* (Lyon, 1767), p. 233; H. Thétard, *La Merveilleuse Histoire du cirque* (Paris, 1978), pp. 32–4; Thiéry, *Le Voyageur à*

Paris, vol. I, p. 188.

20 R. Delort, *Les Eléphants, piliers du monde* (Paris, 1990), p. 89.

21 L. Orsi, 'The Emblematic Elephant: A Preliminary Approach to the Elephant in Renaissance Thought and Art', *Anthropozoologica*, XX (1994), pp. 69–86.

22 C. Luz, *Exotische Welten: Exotische Phantasien: Das exotische Tier in Europäischen Kunst* (Stuttgart, 1987), pp. 1–18 and Catalogue.

23 X. Salmon, *Versailles: Les Chasses exotiques de Louis XV* (Paris, 1995), pp. 38–98, 100–101.

24 *Ibid.*, pp. 136, 164–8.

25 M. Pinault, *La Peintre et l'histoire naturelle* (Paris, 1990), pp. 12–26, 165–81; Haupt, *Le Bestiaire*, pp. 33–44.

26 G. Petit and J. Theodoridès, *Histoire de la zoologie des origines à Linné* (Paris, 1962), p. 253; A. Baümer, *Zoologie der Renaissance – Renaissance der Zoologie* (1991), vol. II, pp. 9–10; P. Delaunay, *La Zoologie au XVIe siècle* (Paris, 1962), pp. 110–29.

27 Y. Laissus, 'Les Voyageurs naturalistes du Jardin du roi', *Revue d'histoire des sciences*, 3–4 (1981), p. 263; C. Perrault, *Mémoires pour servir à l'histoire naturelle des animaux* (Amsterdam, 1736), Preface, n.p.; L. G. Buffon, *Histoire naturelle* (Paris, 1749), vol. I, pp. V–VI, 5–12, 25 (ref.).

28 P. Belon, *L'Histoire de la nature des oiseaux* (Paris, 1555), fol. III; P. Camper, *Œuvres* (Paris, 1803), vol. I, pp. 282, 295–6; Buffon, *Histoire naturelle*, vol. IX, pp. 1–25; C. Temminck, *Histoire naturelle des pigeons* (Amsterdam, 1813–15), vol. I, pp. 9–13; Pinault, *Le Peintre et l'histoire naturelle*, pp. 31–4, 179–80.

29 Buffon, *Histoire naturelle*, vol. IX, pp. 201–2; Vosmaer, *Description d'un recueil exquis d'animaux rares*; E. Turgot, *Mémoire instructive sur la manière de rassembler, de préparer, de conserver et d'envoyer les diverses curiosités d'histoire naturelle* (Lyon, 1758), pp. 1–2, 12–18, 37–9; Laissus, 'Les voyageurs naturalistes', p. 272; 'Les Cabinets d'histoire naturelle', in R. Taton, ed., *Enseignement et diffusion des sciences en France au XVIIIe siècle* (Paris, 1964), p. 669; H. Daudin, *Les Méthodes de la classification et l'idée de série en botanique et en zoologie de Linné à Lamarck* (Paris, 1926), pp. 61–4, 145–7.

30 Delaunay, *La Zoologie au XVIe siècle*, p. 153; C. Perrault, *Description anatomique de divers animaux disséqués dans l'Académie royale des sciences* (Paris, 1682), p. 53; Camper, *Œuvres*, vol. I, pp. 47, 57, 61, 118.

31 F. Bacon, *La Nouvelle Atlantide* (Paris, 1983), pp. 75–6; Vosmaer, *Description d'un recueil exquis d'animaux rares*, p. III; on Temmink, see Le Vaillant, *Voyage de M. La Vaillant dans l'intérieur de l'Afrique* (Paris, 1790), vol. I, pp. 1–2.

32 Belon, *L'Histoire de la nature des oiseaux*, p. 5; G. Rondelet, *La Première Partie de l'histoire entière des poissons* (Lyon, 1558), Preface; C. Kolb, *Graveurs, artistes et hommes de science: Essai sur les traités de poissons de la Renaissance* (Paris, 1996), p. 21; Perrault, *Mémoires*, Preface, n.p.

33 P. Maupertius, *Lettres sur le progrès des sciences*, in *Œuvres* (Lyon, 1756), vol. II, pp. 387–9; Pieters, 'Notes on the Menagerie and Zoological Cabinet of Stadholder William V of Holland', p. 540; Jimenez de Cisneros, *El Parque zoologico de Madrid*, p. 18; Bachaumont, *Mémoires secretes* (London, 1783), vol. XXI, p. 31 (Buffon).

34 Perrault, *Description anatomique de divers animaux disséqués*, pp. 5–20; Vosmaer, *Description d'un recueil exquis d'animaux rares*, pp. 9–15; Camper, *Œuvres*, vol. I, pp. 58–63, 301; vol. II, p. 26.

35 B. de Fontanels, *Histoire de l'Académie Royale des Sciences* (Paris, 1733), vol. I, p. 322. On the dissections, see Petit and Theodoridès, *Histoire de la zoologie*, pp. 307–30; J. Schiller, 'Les Laboratoires d'anatomie et de botanique à l'Académie des Sciences au XVIIe siècle', *Revue d'histoire des sciences*, 2 (1964), pp. 37–114; Daudin, *Les Méthodes de la classification*, pp. 53–9, 153–7.

36 Kolb, *Graveurs, artistes et hommes*, p. 87; Camper, *Œuvres*, vol. I, p. 56; C. Perrault, *Observations*, pp. 49–71.

37 Delort, *Les Eléphants*, p. 93; M. Jimenez de Cisneros, *Discours apologétique en faveur de l'instinct et naturel admirable de l'éléphant* (Rouen, 1627); J. B. Ladvocat, *Lettre sur le rhinocéros* (Paris, 1749).

38 J. Roger, *Buffon* (Paris, 1989), pp. 352–77, 405–37; G. Leroy, *Lettres sur les animaux 1781* (Paris, 1862), pp. 4–12.

39 Buffon, *Histoire naturelle*, vol. VIII, p. 287; vol. IX, p. 133; Camper, *Œuvres*, vol. II, pp. 29–31; Paust, *Studien zur barocken Menagerie*, p. 134.

40 M. de Scudéry, *Célanine* (Paris, 1671), p. 59; Camper, *Œuvres*, vol. I, p. 276; AN, O¹ 1805, no. 207, loge du rhinocéros, 1776; Perrault, *Description anatomique de divers animaux disséqués*, p. 68; Buffon, *Histoire naturelle*, vol. IX, p. 133.

41 Haupt, *Le Bestiaire*, p. 44; Jimenez de Cisneros, *El Parque zoologico de Madrid*, p. 15; G. Forster, *Voyage pittoresque et philosophique* (Paris, an III), vol. II, p. 332; Hervieux de Chanteloup, *Nouveau Traité des serins de canarie* (Paris, 1719), p. 43.

42 Buffon, *Histoire naturelle*, examples of panthers (vol. IX) and of beavers (vol. VIII); W. Blunt, *Linné* (Paris, 1986), p. 201; Jimenez de Cisneros, *El Parque zoologico de Madrid*, p. 14.

5 THE ELITE AND THE INVENTION OF THE ZOO

1 *Encyclopédie*, articles entitled 'Ménagerie', 'Chasse', 'Cabinet'; L. Strivay, 'Manger juste: Les Droits de l'animal dans les encyclopédies de 1750 à 1800: De l'éthique au politique', in L. Bodson, ed., *Le Statut éthique de l'animal* (Liège, 1996), p. 76.

2 J. D. Hunt, 'Emblème et expressionnisme dans les jardins paysagers du XVIIIᵉ siècle', *Urbi* (1983), pp. xvi–xxxii; M. Mosser and G. Teyssot, eds, *Histoire des jardins de la Renaissance à nos jours* (Paris, 1991), pp. 10, 442.

3 J. C. Nemeitz, *Séjour à Paris* (Leiden, 1727), p. 506; Baron d'Oberkirch, *Mémoires* (Paris, 1853), vol. I, p. 209.

4 J.-F. Solnon, *La Cour de France* (Paris, 1987), pp. 428–42; P. A. Lablaude, *Les Jardins de Versailles* (Paris, 1995), pp. 118–22.

5 AN, O¹ 1805, nos 111–16, 130–40, 202–4, 217–20, 229–30; AJ¹⁵ 512, no. 508; Hezecques, *Souvenirs d'un page de la cour de Louis XVI* (Paris, 1873), p. 248.

6 AJ¹⁵ 512, nos 510–11, 19 September 1792 and 17 January 1793; AJ¹⁵ 844, Jussieu, 'Notes relatives à l'établissement d'une ménagerie', n.d.

7 H. Bernardin de Saint-Pierre, *Mémoire sur la nécessité de joindre une ménagerie au Jardin national des plantes* (Paris, 1792); A. Millen, P. Pinel and A. Brongniart, *Rapport fait à la Société d'Histoire Naturelle de Paris* (Paris, 1792); E. De Lacépède, 'Lettre relative aux établissements publics destinés à renfermer des animaux vivants', *La Décade philosophique* (20 Frimaire, Year IV), vol. VII, pp. 449–62.

8 AN, AJ¹⁵ 844, *procès-verbaux* of police commissioners, (Year II), heading XI, art. 3, cited in M. Foucault, *Histoire de la folie à l'âge classique* (Paris, 1981), p. 443; Y. Laissus and J. J. Petter, *Les Animaux du Muséum 1793–1993* (Paris, 1993), pp. 83–7.

9 N. and J. Dhombres, *Naissance d'un nouveau pouvoir: Sciences et savants en France, 1793–1824* (Paris, 1989), pp. 85–90; G. Legée. 'Le Muséum sous la Révolution, l'Empire et la Restauration', *Histoire de l'enseignement de 1610 à nos jours* (Paris, 1974), p. 750; G. Bazin, *Le Temps des musées* (Brussels, 1967), pp. 169–71; D. Poulot, *Musée, nation, patrimoine 1789–1815* (Paris, 1997).

10 AN, AJ¹⁵ 844, Muséum correspondence (Year II–Year VI), F¹³ 1218 B Muséum to the Ministry of the Interior (25 Prairal, Year IX).

11 G. Toscan, *L'Ami de la nature* (Paris, an VIII), pp. 279–94; F. Boyer, 'La Révolution et les sciences de la nature: Des animaux d'Afrique pour le Muséum (1719–98)', *L'Information historique*, V (1972), pp. 219–22; E. Vignier, *Description abrégée des animaux quadrupèdes de la ménagerie de Tipoo Saib nouvellement achetés à Londres* (Paris, an X), p. 7; *Annales de Muséum* (Paris, 1804), p. 171.

12 AN, AJ¹⁵ 844, Muséum correspondence for Versailles, Raincy, Loo, AF^III 420, 2357, *idem* for Loo; A. Thouin, *Voyage dans la Belgique, la Hollande et l'Italie* (Paris, 1841); F. Boyer, 'Le Transfert à Paris des collections du stathouder', *Annales historiques de la rèvolution française* (1971), pp. 389–404; Laissus and Petter, *Les Animaux du Muséum*, p. 94.

13 Laissus and Petter, *Les Animaux du Muséum*, pp. 100–138.

14 W. H. Adams, *Jardins en France, 1500–1800: Le Rêve et le pouvoir* (Paris, 1980), pp. 111–13; M. Moser and G. Teyssot, eds, *Histoire des jardins de la Renaissance à nos jours* (Paris, 1991), pp. 8–11; J. Starobinski, *L'Invention de la liberté, 1700–1780* (Geneva, 1987), p. 194; J. Ehrard, *L'Idée de nature en France dans la première moitié du XVIIIᵉ siècle* (Paris, 1963); R. Girardin, *De la composition des paysages* (Paris, 1777), p. 8.

15 B. Paust, *Studien zur barocken Menagerie in deutschsprachigen Raum* (Worms, 1996), pp. 183–9; C. Percier and P. Fontaine, *Choix des plus célèbres maisons de plaisance de Rome et de ses*

environs (Paris, 1809).

16 C. Chavard and O. Stemler, *Recherches sur le Raincy* (Paris, 1884), pp. 99–106; E. Ganay, 'Les Jardins à l'anglaise de Mesdames de France à Bellevue et à Versailles', *La Revue de l'art* (1926), p. 222; Lablaude, *Les Jardins de Versailles*, p. 155; L. V. Thiéry, *Le Voyageur à Paris* (Paris, 1761), vol. II, pp. 52–8.

17 Girardin, *De la composition des paysages*, pp. 42–68; H. Walpole, *Essai sur l'art des jardins modernes* (Kirgate and Strawberry Hill, 1975), p. 86; C.C.L. Hirschfeld, *Theorie der Gartenkunst* (Leipzig, 1779–85).

18 Moser and Teyssot, *Histoire des jardins de la Renaissance*, p. 442 (ref.); M. Laugier, *Essai sur l'architecture* (Paris, 1753), pp. 277–84; Walpole, *Essai sur l'art des jardins modernes*, pp. 20–26.

19 *Bulletin de la Société Impériale d'Acclimation* (Paris, 1858), p. 160; Archives Municipales de Lyon), 925 WP 264, Letter from Bühler, September 1858; M. Milne-Edwards, *La Ménagerie, rapport au ministre de l'Instruction publique* (Paris, 1891), p. 20; G. Loisel, 'Rapport sur une mission scientifique dans les jardins et établissements zoologiques publics et privés du Royaume-Uni, de la Belgique et des Pays-Bas', *Nouvelles Archives des missions scientifiques et littéraires* (1907), p. 2.

20 M. Jimenez de Cisneros, *El Parque zoologico de Madrid, 1774–1994* (Madrid, 1994), p. 20; Paust, *Studien zur barocken Menagerie*, p. 190; Loisel, 'Rapport sur une mission scientifique' (1907), pp. 26, 87; (1908), p. 207.

21 W. Blunt, *The Ark in the Park: The Zoo in the Nineteenth Century* (London, 1976), p. 32.

22 A. Dauzat *et al.*, *Nouveau Dictionnaire étymologique et historique* (Paris, 1971).

23 List in G. Loisel, *Histoire des ménageries de l'antiquité à nos jours* (Paris, 1912), vol. III, pp. 430–34; S. Flower, *Report on a Zoological Mission to India in 1913* (Cairo, 1914). The dates vary from place to place.

24 M. Chaumelin,' Promenades artistiques autour de Marseille', *Gazette du Midi* (July 1864–February 1855); *Il Giardino zoologico di Roma* (Rome, 1935), p. 45.

25 Blunt, *The Ark in the Park*, pp. 23–31; E. Lamy, *Zoo* (Geneva, 1968), n.p.; *Il giardino zoologico di Roma*, pp. 38–9; J. Rousseau, *Historique du parc zoologique de Paris, 1934–1984* (Paris, 1984).

26 E. A. Hanson, 'Nature Civilized: A Cultural History of American Zoo 1870–1940' (thesis, University of Philadelphia, 1996), p. 12, list and dates of conception and opening.

27 *Rapport de M. le Sénateur chargé de l'administration du Rhône au conseil municipal de Lyon* (Lyon, 1856); O. Teissier, *Marseille et ses monuments* (Paris, 1867), p. 119; J. Hässlin, *Der zoologische Garten zu Köln* (Cologne, 1960), pp. 13, 30–31.

28 A. Brauman and S. Demanet, *Le Parc Léopold, 1850–1950: Le Zoo, la cité scientifique et la ville* (Brussels, 1985), p. 143; H. Ritvo, *The Animal Estate: The English and Other Creatures in the Victorian Age* (London, 1990), pp. 206–10; Blunt, *The Ark in the Park*, pp. 26, 51, 84–98; *Bulletin de la Société Impériale d'Acclimation* (1854), p. XXIX; Archives du Muséum National d'Histoire Naturelle), register 41.

29 AML, 485 WP 12–14; K. Pomian, *Collectionneurs, amateurs, et curieux, Paris, Venise: XVIe–XVIIe siècle* (Paris, 1986), pp. 7–8.

30 Blunt, *The Ark in the Park*, p. 26; Loisel, 'Rapport sur une mission scientifique', pp. 7–8, 65, 73–5, 85–6, 99; A. Esquiros, 'Des jardins zoologiques: Les Sociétés d'histoire naturelle en Belgique', *Revue des deux mondes*, 15 November 1854, pp. 691–2. See also M. Agulhon, *Le Cercle dans la France bourgeoise: 1810–1848* (Paris, 1977).

31 Brauman and Demanet, *Le Parc Léopold*, p. 13; Archives Municipales de Marseille, 64 R 1, Rapport de la société (9 August 1864); Loisel, 'Rapport sur une mission scientifique', (1907), pp. 24–5, 66, 97; (1908), p. 176.

32 Loisel, 'Rapport sur une mission scientifique', pp. 73–4, 85; Brauman and Demanet, *Le Parc Léopold*, pp. 12, 22–4; B. Marrey and J.-P. Monet, *La Grande Histoire des serres et des jardins d'hiver, France, 1780–1900* (n.p., n.d.), p. 161; Hässlin, *Der zoologische Garten zu Köln*, pp. 17, 52; J. Gebbing, *50 Jahre Leipziger Zoo* (Leipzig, 1928), pp. 93ff.

33 Jimenez de Cisneros, *El Parque zoologico de Madrid*, p. 22; Marrey and Monet, *La Grande Histoire des serres*, pp. 43–8.

34 Cited by Brauman and Demanet, *Le Parc Léopold*, p. 141. See also L.-M. Nourry, *Les Jardins publics en province: Espace et politique au XIXe siècle* (Lyon, 1996), vol. I, pp. 230–31.

35 *Rapport de M. le Sénateur chargé de l'administration du Rhône*, pp. 1–3; E. André, *Traité général de la composition des jardins* (Paris, 1879), p. 197; Moser and Teyssot, *Histoire des jardins de la Renaissance*, pp. 369–93. On Germany, see G. Gusdorf, *Le Savoir romantique de la nature* (Paris, 1985).

36 A. Corbin, ed., *L'Avènement des loisirs* (Paris, 1995), pp. 134–9; Teissier, *Marseille et ses monuments*, pp. 37–45; J. Siepi, *Petite Histoire du jardin zoologique de Marseille* (Marseille, 1937), p. 5; *Tête-d'Or: Un Parc d'exception créé par Denis Bülher* (Lyon, 1992); Hässlin, *Der zoologische Garten zu Köln*.

37 Laissus and Petter, *Les Animaux du Muséum*, pp. 94, 102; Ritvo, *The Animal Estate*, pp. 206–14; Blunt, *The Ark in the Park*, pp. 32, 211–12.

38 In 1870. R. J. Stott, *The American Idea of a Zoological Park* (Santa Barbara, 1981), p. 3.

39 J. Spraul-Schmidt, 'Designing the Late XIXth Century Suburban Landscape: The Cincinnati Zoological Garden', *Queen City Heritage*, LI/1 (1993), pp. 40–51.

40 Brauman and Demanet, *Le Parc Léopold*, pp. 13–22; *Il giardino zoologico di Roma*, pp. 45–7; *Zoo: Mémoires de l'éléphant, le zoo de Genève à Saint-Jean entre 1935 et 1940* (Geneva, 1993), pp. 15, 80–114.

41 Loisel, *Histoire des ménageries*, vol. III, p. 164; *idem*, 'Rapport sur une mission scientifique', pp. 8, 11, 74–6, 99; Ritvo, *The Animal Estate*, pp. 213–17.

42 AMM, 64 R 2, Rostant report, 9 October 1877, 64 R 1 and 110 M 4, garden repurchase; AML, 458 WP 12–14, park concessions; Jimenez de Cisneros, *El Parque zoologico de Madrid*, pp. 47–56; Loisel, *Histoire des ménageries*, vol. III, pp. 110–13, 408ff.

43 Loisel, *Histoire des ménageries*, vol. III, pp. 411, 414; AMM, 110 M 4, treatise of 10 October 1877 and repossession, 1889; AN, AJ¹⁵ 844, documents on upkeep of the Jardin des Plantes; Milne-Edwards, *La Ménagerie*, pp. 9–16.

44 AMM, 1 D 101, municipal council, 30 December 1869; Estienne, *Observations présentées … à la commission municipale de la ville de Lyon* (Lyon, 1873); 'Centenaire du parc zoologique et botanique', *Bulletin de la Société Industrielle de Mulhouse*, I (1968), p. 13; R. Oberle and M. Stahl–Weber, *Mulhouse:*

Panorama monumental et architectural (Contades, 1983), pp. 152–6; Loisel, *Histoire des ménageries*, vol. III, pp. 111, 281.

45 Hanson, 'Nature Civilized', esp. pp. 21–3.

46 J. N. Hyson, 'Urban Jungles: Zoos and American Society', thesis (Cornell University, 1999), pp. 66–9.

47 AN, O¹ 1292, list of animals for Mme Bonaparte, Year VII; Paust, *Studien zur barocken Menagerie*, pp. 95, 119, 142, 190; Ritvo, *The Animal Estate*, pp. 213–14; Jimenez de Cisneros, *El Parque zoologico de Madrid*, p. 36.

48 Paust, *Studien zur barocken Menagerie*, p. 135; A. Marotta, *Il Real Giardino Zoologico*, special issue of *Storia dell'urbanistica piemonte* (1989), pp. 5–17; G. Maschietti *et al.*, *Serragli e menagerie in Piemonte nell'ottocento sotto la real casa Savoia* (Turin, 1988), pp. 43–59, 82–3, 121, 135, 138, 155–62.

49 Maschietti, *Serragli e menagerie*, pp. 84–6; Ritvo, *The Animal Estate*, pp. 238–9; L. Lambton, *Beastly Buildings: The National Trust Book of Architecture for Animals* (London, 1985), pp. 39–47; Loisel, 'Rapport sur une mission scientifique', pp. 35–6; Marrey and Monet, *La Grande Histoire des serres*, p. 101; Corbin, *L'Avènement des loisirs*, pp. 90–98; C.-I. Brelot, 'Noblesse et animal domestique au XIXᵉ siècle', *Cahiers d'histoire*, III–IV (1997), pp. 639–53.

50 Sale and gifts of animals in AN, AJ¹⁵ 844–6; AMNHM, registers 29, 31, 41; AML, 485 WP 11, 961 WP 73; AMM, 64 R 3; Blunt, *The Ark in the Park*, pp. 68, 87–9; H. Coupin, *L'Aquarium d'eau douce et ses habitants animaux et végétaux* (Paris, 1893).

51 *Magasin pittoresque* (1900), p. 258. See also F. Gastou, *Sur les traces des montreurs d'ours de Pyrénées et d'ailleurs* (Toulouse, 1987).

52 Loisel, *Histoire des ménageries*, vol. III, pp. 301–4; J. Turner, *Reckoning with the Beast: Animals, Pain and Humanity in the Victorian Mind* (London, 1980), pp. 20–28; C. Hagenbeck, *Cages sans barreaux* (Paris, 1951), pp. 1–17.

53 Lambton, *Beastly Buildings*, p. 147; Loisel, *Histoire des ménageries*, vol. III, pp. 305–16; H. Thétard, *Les Dompteurs* (Paris, 1928), p. 9; Ritvo, *The Animal Estate*, p. 207.

54 P. Jacob, *La Grande Parade du cirque* (Paris, 1992), pp. 55–77; Thétard, *Les Dompteurs* (Paris, 1928), pp. 24, 39; *idem*, *La Merveilleuse Histoire du cirque* (Paris, 1978), pp. 10–14, 34–8,

42–55, 71–3, 152, 174–81; AML, 485 WP 4, Bidel proposition, 1876; Hagenbeck, *Cages sans barreaux*, p. 86.

55 Hyson, 'Urban Jungles', pp. 16–18 etc.

6 IMPERIAL GLORY

1 L. Heck, *Aus der Wildnis in den Zoo auf Tierfang in Ostafrica* (Berlin, 1930).

2 AN, AJ[15] 846, off-season hunting permit for naturalist, 9 March 1914.

3 J. Janin and M. Boitard, *Le Jardin des plantes* (Paris, 1942), p. XXVII.

4 A. Corbin, ed., *L'Avènement des loisirs* (Paris, 1995), p. 98.

5 H. Reichenbach, 'Carl Hagenbeck's Tierpark and Modern Zoological Gardens', *Journal of the Society for the Bibliography of Natural History* (April 1980), pp. 573–85.

6 H. Ritvo, *The Animal Estate* (London, 1987), p. 248.

7 13 March 1891, Société Nationale d'Acclimation, Paris, p. 47.

8 A. Sparman, *Voyage au cap de Bonne-Ésperance autour du monde avec le capitaine Cook* (Paris, 1787), pp. 1, 28.

9 C. Hagenbeck, *Cages sans barreaux* (Paris, 1951), p. 156.

10 H. Thétard, *Les Dompteurs* (Paris, 1928), p. 319; Hagenbeck, *Cages sans barreaux*, pp. 129, 146.

11 H. Velvin, *Le Dressage des fauves par Bostock* (Paris), p. 123; M. E. Fowler, *Restraint and Handling of Wild and Domestic Animals* (Ames, IA, 1995); AN AJ[15] 846, 24 January 1925.

12 *Zoo* (May 1957), pp. 12–23; J. J. Anderson, 'Restoring a Wilderness … Pilanesberg', *International Zoological Yearbook* (1986), pp. 192–9.

13 A. Maillot, 'Méthode d'enrichissement de l'environnement des primates de l'ancien monde en captivité', vet. thesis (Maisons-Alfort, 1994), p. 73; H. Hediger, *Les Animaux sauvages en captivité* (Paris, 1953), pp. 190–203.

14 AML, 961 WP 72, E. Herriot to the Governor-general of Algeria, 2 October 1928; AN, AJ[15] 846, V. Godefroi, Proposition to the Muséum, Danané, 18 February 1926; The Lieutenant-governor to the Director of the Muséum, 28 February 1927; AN, AJ[15] 845, Millet-Horsin, request to hunt off-season; Affaire Fournière, Sergeant-major of the colonial infantry, 6 June

1922; Groleau sur Fournière, 18 September 1921; etc.

15 AMNH, dossier 45, E. Bourdelle, *Notes sur les parcs nationaux de refuge pour les espèces animales en A-OF et sur la réglementation de la chasse en A-OF*, pp. 3, 46.

16 AML, 961 WP 72, Administer-in-Chief of the Cameroon colonies to Pochard, 26 November 1931.

17 E. Bourdelle, IIe Congrès, p. 79; S. Flower, *Report on a Zoological Mission to India in 1913* (Cairo, 1914), pp. 41–3.

18 AN, AJ[15] 846, Director of the Muséum to the Colonial Minister, 7 October 1920; E. Bourdelle, IIe Congrès, p. 79; AML, 963 WP 37, Muséum to the Mayor, 1 January 1933; M. Rondet-Saint, *L'Organisation des colonies françaises au point de vue cynégétique* (Melun, 1931).

19 Y. Laissus and J. J. Petter, *Les Animaux du Muséum 1793–1993* (Paris, 1993), pp. 11, 103, 104, 113, 125; G. Toscan, *L'Ami de la nature* (Paris, an VIII), pp. 279–94; E. Vignier, *Description abrégée des animaux quadrupèdes de la ménagerie de Tipoo Saib nouvellement achetés à Londres* (Paris, an X), p. 7; *Annales du Muséum National d'Histoire Naturelle* (Paris, 1804), p. 171.

20 *Zoo* (January 1983), p. 12 and elsewhere.

21 B. Berg, *Meine Jagd nach dem Einhorn* (Leipzig, 1933); *Le Tigre et l'homme* (Paris, 1938), p. 162; P. Eiper, *Un Cirque en voyage* (Paris, 1941); *Les Bêtes vous regardent* (Paris, 1954).

22 G. Durrell, *Un Zoo dans ma maison* (Paris, 1964), pp. 106–17; idem, *Un Zoo pas comme les autres* (Paris, 1972); idem, *L'Arche immobile* (Paris, 1976).

23 A. Mercier, *Je suis un assassin* (Paris, 1954), p. 33; J.-Y. Domalain, *L'Adieu aux bêtes* (Grenoble, 1976).

24 Hagenbeck, *Cages sans barreaux*, p. 156.

25 F. Cuvier, *Annales du Muséum d'Histoire Naturelle*, XVI (1810), pp. 51–2; C. Sevin, 'La Ménagerie du Muséum d'Histoire Naturelle de Paris', vet. thesis (Maisons-Alfort, 1990), p. 85; W. Blunt, *The Ark in the Park: The Zoo in the Nineteenth Century* (London, 1976), pp. 178–87; AML, 961 WP 72, 1928.

26 AN, AJ[15] 845, expenses for transport of a collection of animals on the German vessel *Drachenfelt* [*sic*] to the Muséum, 1922.

27 AML, 963 WP 37, invoice, 16 September 1924.

28 R. Hartmann, *Les Singes anthropoïdes et leur organisation comparée à celle de l'homme* (Paris, 1886), p. 195; *Zoo* (June

1948), p. 13.

29 Reichenbach, 'Carl Hagenbeck's Tierpark', p. 574; G. Loisel, *Histoire des ménageries de l'antiquité à nos jours* (Paris, 1912), vol. III, p. 327; M. Rondet-Saint, *Rapport sur l'exportation des animaux vivants, visés par la réglementation de la chasse aux Colonies et des dépouilles d'animaux* (Paris, 1931), pp. 129–34.

30 J.-P. Pouvreau, 'Quelques réflexions sur la captivité des animaux'; 'La Confession d'un ancien trafiquant au Laos', *Bulletin herpétologique de J.-P. Pouvreau*, III (n.d.); J. Fisher, *Le Zoo, son histoire, son univers* (Paris, 1967), p. 112.

31 Report BUAV, *Animals International* (1993); G. Loisel, 'Rapport sur une mission scientifique dans les jardins et établissements zoologiques publics et privés du Royaume-Uni, de la Belgique et des Pays-Bas', *Nouvelles archives des missions scientifiques et littéraires*, XIV (1907), p. 77.

32 *Zoo* (January 1958).

33 C. J. Cornish, *Life at the Zoo* (London, 1889), p. 198. Archives du Muséum, Paris, registre 19.

34 Cornish, *Life at the Zoo*, p. 198; H. Ritvo, *The Animal Estate: The English and Other Creatures in the Victorian Age* (London, 1987), p. 24.

35 E. A. Hanson, 'Nature Civilized: A Cultural History of American Zoo 1870–1940' (thesis, University of Philadelphia, 1996), pp. 312–19. R. W. Flint, 'American Showmen and European Dealers', in R. J. Hoage and W. Deiss, eds, *New Worlds, New Animals: From Menagerie to Zoological Park in the Nineteenth Century* (London, 1996), pp. 97–108.

36 AM, Paris, Registres 25, 40, 41. AN, Paris, AJ[15] 845.

37 Reichenbach, 'Carl Hagenbeck's Tierpark', Bibliography; H. J. Tast, 'Projekt "Wild Tiere, frei Haus"', *Kulleraugen-Studium*, XXX (November 1991); 'Franz Kraml, Karrier eines Dompteurs', *Alfelt aktuell*, X/80; 'Hermann Ruhe ist heute 75', *Alfelt aktuell*, 3 June 1970, p. 7; Eiper, *Les Bêtes vous regardent*, p. 172; R. Flint, in Hoage and Deiss, *New Worlds, New Animals*, pp. 97, 102.

38 AN, AJ[15], Director of the Muséum to the Minister, 7 October 1920.

39 A. Esquiros, 'Des jardins zoologiques: Les Sociétés d'histoire naturelle en Belgique', *Revue des deux mondes*, 15 November 1854, p. 691; M. A. Cap, *Le Muséum d'Histoire Naturelle* (Paris,

1854), p. 152.

40 Laissus, *Les Animaux du Muséum*, p. 137; G. Maschietti *et al.*, *Serragli e menagerie in Piemonte nell'ottocento sotto la real casa Savoia* (Turin, 1988), pp. 75–8; A. Brauman and S. Demanet, *Le Parc Léopold, 1850–1950: Le Zoo, la cité scientifique et la ville* (Brussels, 1985), p. 15.

41 P. Street, *The London Zoo* (London, 1965); G. Loisel, 'Projet et études sur la réorganisation et l'utilisation de la ménagerie du Jardin des plantes', *La Revue des idées* (1907), p. 12; M. Milne-Edwards, *La Ménagerie: Rapport au ministre de l'Instruction publique* (Paris, 1891); 'De l'influence des grands froids de l'hiver sur quelques-uns des animaux de la ménagerie du Muséum d'histoire naturelle', *Comptes rendus de l'Académie des sciences*, CXII (26 January 1891), pp. 16–22.

42 *L'Eclair*, 16 December 1904; AML, for example, 485 WP 11, report by the Engineer of Roads, 19 November 1877, 18 July 1981, etc.

43 AN, AJ[15] 845, D. Ahn to Trouessard, 5 April 1913; Professor of Pathology Lucet to the Director, 7 August 1915.

44 AMHN, Delacour mission, ms 44, fol. 202, 28 April 1932; Tchad, R. 30, fol. 73; Shanghai, R. 31.

45

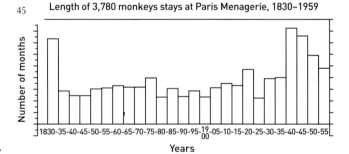

Length of 3,780 monkeys stays at Paris Menagerie, 1830–1959

Number of months

Years

Number of monkeys calculated over five-year periods ('1830–17.' means 17 monkeys on average from 1830 to 1834): 1830– 17. 1835– 154. 1840– 229. 1845– 146. 1850– 152. 1855– 118. 1860– 168. 1865– 165. 1870– 163. 1875– 83. 1880– 171. 1885– 143. 1890– 231. 1895– 216. 1900– 284. 1905– 240. 1910– 231. 1915– 68. 1920– 92. 1925– 152. 1930– 237. 1935– 109. 1940– 20. 1945–104. 1950– 49. 1955– 38.

46 Average number of deaths by month from 1850 to 1899: January 168, February 115, March 127, April 77, May 73, June 72, July 81, August 77, September 101, October 99, November 98, December 137.

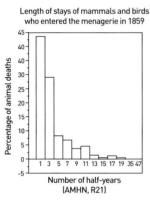

Length of stays of mammals and birds who entered the menagerie in 1859

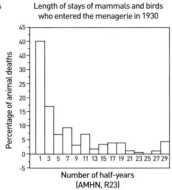

Length of stays of mammals and birds who entered the menagerie in 1930

47 U. Gijzen, in *Zoo* (May 1965), pp. 8–26; AMHN, ms 44, p. 132.

48 AMHN, R 27, 28, 29. Average survival for 16 gibbons: 16.38 months; for 37 orang-utans: 21.16 months; for 39 chimpanzees: 12.46 months; for 4 gorillas: 31.5 months (1837–1965).

49 A. Schultz, *Les Primates*, p. 193.

50 Eiper, *Les Bêtes vous regardent*, p. 213; Hediger, *Les Animaux sauvages*, p. 103.

51 AMHN, ms 44, p. 161; E. Bourdelle and A. Mouquet, 'La Longévité des mammifères à la ménagerie', *Bulletin du Muséum*, II (1930), pp. 288–97.

52 Hediger, *Les Animaux sauvages*, p. 46; L. C. Randall, *Wild Animals in Captivity* (Chicago, 1964); Hoage and Deiss, *New Worlds, New Animals*, p. XIV.

53 U. and W. Dolder, *Le Grand Livre du zoo* (Zurich, 1979), p. 106.

54 F. Doumenge, 'Lettres des téléspectateurs', *Télé 7 jours*, 25 August 1979, p. 1, response to letter of 27 July.

55 A. Dumeril, 'Troisième Notice sur la ménagerie des reptiles du Muséum', *Nouvelles Archives du Muséum National d'Histoire Naturelle* (Paris, 1865), pp. 31–46, esp. p. 40; O. Teissier, *Marseille et ses monuments* (Paris, 1867); AML, 485 WP 11, gifts of animals, 1865, etc.; AMNH, ms 2225, Colonial biological office project, 1900.

56 *Journal des débats*, 7 April 1905.

57 L. Heck, *Führer durch den Berliner zoologischen Garten* (Berlin, 1903), pp. 16, 32.

58 Ritvo, *The Animal Estate*, pp. 229, 231.

59 S. Flower, *Report on the Zoological Service for the Year 1912*, and *Report on a Zoological Mission to India* (Cairo, 1913); *Zoologischer Beobachter* (May 1908), p. 9; (1909), pp. 105, 308 etc.; 'Les Zoos dans le monde' (1909), p. 251; (1914); Loisel, *Histoire des ménageries*, vol. III, pp. 17–23; L. Gulbanks, in Hoage and Deiss, *New Worlds, New Animals*, p. 73.

60 *Zoo*, esp. (October 1952), p. 50; (September–October 1953), p. 29; (May 1954), p. 21; (January 1972), pp. 116–17.

61 Loisel, *Histoire des ménageries*, vol. I, p. 204; Hagenbeck, *Cages sans barreaux*, pp. 60–69; D. Verniquet, *Exposition d'un projet sur le Muséum d'Histoire Naturelle et sur une ménagerie* (Paris, an XI), p. 23; R. Flint, in Hoage and Deiss, *New Worlds, New Animals*, p. 106.

62 Loisel, *Histoire des ménageries*, vol. III, p. 274; G. Bazin, *Le Temps des musées* (Brussels, 1967), pp. 237–8. Unless otherwise indicated, all details on the ethnological exhibition come from H. Thode-Arora, *Für fünfzig Pfennig um die Welt: Die Hagenbeckschen Völkerschauen* (Frankfurt, 1989), esp. pp. 34, 35, 111, 168–75, table, 176–9.

63 AN, F[12] 12600.

64 *Guide de l'Exposition 1900* (Paris, 1902), pp. 348–57; AMHN, R 19; AN, AJ[15] 846, to Manin, 21 October 1921.

65 H. Thétard, *Des hommes et des bêtes: Le Zoo de Lyautey* (Paris, c. 1945).

66 E. Bourdelle, 'Répartition des animaux des colonies …', *Bulletin du Muséum* (1931), pp. 586–7.

67 Boulineau, *Les Jardins animés*, p. 49; Thétard, *Des hommes et des bêtes*, p. 176.

7 THE EXPLOITATION OF NATURE

1 G, Légée, 'Le Muséum sous la Révolution, l'Empire et la Restauration', in *Histoire de l'enseignement de 1610 à nos jours* (Paris, 1972), p. 752; G. Loisel, 'Rapport sur une mission scientifique dans les jardins et établissements zoologiques publics

et privés du Royaume-Uni, de la Belgique et des Pays-Bas', *Nouvelles Archives des missions scientifiques et littéraires* (1907), pp. 107, 163; (1908), p. 135.

2 H. Bernardin de Saint-Pierre, *Mémoire sur la nécessité de joindre une ménagerie au Jardin National des Plantes* (Paris, 1792), pp. 31–6.

3 F. Cuvier, 'Du rut', and 'Description d'un orang-outang et observations sur ses facultés intellectuelles', *Annales du Muséum* (1807), p. 119 (ref.); (1810), pp. 46–65; 'De la sociabilité des animaux', and 'Essai sur la domesticité des mammifères', *Mémoires du Muséum* (1825), pp. 1–27, 406–55; Y. Laissus, *Les Animaux du Muséum 1793–1993* (Paris, 1993), pp. 128–34.

4 Loisel, 'Rapport sur une mission scientifique' (1907), pp. 24, 109.

5 R. Hartmann, *Les Singes anthropoïdes et leur organisation comparée à celle de l'homme* (Paris, 1886), pp. 171–204; G. Thines, *Psychologie des animaux* (Brussels, 1966), pp. 23–5; J. Vauclair, *L'Intelligence de l'animal* (Paris, 1992), pp. 17–19; C. Blanckaert, 'Les Animaux "utiles" chez Isidore Geoffroy Saint-Hilaire: La Mission sociale de la zootechnie', *Revue de synthèse* (1992), III–IV, p. 369.

6 E. de Lacépède and G. Cuvier, *La Ménagerie du Muséum* (Paris, an X); E. Geoffroy Saint-Hilaire, 'Extrait d'un mémoire sur l'orang-outang vivant actuellement à la ménagerie', *Comptes rendus des sciences de l'Académie des Sciences*, III (1836), pp. 601–2; Loisel, 'Rapport sur une mission scientifique' (1907), pp. 24, 87; (1908), pp. 135, 163.

7 M. Pinault, *Le Peintre et l'histoire naturelle* (Paris, 1990), p. 26; W. Blunt, *The Ark in the Park: The Zoo in the Nineteenth Century* (London, 1976), pp. 50–51, 215; R. Taton, ed., *Histoire générale des sciences* (Paris, 1981), vol. III, pp. 405–23; L. Gaillard, 'La Découverte d'espèces de grands mammifères entre 1950 et 1994', thesis (Maisons-Alfort, 1997), p. 188.

8 Loisel, 'Rapport sur une mission scientifique' (1907), pp. 74, 85; AML, 485 WP 4, Commission report, 24 October 1876, Lortet correspondence, 3 May 1881.

9 *Annales du Muséum* (1804), p. 54; *Nouvelles Archives du Muséum* (1870), p. 31.

10 Blunt, *The Ark in the Park*, pp. 44, 45.

11 G. Cuvier, *Leçons d'Anatomie comparée* (Paris, 1799–1805), vol. I, p. IX; M. A. Caped., *Le Muséum d'Histoire Naturelle* (Paris, 1854), p. 154; C. Sévin, 'La Ménagerie du MNIIN, de sa création à son apogée', thesis (Maisons-Alfort, 1986), p. 74; AN, AJ¹⁵ 844, 845.

12 M. Jimenez de Cisneros, *El Parque zoologico de Madrid, 1774–1994* (Madrid, 1994), p. 21; G. Maschietti *et al.*, *Serragli e menagerie in Piemonte nell'ottocento sotto la real casa Savoia* (Turin, 1988), pp. 151–2; AMM, 110 M 4, Treatise of 10 October 1877; Loisel, 'Rapport sur une mission scientifique' (1907), p. 24; (1908), pp. 135, 276; Blunt, *The Ark in the Park*, pp. 164, 198, 201.

13 H. Daudin, *Les Classes zoologiques et l'idée de série animale en France à l'époque de Lamarck et de Cuvier (1790–1830)* (Paris, 1926), pp. 3–19, 52–59, 73–5; F. Dagognet, 'La Situation de Cuvier dans l'histoire de la biologie', *Revue d'histoire des sciences* (1970), pp. 49–62; B. Balan, *L'Ordre et le temps: L'Anatomie comparée et l'histoire des vivants au XIXᵉ siècle* (Paris, 1979), pp. 12–16.

14 R. Taton, ed., *Histoire générale des sciences*, vol. III/1, pp. 485–502; vol. III/2, pp. 665–8; Laissus, *Les Animaux du Muséum*, pp. 139, 154, 174.

15 R. Lancaster, in *Encyclopaedia Britannica*, vol. XXIV (1889), p. 856; G. Loisel, 'Projets et études sur la réorganisation et l'utilisation de la ménagerie du Jardin des Plantes', *La Revue des idées* (Paris, 1907), pp. 9–14; C. Schnitter, 'Le Développement du Muséum d'Histoire Naturelle de Paris au cours de la seconde moitié du XIXᵉ siècle: "Se transformer ou périr"', *Revue d'histoire des sciences*, I (1996), pp. 86–94.

16 M. Milne-Edwards, *La Ménagerie: Rapport au ministre de l'Instruction publique* (Paris, 1891), pp. 10–12; H. Dathe, *Der Zoologische Garten Leipzig: Eine Stätte der Wissenschaft im Auftrage des zoologischen Gartens Leipzig* (Leipzig, 1961), pp. 138–54; J. Rousseau, *Historique du parc zoologique de Paris* (Paris, 1984), pp. 20–23.

17 L. Jauffret, *Voyage au Jardin des Plantes* (Paris, 1798), p. 52; H. Ritvo, *The Animal Estate: The English and Other Creatures in the Victorian Age* (London, 1990), pp. 210–11, 233–4; M. Osborne,

Nature, the Exotic and the Science of French Colonialism (Indianapolis, 1994); *Il giardino zoologico di Roma* (Rome, 1935), pp. 69–70.

18 R. Rey, 'L'Animalité dans l'œuvre de Bernardin de Saint-Pierre', *Revue du synthèse*, III–IV (1992), pp. 312–18; E. de Lacépède, 'Lettre relative aux établissements publics destinés à renfermer des animaux vivants', *La Décade philosophique* (an IV), pp. 456–9; D. Verniquet, *Exposition d'un projet sur le Muséum d'Histoire Naturelle et sur une ménagerie* (Paris, an X), pp. 6–16; AN, AJ¹⁵ 846, National menagerie programme, 27 Pluviose, Year X.

19 *Annales du Muséum* (1803), p. 246; AN, F¹² 1218 B, Molinos's first design, Year X; F¹³ 1218 A, Correspondence on the rotunda, 9 and 13 August 1810; AJ¹⁵ 844, Muséum to Molinos, 11 June 1817.

20 I. Geoffroy Saint-Hilaire, *Note sur la ménagerie* (Paris, 1860), pp. 9–10; Milne-Edwards, *La Ménagerie*, p. 25; P. Bouissac, 'Perspectives ethnologiques: La Statut symbolique de l'animal au cirque et au zoo', *Ethnologie française*, III–IV (1972) p. 254.

21 *Animals at the Zoo* (London, 1907); K. Baedeke, *Londres et ses environs* (Leipzig, 1890), pp. 156–9 (map); AML 485 WP 10, 961 WP 73, 963 WP 39, plans of cages.

22 Blunt, *The Ark in the Park*, p. 88; *Illustration*, 13 October 1860; G. Loisel, *Histoire des ménageries de l'antiquité à nos jours* (Paris, 1912), vol. III, pp. 257, 288–91, 355–8.

23 For a detailed description of zoos of the period, see Loisel, 'Rapport sur une mission scientifique' (1907), pp. 1–112; (1908), pp. 125–282. See also H. Strehlow, 'Zoos and Aquariums of Berlin', in R. Hoage and W. Deiss, eds, *New Worlds, New Animals: From Menagerie to Zoological Park in the Nineteenth Century* (London, 1996), pp. 63–72.

24 B. Denis, 'Les Zootechniciens français et l'éthique animale', in L. Bodson, ed., *Le Statut éthique de l'animal* (Liège, 1996), p. 106; AML, 485 WP 10, 11, 12, for the selection criteria; Ritvo, *The Animal Estate*, p. 208, and 'The Order of Nature: Constructing the Collections of Victorian Zoos', in Hoage and Deiss, *New Worlds, New Animals*, pp. 43–62; Loisel, 'Rapport sur une mission scientifique' (1908), p. 135.

25 Loisel, *Histoire des ménageries*, vol. I, pp. 23, 73–80, 282–4; vol.

II, pp. 16, 19, 322–32; A. Thouin, *Voyage dans la Belgique, la Hollande et l'Italie* (Paris, 1841), vol. II, pp. 429–32 (dromedaries); J. Risse, *Histoire de l'élevage français* (Paris, 1994), pp. 109–10; A. Raillet, *Histoire de l'école d'Alfort* (Paris, 1907); F. Audouin-Rouzeau, 'Les Eléments nouveaux de l'élevage aux temps modernes', *Cahiers d'histoire*, III–IV (1997), pp. 481–509.

26 *Histoire naturelle* (Paris), vol. XII, p. 95; vol. XIII, p. 31; AN, AJ¹⁵ 512, 374, report of 1 July 1774; *Mémoires de l'Académie Impériale et Royale de Bruxelles* (1777); *Voyages en France* (Paris, 1793), vol. I, p. 12; Cuvier, 'Essai sur la domesticité des mammifères', pp. 406–55.

27 Bernardin de Saint-Pierre, *Mémoire sur la nécessité de joindre une ménagerie*, pp. 18–21; Lacépède, 'Lettre relative aux établissements publics', pp. 449–62; L. Daubenton, in *Recueil des séances des Ecoles Normales*, I (1800), p. 108.

28 G. Toscan, *L'Ami de la nature* (Paris, an X), pp. 265–78; I. Geoffroy Saint-Hilaire, *Acclimatation et domestication des animaux utiles*, new edn (Paris, 1986), pp. 8–9; Ritvo, *The Animal Estate*, p. 211; Loisel, 'Rapport sur une mission scientifique' (1907), p. 74; AMM 110 M 4, Report of 6 March 1876; Maschietti, *Serragli e menagerie*, pp. 152–4.

29 A. Déclémy, *Considérations sur l'établissement d'une volière au jardin du roi* (Paris, 1841), pp. 31–3, 62–4.

30 *Dictionnaire historique de la langue française* (Paris, 1992); Geoffroy Saint-Hilaire, *Acclimatation et domestication des animaux utiles*, pp. 5, 15, 52–5, 117, 140–41, 149, 156; Blanckaert, 'Les Animaux "utiles" chez Isidore Geoffroy Saint-Hilaire', pp. 347–82.

31 *Bulletin de la Société Zoologique d'Acclimatation* (1854), pp. V–XXXVIII; (1858), pp. 154–5; (1859), p. XIV; (1860), p. 421; Ritvo, *The Animal Estate*, pp. 239–40; Osborne, *Nature, the Exotic and the Science of French Colonialism*.

32 *Bulletin de la Société Zoologique d'Acclimatation* (1858), pp. 153–60, 236–8; (1859), p. 94; (1860), pp. 290–97, 519–24; (1861), p. XIV; Société anonyme du Jardin d'Acclimatation, *Rapport du conseil d'administration* (Paris, 1861), pp. 3–31; Geoffroy Saint-Hilaire, *Acclimatation et domestication des animaux utiles*, pp. 104–7, 506; M. Soborne, 'The Role of Exotic Animals in the Scientific and Political Culture of Nineteenth

Century France', in L. Bodson, ed., *Les Animaux exotiques dans les relations internationales* (Liège, 1998), pp. 15–32.

33 Jimenez de Cisneros, *El Parque zoologico de Madrid*, pp. 25–9; Loisel, *Histoire des ménageries*, vol. III, pp. 66–86, 293–5; Maschietti, *Serragli e menagerie*, pp. 118–20, 155; P. A. Pichot, *L'Acclimatation en Russie* (Paris, 1861); W. Kazeeff, 'Un immense jardin d'acclimatation en Russie: Askania-Nova', *La Nature* (January 1933), pp. 1–6.

34 P. A. Pichot, *Le Jardin d'Acclimatation illustré* (Paris, 1873), pp. VII, 5–9; J. Boulineau, *Les Jardins animés: Etude technique et documentaire des parcs zoologiques* (Limoges, 1934), pp. 405–7; Ritvo, *The Animal Estate*, p. 235; Sévin, *La Ménagerie du MNHN*, p. 67. On the importance of hybridization, see D. Buican, *Mendel, la génétique d'hier et d'aujourd'hui* (Paris, 1993).

35 Geoffroy Saint-Hilaire, *Acclimatation et domestication des animaux utiles*, pp. 17–18, 48; Pichot, *Le Jardin d'Acclimatation illustré*, pp. 64–103.

36 E. Trouessard, 'Les Conditions de l'hybridité en biologie', *Revue des idées* (1908), pp. 327, 341 etc.; *idem*, 'Acclimatation', *Le Monde et la science*, I (1911), pp. 15–28; Boulineau, *Les Jardins animés*, pp. 30–32; H. Conwentz, *The Care of Natural Monuments* (Cambridge, 1909); AN, AJ¹⁵ 846, Protection of African fauna, December 1920.

37 A. Morton, *History of Botanical Science* (London, 1981); B. Marrey and J.-P. Monet, *La Grande Histoire des serres et des jardins d'hiver, France, 1780–1900* (n.p., n.d.), pp. 26–8; S. Van Sprang, ed., *L'Empire de Flore: Histoire et représentations des fleurs en Europe du XVIᵉ au XIXᵉ siècle* (Brussels, 1996), pp. 18, 13–40, 64, 84–9, 129–31.

8 THE THRILL OF THE WILD

1 Y. Laissus, *Les Animaux du Muséum 1793–1993* (Paris, 1993), pp. 82, 97; W. Blunt, *The Ark in the Park: The Zoo in the Nineteenth Century* (London, 1976), pp. 85–6, 232.

2 *Bulletin de la Société Zoologique d'Acclimatation* (1858), p. 235; (1861), p. XIV; A. Esquiros, 'Des jardins zoologique: Les Sociétés d'histoire naturelle en Belgique', *Revue des deux mondes* (15 November 1854), pp. 691–2.

3 M. A. Cap, ed., *Le Muséum d'Histoire Naturelle* (Paris, 1854), p. 128; J. Hässlin, *Der zoologische Garten zu Köln* (Cologne, 1960), p. 43; G. Loisel, 'Rapport sur une mission scientifique dans les jardins et établissements zoologiques publics et privés du Royaume-Uni, de la Belgique et des Pays-Bas', *Nouvelles Archives des missions scientifiques et littéraires* (1907), p. 28; (1908), p. 131.

4 R. Beck, *Histoire du dimanche* (Paris, 1997); A. Corbin, ed., *L'Avènement des loisirs* (Paris, 1995), pp. 25, 51, 140.

5 L. Crandall, *Wild Mammals in Captivity* (Chicago, 1964), pp. 415–18; P. Bernard et al., *Le Jardin des plantes* (Paris, 1842), vol. I, p. 38.

6 Loisel, 'Rapport sur une mission scientifique' (1907), p. 32; I. Geoffroy Saint-Hilaire, *Acclimatation et domestication des animaux utiles*, new edn (Paris, 1986), p. 8; *Le Jardin zoologique* (Brussels, 1856), cited by A. Brauman and S. Demanet, *Le Parc Léopold, 1850–1950: Le Zoo, la cité scientifique et la ville* (Brussels, 1985), p. 146.

7 Loisel, 'Rapport sur une mission scientifique' (1907), p. 13; (1908), p. 150; A. Feuillée-Billot, 'La Nouvelle Singerie du Muséum', *La Nature'* (1934), pp. 366–8; A. Corbin, *Le Miasme et la jonquille: L'Odorat et l'imaginaire social, XVIIIᵉ–XIXᵉ siècle* (Paris, 1982).

8 AML, 485 WP 10, Plan of the bear cage (1877), general plan (1894), 963 WP 37, plan of the big cat cage, c. 1897; S. Austermühle, *Die Wahrheit über Tierhaltung im Zoo* (Hamburg, 1996), p. 63; J. Siepi, *Petite Histoire du jardin zoologique de Marseille* (Marseille, 1937), p. 7.

9 U. and W. Dolder, *Le Grand Livre du zoo* (Zurich, 1979), p. 145.

10 G. Toscan, *L'Ami de la nature* (Paris, an X), pp. VII, XI; L. Jauffret, *Voyage au jardin des plantes* (Paris, 1789), pp. 1–2.

11 E. Revel, *Leconte de Lisle animalier et le goût de la zoologie au XIXᵉ siècle* (Marseille, 1942), pp. 3–39; V. Hugo, *L'Art d'être grand-père* (Paris, 1995), pp. 49–72; E. Mannoni, *Barye* (Paris, 1996), pp. 19–24, 31–50, 105–8; I. Leroy-Jay, *La Griffe et la dent* (Paris, 1997); C. Luz, *Exotische Welten: Exotische Phantasien: Das exotische Tier in Europäischen Kunst* (Stuttgart, 1987), p. 19. E. Hardouin-Fugier, *Le Peintre et la Palette* (Paris, 2001), p. 131.

12 Bernard, *Le Jardin des plantes*, vol. I, p. 23; AML, 485 WP 2, 13;

B. Paust, *Studien zur barocken Menagerie in deutschsprachigen Raum* (Worms, 1996), pp. 191–2.

13 P. Maclot and E. Warmenbole, 'Bevaugen door Egypte: de Egyptische Tempel in de Antwerpse Zoo', in C. Kruyfhoot, ed., *Zoom op zoo: Antwerp zoo foursing on Arts ans Sciences* (Antwerp, 1985), pp. 359–91; Brauman and Demanet, *Le Parc Léopold*, p. 87; Loisel, 'Rapport sur une mission scientifique' (1908); *Zoo: Mémoires de l'éléphant, le zoo de Genève à Saint-Jean entre 1935 et 1940* (Geneva, 1993), p. 18; Corbin, *L'Avènement des loisirs*, pp. 98, 100.

14 N. and J. Dhombres, *Naissance d'un nouveau pouvoir: Sciences et savants en France, 1793–1824* (Paris, 1989), pp. 347–83; J.-M. Drouin, 'Introduction', *Revue de synthèse*, III–IV (1992), pp. 304–7; Thomas, *Dans le jardin de la nature*, pp. 367–70.

15 Loisel, 'Rapport sur une mission scientifique' (1907), p. 98; H. Perron d'Arc, *Le Jardin des plantes et ses habitants* (Paris, 1860), pp. 5–6; J. Bishop, *Henry and Emma's Visit to the Zoological Garden* (London, 1829); J. Hutinel, *Une visite aux animaux du parc de la Tête-d'Or* (Lyon, 1908). Accounts: E. Vignier, *Vertus morales et description des éléphants de la ménagerie* (Paris, an VIII); E. Oustalet, 'Les Manchots du cap de Bonne-Espérance au Jardin d'acclimatation', *La Nature* (1891), pp. 363–6.

16 M. Ferlus, *Nouvelle Notice sur la girafe* (Paris, 1827); *Animals at the Zoo* (London, 1907).

17 H. Ritvo, *The Animal Estate: The English and Other Creatures in the Victorian Age* (London, 1990), p. 216; Blunt, *The Ark in the Park*, pp. 75–95, 106–48, 163–6, 237, 242; E. Geoffroy Saint-Hilaire, 'Extrait d'un mémoire sur l'orang-outang', *Comptes rendus des séances de l'Académie des Sciences*, III (1836), p. 582.

18 Blunt, *The Ark in the Park*, pp. 74–6, 110–13; G. Maschietti *et al.*, *Serragli e menagerie in Piemonte nell'ottocento sotto la real casa Savoia* (Turin, 1988), pp. 64–7; E. Geoffroy Saint-Hilaire, *Sur la girafe* (Paris, 1827), pp. 1–12; G. Dardaud, *Une girafe pour le roi* (Sceaux, 1984).

19 J. B. Pujoulx, *Promenades au Jardin des plantes* (Paris, 1804), vol. I, pp. XV, 137, 142; M. Jimenez de Cisneros, *El Parque zoologico de Madrid, 1774–1994* (Madrid, 1994), pp. 21, 23; Ritvo, *The Animal Estate*, pp. 223–4; Blunt, *The Ark in the Park*, p. 200; H. Hediger, 'Vom Schauwert der Tiere', *Atlantis* (August 1955), pp. 348–52.

20 Ritvo, *The Animal Estate*, pp. 226–9; Blunt, *The Ark in the Park*, pp. 178–88; L. Heck, *Mes bêtes sauvages* (Paris, 1955), pp. 112–15; T. Lenain, *La Peinture des singes: Histoire et esthétique* (Paris, 1990), pp. 24–6.

21 J. Fischer, *Le Zoo, son histoire, son univers* (Paris, 1967), p. 67; X. Malher, 'Le Parc zoologique et l'enfant', thesis (Maisons-Alfort, 1980), pp. 31–2; J. Boulineau, *Les Jardins animés: Etude technique et documentaire des parcs zoologiques* (Limoges, 1934), p. 92; R. Delort, *Les Eléphants, piliers du monde* (Paris, 1990), p. 92.

22 A. Feuillée-Billot, 'Le Nouvel Aménagement de la rotonde au Muséum d'Histoire Naturelle de Paris', *La Nature* (1933), pp. 249–52. See also E. Vignier, *Epître aux éléphants de la ménagerie nationale* (Paris, an VII), pp. 5–7.

23 Ferlus, *Nouvelle Notice sur la girafe*, pp. 5–7 (giraffes of 1827); Blunt, *The Ark in the Park*, pp. 112–16 (hippopotamus of 1850).

24 Pujoulx, *Promenades au Jardin des plantes*, vol. I, pp. 78–164; V. Hugo, 'Poème du Jardin des plantes'; Hutinel, *Une visite aux animaux*, pp. 20, 71, 77; J.-L. Flandrin and M. Montanari, eds, *Histoire de l'alimentation* (Paris, 1996), pp. 117–32.

25 Brauman and Demanet, *Le Parc Léopold*, p. 146; P. Du Chaillu, *Explorations and Adventures in Equatorial Africa* (London, 1861); R. Hartmann, *Les Singes anthropoïdes et leur organisation comparée à celle de l'homme* (Paris, 1886); J. Martinez-Contrearas, 'L'Emergence scientifique du gorille', *Revue de synthèse* (1992), pp. 399–421.

26 S. Boulch, 'Le Statut de l'animal carnivore et la notion de pureté dans les prescriptions alimentaires chrétiennes du haut Moyen Âge occidental', in L. Bodson, ed., *Le Statut éthique de l'animal* (Liège, 1996), pp. 41–59; F. Burgat, *Animal, mon prochain* (Paris, 1997), pp. 74–107.

27 Jauffret, *Voyage au Jardin des plantes*; AMM 64 R 2, Architect's report, 28 May 1879, 110 M 2, estimate, 7 December 1989; AML, 963 WP 37, Letters to the Director and to the architect, 30 April and 25 June 1927, letter from the director, 13 September 1939; AN, AJ[15] 844, Muséum correspondence, 19 August 1859, 31 August 1906; *Zoo: Mémoires de l'éléphant*, pp. 33, 43.

28 Bernard, *Le Jardin des plantes*, vol. I, p. 39; J. Huret, *En Allemagne: De Hambourg aux Marches de Pologne* (Paris, 1908),
p. 250.

29 Brauman and Demanet, *Le Parc Léopold*, p. 148; Y. Raymond,
'Contribution à l'éthologie des animaux sauvages en captivité',
thesis (Maisons-Alfort, 1986), p. 169; Bernard, *Le Jardin des
plantes*, vol. I, p. 42; I. Eibl-Eibesfeldt, *Contre l'agression* (Paris,
1972), pp. 192–3; D. Buican, *Ethologie comparée* (Paris, 1995),
p. 116.

30 H. Hediger, *Lieu de naissance: Zoo* (Zurich, 1984), p. 88; S.
Winkel and K. Räter, *Das Betteln des Zootiere* (Bern, 1960);
Bernard, *Le Jardin des plantes*, vol. I, pp. 38, 42–50; R. Riet-
mann, *Mes amis du zoo* (Lausanne, 1947), p. 183, 197; Malher,
'Le Parc zoologique et l'enfant', pp. 32–4.

31 Blunt, *The Ark in the Park*, p. 205; AML, 486 WP 12, Prefect to
Mayor, 10 September 1887; AMM, 64 R 3, Management to the
Mayor, 18 June 1965.

32 Loisel, 'Rapport sur une mission scientifique' (1907), p. 30;
(1908), p. 206; AMMU, A XV R, Instructions, 5 June 1968 and
February 1969; AML, 877 WP bundle 272, Letter from the
director, 18 June 1965.

33 L. Rookmaaker, 'Histoire du rhinocéros de Versailles
(1770–1793)', *Revue d'histoire des sciences*, III–IV (1983), p. 311;
AN, AJ[15] 846, Ménagerie plans, 27 Pluviôse, Year X; M. Agulhon, 'Le Sang des bêtes: Le Problème de la protection des
animaux en France au XIXe siècle' *Romantisme* (1981),
pp. 81–109.

34 M. Milne-Edwards, *La Ménagerie, rapport au ministre de l'Instruction publique* (Paris, 1891), p. 18; AN, AJ[15] 844, Letter from
the menagerie director, 2 July 1859; AJ[15] 845, *idem*, 12 June
1907; AML, 485 WP 4, Management to the Mayor, 3 March
1903; 485 WP 10, *idem*, 20 May 1860; 963 WP 37, *idem*, 2
March 1928, 28 April 1941; V. Hegi, *Les Captifs du zoo*
(Lausanne, 1942), pp. 155–16, 13 (ref.); Blunt, *The Ark in the
Park*, pp. 220–29.

35 *Illustration*, 23 May 1931; Corbin, *L'Avènement des loisirs*, p. 12;
P. Giberne, 'La Protection juridique des animaux', thesis
(Nîmes, 1931); AMM, 3 D 29, Decree, 13 September 1904.

36 C. Hagenbeck, *Cages sans barreaux* (Paris, 1951), pp. 5–13. Similarly in Italy and England: Ritvo, *The Animal Estate*, pp. 207–8,
216.

37 H. Thétard, *Les Dompteurs* (Paris, 1928), pp. 18–48, 55–72;
Hagenbeck, *Cages sans barreaux*, pp. 90–91.

38 G. Dumur, ed. *Histoire des spectacles* (Paris, 1965), p. 1458
(cinema); P. Pichot, *Les Mémoires d'un dompteur* (Paris, 1877),
Preface, pp. 171ff; E. Velvin, *Le Dressage des fauves par F. Bostock*
(Paris, 1904), p. V; C. Mertens, 'Les Animaux dans la musique',
Zoo (Journal du Jardin d'Anvers) (October 1978), pp. 76–7;
Delort, *Les Eléphants*, pp. 90–91.

39 Toscan, *L'Ami de la nature*, p. 283; Loisel, *Histoire des
ménageries*, vol. III, p. 291; Huret¸ *En Allemagne*, p. 246; J.
Rousseau, *Historique du parc zoologique de Paris* (Paris, 1984),
p. 19; *La Vie des bêtes* (August 1964), p. 18; *Zoo: Mémoires de
l'éléphant*, p. 28; P. Bouissac, 'Perspectives ethnologiques: Le
Statut symbolique de l'animal au cirque et au zoo', *Ethnologie
française*, III–IV (1972), pp. 255–62.

40 AMM, 110 M 4, Management to the Mayor, 8 October 1878;
Ritvo, *The Animal Estate*, p. 222; AMMU, R XV A, Commission, 12 March 1956; Jimenez de Cisneros, *El Parque zoologico
de Madrid*, p. 56; Loisel, 'Rapport sur une mission scientifique'
(1907), pp. 76, 100; (1908), p. 143; Loisel, *Histoire des
ménageries*, vol. III, p. 317; *Der Zoologische Tiergarten* (1934),
p. 280–85; X. Pasquini, *La France des animaux* (n.p., 1991),
pp. 121, 140.

41 P. Belon, *L'Histoire de la nature des oiseaux* (Paris, 1555), p. 5;
B. Paust, *Studien zur barocken Menagerie in deutschsprachigen
Raum* (Worms, 1996), pp. 183–7; Prince de Ligne, *Coup d'œil
sur Belœil* (Belœil, 1781), pp. 109–10.

42 E. de Lacépède, 'Lettre relative aux établissements publics
destinés à renfermer des animaux vivants', *La Décade
philosophique* (20 Frimaire, Year IV), pp. 452, 454; A. Millin, P.
Pinel and A. Brongniart, *Rapport fait à la Société d'Histoire
Naturelle de Paris sur la nécessité d'établir une ménagerie* (Paris,
1972); L. Strivay, 'Manger juste: Les Droits de l'animal dans les
encyclopédies de 1750 à 1800: De l'éthique au politique', in
Bodson, *Le Statut éthique de l'animal*, pp. 61–99; Jauffret,
Voyage au Jardin des plantes, p. 53; Pujoulx, *Promenades au
Jardin des plantes*, vol. I, pp. 76–84.

43 Bernard, *Le Jardin des plantes*, vol. I, pp. 23–4, 30–31, 50; Laissus, *Les Animaux du Muséum*, pp. 140–2.

44 Bernard, *Le Jardin des plantes*, vol. I, p. 52; Loisel, *Histoire des ménageries*, vol. III, p. 115; AML, 485 WP 10, Plan of the bear cage, 1877; J.-L. Pinol, *Les Mobilités de la grande ville: Lyon fin XIXᵉ siècle–début XXᵉ* (Paris, 1991), pp. 33–6.

45 J. Manilli, *Villa Borghèse, Fuori di porta Pinciana* (Rome, 1650); Bernard, *Le Jardin des plantes*, vol. I, p. 26; G. Toscan, *Histoire du lion de la Ménagerie … et de son chien* (Paris, an III), p. 30; *Magasin pittoresque* (1807), p. 402.

46 *Bulletin de la Société Protectrice des Animaux* (1855), pp. 6, 13; (1856), pp. 8, 13, 78; (1860), pp. 76, 314; (1861), pp. 258–70, 628–9; A. Godin, *Le Protecteur, le législateur et l'ami des animaux* (Paris, 1856), pp. 15–27; C. Blanckaert, 'Les Animaux "utiles" chez Isidore Geoffroy Saint-Hilaire: La Mission sociale de la zootechnie', *Revue de synthèse*, III–IV (1992), pp. 347–82; E. Pierre, 'Amour des hommes: Amour des bêtes: Discours et pratiques protectrices dans la France du XIXᵉ siècle', thesis (Angers, 1998), pp. 64–88; M. Fleury, *La Belle Histoire de la SPA* (Paris, 1995), pp. 45, 47.

47 Pelican Island in 1903. Stott, *The American Idea of a Zoological Park*, p. 227.

48 H. Kean, *Animal Rights: Political and Social Change in Britain since 1800* (London, 1998), pp. 39–48 ff.

9 A PUBLIC QUEST

1 W. Blunt, *The Ark in the Park: The Zoo in the Nineteenth Century* (London, 1976), p. 212.

2 J. Lerclerq, 'Le Nombre de visiteurs des jardins zoologiques d'Europe', *Les Naturalistes belges*, I (1965), pp. 3–8; U. and W. Dolder, *Le Grand Livre du zoo* (Zurich, 1979), pp. 61, 149, 152; D. Barreau, *Insertion spatiale des parcs zoologiques dans la région d'Île-de-France* (Paris, 1985); *Le Figaro*, 3 April 1900; *Zoo: Revista del parque zoologico de Barcelona* (March 1971), p. 3.

3 A. Corbin, ed., *L'Avènement des loisirs* (Paris, 1995), pp. 376–7, 394–8, 408.

4 Barreau, *Insertion spatiale*; *Zoo: Revista del parque zoologico de Barcelona*, IX (1970), p. 20; *Zoo Mulhouse: Rapport annuel d'activités* (Mulhouse, 1965), p. 28.

5 Archives of the zoological gardens at Vincennes, typewritten reports on French parks (1970–80); N. Lippi, 'La Pédagogie dans les parcs zoologiques', thesis (Maisons-Alfort, 1977), p. 12 (Frankfurt); A. Marchand, 'Enquête sur les parcs zoologiques français', thesis (Maisons-Alfort, 1992), pp. 27–9; *Zoo: Mémoires de l'éléphant: Le Zoo de Genève à Saint-Jean entre 1935 et 1940* (Geneva, 1993), p. 15.

6 Marchand, 'Enquête sur les parcs zoologiques français', p. 27; AML, 485 WP 11, Correspondence, 27 May 1897; 961 WP 72, Management to the Mayor, 23 January 1923, 4 October 1929; *Zoo Mulhouse: Rapport d'activités* (Mulhouse, 1977); E. Becchi and D. Julia, eds, *Histoire de l'enfance en Occident* (Paris, 1998), vol. II.

7 J. M. Bradburne, 'Où sont les bêtes sauvages? Du rôle des jardins zoologiques', *Alliage* (1991), pp. 139–42; A. Jourcin, *La Vie des bêtes au zoo* (Paris, 1947), pp. 15, 26; X. Malher, 'Le Parc zoologique et l'enfant', thesis (Maisons-Alfort, 1980), pp. 30–40.

8 N. Lippi, 'La Pédagogie dans les jardins zoologiques', thesis (Maisons-Alfort, 1977), p. 46.

9 AML, 961 WP 72, Society of Friends to the Mayor, 7 October 1935; E. Tylinek and O. Stepanek, *Les Animaux au zoo* (Paris, 1957), p. 10; G. Miararet and J. Vial, eds, *Histoire mondiale de l'éducation* (Paris, 1981), vol. III, pp. 152–70; Corbin, *L'Avènement des loisirs*, pp. 306–16, 389–91.

10 P. Bourdieu, *La Distinction: Critique sociale du jugement* (Paris, 1979); *Zoo: Mémoires de l'éléphant*, p. 37; J. Siepi, *Petite Histoire du jardin zoologique de Marseille* (Marseille, 1937), pp. 10–11.

11 *Zoo: Mémoires de l'éléphant*, p. 39; Barreau, *Insertion spatiale*; S. Austermühle, *Die Wahrheit über Tierhaltung im Zoo* (Hamburg, 1996), pp. 277–9.

12 J. N. Hyson, 'Urban Jungles: Zoos and American Society', thesis (Cornell University, 1999), chap. 4, esp. p. 89.

13 *New York Zoological Society Report* (1899), p. 79, cited in Stott, *The American Idea of a Zoological Park*, p. 53.

14 *Worcester Telegram*, cited in Stott, *The American Idea of a Zoological Park*, p. 149.

15 Hyson, 'Urban Jungles', pp. 179–82ff.

16 W. C. Sharp, *In Search Of a Preservation Ethic: William Temple Hornaday and American Environmental Education* (Kansas City, 1997).

17 *The Extinction of the American Bison* (report to the US National Museum under the direction of the Smithsonian Institution, Washington, DC, 1889), cited in Stott, *The American Idea of a Zoological Park*, p. 223.

18 *Illustration*, 23 May 1931, 2 June 1934, 22 June 1934; J. Rousseau, *Historique du parc zoologique de Paris, 1934–1984* (Vincennes, 1984), pp. 15–18, 48–50; R. Riedtmann, *Mes Amis du zoo: Souvenirs d'un gardien* (Lausanne, 1947), p. 209.

19 *Les Amis du zoo* (1956), p. 1; I (1975), p. 7; Marchand, 'Enquête sur les parcs zoologiques français', pp. 28, 46, 132; *Parc zoologique de Vincennes*, special issue of *La Documentation française illustrée* (June 1957), p. 27; E. Lamy, *Zoo* (Geneva, 1968).

20 Hyson, 'Urban Jungles', p. 320.

21 E. A. Hanson, 'Nature Civilized: A Cultural History of American Zoos 1870–1940' (thesis, University of Philadelphia, 1996), pp. 182, 284.

22 J. Brooke, 'A Rocky Mountain High: Twin Polar Bears', *New York Times*, 26 December 1995.

23 Hyson, 'Urban Jungles', p. 277.

24 S. Pairault, *Le Livre du zoo* (Paris, 1951), pp. 3, 44–5, 95; Jourcin, *La Vie des bêtes*, pp. 38–60; E. Vignier, *Phénomène d'histoire naturelle: Récit de la deuxième gestation de Constantine* (Paris, an X), pp. 30–33; Blunt, *The Ark in the Park*, pp. 119, 203; *Zoo: Ami des bêtes* (Paris, 1951), vol. III, p. 7.

25 Jourcin, *La Vie des bêtes*; P. Loewenbruck, *Animaux captifs: La Vie des zoos* (Paris, 1971); Riedtmann, *Mes Amis du zoo*; P. Eiper, *Les Bêtes vous regardent* (Paris, 1954).

26 C. Hagenbeck, *Cages sans barreaux* (Paris, 1951); L. Heck, *Mes bêtes sauvages* (Paris, 1955); J. Bouillault, *Mes amis du Tertre Rouge* (Paris, 1971); Riedtmann, *Mes amis du zoo*; M. Leclerc-Cassan, *Vivre avec eux* (Paris, 1978); D. Taylor, *Au suivant de ces pandas: Un vétérinaire de zoo raconte* (Paris, 1985).

27 J. Hutinel, *Une visite aux animaux du parc de la Tête-d'Or* (Lyon, 1908), p. 83; Tylinek and Stepanek, *Les Animaux au zoo*; AML, 961 WP 72, Society of Friends to the Mayor, 7 Octobre 1935;

Tribune de Genève, 31 June 1936.

28 *La Vie des bêtes* (November 1958), pp. 9–11; *Bêtes et nature* (January and April 1965); Hagenbeck, *Cages sans barreaux*, pp. 101–4.

29 Tylinek and Stepanek, *Les Animaux au zoo*, pp. 9–10; J.-M. Lernoult, 'Contribution à l'étude de la traumatologie chez les animaux sauvages en captivité', thesis (Maisons-Alfort, 1968), p. 15; C. Caille, *Mon zoo … ma vie: Zoo de la Palmyre* (Artigues, 1983), p. 78.

30 Stott, *The American Idea of a Zoological Park*, chap. 4, p. 153.

31 'Elephant in Captivity, a Dark Side', *Los Angeles Times*, 5 October 1988.

32 In Philadelphia in 1941. Hyson, *Urban Jungles*, esp. p. 225 etc.

33 The reason being that they were used to give rides in zoos. Hanson, 'Nature Civilized', pp. 100, 112.

34 'Survival of the Kindest', *New York Times*, 22 August 1996; articles in *People, Life, Time* and *Discover* between September 1996 and January 1997

35 *Parc zoologique de Vincennes*, p. 30; M. Harvey, 'Rembrandt Bugatti, A Great Animal Sculptor', in C. Kruyfhoot, ed., *Zoom op zoo: Antwerp zoo foursing on Arts ans Sciences* (Antwerp, 1985), pp. 235–7.

36 AMMU, 44 W 68, Various nos, 1949–54; P. Cereja *et al.*, *Mulhouse: Parc zoologique et botanique* (Mulhouse, 1991), pp. 67–8; *Zoo Mulhouse*, XXIV (1994), pp. 4, 25; (1995), pp. 2–3; *L'Espace zoologique (Saint-Martin)*, XIII (1989), p. 3.

37 *Zoo: Ami des bêtes*, III (1951), p. 7; IV, p. 8; (January 1960), p. 34.

38 A. Feuillée-Billot, 'La Nouvelle Fauverie du Muséum', *La Nature* (1938), pp. 367–8.

39 E. Pierre, 'Amour des hommes: Amour des bêtes: Discours et pratiques protectrices dans la France du XIXᵉ siècle', thesis (Angers, 1998), chaps IV, VII; M. Fleury, *La Belle Histoire de la SPA* (Paris, 1988), pp. 192, 205, 228, 272, 275, 282; H. Thétard, *Des hommes et des bêtes: Le Zoo de Lyautey* (Paris, *c.* 1945), pp. 28, 67.

40 *L'Excelsior*, 6 September 1921; AML, 485 WP 11, Correspondence of 3 May 1881, 14 April 1895; 963 WP 37, Director to the Mayor, 4 November 1926, letter to the Mayor, 3 June 1938; 961 WP 72, Director to the Mayor, 4 October 1929, letter to the

Mayor, 23 March 1932.

41 AMMI, R XV A, Internal directive, 29 September 1969; *Que sera le zoo de l'an 2000?* (Mulhouse, 1969), p. 13.

42 Riedtmann, *Mes Amis du zoo*, pp. 11–12; *Tribune de Genève*, 27 December 1929; Colette, *Paradis terrestre* (Lausanne, 1953), pp. 87–9; G. Loisel, *Histoire des ménageries de l'antiquité à nos jours* (Paris, 1912), vol. III, p. 281; *Zoo: Mémoires de l'éléphant*, pp. 54, 67.

43 Hyson, 'Urban Jungles', p. 415.

44 P. Batten, *Living Trophies* (New York, 1976), p. 172; *Animal Law Journal* lists of environmental resources, http://www.earthsystems.org/all.shtml.

45 M. Kernan, 'Animal Old Folks (Washington Zoo)', *Smithsonian* (December 1999).

46 The Captive Animals' Protection Society, *Annual Report* (1988–9), (1991–2); V. McKenna *et al.*, *Beyond the Bars: The Zoo Dilemma* (Wellingborough, 1987). pp. 25–39; D. Morris, *Des animaux et des hommes* (Paris, 1992), p. 53.

47 E. Bronzini, 'Serve ancora in zoo?', *Epoca*, 17 September 1972; E. Sanna, *Cet animal est fou* (Paris, 1976); Austermühle, *Die Wahrheit*.

48 P. Amitabh, 'Cut the Monkey Business', *Progressive*, 14 March 1998.

49 R. Flamm and G. Wyler, *Los Angeles Times*, 17 February 1995.

50 D. Jordan, 'Living Trophies', *Animal's Voice Magazine*, II/5.

51 *The News and World Report*, 24 August 1992.

52 C. C. Robbins, 'A Zoo in Peril Stirs a Debate about Navajo Tradition', *New York Times*, 28 March 1999.

53 D. Jamieson, 'Against Zoos', in P. Singer, ed., *In Defense of Animals* (New York, 1985).

54 F. T. Mapel, *Zoo Biology* (1986), pp. 261–8.

55 Johnson, 'Attempts to Clone Pandas', *Discover*, 21 October 1999.

56 T. Fields Mayer, 'Doctor Zoo', *People*, 7 February 2000.

57 J. Dorst, *Avant que nature ne meurt* (Neuchâtel, 1965), pp. 508–11; *Bêtes et nature* (January, February, June 1973), pp. 40, 4, 56; *Le Figaro*, 7 January 1974; *Le Monde*, 8 January 1974; Leclerc-Cassan, *Vivre avec eux*, p. 47; P. Diolé, *Les Animaux malades de l'homme* (Paris, 1974), pp. 31–49.

58 *La Vie des bêtes* (June 1974), pp. 40–43; (July 1974); (August 1971), p. 23 (Diolé); (April 1978), pp. 11–16, 38. See also Morris, *Des animaux et des hommes*, pp. 50–56.

59 *La Protection des animaux: Revue de la Société Protectrice des Animaux de Lyon et du Sud-Est*, LXIII (1974), pp. 9–13; LXVI (1975), pp. 17–18; LXVIII (1975), pp. 15, 27; LXIX (1976), p. 17; LXXXV (1980), p. 22; XCIII (1982), p. 23.

60 Colette, *Paradis terrestre*, pp. 105–7; Diolé, *Les Animaux malades de l'homme*, p. 50; Sanna, *Cet animal est fou*, p. 206; Morris, *Des animaux et des hommes*, p. 58; *La Protection des animaux*, LXXII (1976), pp. 26–7.

61 G. Thines, *Psychologie des animaux* (Brussels, 1966); S. Godlovitch and J. Harris, eds, *Animals, Men and Morals* (New York, 1974); P. Singer, *Animal Liberation* (New York, 1975).

62 D. Morris, *Le Zoo humain* (Paris, 1970), pp. 7–11; H. Ellenberger, 'Jardin zoologique et hôpital psychiatrique', in A. Brion and H. Ey, eds, *Psychiatrie animale* (Paris, 1964), pp. 559–78 (trans.); J. Berger, *Why Look at Animals?* (New York, 1981); D. Mainardi, 'Il comportamento anormale degli animali', *Sapere* (June 1973); Sanna, *Cet animal est fou*, pp. 79–81, 179.

63 *30 Millions d'amis* (1986); (1990); (October 1995), p. 15; *La Protection des animaux*, LV (1975), p. 27; CVI (1985), p. 15; *La Voix des Bêtes* (December, 1995, February, 1996).

64 Morris, *Des animaux et des hommes*, p. 53; C. Juliet, in *Le Voyage singulier: Regards d'écrivains sur le patrimoine* (Geneva, 1996); J.-P. Reverdot, *Zoo* (n.p., 1986); C. Höfer, *Zoologische Gärten* (Bern, 1993); *Aillaud by Olbalk* (Paris, 1987).

65 Loisel, *Histoire des ménageries*, vol. III, pp. 430–34; *International Zoo Yearbook* (1965), pp. 257–318; *El Pais*, 31 May 1993; M. Jouve and P. Osusky, *La France et ses animaux* (Paris, 1961).

66 A. Grandremy, *Guide des parcs, jardins, réserves zoologiques* (Pinou, 1970); *La Protection des animaux*, LXVII (1975), p. 6; M. Jimenez de Cisneros, *Guia de los zoos, safaris y acuarios de Espana* (Madrid, 1986); *International Year Book* (1995), pp. 33–43.

67 *La Vie des bêtes* (February 1972), pp. 37–8; (May 1972), p. 68; (September 1972), p. 63; Bouillault, *Mes amis du Tertre Rouge*, pp. 35–7, 52, 59–60, 69; Caille, *Mon zoo*, pp. 6, 24–31; Riedt-

mann, *Mes Amis du zoo*, pp. 7–10; Leclerc-Cassan, *Vivre avec eux*, p. 9.

68 Jouve and Osusky, *La France et ses animaux*, pp. 68, 82, 98–116; *Les Amis du zoo*, III (1975), pp. 2–3; *Le Journal du zoo (de Saint-Martin)*, V (1987), p. 6; Diolé, *Les Animaux malades de l'homme*, p. 49.

69 Captive Animals' Protection Society, *Annual Report* (1988–9), p. 15; S. Peppler-Surer, 'Aspects de la protection animale et de la conservation des espèces européennes menacées dans les jardins zoologiques suisses', thesis (Bern, 1992), pp. 4, 63–5; G. Devierne, 'Loi du 10 juillet relative à la protection des animaux', thesis (Lyon, 1980), pp. 62–6.

70 P. Giberne, 'La Protection juridique des animaux', thesis (Nîmes, 1925), p. 51; O. Pinguet, 'Animaux et spectacle à travers l'histoire', thesis (Lyon, 1996), p. 100.

71 Grandremy, *Guide des parcs*, p. 6 (Richard); H. Hediger, *Lieu de naissance: Zoo* (Zurich, 1984), p. 7; Caille, *Mon zoo*, p. 32; *Les Amis du zoo*, I (1975), pp. 1, 5; *Zoo: Revista del parque zoologico de Barcelona*, I (1962), p. 30.

72 A. Urbain, 'Le Parc zoologique du bois de Vincennes', *La Revue de Paris*, 15 August 1934, p. 934; Hediger, *Lieu de naissance*, pp. 7–27; Bouillault, *Mes Amis du Tertre Rouge*, pp. 112–13; Riedtmann, *Mes Amis du zoo*, p. 11.

73 H. Thétard, 'Le Jardin zoologique d'Anvers', *Revue des deux mondes* (January 1954), p. 122; Lippi, *La Pédagogie dans les parcs zoologiques*, pp. 25–49; *Zoo: Journal de la Société Royale de Zoologie d'Anvers*; *Zoo: Revista del parque zoologico de Barcelona*.

74 Riedtmann, *Mes Amis du zoo*, p. 294; Malher, 'Le Parc zoologique et l'enfant', pp. 52–60; *La Protection des animaux*, CIV (1984), p. 25.

75 K. Svitil, 'Virtual Gorillas in Atlanta Zoo', *Discover* (April 1997).

76 T. C. Davis, 'Theatrical Antecedents of the Mall (Edmonton, Alberta)', *Journal of Popular Culture*, XXIV/4 (1991), pp. 1–15.

77 *Zoo: Revista del parque zoologico de Barcelona*, IX, (1970); *Zoo Mulhouse: Rapport annuel d'activités* (1965), pp. 29–30; T. Lenain, *La Peinture des singes: Histoire et esthétique* (Paris, 1990), pp. 10, 27, 45–51; F. de Waal, *La Politique du chimpanzé* (Monaco, 1987); *De la réconciliation chez les primates* (Paris,

1992), pp. 48–58.

78 A. Mouquet, 'Animaux de ménagerie: Notes de pathologie', thesis (Maisons-Alfort, 1925); J.-M. Lernoud, 'Contribution à l'étude de la traumatologie chez les animaux sauvages en captivité', thesis (Maisons-Alfort, 1968).

79 E. Trouessard, 'Acclimatation ', *Le Monde et la science*, I (1911), pp. 15–28; A. Milice, 'Le Parc zoologique de Clères', *La Nature* (1934), pp. 535–6; *Zoo: Revista del parque zoologico de Barcelona*, IX (1970); Parc zoologique de la Haute-Touche, *Guide d'observation* (Tours, 1992), p. 5.

80 *Le Journal de zoo (Saint-Martin)*, V (1987), p. 7; VI (1987), p. 7; *Zoo Mulhouse*, XXI (1992), p. 5; *Bêtes et nature* (January 1973), p. 40; 'Les Zoos aujourd'hui: Des instituts de conservation', *Science et avenir* (July 1985), pp. 36–9.

81 *Le Figaro*, 9 April 1991; Marchand, 'Enquête sur les parcs zoologiques français', pp. 46–50; Lippi, 'La Pédagogie dans les parcs zoologiques', pp. 12, 36; Bradburne, 'Où sont les bêtes sauvages?', p. 138.

82 *Le Journal du zoo (de Saint-Martin)*, V (1987), p. 6; *Réserve africaine de Sigean* (Millau, 1989), p. 172.

10 THE ILLUSION OF LIBERTY

1 J. Huret, *En Allemagne: De Hambourg aux Marches de Pologne* (Paris, 1908), p. 249; P. Morand, *Jungles pour rire* (Paris, 1937), pp. 187–9.

2 H. G. Klös, *Wegweiser durch den zoologischen Garten Berlin* (Berlin, 1959), p. 122; *Von der Menagerie zum Tierparadies: 125 Jahre Zoo Berlin* (Berlin, 1959), p. 122; S. Waetzoldt, *Bibliographie zur Architektur im XIX^{ten} Jahrhundert, 1789–1918* (Nendeln, 1977), nos 36837, 36841–79.

3 Y. Laissus and J. J. Petter, *Les Animaux du Muséum 1793–1993* (Paris, 1993), p. 16; *Zoo* (July 1984), p. 22.

4 H. Reichenbach, in R. Hoage and W. Deiss, eds, *New Worlds, New Animals: From Menagerie to Zoological Park in the Nineteenth Century* (London, 1996), p. 61; P. Boulineau, *Les Jardins animés* (Limoges, 1934), p. 343; C. Hagenbeck, *Cages sans barreaux* (Paris, 1951), p. 264; V. Dröscher, *C'est arrivé au zoo* (Paris, 1971), p. 175.

5 M. Seiler, 'Peter-Joseph Lennés erster Entwurf für den Berliner Zoo in nicht-realisierte Projekt, eine Pfauen Insel vor die Tor der Stadt zu holen', *Bongo-Heft*, III (1979); *Zoo Report* (Berlin, 1978), pp. 62–74; Boulineau, *Les Jardins animés*, no. 17; H. Strehlow in Hoage and Deiss, *New Worlds, New Animals*, p. 63.

6 J. Hässlin, *Der zoologische Garten zu Köln* (Cologne, 1960), p. 48; G. Bazin, *Le Temps des musées* (Brussels, 1967), pp. 237–8.

7 G. Loisel, 'Rapport sur une mission scientifique dans les jardins et établissements zoologiques publics et privés du Royaume-Uni, de la Belgique et des Pays-Bas', *Nouvelles Archives des missions scientifiques et littéraires*, XV (1908), pp. 125–282.

8 Huret, *En Allemagne*, p. 26; F. Chaslin, 'Résidences surveillées', *Feuilles*, II (Autumn 1982), pp. 6–21; J. Gebbing, *50 Jahre Leipziger Zoo* (Leipzig, 1928), p. 24.

9 Hässlin, *Der zoologische Garten zu Köln*, pp. 28, 69; G. Loisel, *Histoire des ménageries de l'antiquité à nos jours* (Paris, 1912), vol. III, p. 317; Boulineau, *Les Jardins animés*, p. 478.

10 F. Katt, 'Hagenbecks Tierparadies', *Zoologische Beobachter* (1909), pp. 370–72.

11 Huret, *En Allemagne*, p. 240; Loisel, *Histoire des ménageries*, p. 326; AMHN, Box no. 16, p. 17; Laissus and Petter, *Les Animaux du Muséum*, p. 180.

12 Hässlin, *Der zoologische Garten zu Köln*, p. 63; G. Lisch, 'Le Nouveau Jardin zoologique', *L'Architecture* (June 1934), pp. 222, 227; R. Holl, 'Construire au zoo', *Bulletin de la ville de Mulhouse*, I (1968), p. 30.

13 W. Kourist, *Kultur, Zivilisation und Wildtierhaltung (WTH) in Europa* (Linz, 1989), p. 49; AMMU, 44 W 47, 'Problème du jardin zoologique', 27 December 1952.

14 P. Eiper, *Les Bêtes vous regardent* (Paris, 1954), p. 255; M. Butor, *Les Naufragés de l'arche* (Paris, 1981).

15 Hässlin, *Der zoologische Garten zu Köln*, p. 65; Gebbing, *50 Jahre Leipziger Zoo*, p. 93; L. Heck, *Der Builderzoo, Bildauswahl und Zusammenstellung Fritz* (Ulm, 1934); U. and W. Dolder, *Le Grand Livre du zoo* (Zurich, 1979).

16 A. Weill, *Affiches et art publicitaire* (Paris, 1987).

17 L. Crandall, *Wild Mammals in Captivity* (Chicago, 1964), p. 359; Loisel, 'Rapport sur une mission scientifique', pp. 110, 178, 295 (Rome); H. Reichenbach, 'Carl Hagenbeck's Tierpark and Modern Zoological Gardens', *Journal of the Society for the Bibliography of Natural History* (April 1980), p. 582.

18 Hässlin, *Der zoologische Garten zu Köln*, p. 53; *Il giardino zoologico di Roma nel XXV anniverario, 1910–1935* (Rome, 1935), pp. 38, 87; P. Street, *The London Zoo* (London, 1965), pp. 39–40; D. Laouénan, 'La Place du zoo de Stellingen dans l'histoire de l'architecture des zoos', M.A. thesis (Tours, 1997), pp. 32, 60 (*L'Illustration*); H. Gillespie, 'The National Park of Scotland', *Zoologischer Garten* (1938), pp. 141–7.

19 J. Rousseau, *Historique du parc zoologique de Paris, 1934–1984* (Vincennes, 1984), p. 28; A. Urbain, 'Le Parc zoologique du bois de Vincennes', *La Revue de Paris*, 15 August 1934, p. 937; AMHN, Bourdelle project, box 43, fols 227–5; Lisch, 'Le Nouveau Jardin zoologique', pp. 220–21.

20 Rousseau, *Historique du parc zoologique de Paris*, p. 34; *Guide officiel avec plan du parc zoologique du bois de Vincennes* (Paris, c. 1935), p. 4; AMHN, Box 43, Dechambre, 22/3/1933; Urbain, 'Le Parc zoologique du bois de Vincennes', p. 637.

21 *Le Monde*, 27 March 1995.

22 AMMU, F. Duprat, August 1952; Parc Zoologique et Botanique de la Ville de Mulhouse, *Le Complexe pour animaux de la zone holarctique* (Mulhouse, 1974), p. 1; AML, 977 WP, bundle 271, elephant pavilion plans, 1964; B. Montsai, *Les Besties del parc: Una visita a la collecio zoologica de Barcelona* (Barcelona, 1931); *Zoo* (Barcelona), I (1962), p. 28; VIII (1963), pp. 25, 28; IV (1964) p. 14; IV (1965); IX (1970), p. 26.

23 Morand, *Jungles*, p. 187; P. Coe and M. Reading, *B. Lubetkin and Tecton Architecture and Social Committment* (Paris, 1983); K. M. Schneider, 'Von Daseinsrecht der Zoologischen Garten', in *Der Zoologische Garten* (1936), pp. 173–9.

24 'Warshau Zoo', *Der Zoologische Garten* (1937), 1/2, pp. 10–14; Holl, 'Construire au zoo', pp. 28–39; P. Cereja *et al.*, *Mulhouse: Parc zoologique et botanique* (Mulhouse, 1991), pp. 45–9; AMMU, 44 W 10, Interview with Nouvel, 10 September 1958; 44 WW 45–46, Planning of the monkey houses, 1960–61.

25 V. McKenna, *Beyond the Bars* (London, 1987), pp. 182–3, citing *Daily Mail*, 5 October 1982, Letter from J. Adams.

26 H. Hediger, *Wildtier in Gefangenschaft* (Basle, 1942), pp. 189–94; *Exploration des parcs nationaux du Congo belge, mission Hediger–Verschuren, 1948* (Brussels, 1951); *Les Animaux sauvages en captivité* (Paris, 1953); *Nos amis exotiques au zoo* (Paris, 1954); *Studies of the Psychology and Behaviour of Captive Animals in Zoos and Circuses* (London, 1965), *Lieu de naissance: Zoo* (Zurich, 1984).

27 Dröscher, *C'est arrivé au zoo*, p. 80.

28 Hediger, *Les Animaux sauvages*, p. 12.

29 G. Durrell, *L'Arche mobile* (Paris, 1976), p. 55; I. Debyser, *Juvenile Mortality in Captive Populations of Primates ... 1990–1992* (Bilthoven, 1992), p. 12.

30 F. Burgat, *Animal mon prochain* (Paris, 1997); all citations and the bibliography come from chap. III, esp. pp. 129–33.

31 J.-C. Guyomarch, *Ethologie* (Paris, 1995), cover, p. 4.

32 D. McFarland, N.B.D., 'Territoire', *Dictionnaire du comportement animal* (Paris, 1990), pp. 833–91.

33 Hediger, *Les Animaux sauvages*, p. 54; B. Grzimek, *Education des singes* (Paris, 1953); V. Hugo, 'Liberté', cited in J. Charpentreau, *Les Oiseaux et les animaux sauvages en poésie* (Paris, 1982), pp. 90–91; P. Grassé, *Précis de zoologie* (Paris, 1977).

II THE IMITATION OF NATURE

1 V. Pelazza, 'Les Cercopithèques, zoologie, éthologie, maintien en captivité', thesis (Nantes, 1992), p. 142.

2 H. Thétard, *Des hommes et des bêtes: Le Zoo de Lyautey* (Paris, *c.* 1945), p. 211.

3 Colette, *Paradis terrestre* (Lausanne, 1953), p. 107.

4 J. Hässlin, *Der zoologische Garten zu Köln* (Cologne, 1960), pp. 70–71.

5 *J. Beuys et l'animal* (Düsseldorf, 1965); *Joseph Beuys* (Paris, 1994).

6 G. Le Bolzer, *Le Figaro*, 24 December 1973; *Safari de Peaugres* (*c.* 1997); Advertisements, 1997; FR3, News bulletin, 1 April 1997.

7 D. O'Donovan and J. E. Hindle, 'Effects of Visitors on the Behaviour of Female Cheetahs and Cubs', *International Zoo Yearbook*, XXXII (1993), pp. 238–44; *Var-Matin*, 6 May 1979.

8 F. Bel and G. Vienne, *Caméras dans la brousse, du territoire des autres à la griffe et à la dent* (Paris, 1976); H. Markovitz, 'Enviromental Enrichment and Behavioral Engineering', in *Captivity and Behavior: Primates in Breeding, Colonies, Laboratories and Zoos* (New York, 1978), pp. 229–35.

9 H. Dathe, *Der zoologische Garten Leipzig* (Leipzig, 1961); *Wegweiser durch den Tierpark Berlin* (Berlin, 1966); *Heinrich Dathe: Ein Leben für die Tierwelt* (Berlin, 1995–6); B. Grzimek, *Hundertähriger Zoo in Frankfurt-am-Main* (Frankfurt, 1958), pp. 10–11.

10 Cited in D. Laouénan, 'La Place du zoo de Stellingen dans l'histoire de l'architecture des zoos', M.A. thesis (Nantes, 1997), p. 48, based on *Zoo monde animal* (September–October 1934); K. Lemke, *Tiergarten, Zoos, Aquarien, Wildgehege* (Berlin, DDR, 1985).

11 S. McDonald, 'The Detroit Zoo Chimpanzees', *International Zoo Yearbook*, XXXIII (1994) pp. 236–47.

12 D. Maleyran, 'Les Ours, situation actuelle en France, à l'état sauvage et en captivité', vet. thesis (Maisons-Alfort, 1995); *Varmatin*, 15 July 1997; '300 crocodiles en liberté dans une serre exotique', pamphlet (Pierrelate, n.d.).

13 TF1, 30 July 1995; *VSD*, 'Spectacles', 26 April 1979; 'Castel Rock', *Sciences et nature*, LXXI (December 1996), p. 455.

14 H. Dathe, 'Architecture and Construction: The Alfred Brehm House at East Berlin Zoo', *International Zoo Yearbook*, V (1965), pp. 230–32; A. S. Embury, 'Gorilla Rainforest at Melbourne zoo', *International Zoo Yearbook*, XXXI (1992), pp. 203–13.

15 R. Davidson and J.-J. Lincourt, 'Designing the Montreal Biodome: Tropical and Boreal Forest Exhibits', *International Zoo Yearbook*, XXIX (1990), pp. 39–41; M.-N. Dufrenne, '42 000 animaux ... le plus beau musée du monde', in *30 Millions d'amis*, p. 25; *Guide de visite* (Montréal, 1992).

16 S. Austermühle, *Die Wahrheit über Tierhaltung im Zoo* (Hamburg, 1996), p. 284.

17 P. Street, *The London Zoo* (London, 1965), p. 40; W. Schoenichen, *Naturschutz: Ihre Begründung durch E. Rudorf, H. Conwentz und ihre Vorläufer* (Stuttgart, 1954), p. 97; C. J. Cornish, *Life at the Zoo* (London, 1889), p. 196; H. Lefkowitz, in R. Hoage and W. Deiss, eds, *New Worlds, New Animals: From*

Menagerie to Zoological Park in the Nineteenth Century (London, 1996), pp. 126–35, 151–3.

18 J. N. Hyson, 'Urban Jungles: Zoos and American Society', thesis (Cornell University, 1999), p. 463.

19 M. Holloway, 'Congo City', *Scientific American* (September 1999).

20 H. Goetschy, 'Les Effects de la captivité sur les animaux des parcs zoologiques', vet. thesis (Maisons-Alfort, 1952); J. Crestian, 'Contribution à l'étude des oiseaux en captivité, recherche d'un moyen chirurgical pour les empêcher de voler', vet. thesis (Maisons-Alfort, 1968); J. Vercruysse, in *Zoo* (October 1970), pp. 153–5.

21 C. Wiedemmayer and R. Tanner, 'Untethered Housing of Asian Elephant at Zurich Zoo', *International Zoo Yearbook*, XXXIV (1995), pp. 300–05.

22 *Rapport sur la mortalité et la natalité enregistrées au parc zoologique du bois de Vincennes* (1944–69) (Paris, 1970).

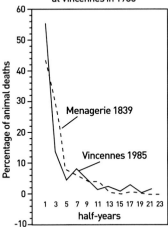

Number of half-years spent by mammals and birds at the menagerie in 1839 and at Vincennes in 1985

23 Austermühle, *Die Wahrheit*; Agence France–Presse, Beijing, no. 220914, 22 October 1997.

24 P. Batten, *Living Trophies* (New York, 1976). Symposium of the US Humane Society, October 1995, Seattle; Planète mer, SOS Grand bleu, 1995–8.

25 J. Fisher, *Le Zoo: Son histoire, son univers* (Paris, 1967), p. 207; O'Donovan and Hindle, 'Effects of Visitors on the Behaviour of Female Cheetahs and Cubs', p. 32.

26 For example, Przewalski horses: 32.3 per cent had 186 m^2 per animal; 21.6 per cent, 506 m^2; 26.3 per cent, 2,490 m^2; 19.8 per cent, more. Consanguinity 0.151 = lifespan of more than ten years; 0.242 = lifespan of less than ten years; this analysis comes from Inge and Jan Bouman, 'Dès la seconde génération, la consanguinité cause des déformations, une diminution du poids du cerveau est lié à la captivité. Les espaces consacrés à l'élevage du cheval Przewalski sont insuffisants', in *Die Illusion der Arche Noah* (Göttingen, 1988), pp. 269–80. See also L. Crandall, *Wild Mammals in Captivity* (Chicago, 1964), p. 377; L. Blomquist, 'Three Decades of Snow Leopards in Captivity', *International Zoo Yearbook*, XXXIV (1995), pp. 178–85; E. Flachetti and B. Mostaci, 'A Case Study of Inbreeding and Juvenile Mortality in the Population of Nile Lechwer', *International Zoo Yearbook*, XXXIV (1995), pp. 225–31.

27 H. Oelke, 'Morphologische und ethnologische Veränderungen bei Vögeln in Gefangenschafshaltung', in *Die Illusion der Arche Noah*, pp. 169–70; H. Pechlaner, 'Anforderung an Haltungsbedingungen und Haltungspraxis', in *ibid.*, pp. 67–77; Austermühle, *Die Wahrheit*, p. 211.

28 Austermühle, *Die Wahrheit*, p. 68; F. Bourlière and B. Faucheux, *Biology of Behaviour* (Paris, 1976), p. 329.

29 H. Ellenberger, 'Jardin zoologique et hôpital psychiatrique', in A. Brion and H. Ey, eds, *Psychiatrie animale* (Paris, 1964), p. 571.

30 A. Proust, ed., 'Pathologie humaine et pathologie animale en milieu prisonnier et le primate de zoo', *Assises internationales de l'environnement* (1976). 1. Ulcers, in a third of prisoners and of zoo primates; 2. Skin conditions, acne in humans and alopecia in animals; 3. Respiratory and psychosomatic conditions, asthma in prisoners, similar problems in laboratory rats; 4. Cardio-vascular; 5. Mental conditions.

31 J. Erwin, 'Strangers in a Strange Land', in *Captivity and Behavior*, pp. 4–26.

32 J.-Y. Domalain, *L'Adieu aux bêtes* (Grenoble, 1976), p. 183.

33 J.-P. d'Huart, 'La Convention de Washington', in *Zoo* (Paris, 1984), pp. 6–12.

34 American Association of Zoological Parks (AAZP); Species Survival Plan (SSP); Europäische Erhaltungzucht Programm (EEP); Species Survival Plan (SSP); Australian Species Management Programme (ASMP).

35 Pelazza, *Les Cercopithèques*, pp. 138–42.

36 Austermühle, *Die Wahrheit*, pp. 184–5.

37 'Life after Extinction', *Symposium of the Zoological Society of London* (1991), pp. 41–55.

38 A. Bertrand, 'Contribution des parcs zoologiques à la sauvegarde des espèces en voie de disparition', vet. thesis (Lyon, 1988), p. 41; G. Kleiman *et al.*, 'Coast of a Reintroduction ...', in *Symposium of the Zoological Society of London*, pp. 125–42.

39 *China Daily*, Agence France-Presse, 22 October 1997; Austermühle, *Die Wahrheit*, p. 214.

40 Bertrand, 'Contribution des parcs zoologiques', p. 139.

41 H. Oelke, Préface, and H. Hölder, 'Espèces des temps reculés, leur devenir dans l'évolution', in *Die Illusion*, pp. 7–9, 26.

42 Bertrand, 'Contribution des parcs zoologiques', p. 189; Austermühle, *Die Wahrheit*, p. 131.

43 J.D. Kelly, 'Guest Essay', *IZY*, 35 (1997), pp. 1–14.

44 *Le Figaro*, 4 November 1993.

45 M. Ancrenaz, 'Retour à la nature', *Pour la Science*, no. 246 (April 1998), p. 26; 'Contribution à l'étude éco-éthologique du aye-aye', vet. thesis (Maisons-Alfort, 1991).

46 C. J. Cornish, *Life at the Zoo* (London, 1899), p. 196.

47 J. Lafleur and L. Goldston, 'The Animal Business', *San Jose Mercury News* special investigation, 2 February 1999.

48 Lafleur and Goldson, 'The Animal Business'; A.M. O'Neill, 'Animal House', *People Weekly*, 2 March 1997, pp. 81–2; anon., *The New York Times* (December 1996); Michael Lipton and A. Arkangel, *People Weekly*, 31 March 1997, pp. 78–80.

49 Betsy Carpenter, in 'The Animal Business'.

PHOTOGRAPHIC ACKNOWLEDGEMENTS

The authors and publishers wish to express their thanks to the following sources of illustrative material and/or permission to reproduce it. They would also like to thank the staff of many additional zoos for their assistance; and to thank especially the Zoological Society of London. (As the captions for works of art do not give the physical locations of artworks, such locations, where known, are also listed below.)

Alte Pinakothek, Munich (photo Bayerische Staatsgemäldesamlungen, Munich): p. 63 (bottom); photos courtesy of Artis Zoo, Amsterdam (Artis archives): p. 307; photos by or courtesy of the author: pp. 10, 56 (top), 106, 126, 127, 130, 144, 148 (bottom), 151, 176 (bottom), 178 (top), 181, 210, 215 (top), 231 (top), 245, 246, 251 (top right), 252 (top), 274 (left), 317, 331, 332, 334; courtesy of Berlin Zoological Gardens: p. 128, 165 (top right); © Bildarchiv Preussischer Kulturbesitz, Berlin - Kupferstichkabinett (photos Jörg P. Anders): pp. 202, 348; Sarah Campbell Blaffer Foundation, Houston, TX: p. 57; courtesy of Budapest Zoo & Botanical Garden: p. 89 (top); Citymuseum of Helsinki: p. 166; photos Phillip Coffey/© Durrell Wildlife Conservation Trust: p. 117; City Art Gallery, Manchester (photo Manchester City Art Galleries): p. 65); Deutsches Historisches Museum Berlin (photo © DHM), p. 339; John Edwards Collection: pp. 85 (bottom), 87 (top), 91 (bottom), 92 (top left, top right and middle right), 93 (top), 98 (top), 103, 107, 110 (top), 138 (bottom), 145, 146, 150, 154, 155, 156 (bottom), 157, 163, 164, 172 (bottom), 174, 182 (bottom), 191 (top), 192, 208, 213, 214, 239, 240, 242, 289, 325, 326, 327, 333, 335 (bottom); Galerie de France, Paris archives/J. Hyde (© ADAGP, Paris and DACS, London 2002): pp. 227, 228, 229, 278; Galerie Neue Meister, Dresden (photo Staatliche Kunstsammlungen, Dresden): p. 189; Gemeentearchief Amsterdam: pp. 82 (top), 201 (Dreesmann Collection no. XXIX-950a), 308, 309, 310, 311, 312; Graphisches Sammlung Albertina, Vienna: p. 63 (top); Hagenbeck-Archiv, Hamburg: pp. 110 (bottom), 120, 121, 190, 193 (top), 238, 244; Hessisches Landesmuseum Darmstadt (photo Wolfgang Fuhrmannek/© DACS, London 2002): p. 207; © Historisches Museum Hannover Digitales Bildarchiv: pp. 9, 270; courtesy of Candida Höfer: pp. 7, 11, 12 (top), 165 (bottom), 226, 257 (top), 260, 266, 353, 354, 355, 356, 357, 358, 359, 360, 361, 362, 363; courtesy Britta Jaschinski: pp. 12 (bottom), 177 (top), 199, 225, 243, 256 (top), 261, 280, 364, 365, 366, 367, 368, 369, 370; © John Shedd Aquarium, Chicago: p. 93 (middle and bottom); Kunsthalle Bremen: p. 345 (© DACS, London 2002); Kunsthistorisches Museum Vienna: p. 15; photos M. Leaman/Reaktion: pp. 90, 159, 160, 161, 248, 250, 251 (top left), 253 (bottom left and right), 254, 274 (right), 305, 306, 314, 315, 316, 328, 329, 330, 336, 337; courtesy of Ljubljana Zoo: p. 231 (bottom); courtesy of Montréal Biodome: pp. 212 (top right) (photo Michel Tremblay), 265; courtesy Moscow Zoo (Educational Department): pp. 88, 162 (bottom), 297, 298, 299, 300, 301 (bottom), 302, 303, 304; Musée d'Art Moderne (Petit Palais), Geneva (photo Studio Monique Bernaz/© ADAGP, Paris and DACS, London 2002): p. 351; courtesy of the Musée Nationale d'Histoire Naturelle (Menagerie du Jardin des Plantes): p.252 (bottom); Museen der Stadt Nürnberg (Abteilung Beweglicher Kunst- und Kulturbesitz: © DACS, London 2002): p. 98; Museo Ca' Rezzonico, Venice (photo Osvaldo Böhm): p. 58; Museu de Arte de San Paulo: p. 114; Museum der bildenden Künste, Leipzig (photo Gerstenberger): p. 188; Museum Folkwang, Essen (photo J. Nober/© DACS, London 2002): p. 344; courtesy of the National Zoological Park, New Delhi: p. 249; Niedersächsische Landesgalerie Hannover (© DACS, London 2002): p. 275; courtesy of Nikolaev Zoo: p. 232; Öffentliche Kunstsammlung Basel, Kunstmuseum: p. 18 (photo Martin Bühler; © DACS, London 2002); Pierpont Morgan Library, New York: p. 340 (photo David A. Loggie; PML IV 151B); courtesy of Riga Zoological Garden: pp. 89 (bottom), 141; courtesy of the Royal Zoological Society of Antwerp: pp. 82 (bottom), 83, 154 (bottom), 212 (top left), 216, 318, 319, 320, 321, 322, 323, 324; Sammlung Frieder Burda, Baden-Baden (photo Ralf Cohen): p. 347; courtesy of Schauer + Volhard architects: p. 235; courtesy of the Sladmore Sculpture Gallery, London: p. 220; Stadtmuseum Berlin: pp. 84 (photos by Carl Friedrich Höge, rephotographed by Hans-Joachim Bartsch), 85 (top), 108 (bottom), 111 (Collection of Inge and Werner Kourist, photo Christel Lehmann), 119 (photo Hans-Joachim Bartsch), 156 (top), 158 (photo Hans-Joachim Bartsch), 183 (photo Friedrich Siedenstücker), 241 (photo Hans-Joachim Bartsch), 247, 346 (photo Christel Lehmann); Städtische Galerie im Lenbachhaus, Munich: p. 175, 268, 349 (© DACS, London 2002); State Hermitage Museum, St Petersburg: p. 56 (bottom); Tate Britain, London: p. 343 (bequeathed by Thomas Hyde Hills; photo © Tate Gallery 2001); Westfälisches Landesmuseum für Kunst und Kulturgeschichte, Münster: p. 269 (top); Wilhelm-Lehmbruck-Museum Duisberg: p. 350; Zoo Leipzig Archives: pp. 218, 283; courtesy of the Zoological Park of Barcelona: pp. 193 (bottom), 203, 212 (bottom), 253 (top); photos © Zoological Society of London: pp. 40, 41 (bottom), 78, 81, 86, 87 (bottom), 88 (top), 91 (top), 95, 96, 97, 108 (top), 109, 132, 133, 137, 138 (top), 139, 140 (bottom), 143, 148 (top), 149, 168, 169, 171, 172 (top), 173, 176 (top), 177 (bottom), 178 (bottom), 179, 182 (top), 186, 191 (bottom), 206 (top), 217, 237, 255, 256 (bottom), 257 (bottom), 267, 271, 285, 286, 287, 288, 290, 301 (top), 335 (top), 352; courtesy of the Zoological Society of San Diego (© Zoological Society of San Diego): pp. 291, 292, 293, 294, 295, 296.

posters 246

prehistoric animals 188, 194, 213

preservation of species 145, 227, 235–6, 272–7, *see also* endangered species

preserved animals 29–32, 56, 64–5, 244, *see also* taxidermy

princes' collections 30–32, *see also* courts and courtiers

prison analogy 224–7

private menageries 107–8

private sanctuaries 279–80

promenading 100, 147

protection societies 196, 220–30, 232

psychology 185, 235, 262, 263, *see also* behavioural studies

psychopathologies 115, 222–3, 274–6

public attitudes, interests and preferences 9–10, 13, 147, 170–86, 220–30

public opening begins 55–6, 58

publicity for zoos 213–16, 219, 220, 234, 246–7

rarity value 31, 32, 114, 141

realism 64, 152, 246

recreation 147–97, 204, 233, 235

Regent's Park (London Zoo) 80, 101, 102, 125, 201, 203, 249, 272

popularization 147, 167, 190

scientific work 132, 133, 134, 137, 139

reintroduction into the wild 236, 272, 276, 277, 279, 280

Renaissance collections 29–42

reproduction and breeding 136, 139, 142, 216, 220, 222, 236, 271–80, *see also* cross–breeding

reptiles 112, 173, 213, 242

research *see* scholarly and scientific study

rocks, fake 237–44, 247–52

Romanticism 151–3

Roosevelt, Theodore 197, 218–19

safari parks 211, 230, 266–8

scholarly and scientific study 64–9, 94–5, 116, 131–46, 223

science, popular 167, 197, 204, 211, 224

Scotland 249, 270

sculpture 152, 219–20, 241, 258

security 181–3

sensationalism 60

seraglios 17–22, 39–40

shipwrecks 23–4

showmen 56–61, 108–12, 126–7, 187–94

smuggling 223, 227

social functions of zoos 99–104

societies

acclimatization 136, 141–4, 196, 236

animal protection 196, 220–30, 232

environmental 223

friends of zoos 220

horticultural 146

see also zoological societies

souvenirs 170, 213

Stellingen (Hamburg) 237–42

influences 242–54

see also Hagenbeck family

stress 115

taming 113, 187, 211, 219, 232, 238

taxidermy 56, 64, 65, 114, 135, 244

terracing 249

territory theory 262, 263

theatrical scenery 34, 251–2

theme parks 265, 270–71

tourism 204, 205

trade and transportation 22–4, 113–22, 223, 227, 276–80

training of animals *see* performing animals

trans-location 276

trapping 115, 197

travelling exhibitions 56–61, 108–12, 126–7

trees 45, 47, 106, 141

trophy-hunting 113–14

urban renovation programmes 101

USA

first zoological parks 92, 102–4, 111–12, 122

illegal sales 279–80

modern zoos 209–16, 218–19, 233–4

opposition to zoos 222–3

Versailles 37, 40, 42, 48–52, 55, 68–9

influences 52–4

last days 73–6

villa gardens, Italy 43–7, 55

violence 185–6, 219, 221

visitor numbers 147, 167, 201–4, 205, 216, 230, 234

vivariums 230

vivisection 223

Whipsnade, England 265–6, 272

wildlife parks 230–31, 249, 265–72

wildlife reserves *in situ* 272

working classes 105, 147–8, 205, 209

zoo-psychology 185, 235

zoological gardens

invention 73, 80

in colonies 125–6

spread across Europe 80–83

'zoos without bars' 211, 218, 224, 237–62

zoological sciences, early 66–8, *see also* scholarly and scientific study

zoological societies 94–5, 97–9, 104

scientific work 131, 136, 141, 142, 143–4